STAPLETON'S
POWERBOAT
BIBLE

STAPLETON'S POWERBOAT BIBLE

How to Buy, Equip, and Organize a Boat for Coastal and Bluewater Cruising

Sid Stapleton

With a Foreword by Carleton Mitchell
Illustrations by Jeff Landis

Hearst Marine Books
New York

Library of Congress Cataloging-in-Publication Data

Stapleton, Sid.
    [Powerboat bible]
    Stapleton's powerboat bible: how to buy, equip, and organize a
boat for coastal and bluewater cruising / Sid Stapleton.
        p.   cm.
    Includes index.
    ISBN 0-688-08448-6
    1. Motorboats—Handbooks, manuals, etc.   I. Title.   II. Title:
Stapleton's powerboat bible.   III. Title: Powerboat bible.
GV835.S73   1989
797.1'25—dc20   89-34407
                                                        CIP

Printed in the United States of America

First Edition

1 2 3 4 5 6 7 8 9 10

BOOK DESIGN BY ARLENE GOLDBERG

FOREWORD

In the introduction to *Stapleton's Powerboat Bible*, Sid Stapleton truthfully notes: "In a perfect world, you wouldn't need a book like this." The *you* is defined elsewhere in the text as a prospective buyer, equipper, owner, and operator of a power yacht suited to the preferred type of cruising and the lifestyle of its owner. But alas! There are more sharks ashore in blue blazers in the guise of yacht brokers than ever swam the ocean, and more pirates behind counters vending marine equipment and electronics than once sailed the Spanish Main. Worse, many of both species have never white-knuckled a craft offshore on a blowy night, and thus have no real knowledge of how their shiny products would perform in the real world of blue water. Their blandishments are often based on ignorance rather than dishonesty, but the result can be equally disastrous for the uninitiated.

To me, the greatest strength of this book is the way Sid Stapleton takes the reader by the hand to go "tiptoeing through the minefield," dealing with all the different issues involved in selecting the right vessel. Before even considering types, he suggests giving thought to how much boat is really needed in terms of where and how it will be used, and the capabilities of the prospective captain and mate. Then comes "the first cross-roads," whether you will be best served by a boat with a planing hull, a semidisplacement hull, or a full-displacement hull, with explanations of the characteristics and advantages of each in terms anyone can understand. This leads into a discussion of functional layouts, both on deck and below; and choice of systems, from fire extinguishing to refrigeration. In every case, options are listed and dissected, so the ultimate decision can be made by an informed buyer—*you*. Not forgotten is an analysis of cost, an all-important consideration to most of us, notwithstanding J. P. Morgan's famous remark: "If you want to know how much a yacht will cost, you shouldn't own one."

Practically nothing relating to powerboat cruising is omitted, from a thorough review of the bewildering array of modern high-tech marvels in the communications and navigation fields, through staying safe and healthy and taking care of money and mail when going off into the wild blue yonder. Throughout are bits of advice that might not only prevent mistakes ruining the dream cruise, but which could save many times the cost of this book.

However, at the crossroads of choice, where Sid Stapleton quite properly explores the pros and cons of various hull types for serious cruising, I must come down unequivocally on the side of the full-displacement miniship for extended offshore voyaging. As I have always believed a boat should be matched to its owner's purpose and way of life, my present vessel is a Hatteras 58-foot Yacht Fisherman powered by twin diesels turbocharged and aftercooled. It is a far cry from the first motorboat I owned after the transition from sail over twenty years ago, a Grand Banks 42 of the trawler persuasion. A shakedown passage for the latter took me from Los Angeles to Miami, with a side trip to the Galapagos and a thrash along the coast of South America from the Panama Canal to Grenada. We dropped anchor in every gunkhole along the way—three years of live-aboard cruising and some 12,000 miles of offshore passage-making at an average speed of 6.2 knots. Now my voyaging is limited to quick dashes across the Gulf Stream to the Bahamas, or down through the Florida Keys inside the reefs. Both boats can be affectionately called "just right" for their eras—but neither would be suitable for the other's role. Thus I recommend careful reading of the paragraphs asking how and where you will really use your vessel, and study Sid's whys and wherefores of the alternatives.

Herein lies the basic and fundamental decision on which all else depends. But take it from me: if you have the time, just remember that when you are happy where you are, there is no reason to be in a hurry to get somewhere else!

Carleton Mitchell
Aboard Pied-à-Terre
Key Biscayne, Florida

ACKNOWLEDGMENTS

This book could not have been written without the cooperation of hundreds of people who shared their particular areas of expertise in virtually every aspect of cruising under power and generously took their time to answer my interminable questions. Much as I appreciated their input, I hasten to add that any errors that might have crept into the book are due not to what they told me but to my failure to properly comprehend it.

While it is impossible to name everyone who contributed to the effort, a number deserve special mention.

On the topic of cruising powerboat hulls, naval architect Jack Hargrave kindly reviewed the entire section and offered trenchant and knowledgeable comments. Dick Loh of Grand Banks Yachts, Ltd., Dick Lazzara of Viking Yachts, Greg Burdick of Stuart Yachts, Ken Kranz of Hatteras Yachts, and delivery captain Rob Alexander also contributed information and suggestions. John Brock of Brock's Engine Service, Bill Maerlender, Tommy Kinney, and Don Wilcox of Covington Diesel, Bill Knapp of Detroit Diesel, and Gene Wineland and Dave Jackson of Caterpillar provided much useful information on the proper operation and maintenance of marine diesel engines. Phil McCarthy of Exxon Company, USA, and Howard Chesneau of Fuel Quality Services, Inc., provided much helpful advice on the handling of diesel fuel.

Dave Parker, former president of Hatteras Yachts and now

president of Stuart Hatteras, Mike Howeter of Great American Boat Yards, Chuck Hovey of Chuck Hovey Yachts, and Tom McElhatten of Mariner Yacht Sales provided valuable insights into the yacht sales and brokerage business. William J. Kramer, vice-president of NCNB National Bank's Marine Division discussed with me the ins and outs of yacht financing, while Yvonne Wisely of Rodgers and Cummings Insurance and Neal Kratzer of Travelers Insurance led me through the labyrinth of marine insurance. Marine surveyors Frank Hamlin, Dean Greger, Ted Ezell, and Captain Kent Savage, former president of the National Association of Marine Surveyors, increased my understanding of the important role their profession plays in the purchase of a used cruising vessel.

Elayne Hebner, chief of the Bureau of Registration and Titling of Florida's Department of Natural Resources, and Steve Brown, special program supervisor of the Florida Department of Revenue's Bureau of Enforcement, helped me understand the intricacies of cruising vessel registration and taxation. Debbie Rich of Specialized Yacht Services, Inc., helped update me on the federal documentation procedure.

Those who offered technical information for the section on navigation electronics include Bob Merry and Jeffery S. Morris of Digital Marine Electronics; Ely Hammaty, executive director of the National Marine Electronics Association, and his staff; Mike Buonopane of the Cetec Benmar division of Cetec Corporation; Jim Dodez and Karen Belinski of KVH Industries, Inc.; Dayna Risebrow of Robertson-Shipmate, Inc.; Hobie Zeller of Laser Plot, Inc.; Gene Brusin of Megapluse, Inc.; Commander James R. Nagle II, chief of the U.S. Coast Guard's Radionavigation Division; and the Coast Guard's Gary Desilets and Paul Miller.

Paul Newland of AT&T's Consumer Products Laboratories was an invaluable resource who reviewed and offered helpful comments on the chapter on cruising communications. Bill Clark of Standard Communications and Don Henry of the Shakespeare Company provided similar assistance on the discussion of VHF marine radios, as did Jack F. Worbass of Stephens Engineering Associates on marine single sideband radios. Others who contributed to the cruising communications chapter are Peter Scott of AT&T's High Seas Service and Doris Bean, manager of AT&T's high seas station WOM; John D. Klemm, manager of Mobile Marine Radio, Inc.'s, High Seas station WLO, along with the station's engineer, Tim Urban; Craig Williams of Harris Corp.'s RF Communications Group; Charles S. Carney, editor of *NMEA News;* Julie Klein of GTE; Kirby Cantrell of Miami Telephone, Inc.; Dave Johnson of Jackson Marine Electronics; and Jack Carleson of Alden Electronics, Inc. Those who helped with the sections on SITOR and satellite communications include John Bloom of Radio Holland, USA; Kenneth J. Sartin of Hal Communications Corp.; Ray Brooks of Mackey Corp.; and Patricia T. Whalen of Communications Satellite Corp. At the Federal Communications Commission, Bob McIntyre, Kathryn S. Hosford, William Berges, Betty Reedy, and Carol Ball were most patient in helping me understand their agency's regulations and procedures. Amateur radio operators John Hennessee, KJ4KB; Ruth Hoffman, N4LCM; and Steve Korn, K2MDD, offered useful background on their fascinating hobby. Pat McFaden, manager of electronic services for Great American Boat Yards, offered a wealth of ideas on electronics selection and installation.

For the chapter on ground tackle, Jay Stuart Haft of Jay Stuart Haft Co.; Paula Vendetuoli of Ideal Windlass; Bob Culbertson of American Chain and Cable Co.; Walt Wecal of the Danforth Division of Rule Industries, Inc.; and Betty Mooring of Mooring, Inc., provided a great deal of useful information. Much of the data and illustrative material on yacht tenders was gleaned from Tom Bridges of The Boat Doc, Paul Foster of Boston Whaler Corp., Mark Ibsen of Novurania, and Eric Braithmeyer of Imtra Corp.

Kelsey Burr and Ardith Bonner of Survival Technologies Group devoted hours to discussing marine safety with me, while William R. Kuenzel of ACR Electronics, Inc., and Richard Switlik, Jr., of Switlik Parachute Co. were kind enough to share their ideas and suggestions on the topic.

For the chapter on cruising health, information was supplied by Ron Pickett, president of Medical Advisory Systems, Inc., and Dr. Tom Hall and Dave Monahan of his staff; Chris Wachholz of Diver's Alert Network provided information on dealing with diving accidents. Bill Stack of National Welders Supply Co., Inc., and Vickey Lewis, RN, BSN, and Dianne Wheaton, RN, BSN, both of North Carolina Baptist Hospital/ Bowman Gray School of Medicine, offered valuable suggestions on emergency medical equipment and procedures.

In addition to these experts, those who contributed to the meat of the book are the cruisers themselves, who over the years have been kind enough to share their cruising experiences with me aboard their vessels and in the process broadened my knowledge of what cruising under power is all about. Those from the United States include Frank and Lee Glindmeier; Carleton Mitchell; John and Mary Matthews; Don, Donna, and Bob Baumgartner; Rob and Nina Hixon; Joe and Evelyn Columbus; Sumner and Virginia Pingree; Bob and Eunice Stephens; Pete Benoit; Nat and Mary Robbins; John and Ginny Schlegel; Frank and Charlene Mascuch; Brig and Louise Pemberton; Bill and Alice Templeman; and Denny and Dianne Boyce. Those from other countries include Count Franco Antamoro of Switzerland and Italy; Australia's Neville and Andrew Green; England's Joe and Pat Arnold; Austria's Sepp and Christl Wagner; and Germany's Fritz Stahl. Though I have never had the opportunity to cruise with them, I am also grateful to Charlie and Nancy Bowen for the information they provided on their Caribbean excursion, and to Jim and Karen Eckles for permission to photograph details aboard their cruiser, *Priority*. Thanks also to Jeff Landis for working my incomprehensible scribbles into the book's illustrations, which add greatly to its usefulness.

A special word of thanks must go to Frank Glindmeier and to Dan Fales, executive editor of *Motor Boating & Sailing*, both of whom read the manuscript and offered invaluable advice and guidance and honest, informed criticism.

Last, I owe a special debt of gratitude to Anne Smith, who was unflagging in her support and encouragement and saintly in her understanding and patience.

CONTENTS

PART I: TIPTOEING THROUGH THE MINEFIELD

How much boat do you need? Hull and engines come first. Planing, semidisplacement, and full-displacement cruising hulls and their engines. Hull materials: What's best? Are stabilizers necessary?

The main deck and cruising cockpits. Upper deck, interior accommodations, and engine-room layout.

Fire-extinguishing and alarm systems. Hydraulic vs. mechanical steering. DC and AC electrical systems. Heating and air conditioning. Handling water and waste. Cooking and refrigeration alternatives.

Creating boat-buying and operating budgets. Will she be new or used? Domestic or import?

checkup. Emergency medical services afloat. Helicopter evacuation.

PART IV: THE FINAL PREPARATIONS

INTRODUCTION
Welcome to the Dream

So you've been bitten by the cruising bug. You've heard the siren song of the waves lapping against that rocky coast in Maine or that island in the Caribbean, and you are determined to go. Now you are setting out to acquire that perfect power cruiser which will carry you in safety and comfort to distant ports and romantic anchorages. From one who has suffered from the malady for years, welcome to the dream.

Whether you plan to stick close to the coast or head well offshore, as you begin your search for the vessel that best fits your lifestyle and cruising plans you will face a bewildering array of decisions on such topics as the hull form, propulsion package, and layout best suited to the voyage you have in mind. When it comes to outfitting the boat you finally select with navigational aids, communications equipment, safety gear, and the hundreds of other accessories you will need to turn her into a safe and comfortable home on the water, you will encounter an even more confusing tangle of choices.

In a perfect world, you wouldn't need a book like this. Every yacht broker, marine electronics salesman, and boating accessories store clerk you dealt with would listen carefully to your description of the kind of cruising you plan to do, would have thousands of miles of cruising experience under his keel and would sell you the exact boat and the precise equipment you really need at a fair price and fully brief you on how to use it.

Unfortunately, we don't live in a perfect world.

I'm not saying there aren't knowledgeable people with the highest levels of integrity in all three areas. But face it, the person you are about to hand thousands—maybe hundreds of thousands—of your hard-earned dollars to may never have been closer to a serious coastal- or bluewater-cruising powerboat than the display at the most recent boat show. Even if they are extremely experienced and knowledgeable, they are in business to sell you the boats in their line or at their dock or on their listing sheet, the radios and radars and depth-sounders on their store's shelves, the anchors and rodes and life rafts on their company's sales floor. What they are not in business to do is to send you down the street to buy the competition's products.

In buying a seaworthy power cruiser, you may well be making the largest single financial investment of your lifetime, with the possible exception of your home. At best, a significant mistake anywhere in the process of selecting and outfitting her could be horrendously expensive. At worst, you could find that your life and the lives of those you love depend on the choices you make. Before you even start looking for your boat or choosing a radio or a life raft, you'd better make sure you know at least enough to decide for yourself whether you're getting wise, dependable counsel or are being handed a slick sell.

Once you've bought your boat and have her rigged, you'll still have hundreds of questions about planning your itinerary, handling your finances, getting mail forwarded, and dealing with water, fuel, and provisioning.

Suppose, before you launch yourself into the world of cruising, you could sit down and talk at length with a room full of powerboat experts—naval architects who design them, plant managers who build them, dealers and brokers who sell them, bankers who finance them, agents who insure them, and service personnel who repair them. Suppose also you could engage in some long, relaxed chats with a healthy contingent of robust, tanned owners who have cruised thousands of miles in just the type of boat you're considering and are happy to share with you their accumulated wisdom about the equipment and techniques they have discovered that will help make your time on the water a relaxed adventure instead of a nightmare of broken gear and anchors that drag in the night. And suppose they were willing to give you at least some idea of what all this is going to cost.

That's exactly what this book is all about.

For the past twenty years or so, in addition to owning and cruising several boats of my own, I've made a good part of my livelihood writing about boats and the people who love them. In that connection, I've had the opportunity to cruise thousands of miles with a broad cross section of owners through some of the world's most beautiful cruising grounds. In the Virgin Islands, for instance, I visited with Carleton Mitchell, holder of the Cruising Club of America's prestigious Blue Water Medal and the only sailor to win the fiercely competitive Southern Ocean Racing Circuit and the prestigious Newport-Bermuda Race three times. Aboard his displacement-hull yacht, *Coyaba,* which was shaped by everything he had learned in a lifetime of cruising the waters of the world, we talked long into the night about what works and what doesn't work, and he showed me the slickest anchoring setup I've ever seen on a pleasure yacht. As I accompanied Bob and Don Baumgartner aboard their 58-foot *Trenora* during portions of their trans-Atlantic voyage from Florida to the Mediterranean, I had a chance to learn from their experience. While cruising from Sardinia to Corsica with Count Franco Antamoro, I found out much of what he learned captaining his 65-footer across the Atlantic on her own bottom. With Frank and Lee Glindmeier on segments of their 18,000-mile odyssey from Florida to Alaska and back or running the Mississippi River with Nat and Mary Robbins, I gained from what they had learned.

Through these experiences and hundreds of others in cruising areas ranging from the Gulf of Aqaba in the Middle East to Australia's Great Barrier Reef, from the islands of Greece and the coast of Norway to the Galápagos Islands off Ecuador, I've had the opportunity to see how owners of differing backgrounds tailored the selection of their boats to fit their distinctive lifestyles and cruising plans and to learn how they rigged and equipped their yachts to function anywhere—from the frigid zone to the tropics.

In addition to that on-the-water experience, in researching material for my columns on seamanship and boat handling in *Motor Boating & Sailing* magazine and for hundreds of other boating articles, I've roamed through the factories where many of the finest cruising yachts are built and inspected these boats at all stages of construction, inquired about their hull lay-up schedules, hull-to-deck joints, electrical generation and distribution systems, and the other elements that go into a proper cruising vessel. I've questioned naval architects, yacht designers, marine engineers, and boat-manufacturing and service personnel about the thinking that goes into a cruiser designed and built for dependability, economy of operation, seaworthiness, and comfortable accommodation under way, at anchor, and at the dock.

In this book I've tried to distill what I have learned into a volume which will allow you to profit from the experience of those who have gone before you and avoid unnecessary difficulties.

You'll find here a wealth of advice starting with such basics as how to decide how much boat you really need. We'll consider the question of whether a planing hull, semidisplacement vessel, or a deep-bilged full-displacement yacht would be better suited to your plans. Should your dream boat have a single engine or twin screws? Should you buy a new boat or one that has been— as one creative broker puts it—"previously loved"? Should you consider only American-built vessels, or do some of the imports offer better value?

If you decide to buy a new boat, we'll show you how to look beneath the sleek gel-coat and the varnished brightwork to choose a well-built vessel instead of a piece of glorified cardboard that will fall apart on you. If you're thinking about buying a used boat, we'll point out the difference between merely cosmetic shortcomings that can be repaired inexpensively and those problems that will require major outlays of cash before you can safely take her to sea. We'll tell you when a marine survey is necessary, what you can expect it to tell you, and how you might use its information to negotiate a better price.

Once we've helped you find the boat of your dreams, we'll give you an insider's look at the economics of the yacht-selling business to help you figure out whether you are being offered a fair deal or are putting too many unnecessary dollars in the seller's pocket. We'll show you how to make the best financing arrangements and tell you about pitfalls to look out for in marine insurance. We'll help you decide whether state registration will be sufficient, or whether you should go to the time and expense of documenting your vessel with the Federal Government.

We'll also guide you through the bewildering array of optional equipment now on the market. When it comes to navigation equipment, for instance, we'll make specific suggestions on choosing everything from autopilots and a Loran C receiver to satellite navigators and video chart plotters. We'll help you decide what items in this electronic cornucopia you really need and what amounts to overkill. A good VHF radio may be all you need for coastal cruising, but offshore voyaging will take you well beyond its range. We'll explain the options in long-range communication through single sideband or ham radios. If your current boat's range has limited you to cruising United States coastal waters and you now are preparing to strike off for foreign shores, we'll tell you whether you need an inverter, a converter, or an isolation transformer to adapt to queer dockside power supplies. If you plan to cruise areas where the water supply may be limited or suspect, we'll familiarize you with water-makers. Stabilizers are expensive. We'll tell you when they're a needless expense and when they are absolutely necessary and well worth the investment.

Once we've helped you choose the right boat and rig her properly, we'll cover all the things you need to know before you shove off: everything from how to plan your cruise to avoid predictable bad weather to how to prepare for medical emergencies.

One note: Throughout this book, I call a spade a spade. I mention brand names of the boats and equipment commonly sold in this country—whether built here or imported—that I and other experienced cruisers have found to perform satisfactorily and those that have failed the test of time and continuous use in the corrosive marine environment. I'm not interested in promoting or slamming any particular manufacturer of yachts or accessory equipment. But if a boat is lightly built or has an inefficient hull form, if an inflatable dinghy is not up to the rigors of the cruising life, or if a life raft is likely to come unglued just when your life depends on it, I think you should know it.

My purpose in writing this book is to help you select, outfit, and operate the yacht best suited to your lifestyle and cruising plans in comfort and safety. I hope—whether you are a first-time buyer of a cruising yacht or an experienced yachtsman who has already left thousands of miles of open water in your wake— that you will find in these pages a wealth of information, ideas, and suggestions which will help make your cruising dreams come true.

Sid Stapleton
Coquina Key, Florida
May, 1989

PART I

Tiptoeing Through the Minefield

1

START WITH
THE BASICS

On the west coast of Florida not long ago I met a most engaging couple who were making their home aboard a boat they
had recently purchased for a long-dreamed-of retirement years'
cruise through the Bahamas and, if all went well, on down

through the Leeward and Windward islands. The gentleman in the couple was bright and articulate, a former corporate-jet pilot for a large company in the Northwest. He had virtually no boating experience, but when he began making plans for this retirement he had been put in contact with a pleasant-sounding Gulf Coast boat dealer who had assured him he had "just the boat you need."

On a quick flight down for an inspection, the boat's roomy interior and such amenities as reverse-cycle air conditioning, a washer/dryer, and a microwave oven easily convinced my friend it was worth the $100,000-plus asking price and assured his wife it was a vessel she could make into a comfortable floating home. On the checkout run, the vessel proceeded sedately across the calm waters of the bay opposite the dealer's dock. The deal was made, checks were passed, and within a few weeks my friends had sold their home, stored the possessions they would not need on board, taken delivery of the vessel, and set off to live out their dream. The trip along the protected waters of the Gulf Intracoastal Waterway was idyllic—gulls wheeling in the bright air amid the glories of a golden sunset across the marshland. At Apalachicola, with the wind out of the southeast, the Gulf of Mexico was kicking up a light chop, but my friend was certain it would present no problem to a boat the dealer had assured him was capable of carrying him and his wife in comfort and safety to the Virgin Islands and beyond. He set a course for Cedar Key, and they were off on their first open-water passage. The moment they cleared the inlet, the boat began to pound unmercifully. Even cutting his cruising speed well below what the dealer had assured him he could count on in virtually any weather helped little. By the time my bruised and battered friends reached Clearwater, they realized they had been sold a vessel that was entirely unsuited to the kind of cruising they had in mind.

What had the dealer sold them for their cruise-of-a-lifetime through the Leewards and Windwards? A 50-foot flat-bottomed houseboat!

This may be an extreme example of a couple with the best of intentions being sold a totally inappropriate vessel for the type cruising they had in mind, but from Maine to Florida, from California to Washington State, it is repeated to some degree almost daily.

Before you plunge into the glittering world of the boat shows or head for the broker's dock to seek the cruiser of your dreams, make certain you are looking for a boat of the right size and with the type of hull, layout, propulsion system, and basic systems best suited to the kind of cruising you have in mind, and a vessel you can afford to buy and operate comfortably.

HOW MUCH BOAT DO YOU NEED?

If you plan to operate your boat yourself rather than hire a crew, you need to look for a vessel that is large enough to deal with the seas you will surely encounter and allow you to accommodate guests in comfort yet is small enough for you and your mate to operate easily.

How much boat is "too much" depends not only on the amount of money you can spend but on how energetic and mechanically inclined you are. I know several couples in their late fifties or early sixties who handle 58- to 64-footers by themselves with no problems. I've also known couples who have bought elaborate 50-footers and later sold them because they found them too complex to maintain and operate. At least one of the couples subsequently acquired a 42-footer with only minimal amenities and found what they called their "second honeymoon cottage" was far better suited to their needs.

How much boat is "too little" is a somewhat more objective matter. For cruising protected waters, a solidly constructed boat around 35 feet in length might be adequate for the sea conditions you are likely to face. If you can go ashore frequently to stretch your legs, and can easily find fuel, water, and provisions, you don't necessarily need a boat with spacious accommodations and voluminous storage capacities. For handling the sea conditions encountered in open-water voyaging, however, I personally feel a vessel of about 40 feet overall is the practical minimum, and I'd really rather have a boat closer to 50 feet. People regularly venture offshore in powerboats under 40 feet, but I think they are foolishly taking their lives in their hands. It's not merely a question of the expanse of open water to be covered. It's only about 50 nautical miles from the east coast of Florida to the Bahamas, for instance, but to get there you have to cross the Gulf Stream. I've been in the Stream with 30 knots of wind opposing current and found it a frightening experience even in a well-found boat of 50 feet or so. I shudder to think what it would be like in a lesser vessel. Further, I think it takes at least a 40-footer to provide a safe fuel reserve and adequate living space and storage capacity for at least two people and occasional guests to cruise in relative comfort for a month or more.

A good way to get a feel for how much boat you need is to add up the number of people you will have aboard on a typical cruise and base your decision initially on providing comfortable sleeping accommodations for them all. If there will be just you and your "significant other" with only infrequent guests, a two-stateroom boat will probably be adequate. For those rare times when you have more than one other couple aboard, put a sofa in the main salon that will fold out into a bed. On the other hand, if you often will have loads of kids and grandkids aboard, you may need three or four staterooms.

HULL AND ENGINES COME FIRST

According to the extensive marketing surveys that American yacht manufacturers periodically conduct, when most people begin the search for the cruiser of their dreams, the first thing they focus on is a boat's exterior styling. Does it really look like their idea of a proper cruising vessel? From styling, they progress to studying the interior. Does the layout offer enough space for mom, pop, and all the kids? Does it have enough heads? Is the galley big enough? After that, they spend hour after hour choosing the right color combination for the drapes and carpet in the main salon. Only then do they take a cursory glance at the boat's deck layout and anchoring setup and wonder if there is enough space in the engine room to get around to the backside of the power plants.

I suggest that when you start out on your quest for the perfect cruising boat, you work literally from the bottom up rather than the top down. As a first step, put out of your mind for the moment all thoughts of styling, accommodation plans, galley arrangements, and deck layouts. Concentrate solely on selecting the hull form and engine package that will best suit your needs. If the hull form and power plants of the boat you eventually buy are right for the kind of cruising you have in mind, most other factors can be modified or lived with. If the hull form is wrong or the boat is seriously underpowered, no amount of cosmetic surgery or electronic gadgetry is going to make that boat do the job you expect it to do. By concentrating on a boat's hull form and engines, I mean far more than just flipping through the builder's fancy brochure or taking a quick walk around the boat in its cradle or sling and poking your head into the engine room. After reading this chapter, you won't be a naval architect or a marine engineer, but you should be able to analyze the configuration of a particular vessel's underbody and its propulsion system to determine whether she can be counted on to perform the way you want her to under the less-than-perfect conditions you will encounter at sea.

In making your hull-form evaluation, it would be ideal if you could obtain station drawings of the hull you are considering, but dragging that kind of information out of most boatbuilders is difficult. In the case of a new boat, you should insist on a close inspection of the boat you are thinking of buying, or one identical to it, out of the water. In the case of a used boat which is already lying at a dock, try to get a good look at the underbody of a sister ship before you get into serious deliberations.

The first crossroads you will come to is deciding whether you will choose a boat with a planing hull, a semidisplacement hull, or a full-displacement hull (Fig. 1.1) and which propulsion package is appropriate to power it.

Twenty years ago, a full-displacement boat with a relatively low-horsepower engine was considered the only proper vessel for extended voyaging, and this type of boat still has strong advocates among some of the world's most experienced cruisers. Planing-hull advocates scoff that the full-displacement boat's snail's-pace cruising speed and the rolling inherent in its rounded bottom should be relegated to some maritime museum. The only proper cruising vessel, they argue, is a planing-hull motor yacht with a pair of husky turbocharged diesels. My California friend Rob Hixon expresses the planing-hull cruiser's viewpoint clearly. Rob cruised his 60-foot planing yacht *Dorado*, which was equipped with General Motors 12V-71 turbocharged diesels, from New England to his home in Newport Beach by way of the Caribbean and the Panama Canal, made a number of runs north to Alaska, and successfully voyaged 600 miles into the Pacific to visit the Galápagos Islands. "On the long hauls," Rob told me once as

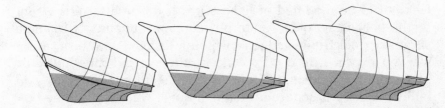

Fig. 1.1: *A typical planing hull (left) has relatively flat surfaces, hard, full-length chines and a cut-away forefoot. In a semidisplacement hull (center), the chines often disappear forward but resume amidships, the hull bottom is rounded in the forward sections, and the forefoot is somewhat more pronounced. In a full-displacement hull (right), the chine virtually disappears, hull sections are almost completely rounded, and the forefoot is even deeper.*

we lolled stern-to at the quay of Nelson's Dockyard in English Harbour, Antigua, "we can pull her back to about eleven hundred rpm to make ten knots while burning about twenty gallons of fuel per hour. If the weather turns sour, we can crank her up to twenty-one hundred rpm and scoot out of its way at twenty knots."

Owing primarily to our national obsession with speed, in recent years the planing-hull boys have had much the better of the planing-versus-displacement argument. Planing cruisers now outsell full-displacement boats in the United States by a vast margin. Many major U.S. boatbuilders, in fact, say they can't sell a boat that isn't of the planing or semiplaning variety and doesn't cruise at about 15 to 20 knots. As a result, most companies that once offered full-displacement boats have either gone out of the business all together or have hardened up the lines of their boats and transformed them into semidisplacement hulls. This underbody, they claim, provides the option of cruising at economical displacement speeds or zipping along at planing speeds by merely advancing the throttles. We'll examine those claims in more detail than these builders provide in their sales literature.

Some people say that potential cruising boat-buyers instinctively know which type of hull will suit them best. My experience indicates otherwise. I have known a number of first-time buyers—particularly older people moving from sailboat to powerboat voyaging—who bought a sizable planing boat and quickly found that it pounded too much, made too much noise under way, slurped down too much fuel, and had too limited a range. When they shifted to a displacement-hull boat they found they were happy as larks. Conversely, during the Arab oil embargo of the 1970's when diesel fuel prices went through the roof and there were serious doubts about its long-term availability for pleasure marine use, a number of planing-boat owners traded in their fuel-thirsty motor yachts for displacement boats. Some made the adjustment well. Others found they were driven close to insanity by chugging along at 8 to 10 knots. As soon as diesel fuel prices came down to around a dollar a gallon, they couldn't wait to get back into a planing boat and feel they were really moving again.

My point is that the choice between a planing cruiser versus a semidisplacement or full-displacement cruiser should receive careful consideration. And I further suggest that the process of deciding which way you will go should not begin with the glitz and glitter of boat shows or Saturday afternoon meanderings along the used-boat broker's dock. It should begin with finding the answers to some basic questions about yourself.

How will you use this vessel? If you have the luxury of sufficient time and income to strike off for several months at a whack, enjoy lazing along drinking in the patterns of wind and sea, and feel the best part of cruising is glorying in the colors of sunset in a secluded anchorage far from the madding crowd, you probably would be quite happy with a displacement vessel. On the other hand, if family and business responsibilities will limit your cruising to shorter voyages of a few days or weeks at a time and you prefer to get the boring open-water passages behind you quickly, you probably should opt for a planing vessel.

Where will you do your cruising? If the area or route you plan to cruise allows frequent refueling and reprovisioning stops, a planing motor yacht might be practical. If you plan to seek out remote areas where fuel and provisions may well be hard to come by, you probably need a displacement boat that can carry enough fuel and provisions to allow you to stay away from fuel docks and supermarkets for weeks or even months at a time. In the following pages, we'll cover the basic characteristics of planing, semidisplacement and full-displacement cruising hulls. For a more detailed technical discussion, see Appendix I.

PLANING-HULL CRUISERS

First, let's clarify what we're calling a "planing" hull. From the standpoint of the distinguished naval architect Jack Hargrave, a vessel is planing when it is lifted far enough out of the water to reduce its wetted surface to the point that the effort needed to propel it forward equals the effort needed to overcome surface friction. "I compare planing to flying," Jack says. "It's easy to tell when an aircraft is flying. You can see daylight beneath the wheels." Under Jack's definition, about the only true planing hulls around are on extremely-high-speed racing boats and the over-30-knot hot rods.

While Jack's definition is doubtless technically accurate, when most yachtsmen refer to a planing hull, they are thinking of something a bit less dramatic. They are thinking more of a vessel (Fig. 1.2) that reaches a speed sufficient for it to overcome the resistance of the bow wave it creates and "climb out of the hole" to operate more or less on top of the water rather than in it. The technical types who subscribe to this view would say a vessel

Fig. 1.2: *Planing hull cruisers like this 63-foot Viking cockpit motor yacht have sufficient power to overcome the resistance of their own bow wave and typically operate at cruising speeds of seventeen to twenty knots or more.*

reaches that speed and is planing when its speed in knots equals twice the square root of its load waterline (LWL). Though this may not be completely accurate, since that is what most people consider a planing hull, that's the definition we'll use.

If a planing hull is the route you want to pursue, you immediately come to a second fork in the path: Should you go with some variation of a deep-vee hull that carries a high degree of dead rise all the way aft (in extreme cases as much as 24 degrees at the stern), or would you be better off with a modified-vee hull whose aft sections flatten out to 15 degrees of dead rise or less (Fig. 1.3)?

Those who favor deep-vee cruising hulls argue that they pound less in a head sea and track better in a following sea. Devotees of modified-vee cruising hulls counter that their boats come up on plane faster, carry a load better, and do not roll as much under way, at the dock, or at anchor.

For cruising, I have to come down on the side of the modified-vee hull. It's true that deep-vee hulls tend to pound less in a head sea, but that is far less important in a boat that is likely to cruise at 20 knots or less than it is in a high-performance sportfishing boat operating in the 30-knot range. The key factor in a comfortable cruising boat, to me, is controlling its tendency to roll. On a lengthy voyage, reducing roll by even 5 or 6 de-

Fig. 1.3: *A typical deep-vee planing hull (left) carries a significant degree of dead rise well aft while a modified-vee planing hull (right) begins to flatten out amidships.*

grees, as most modified-vee hulls tend to do, is an advantage that outweighs a reduction in pounding. I grant that the broad, flat stern a modified-vee hull presents to a following sea can cause her to slew significantly more than the tapered stern of a deep-vee hull, but I'm willing to make the trade to have a boat that stays on her feet rather than rolling drunkenly in even moderate seas, especially when they are beam-on.

In searching for a good, serviceable underbody on a planing-hull motor yacht, avoid extremes. Look for a hull with a fine entry forward, then lines that broaden gradually amidships and terminate with 15 degrees or less of dead rise at the stern. From just forward of amidships to her stern, she should have at least a moderate keel which will materially aid her tracking and help to further reduce her tendency to roll. It is unlikely you will find a keel on a true planing hull that will offer significant protection to props, struts, and rudders, but that is one of the compromises you have to make if you elect to go with this type of vessel. In checking over the hull of any planing boat, look out for obstructions such as excessively wide struts or water intakes forward of the props, since they will significantly interfere with the props' performance.

Aside from underbody configuration, the other major aspect you should consider in selecting a serviceable planing hull is the degree of flare at the bow. It should be deep and generous to turn back your bow wave and cut down on wind-blown spray. I've seen quite expensive motor yachts whose manufacturer gave way to a designer who obviously knew next to nothing about real-life conditions at sea. They have virtually no flare at the bow because a straighter line was more esthetically pleasing to the designer's eye. In any kind of a head sea, they will take heavy spray over the flying bridge.

Diesel Engines and Turbochargers: I strongly recommend that for a cruising vessel, you consider boats powered only by diesel- rather than gas-fueled engines. Diesels are much safer, more dependable, and have a longer service life because they operate at much lower revolutions-per-minute (rpm) than gasoline engines, which puts less stress on their internal parts. Diesel engines long have been the power-of-choice for yachts over about 40 feet, and the compact, lighter-weight models now available make them practical for vessels in the 30-to-40-foot range as well. Diesels typically are 25 to 30 percent more expensive than gasoline engines but are well worth the additional cost. For a more technical discussion of diesel engine horsepower ratings and designations and the basics of propellers, see Appendix II. Suffice it to say here that when we discuss horsepower, we'll refer to *shaft horsepower*, which is the net power a marine diesel actually delivers to a vessel's shaft and prop.

In a planing cruiser, you are unlikely to have to worry about the question of single versus twin engines. So far as I am aware, no manufacturer builds a planing-hull yacht large enough to be considered a serious cruising vessel that is equipped with anything other than twin engines. A growing trend among manufacturers of boats around 30 feet in length is to combine diesel engines with outboard drives rather than conventional shafts and props. While the ability to raise an outboard drive clear of the water might be an advantage for gunkholing, over the long haul the conventional shaft-and-prop arrangement will give you more trouble-free service.

A number of manufacturers of planing-type yachts now offer their boats with a standard propulsion package, then provide buyers the opportunity to plunk down another ten or twenty thousand dollars for an optional package that provides larger-horsepower engines. Some manufacturers create the option by offering the next larger engine available from their supplier. Others create the option by offering naturally aspirated diesels in their standard package, then boosting horsepower in the optional package by adding turbocharging. (You may also run across the terms "turbo-injected" and "turbo-assisted." All three terms refer to the same process.) Since you are going to be buying a boat with diesel engines, if you are not already familiar with the beasts, you need to know at least the basics of how they operate. If you are considering a boat with turbocharged diesels, you should know a little about how they work as well and the different versions of cooling turbocharged engines that are available.

In order to operate, any internal-combustion engine must mix its fuel with air to create an explosive mixture inside its cylinders. A gasoline engine sucks in the air it needs through intake valves, mixes it with fuel that has been vaporized by the carburetor, compresses the air-fuel mixture on the upstroke of the piston, then ignites it by means of a spark plug.

Diesel engines are similar in certain ways to gasoline engines, but they also have several important differences. Like gasoline engines, they come in two-cycle and four-cycle versions. In a two-cycle diesel (such as most of the Detroit Diesel marine engines), the injector fires on every stroke (Fig. 1.4). Two-cycle diesels don't have intake valves to suck air into the combustion chamber. Instead, they take in outside air and feed it into the cylinder with a simple blower. Four-cycle diesels (Caterpillar and Cummins, for instance) do have intake valves and the injector fires on every other stroke (Fig. 1.5). On the nonfiring stroke, the piston exhausts burned fuel and sucks fresh air through the intake valves to prepare for the next firing stroke.

Diesel engines don't have the carburetors that gasoline engines use to vaporize fuel. Instead, fuel in a diesel engine is vaporized by an injector. Diesel engines also don't use spark plugs. Instead, they compress the air-fuel mixture with such force that the heat caused by the friction of compression causes it to ignite.

Naturally aspirated diesel engines use only intake valves or a blower to suck in outside air and feed it into the combustion chamber under atmospheric pressure.

Since compression is so important in the diesel engine's combustion process, the engine will be able to operate more efficiently if the air that is fed into the combustion chamber is already compressed to some degree. That's what turbochargers do: compress the air and force it into the combustion chamber under up to twice atmospheric pressure. Adding turbocharging to a naturally aspirated diesel has the effect of increasing its shaft horsepower on the order of 25 to 50 percent. (Some people refer to turbochargers with the slang expression "blowers." To differentiate between high-speed, high-pressure turbochargers and the relatively low-speed, low-pressure blower used to suck air into a naturally aspirated diesel, when we mean turbochargers we'll call them turbochargers, not "blowers.")

As turbochargers compress the air, however, friction between its molecules causes its temperature to rise. The engine will be more efficient if the air is cooled down again (and its density thus increased) after it is compressed but before it enters the combustion chamber. So you have diesel engines that are intercooled and those that are aftercooled. In an *intercooled* turbocharged diesel, the air is cooled between the turbocharger and the blower or intake valves in a heat exchanger mounted on top of the engine. This external heat exchanger is cooled by circulating raw water.

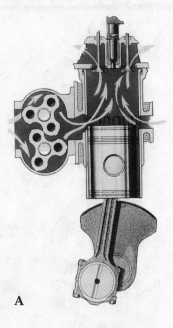

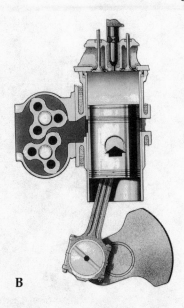

A

B

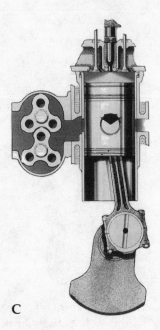

C

Fig. 1.4: *In a two-cycle diesel engine, the injector fires on each revolution of the crankshaft. At the lower end of its power stroke (A), the piston simultaneously exhausts burned gases and takes in air fed into the cylinder by the blower. On the upstroke (B), it compresses the air. The cylinder is injected with fuel which ignites under compression and (C) forces the piston downward for its power stroke. Note the absence of intake valves.*

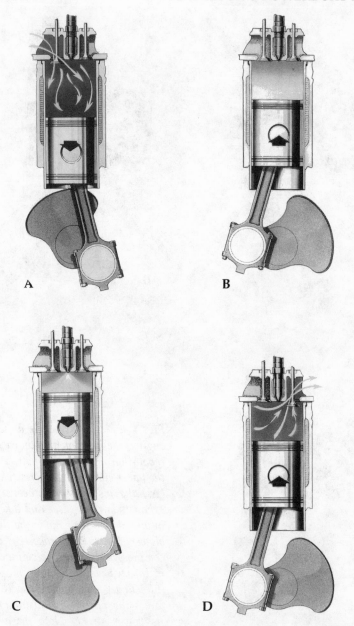

Fig. 1.5: *In a four-cycle diesel engine, the injector fires on every other revolution of the crankshaft. On the piston's first downstroke (A), it draws air into the cylinder through the intake valve. On its first upstroke (B), it compresses the air. Fuel is injected and ignites (C) which forces the piston down on its power stroke. On the piston's second upward stroke (D), it exhausts burned gases through the exhaust valve and is poised to repeat the sequence.*

In an *aftercooled* turbocharged diesel, the air is cooled between the blower and the combustion chamber in a heat exchanger that is an integral part of the engine itself. This internal heat exchanger is cooled by the engine's freshwater cooling system. Adding intercooling or aftercooling to a turbocharged diesel increases its horsepower on the order of 5 to 10 percent. (In a few cases, turbocharged diesels are both intercooled and aftercooled to wring every possible ounce of horsepower out of them. Most of these engines are used in high-performance boats and are pushed so close to their tolerances that they are not practical for use in cruising vessels.)

An aftercooled diesel generally is more expensive because the heat exchanger is inside the engine rather than mounted on top of it. In the event of trouble, aftercooled diesels are also likely to be more expensive to repair because more of the engine must be stripped away to get at the heat exchanger.

Our fascination with speed has made the addition of turbochargers to cruising yachts extremely popular, and they are coming into even wider use. In the process, a couple of misconceptions have grown up about them that need to be corrected: They are not high-maintenence items, nor do they materially affect the useful lifespan of a well-maintained engine. A few cautions regarding them are appropriate, however.

They operate at incredibly high speeds (75,000 to 100,000 rpm) and high temperatures (1,000 to 1,200° F.). To reduce the dissipation of that heat into the engine room, some turbochargers (especially on boats built prior to about 1987) are encased in "blankets" made of heavy insulating material covered with an aluminized fabric. Because of the high temperatures and pressures at which they operate, they must be lubricated by oil which the engine heats to about 215 degrees and circulates around them at 50 to 60 psi. The fittings in this lubrication system have been known to leak and soak the blankets, which can then catch on fire. If you elect to purchase a used boat whose turbochargers have insulating blankets, be certain you have the installation checked out carefully by a qualified marine surveyor or diesel mechanic before you head to sea, and keep a close eye on the integrity of their oil lines and fittings. Change them immediately at the least sign of fraying, cracking, or leaking.

Since about 1987, some manufacturers have switched to cooling their turbochargers by encasing them in cast-iron jacket manifolds through which water circulates. That's fine in quality installations that use fresh water for cooling, but some cheaper installations use raw salt water which in contact with the cast iron is an almost certain prescription for major problems down the road. The only place raw salt water should be used for cooling is in fuel coolers, intercoolers, and heat exchangers made of copper or a copper-nickel alloy, not cast iron.

If you purchase a cruising yacht with turbocharged engines, there are two simple things you can do to extend their life and reduce maintenance appreciably. Because turbos are lubricated under pressure, when the engine is shut down all their lubricating oil drains away and they are dry, which leaves metal rubbing against metal. When you start the engines, run them up to 800 or 900 rpm for a couple of minutes; this assures that the turbos will be adequately lubricated before they are operated at normal cruising speeds. Merely cranking the engines and letting them idle at 500 to 600 rpm does not ensure adequate turbo lubrication. *Never* exceed 900 rpm in the first couple of minutes after starting the engines or you could burn out the turbos' shafts. Conversely, when you end a day's run, don't shut your engines down immediately, but allow them to idle at 500 to 600 rpm for five minutes or so to allow the oil inside the turbo housing to drain away and carry excess heat with it. Abrupt shutdown leave the turbos spinning without oil and trap oil in the housing which can be baked into a sludge by the high heat levels.

Another way of increasing a diesel engine's shaft horsepower is to install larger injectors. By increasing the injectors in turbocharged Detroit Diesel 8V-92 from 115 mm to 125 mm, for example, you increase its maximum rating at 2,300 rpm from 585 shaft horsepower to 625 shaft horsepower, a gain of 40 horsepower or 6.8 percent.

Whether you elect a standard engine package or choose the next larger engine size, whether you opt for naturally aspirated or turbocharged engines, whether or not you go to larger injectors—all comes down to the question of how fast you want to go and how much you are willing to pay for increases in speed. The following examples may offer some guidance:

On the smaller-versus-larger-engine option: A pair of naturally aspirated Detroit Diesel 8V-71 engines equipped with 70 mm injectors will develop 325 shaft horsepower at 2,300 rpm. At a cruise setting of 2,100 rpm, they will propel a typical 50-foot planing-hull motor yacht at around 18 knots while consuming a total for both engines of about 30 gallons per hour. If you increase the engine size in that same boat to naturally aspirated 8V-92 diesels with 85 mm injectors, at 2,300 rpm the engines will develop 375 shaft horsepower each. At a cruise setting of 2,100 rpm, they will propel the boat at about 20 knots while consuming a total for both engines of about 34.5 gallons per hour.

On the question of natural aspiration versus turbocharging: If you add turbochargers to the 8V-71 engines in the 50-footer mentioned above and increase the size of the injectors from 70 mm to 85 mm, the engines will develop 450 shp each at 2,300 rpm. At a cruise setting of 2,100 rpm, they will increase the vessel's speed from 18 to about 22 knots, and their joint fuel consumption will increase from 30 gallons per hour to just a shade under 42 gallons per hour.

As for the effects of adding larger injectors: By increasing the injectors in the naturally aspirated 8V-71 above from 55 mm to 65 mm, you will increase speed by about one knot and fuel consumption for two engines by about 8 gallons per hour.

Bear in mind that as you increase fuel consumption for a particular boat by going to larger engines, adding turbochargers, or increasing injector size, you not only are increasing your operating costs but are reducing the vessel's cruising range as well.

Is it true, as planing-hull advocates claim, that they can throttle their engines back and get close to displacement-hull economy when they want it? It depends on what you call "close." One day I'd like to stage a test run from Ft. Lauderdale, Florida, to Bimini in moderate weather with three boats in identical condition and carrying full loads of fuel and water. Boat No. One would be a full-displacement cruiser with an LWL of 52 feet powered by twin, naturally aspirated 4-71 diesels equipped with 55 mm injectors and operated at her theoretical hull speed of 9.66 knots. Boat No. Two would be a planing-hull motor yacht of the same LWL powered by naturally aspirated 8V-71 diesels with 70 mm injectors. Boat No. Three would be a planing hull identical to boat No. Two but equipped with turbochargers and 90 mm injectors. The two planing-hull boats would match their speed to that of the displacement-hull boat. When the three vessels pulled into Bimini, I'll bet you a dime to a sack of doughnuts that Boat No. One would have consumed very close to 10 gallons per hour, Boat No. Two would have consumed close to 12

gallons per hour, and Boat No. Three would have consumed 14
gallons per hour. Any way you slice it, at displacement speeds
the planing-hull people are paying a 20- to 40-percent penalty
for their reserve power to plane. If that's "close" to displacement-hull economy, their claim is valid. But a few other observations need to be made about this experiment. The displacement-
hull boat is designed to operate at the speed of the crossing and
it will have handled well; the planing hulls are not and they will
have wallowed all over the place. The displacement-hull boat is
beamy enough to carry all the stores and provisions needed for
extended cruising. The planing-hull boats are not. At Bimini, the
displacement boat will have enough fuel left to cruise at least
another 1,500 miles, while the planing boats, even if their helms-
men continue to operate them at displacement speeds, will be
looking for a fuel dock after about half that distance. More likely,
their operators will get bored and antsy at 10 knots and will push
the throttles up to around 2,100 rpm, will do most of their cruising at 18 to 22 knots burning about 35 to 42 gallons an hour, and
their tanks will be bone dry after they have gone less than 600
miles. My point is that for relatively short-range cruising in areas
where fuel and provisions are readily available, I have no quarrel
with the planing-hull advocates' claim. If the plan is to do extended cruising in the boondocks, there is no way a planing vessel can touch a displacement boat's overall economy and
practicality.

SEMIDISPLACEMENT-HULL CRUISERS

Some manufacturers advertise their boats as having semidisplacement hulls which can be operated at low engine power to
achieve displacement-hull fuel economy or at higher engine output for planing-hull speeds (Fig. 1.6). In theory this sounds like
the answer to a cruising man's dreams, and this type boat has a
number of very satisfied adherents. There are, however, a few
points to remember.

The basic difference between a semidisplacement and a true
planing vessel is that the semidisplacement hull (Fig. 1.7) will
have a significantly deeper forefoot to give her a soft entry, forward sections that are slightly fuller than a planing hull but not
nearly so rounded as those of a full-displacement hull, a hard
chine that in most cases runs for the hull's full length, and a
significant keel. The aft half of most semidisplacement hulls has

Fig. 1.6: *A semidisplacement yacht such as the Grand Banks 42 normally has a maximum cruising speed of around fourteen to seventeen knots.*

Fig. 1.7: *Two versions of semidisplacement hulls: The Grand Banks 42 (left) shows a pronounced forefoot and flat planing sections aft but carries her hard chine well forward. The Hatteras 48 Motor Yacht (right) exhibits less forefoot, somewhat rounded sections forward, and planing surfaces aft.*

essentially the same flat sections found in a modified-vee planing hull.

Certainly, this configuration offers some factors that are very positive in cruising. At displacement speeds, its flatter underbody sections make it roll less than would a full-displacement hull, though the boat will tend to snap back to the vertical rather sharply when its hard chine hits the water. The semidisplacement hull's deep keel is a significant aid in tracking and offers valuable protection to struts, props, and rudders.

Whether a semidisplacement vessel operates as a displacement hull or a planing hull depends on its engine power. As an example, let's consider a semidisplacement hull of about 40 feet length over all (LOA) with a waterline length of 36 feet. Suppose it has tankage for 550 usable gallons of fuel. If we use the definition of planing as a speed in knots equal to twice the square root of the waterline, the boat in our example would begin to plane at 12 knots ($\sqrt{36} = 6$; $6 \times 2 = 12$ knots).

If powered by twin diesels of 120 horsepower each and cruised at 2,000 rpm, the vessel will not plane at all but will operate essentially as a full-displacement hull at about 7.5 knots. Fuel consumption will be about 1.25 nautical miles per gallon and maximum range will be just under 700 miles.

Suppose you increase the horsepower in that same boat by replacing the 120-hp engines with naturally aspirated twins developing 215 horsepower each. If the throttles are set at about 1,800 rpm, the vessel will operate essentially as a full-displacement hull at a speed of about 8 knots. Fuel consumption will be around 1.1 nautical miles per gallon and maximum range will be about 600 miles. If the engines are run up to their maximum cruise setting of about 2,150 rpm, the boat will achieve a top speed of about 12.5 knots and begin to come up on plane. At that speed, however, the boat has just barely come up onto the planing "hump" and doesn't really have the power to overcome the resistance of its own bow wave and get fully up on plane. It is operating as a planing hull but at a planing hull's least efficient attitude. The result is that its fuel consumption rate is not likely to be better than about 0.8 nautical miles per gallon and its range will be cut to just under 450 miles.

Suppose you add turbochargers to the 215-hp engines to boost their output to 300 horsepower each. At 1,600 rpm, the boat will still function as a displacement hull at around 8 knots. Fuel consumption will be about 0.8 nautical miles per gallon with a range of about 450 miles. Run the throttles up to 2,100 rpm and she will come up fully on plane, but her fuel consumption rate will soar to less than 0.5 nautical miles per gallon and her range will drop to under 300 miles.

One tip: If you purchase a vessel that is capable of planing and plan to operate it at displacement speeds for extended periods of time, make the last half hour of each day's run at the boat's normal planing speed. This will help clean the injectors and scavenge out any oil which has slobbered into the air boxes to keep it from turning into a sticky sludge.

Semidisplacement boats are available with both single- and twin-engine configurations, and we'll discuss the pros and cons of each in the next section. Suffice it to say here that a semidisplacement boat equipped with a single engine will operate only in a displacement mode and will not have sufficient power to plane.

If your choice comes down to either a semidisplacement or a planing-hull cruising boat, bear in mind that because of her deeper forefoot and keel, the semidisplacement boat operated at planing speeds will not cruise as fast for a given horsepower or be nearly as fuel-efficient as the planing boat.

If you find yourself trying to choose between a semidisplacement and a full-displacement vessel, recognize that in order to get the option of both displacement and planing cruising speeds, you are going to have to put larger engines in the semidisplacement boat and pay a price in fuel economy, even if you operate her primarily at displacement speeds. Recognize also that because a semidisplacement boat lacks the deep bilges of the full-displacement boat, she will carry less fuel and her larger engines will consume it faster. Those two factors together will cut your cruising range significantly.

FULL-DISPLACEMENT-HULL CRUISERS

If you are leaning in the direction of buying a full-displacement vessel (Fig. 1.8) and are not familiar with the genre, I'd strongly recommend you spend several days aboard a friend's boat of that type or charter one for at least a week to make certain you will be happy with two key aspects of this kind of cruiser: its limited speed and its tendency to roll. Going from planing to

Fig. 1.8:   A full-displacement yacht such as this Hatteras 58 Long Range Cruiser normally cruises at ten knots or less but can carry massive amounts of fuel and provisions for extended operation away from the dock.

full-displacement speeds produces quite a psychological jolt, so be sure you can make the adjustment before you sign any contracts.

You'll notice that throughout the book, we refer to "full-displacement vessels" rather than "trawler yachts." The reason is that technically a "trawler" is a commercial vessel with a fully rounded bottom, most often a boat used for fishing well offshore which must incorporate every possible square foot of space to hold its catch. Rolling is not a major problem in these vessels because their trawling rig almost invariably includes outriggers that act as very effective paravane stabilizers. If you watch these boats head to sea, you will note that they drop their outriggers the minute they venture into open water, even though they may be hundreds of miles from their fishing grounds.

Builders of full-displacement vessels for pleasure use realized early that a fully rounded bottom produces more rolling action than the average yachtsman is willing to endure. To reduce rolling to an acceptable level, they flattened the aft fourth or so of their hulls to produce the designs commonly marketed as "full-displacement" or "trawler" yachts seen today. You might find a fully rounded bottom on a pleasure yacht—probably one built in Scandinavia or a true commercial trawler that has been converted to pleasure use—but it will be a rarity. The term *trawler yacht* becomes even more confusing when it is applied to hard-chined semidisplacement cruising boats whose only resemblance to a true trawler ends just aft of its deep forefoot. Even the term *full-displacement hull* is not totally accurate, but it is closer than *trawler*, so that's the one we'll use.

In considering a specific full-displacement boat, the first thing to do is to make certain you know at what speed you actually will be voyaging. Don't rely on the manufacturer's brochure to give you that information because copywriters sometimes wax a bit creative. To determine for yourself the hull speed of a full-displacement pleasure yacht, take the square root of its LWL and multiply the result by 1.34, which is the formula marine engineers generally use to compute the maximum practical speed-to-length (S/L) ratio of this type hull. For a full-displacement vessel with an LWL of 40 feet, that computes out at just under 8.5 knots ($\sqrt{40} = 6.32$; $6.32 \times 1.34 = 8.47$ knots). Up to a point, applying additional horsepower to propel a full-displacement vessel above its hull speed is simply going to create a larger bow wave, force the stern to sink deeper into its own wake, and sharply increase fuel consumption. It is possible, of course, to keep piling on the horsepower until you force a full-displacement hull to exceed its practical maximum speed, but then it ceases to be a true displacement hull and its fuel consumption rate goes off the chart.

In practice, you probably will wind up cruising a full-displacement vessel at something less than its S/L ratio of 1.34. The actual ratio is more likely to be around 1.2 which, for a vessel with a 40-foot LWL, comes up to around 7.6 knots—better than three fourths of a knot slower than its practical maximum.

Once you have worked out the numbers for a specific full-displacement boat, accept the result as the speed at which you actually will be voyaging and make certain you can live with it. If a salesman or owner says you will cruise faster than that while still enjoying the range and fuel economy that are primary reasons for buying a vessel of the type, don't believe him. You will exceed the figures you come up with only by fractions, and even then at stiff increases in fuel consumption.

The experience of the father-son team of Bob and Don Baumgartner who took the Hatteras 58 Long Range Cruiser *Trenora* across the Atlantic on her own bottom provides some hard data with regard to speed and fuel consumption in the real world of full-displacement cruising. The boat was powered by twin, naturally aspirated Detroit Diesel 4-71 engines with N55 injectors that developed 160 shaft horsepower each at 2,300 rpm, and she had total fuel tankage of 2,300 gallons with about 2,000 gallons usable. In order to make sure they had an adequate fuel reserve for the longest leg of the voyage—the 1,779-mile run from Bermuda to the Azores—the Baumgartners equipped the vessel with a 100-gallon day tank graduated in one-gallon increments and did a number of carefully measured runs over a test course in calm seas at different rpm settings. With her 52-foot waterline, the vessel's practical maximum hull speed would be 9.66 knots. During the tests, the boat was fully loaded with fuel, water, and stores, and the fuel consumption figures included the operation of a 15-kw generator. They developed the following numbers:

RPM	Speed	S/L Ratio	GPH	Nautical Miles/Gal.
1,400	8.3 knots	1.15	6.6	1.25
1,500	8.5 knots	1.18	8.5	1.00
1,800	10.7 knots	1.48	12.0	0.89

Notice that, even on the test runs, increasing the throttle setting from 1,400 to 1,500 rpm yielded only a 2.4-percent increase in speed but boosted fuel consumption by almost 30 percent. In going from 8.5 knots—well under the boat's practical maximum hull speed of 9.66 knots—to well over it at 10.7 knots, they achieved a 25-percent speed increase but at the heavy cost of a 41-percent increase in fuel consumption.

Contrast the test figures with those produced under the actual conditions *Trenora* experienced during the voyage, which included 20-foot seas off Bermuda and 40-knot winds gusting to 60 on her approach to the Azores. She covered a total of 3,818 nautical miles from Ft. Lauderdale, Florida, to Vilamora, Portugal, in 460.8 hours running time at an average speed of 8.28 knots (an S/L of 1.148). According to the test run figures, at that average speed she should have burned about 6.5 gph or a total of just under 3,000 gallons of fuel for the entire voyage. Actually, her total fuel consumption, including that used by her 15-kw generator, was more than one and a half times that—4,588.7 gallons—an average of 9.96 gallons per hour or only 0.83 nautical miles per gallon. "On the run from Bermuda to the Azores," Don says, "we kept our speed just under eight knots to stretch our fuel. But with the heavy seas we encountered, we still got a touch less than one nautical mile per gallon. Toward the end of the trip we were very tired and anxious to have the trip behind us. On the relatively short runs from the Azores to Madeira and Madeira to Vilamora, where we were not concerned about range, we ran the engines up to eighteen hundred rpm which gave us about nine knots but increased our fuel consumption to around twelve gallons per hour. At that rate, we were only getting about three quarters of a nautical mile per gallon." The point here is that real-life cruising rarely produces average speed and fuel consumption figures anywhere close to those developed in test runs under controlled conditions. To get the range you may need, you will have to keep the throttles pulled back, and you should always allow yourself a 20 to 25 percent safety margin to deal with any adverse weather you might encounter.

As for the hull form of a full-displacement cruiser (Fig. 1.9), you should look for full, well-rounded sections with no chine forward where she does her work shouldering aside the water. The lines will flatten out somewhat into a moderately hard chine in the aft fourth of the hull. The hull also should incorporate a generous keel to help her track properly and provide protection to the props, struts, and rudders in a grounding.

The comments on the desirability of a generous flare in the bow to turn back the bow wave and windblown spray made earlier in the section on planing-hull boats applies equally to both displacement and semidisplacement cruisers. The more the better. You may notice that there are designers—especially of some boats built in the Far East—who incorporate almost no flare into the bow and rely instead on exceedingly high bulwarks forward to keep the foredeck reasonably dry. Practically speaking, a bow with high bulwarks tends to restrict the forward vision of the helmsman, particularly from the pilothouse, and the boat is likely to take spray across her foredeck in even minimal sea conditions.

Engines: Single vs. Twins: The engines used on full-displacement cruisers are almost invariably naturally aspirated diesels

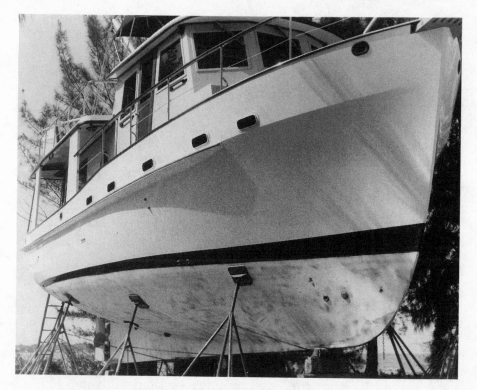

Fig. 1.9: *This Kady Krogen 42 exhibits a full-displacement yacht's typical deep forefoot and well-rounded bilge sections.*

fitted with small injectors, and you normally don't get into considerations of turbochargers. Some manufacturers of full-displacement cruisers do, however, offer their boats with either a standard engine package or optional higher-horsepower power plants. In most cases the standard package will push the boat to its maximum efficient hull speed and is all the power you need. The option of larger engines is offered primarily as a marketing ploy to attract marginal buyers. It might provide a couple of extra knots of speed but only at a sharp increase in fuel consumption.

Several manufacturers of full-displacement boats offer both single- and twin-engine setups—sometimes in the same model— and there are a number of single-engine full-displacement boats on the used-boat market, so this is an appropriate place to take up the single-versus-twin-engines controversy.

Whether a full-displacement boat should be powered by

one engine or two is not really a matter of speed. A full-displacement-hull yacht having an LWL of 36 feet and powered by a single 135-hp diesel engine turning at 1,800 rpm, for instance, will cruise at about 7 knots in calm seas. That same boat with twin 135-hp engines operating at the same rpm setting will cruise only about 1.5 knots faster. The reason the vessel won't achieve anything like twice the speed even though it has twice the power is that the added force will push the vessel to its maximum practical S/L ratio but will not be sufficient to overcome the resistance of its bow wave and allow it to plane. The twin-engine vessel, of course, will burn almost—but not quite—twice as much fuel.

The question of single versus twin engines really comes down to two factors: safety and maneuverability.

As for safety, the advocates of cruising on one engine point out that properly-maintained diesels aboard single-engine commercial fishing and shrimping boats operate mile after mile, year after year, with no significant problems. That is true. But bear in mind that there is usually a pretty fair mechanic aboard who constantly maintains the engine and corrects potential problems before they cause a breakdown. Even these vessels suffer situations where an oil or fuel pump fails or a fuel or water filtration system clogs and brings the engine to a shuddering halt. There is also the danger of a line ensnaring the prop and shaft and bringing the boat to a stop. I grant the adherents of single-engine cruising that their approach consumes less fuel for approximately equal cruising speeds and that because a single shaft and prop can be mounted directly behind the keel they are better protected. But I am a firm believer in Murphy's Law and its First Corollary—whatever can go wrong will, and at the worst possible moment. For that reason, I am a strong advocate of building in redundant systems wherever possible. The first place I would insist on that redundancy in a cruiser on which my life could depend would be twin engines for its main propulsion system.

When maneuverability is brought up in the single-versus-twin-engine debate, the discussion usually revolves around docking. Some single-engine boats handle so poorly in close quarters that in adverse conditions they can only be brought to the dock with the use of a spring line or bow thruster. Certainly there is no question that the twin-engine boat handles far more easily in tight quarters, particularly when you are trying to back into a slip with a stiff crosswind or crosstide running. But where maneuverability is even more critical is in inlet running, particularly in a stiff following sea. Chances are, a full-displacement boat will not be fast enough to run inside on the back of a single wave which is the best approach with a planing-hull boat. With a displacement-hull boat, the best you can do is let the successive waves pass under you while keeping your vessel as nearly as possible over deep water. Since many displacement-hull boats have a broad, flat stern with essentially no dead rise, their tendency in a strong following sea is to slew rather dramatically from side to side. Bear in mind that in such a circumstance the sea will be running from the stern forward at a speed greater than your vessel's forward progress, which will make its rudder essentially useless. The only way you are going to stay centered in the channel under those conditions is to have twin engines and use bursts of power first on one engine, then on the other to overcome the boat's tendency to broach. In extreme conditions, if you get well into a broach, you may even have to put the windward engine in full forward and the leeward engine in full reverse to bring her back on track. If you are caught in that condition with only a single engine, about all you can do is hang on tight and pray.

Advocates of single-engine cruising bring up the question of range. My California friend Peter Fowler, for instance, argues that by sharply throttling back the single 135-horsepower engine in his Kady-Krogen 42 he could wring a 2,800-mile range out of its 700-gallon fuel capacity—enough to reach Hawaii. "I could never do that," he says, "if the fuel were being consumed by two engines." My response is that, if necessary, twin-engine vessels can be operated very effectively on only one engine. If run that way, a twin-engine boat of equal fuel capacity would have very nearly the same range but would still have the backup of a totally separate engine, transmission, shaft, and prop if they were needed.

If you select a single-engine boat, I'd suggest you create emergency "get home" power by rigging it to run off its electric generator if the main engine should fail. Most installations of this type use an electric motor which in an emergency can be connected to the drive shaft with a cog-wheel belt. A 7.5 kw generator, for example, could power about a 10-horsepower motor which would propel a 42-footer at around three knots.

Our discussion to this point has assumed that a boat with two engines would also have two props and shafts. You might come across a boat with twin engines set up to power a single shaft and prop either alternately or in tandem. That arrangement provides a backup source of power if one of the engines fails, but the vessel is still helpless if a significant problem develops with its underwater gear.

HULL MATERIALS: WHAT'S BEST?

If the initial expense of a boat is a primary consideration, you may be attracted to the bargain-basement prices offered on used boats with wooden hulls, which often are 25 to 35 percent less than a boat of comparable size and age with a hull of more modern material such as aluminum or fiberglass. With proper care, wood-hulled vessels can function effectively for coastal cruising in cold northern waters. For offshore voyaging or cruising in warm tropical waters, however, I would advise against their purchase. You'll find it extremely difficult if not impossible to obtain insurance on a wood-hull boat. If you do find someone to insure it, the premiums will be substantially higher than the cost of insuring a comparable boat with a hull constructed of more durable materials, and the insurer may well insist on a significantly higher deductible and annual surveys. In addition, many yacht financing agencies are reluctant to lend money on a cruiser with a wooden hull. In a wood-hulled boat, you also may find you spend more time and money fighting dry rot and wood borers than you do cruising.

You occasionally will encounter full-displacement cruisers with steel hulls. A steel hull may be fine if you plan to venture toward the Arctic Circle and use your boat to bust through ice floes. For the more typical cruiser, however, steel's vulnerability to the problems of rust, galvanic corrosion, and electrolysis severely limits its practicality. Most insurance companies will require an audio-gauge survey on a steel-hull vessel before they will write a policy on it. Such a survey can cost upwards of a thousand dollars and the insurer may require a new one every couple of years. Some people who own and cruise steel-hull displacement vessels argue that the weight of their boats is an advantage. My view is that the weight differential between steel and fiberglass results in an unnecessary expenditure of power—and hence, of fuel—to push a lot of dead weight through the water. Again, I wouldn't recommend it to the average cruiser.

Aluminum is a popular material for building one-off custom planing yachts since it does not require the construction of an expensive plug and mold before you start building the hull. Aluminum is only rarely used in displacement cruisers, though from time to time a few custom creations using this material will pop up on the used-boat market. The basic drawback of aluminum, like steel, is its susceptibility to damage from galvanic corrosion and electrolysis. Most of the owners of aluminum-hull yachts employ professional captains who are well versed in fighting these underwater villains and are not bothered with the problem beyond paying the bills. Aluminum-hull cruising boats also involve insurance difficulties similar to those of steel-hull boats. Aluminum, hence, is not my first choice for the typical owner-operated cruising boat.

By far the most practical hull material for cruising yachts is fiberglass. It is inert and thus is not itself subject to damage from galvanic corrosion and electrolysis (though the shafts, struts, props, and rudders of a fiberglass yacht are). It is relatively inexpensive and easy to maintain and is tough as hell for its weight. But even fiberglass can be subject to problems, most of which result from poor practices in the lay-up process.

The major potential problem with fiberglass is damage resulting from osmosis—the physical principle that a fluid will migrate from an area of higher osmotic pressure to an area of lower osmotic pressure. Osmosis causes damage in fiberglass hulls primarily because the builder fails to put down a thick enough layer of gel-coat in the mold before beginning the hull lay-up process. If that happens, once the boat is launched, the water outside the hull tends to be forced through the relatively porous gel-coat and form a pocket between the gel-coat and the first layer of laminate. In time the gel-coat will bulge up and leave the surface of the vessel's bottom pitted with blisters. Ultimately these blisters rupture, allowing water to reach the fiberglass beneath the gel-coat. The problem can become extremely serious if the woven roving in the underlying laminate was not thoroughly saturated with resin and all the air bubbles squeezed out before the next layer of roving and resin was added. (Builders of less expensive boats often don't get all the air out because about the only way to do it is to use expensive labor to hand-squeegee the air bubbles out of each layer.) In that case, through a wicking action, the water will actually be sucked into the laminate by the woven roving. The result, over time, is that the water creates voids within the laminate itself, which can seriously weaken the hull's integrity.

The best way to avoid osmosis is to use a substantial layer of gel-coat (which is expensive) and plenty of resin in the lay-up process (which is likewise expensive and also adds substantial weight). Another help in retarding osmosis is to spray the hull (at least the bottom up to the waterline, preferably the entire exterior) with a coat of polyurethane or epoxy paint. In addition to reducing the gel-coat's porosity below the waterline, the coating will also counter the gel-coat's tendency above the waterline to chalk and develop hairline cracks, especially under the relentless heat of a tropical sun. Coating a hull with polyurethane or epoxy paint makes a boat more expensive, but it's well worth the added cost in reduced maintenance and added resale value.

One other caution regarding boats with fiberglass hulls: Make certain the hull below the waterline is solid fiberglass, not cored with balsa or some synthetic material. Some builders employ cored fiberglass below the waterline to reduce the weight of their boats and thus increase their speed. It is extremely difficult to completely bond fiberglass to coring materials. Once seawater finds a way into the coring material, it will keep on coming in until it thoroughly soaks the core material. In my judgment, a boat that has a cored hull below its waterline is far more susceptible to delamination than one with a solid fiberglass hull. (Lawyers, in fact, are still trying to settle damage claims on some boats with cored hulls that delaminated, took on water, and wound up on the bottom.) A hull that is cored from the sheer down to within about 6 inches above the waterline is not objectionable, but I would never buy any boat that employed core material in the underbody itself. Some builders claim they have licked the problem of bonding fiberglass to coring material by curing their hulls in a vacuum. I will not be convinced this process solves the bonding problem until I have seen a number of hulls built this way hold together under the punishment the open sea can inflict for five years or so. Until then, I would not care to be part of their experiment.

ARE STABILIZERS NECESSARY?

Stabilizers (Fig. 1.10) are extremely expensive—on the order of $16,000 installed on a 40-footer and up to $28,000 for a 60-footer. A number of planing-hull and semidisplacement-hull yacht owners install them, which is fine if money is no object. I personally don't consider stabilizers essential for either type of vessel. Because of their hard chines, I find the degree of rolling normally experienced in either type is acceptable.

If you decide to purchase a full-displacement-hull cruiser, however, stabilizers are indispensable to help counter the natural rolling tendency of a basically round-hulled boat. On such a boat of 45 to 50 feet cruising at around 8 knots, a proper stabilizer installation can be expected to counter the effects of waves up to about 8 feet high and reduce roll by about 15 degrees either side of the vertical. Even with stabilizers, in extreme conditions you still can find your heart in your throat. On *Trenora*'s voyage across the Atlantic, Don Baumgartner was basically pleased with

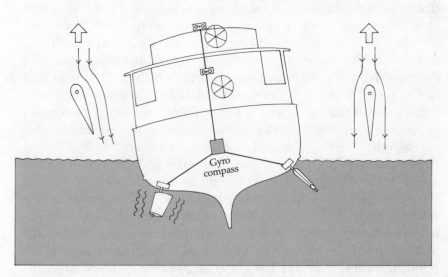

Fig. 1.10: *As a vessel equipped with stabilizers begins to roll to port, the system's gyrocompass activates the port fin to bring her back to a horizontal plane. The starboard fin is inactive until the vessel rolls in its direction.*

the performance of her Naiad stabilizers. But even with them working well, the 20-foot seas he encountered approaching Bermuda rolled the boat up to 40 degrees off the vertical.

You can spark quite an argument as to which is better: stabilizer systems powered by hydraulic oil pressure or those powered by pneumatic air pressure. The arguments in favor of air-powered stabilizers seem to make sense: Their operating pressures are around 120 psi rather than the 1,200 psi of most hydraulic systems, which should mean less stress, less maintenance, and longer life; in the event of hose failure you must deal only with air, not a potentially flammable or explosive oil/mist mixture; and air is compressible which means smoother operation. Despite all this logic, I would opt for the hydraulic type based on several factors: I have heard of a number of cruisers who have had frustrating problems with air-actuated stabilizers but few who have had problems with their hydraulic systems; I would probably have hydraulic steering and clutches on my boat anyway and wouldn't care to introduce another system; and I am more likely to find service for a hydraulic system in remote areas.

Based on the experience of Frank Glindmeier, if you have stabilizers installed on a full-displacement cruiser I suggest you specify pistons and fins one size larger than the manufacturer recommends. The problem stems from the fact that stabilizer manufacturers' recommendations of fin and piston sizes are based on planing-hull vessels, and full-displacement vessels simply don't move water past the fins fast enough to achieve optimum efficiency. When Frank and his wife Lee set out on their 48-foot displacement cruiser *Summer Wind* for their 18,000-mile voyage from Florida to Alaska and back, Frank initially equipped it with air-powered stabilizers which on a shakedown cruiser proved totally unsatisfactory. Before departing on the cruise itself, he changed to hydraulically powered stabilizers which performed much better so long as he was running southward in beam seas down through the Leewards and Windwards. But when he turned east to run with the prevailing wind and current along the northern coast of Venezuela, his vessel put such a strain on the system that he found the 4-foot-square fins he had installed based on the manufacturer's recommendation were not large enough to give him the stabilization he wanted. At Bonaire he replaced the fins with the next larger, 6-square-foot size. On the run from the ABC islands to Panama, the new fins put so much pressure on the piston rams that they broke. At Panama City he installed the next-larger-size pistons and found that the modified configuration served him well for the remainder of the voyage.

By now you should be getting a pretty good idea of how much boat you really need; whether you will be better off with a planing, full-displacement, or semidisplacement hull; the number and size of her engines and whether they will be naturally aspirated or turbocharged; your preferred hull material; and whether the boat will require stabilizers. Next you should consider what to look for in a functional layout.

2

SELECT A
FUNCTIONAL LAYOUT

Hopefully, you will have the luxury of spending weeks at a time aboard whatever cruising vessel you decide to purchase—perhaps even months or years. During that time, through fair weather and foul, she is going to be your floating home complete with a patio and a swimming pool literally as big as the ocean. You are going to have to live with the choices you make for a long time, so approach the selection of her exterior and interior layout with the same degree of care you would give to selecting your home on shore.

MAIN DECK LAYOUT

The main deck of a cruising boat (Fig. 2.1) serves two primary functions: It provides a base for your ground tackle, windlass, docking cleats, and safety rails or lifelines; and it provides a surface for you or your crew to walk on safely when you are docking or anchoring the boat. In addition to these primary functions, either on the bow or well aft, it may also provide a place for you and your guests to sit or lounge when the weather is so pretty you don't want to be inside.

Make certain the foredeck of any cruising boat you consider provides a clear, unobstructed area for handling dock lines and ground tackle. It should be set up to carry at least one anchor on deck which is always attached to its rode and can be deployed instantly in an emergency and easily when it comes time to drop the hook for lunch or overnight. That means the boat

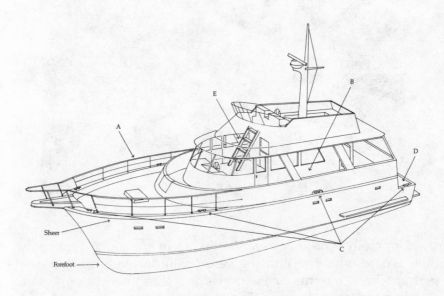

Fig. 2.1: *A functional cruising boat will show such desirable aspects as (A) safety railings with thru-bolted stanchions and an intermediate lifeline, (B) walk-around side decks, (C) good cleat placement and access, (D) a roomy cruising cockpit and (E) interior access to its flying bridge.*

should have either a bow roller or a bow pulpit. I personally prefer a bow pulpit because it allows the crew on the foredeck to be positioned directly over the anchor if necessary during setting and retrieval rather than behind it. The bow pulpit should be firmly affixed at the bow or molded into it, should project about 3 feet past the bow, and should accommodate at least one anchor in self-deploying chocks. It would be even better if it accommodated two—one a fluke type for anchoring in hard sand, the other a plow or Bruce style for anchoring in mud or coral (Fig. 2.2). The pulpit should be capable of supporting at least a 500-pound load in case you have to send a couple of crew members out on it to help free a fouled anchor, and they should be securely protected in the process by a single waist-high railing.

Fig. 2.2: *A stout bow pulpit which carries a primary anchor ready for instant deployment is a must on a practical cruising powerboat. Even better is this pulpit which carries a secondary anchor in the same manner. Deep bulwarks also provide a welcome measure of safety.*

(Here we're concerned only with the structural elements of the boat itself. For a discussion of ground tackle and anchor-handling equipment, see Chapter 10.) The area just aft of the pulpit should have room to accommodate a hefty power winch. Directly below the mounting area for the winch, a coastal cruiser of 30 to 40 feet LOA should have a locker capable of holding six fathoms (36 feet) of ⅜-inch chain and at least 200 feet of ½-inch nylon anchor line. An offshore cruiser should have two lockers: one for handling about 300 feet of ⅜-inch chain; and a second for holding an equal length of ¾-inch nylon line. The lockers should be accessible through separate deck pipes, and it is best if their bottom surface is vee-shaped rather than flat. As rope or chain is fed into a locker with a flat bottom, it tends to pile up in a pyramid. In a heavy sea, it will fall over on itself and be tossed about like spaghetti. The result is a god-awful tangle, and you have to crawl into the locker and straighten it out by hand.

A number of yachts also incorporate some type of lounge seating on the foredeck. That may be fine on a coastal cruiser, but on an offshore boat I find such arrangements tend not to be very functional. For the offshore cruiser, a much better use of that space—seldom found on planing-hull motor yachts but sometimes seen on displacement-hull cruisers—is a Portuguese bridge, which allows the crew to go at least part of the way forward in foul weather without being in danger of being swept overboard.

Most cruising boats provide adequate line-handling space in the bow, but aft is another matter. Many motor yachts today have an aft deck which extends all the way to the stern and is enclosed by a railing, weatherboards, and side curtains or even permanent structures of molded fiberglass and fixed glass panels. The aft cleats on these boats are recessed into the lower corner of these structures and are extremely difficult to reach from inside the aft deck enclosure. An open aft deck that can be enclosed with side curtains in inclement weather provides a natural and valuable gathering place for the children's hour or even meals, but it should not extend all the way to the stern of the vessel. An area just forward of the transom should be reserved for an open space all the way across the width of the boat which is readily accessible from either side of the vessel and is enclosed only by a coaming or a railing and lifeline. Such an area can be on the main deck level or it can be a water-level cockpit. This arrangement allows the person handling the dock lines to get to the aft cleats on either side of the boat quickly and easily without having to reach over or around weatherboards, roll up side curtains, move furniture around, or open glass windows.

The next thing to check for is a convenient way around the outside of the boat to get between the bow and the stern quickly. That means side decks. In recent years, the manufacturers of cruising boats have started offering designs that widen the main salon at the expense of the side decks. I think this is a mistake. If you cruise long enough in a boat without side decks, the day is sure to come when you are trying to dock in a stiff crosswind, or you are trying to fend off a boat whose anchor has dragged and is about to slam into you amidships. You'll be stuck in the main salon powerless to do anything—except cuss—as you watch your beautiful boat slam into the dock or the offender bear down on you.

The manufacturers of some of these boats try to get partially around the problem by building a ledge along the sheer barely wide enough for a mountain goat to negotiate. Side decks don't have to be the width of a sidewalk, but they should be at least 18 inches wide to allow a person of average build to walk fore and aft easily while both of his or her hands are occupied with a large coil of line or a spare anchor; you shouldn't have to crab along sideways while holding on to a safety rail with one hand.

On an offshore boat, the walk-around areas should also incorporate significant bulwarks at the sheer—preferably 4 to 6 inches deep from stern to amidships and gradually rising to 8 inches or more at the bow. A number of cruising boats provide only a teak toe or cap rail at the sheer. Again, if you cruise long enough, the time will come when you or a crew member has to go on deck in a stiff blow. One slip on a wet deck and that person can shoot right over such an insignificant rail and below the lower lifeline to plunge overboard. Even if he or she is wearing a safety harness, it can be a hazardous and potentially life-threatening situation.

The deck of a cruising boat should be entirely encircled by a stout safety railing of teak, stainless steel, or aluminum, and the railing's stanchions should be through-bolted to backing plates. Stanchions that are simply screwed into the deck could well give way if a crew member is thrown hard against them in a heavy sea. The top of this railing should strike a person of average height at the waist or higher. If it is much lower, his center of gravity will be above it. If the boat rolls heavily in his direction and he is slammed into it, he would stand a better than fair chance of being pitched over the railing into the sea.

The area between the top of the rail and the deck should be transected by a lifeline, most often a stainless steel cable encased in plastic that passes through holes drilled in the stanchions or pass-throughs welded to the inside of them. Again, if anyone must go on deck in a blow and slips on a wet deck, he has a much better chance of grabbing onto something if he has a railing and lifeline rather than a single railing. There also should be boarding gates in the railing port and starboard which should likewise have lifelines. One end should be permanently affixed to one stanchion with a hinge or welded chain link, and the opening end should be secured firmly to the next stanchion with a stout bolt lock or a pelican hook.

The deck should have hefty cleats on each side to accommodate dock lines at the bow and stern and spring lines amidships. Cruising boats over about 40 feet should have two spring cleats on each side which divide the hull length into about thirds. All deck cleats should be through-bolted to stainless-steel backing plates, and the sheer of the boat outboard of them should be protected with a rub or chafe plate. The horns of the cleats should be at least 6 inches long and there should be a minimum of 4 inches between the bottom of the horn and the top of the base to accommodate up to ¾-inch-diameter dock lines. A nice touch offered by some higher-quality cruising-boat manufacturers is the added fittings on a sliding track just below the sheer which allows dockside fenders to be placed wherever they are needed.

All horizontal surfaces of the deck should be covered with nonskid material to provide secure footing. Teak decks and cockpit soles are beautiful, but they are difficult to keep looking good, over time they tend to crack and buckle, and under a tropical sun they get hot as the devil.

CRUISING COCKPITS

In an effort to get the maximum use out of every inch of space, the designers of many cruising motor yachts run an aft master stateroom right to the stern of their boats, then top it with some type of fully or partly enclosed aft deck. With this arrangement, access to the water at anchor for swimming, diving, or boarding the tender involves walking backward down a narrow ladder and perching on a swim platform.

A much more practical arrangement is a water-level cruising cockpit incorporating a transom door that leads directly onto a swim platform (Fig. 2.3). With that arrangement, boarding, loading, and unloading the tender, especially in rough weather, is far easier. A cruising cockpit also solves the problem of adequate line-handling space aft and provides an ideal way to leave and reboard the boat for swimming and diving. If properly organized, it can also offer a handy place to store diving, snorkeling, and fishing equipment without dragging it through the interior of the vessel. For safety, the cockpit of a cruising vessel should be enclosed by a coaming which is at least waist-high, not the type of low coaming found on sportfishing boats, which strikes a person of average height about midthigh.

Fig. 2.3: *A roomy cockpit or aft deck close to the water, along with a transom door and swim platform, will greatly simplify the process of boarding and exiting a vessel at anchor.*

UPPER DECK LAYOUT

A good cruising vessel will have a flying bridge as the primary station from which it will be helmed in fair weather (Fig. 2.4). For safety in rough seas, you should be able to reach it by way of a protected ladder from the pilothouse rather than having to go on deck. A Bimini top for the flying bridge is a virtual necessity for providing shade in the tropics (especially in light of the recent warnings about the sun causing skin cancer), but you should be able to fold it down easily to secure it in high winds. On a full-displacement-hull boat I recommend you stay away from elaborate flying-bridge enclosures. They create significant wind resistance at the worst possible point—high above the vessel's center of gravity—which contributes to her natural tendency to roll. Flying-bridge enclosures are necessary only in foul weather, and under those conditions you probably will be commanding the vessel from its lower steering station anyway.

Fig. 2.4: *The flying bridge of a cruising powerboat should provide generous space in its console for installing instruments and a comfortable seating arrangement for both the helmsperson and at least one companion.*

Check the flying bridge for good visibility forward and to each side. For docking, other than stepping around a companion chair next to the helm chair, you should be able to move quickly to either side and look down on your vessel's sheer without having to climb over or move anything. Also make sure the console provides enough space to accommodate a full array of engine instruments, compass, and navigation and communications electronics. At the very least, you will need room to mount a depth-sounder repeater (as you will see, maybe even two) and a VHF radio convenient to the helm. Many cruisers also like to install a radar screen and SSB radio topside as a backup to their main units in the pilothouse. It would be nice if the flying-bridge console also provided a reasonable area on which to spread a chart, but few builders seem to plan for that amenity.

Seating for the helmsperson should be in the form of an

Fig. 2.5: *An offshore cruising powerboat should have a stout mast for carrying its radar antenna. It should also allow the installation of halyards for hoisting a quarantine flag when entering foreign ports and a courtesy flag once clearance has been completed.*

adjustable pedestal chair rather than bench seat, which usually will not allow adequate visibility or comfortable access to the steering wheel and controls. It's also nice if there is room to install a companion chair next to your helm chair. On long passages, you'll be grateful for a little company.

On many cruising boats, the flying bridge or the cabintop just aft of it is also used as an additional outside lounging area and tender storage area. So long as it does not interfere with the helmsman's visibility, lounging space topside is a plus. For reasons we'll go into in a later section, I don't think the cabintop is an ideal place to store a cruising vessel's tender.

The upper deck level of the bluewater cruiser also should support a sturdy mast (Fig. 2.5) which provides secure mounting for a radar antenna, lightning protection, and halyards for hoisting a courtesy flag of the nations whose waters you cruise and the quarantine flag you will be required to fly when entering a foreign port. The arch seen on some motor yachts is a good place to mount a radar antenna but an arch alone normally won't allow the installation of a lightning rod high enough to provide an adequate zone of protection. It also doesn't give you any place to attach flag halyards.

INTERIOR LAYOUT

A current trend in cruising-yacht interior layout is to create a lower helm station that is little more than a bench seat in the forward part of the main salon or in one of its forward corners. The theory behind the design is that the helmsperson, who usually is also the boat's owner, doesn't want to be separated from his guests while the vessel is under way. That may be fine if the boat will be used only for in-shore day cruises, but it's a mistake in an offshore cruising boat. There are several reasons the offshore cruiser should have a separate pilothouse that can be closed off from the other interior areas of the boat.

In the first place, commanding a cruising vessel at sea is a job that should have the helmsperson's primary attention. He or she should be able to operate in a relatively private area, not in the main salon where he/she could be distracted by extraneous activities going on around him or her. It's fine for crew and guests to visit the pilothouse and keep the helmsperson company while the vessel is under way, but a separate pilothouse communicates the idea that it is the vessel's command center and that the vessel's safe operation takes first priority. A separate pilothouse also provides a necessary area where the charts, binoculars, compass protractor, and parallel rules required for the vessel's navigation can be kept instantly within the helmsperson's reach, not scattered about the salon because someone set them aside to make room for a tray of hors d'oeuvres. Another significant reason for having a separate pilothouse is that on night runs it can be properly darkened to preserve the helmsperson's vision while the normal life of the vessel goes on in a fully lighted salon. And make no mistake; in offshore cruising, night runs will become a way of life.

A well-thought-out pilothouse offers good visibility to each side and forward. Visibility aft is not so important because docking normally should be done from the flying bridge. Its console should also provide generous space for navigational and communications electronics as well as space for full-sized charts to be plotted and stored unfolded.

The pilothouse should offer space for a comfortable helm chair directly behind the wheel, and I've seen some rather interesting approaches.

In Frank Glindmeier's *Summer Wind*, the dinette was immediately aft and to port of the pilothouse wheel and the passageway up from the galley was to starboard. The space between the wheel and a cabinet directly behind it was so narrow that installing a permanent helm seat would have made it impossible for Frank's wife Lee to reach the dinette from the passageway. For most of the trip, the lack of a pilothouse helm seat was no problem, as Frank normally operated the vessel from the flying bridge. For the long run up and down the Inside Passage to Alaska and back, where cold, damp weather could be expected as the norm, Frank installed in the pilothouse sole just behind the wheel a second socket to accept the pedestal-mounted helm seat on the flying bridge. In good weather, the socket was sealed with a screw-in cover to keep it flush with the sole. In bad weather, he brought his flying-bridge helm seat down to the pilothouse, installed it in the socket, and settled in to run the boat in sheltered, heated comfort.

Another cruising friend's motor yacht did not have a pilothouse but simply a lower steering station at the forward end of the main salon. For visibility under way, he wanted an elevated, forward-facing helm seat. For conversing with his guests at anchor or the dock, he wanted a chair at normal seating height that faced aft. His solution was to install a barber's chair behind the lower helm which he could pivot in either direction and raise or lower with a few strokes on its hydraulic foot pump.

The pilothouse should also provide some sort of seating for those who want to visit with the helmsperson while the vessel is under way. Some builders provide this seating by putting the dining area in the pilothouse. A number of people whose boats are arranged this way think it's fine. I personally find it rather cumbersome as it makes serving meals from the galley awkward and demotes the pilothouse from its function as a separate area of the vessel. To me, if space permits, a better approach is a companion chair next to the helm chair or a raised bench against the pilothouse's aft bulkhead.

You will find it far more convenient if the pilothouse, the main salon, and the galley are on a single level. Some cruising-boat designs incorporate a pilothouse whose sole is raised above the rest of the main deck level. You'll find that after months of cruising, going up and down even three or four steps every time you enter and leave the pilothouse gets to be something of a hassle.

A troubling trend among cruising-yacht builders is to produce an open, airy feeling by designing salons with expansive areas of glass both on the sides and aft. If these boats ever take green water over the side rails or stern, those windows could easily be smashed in and the boat flooded with thousands of gallons of water. The danger is especially acute in the so-called wide-body motor yachts whose windows are not protected by a side deck overhang and whose salons run all the way to the stern of the vessel. These boats may be fine for cruising protected waters, but I personally would not buy one for bluewater passage-making. If you are considering a boat with that kind of exposure, make certain its windows are of tempered safety glass or, better still, of a Lexan-type plastic material. If you are planning to take it offshore, you would be wise to carry stout shutters of Lexan or plywood that could be quickly and easily secured to the outside of the windows in a blow, but the only people I've ever known to carry them are deepwater sailors who have an appreciation for the damage several hundred thousand gallons of seawater slamming down on a vessel at freight-train speeds can inflict.

Fig. 2.6: *A galley equipped with all the amenities and placed in reasonable proximity to the dinette or dining area will greatly simplify the cruising cook's job of preparing and serving meals.*

We'll discuss cruising galleys (Fig. 2.6) in detail later, but I'd suggest you look for a boat with its galley on the main deck level rather than belowdecks. This arrangement allows the cook to be involved with guests during meal preparation and makes getting food to the dining area easier.

BELOWDECKS ACCOMMODATIONS

The decisions you make regarding the number of state-rooms you need will largely determine what you look for in the arrangement of sleeping accommodations. Just make certain all the bunks are large enough for a grown person to stretch out in comfort and that at least one is a good sea-berth where the off-watch can get a decent night's rest without being thrown on the cabin sole.

Check the heads carefully for sufficient operating room. In extended cruising, you'll find stall showers a great blessing. There are few more unpleasant experiences in cruising than having to pull a cold, clammy curtain around you in order to take a shower without inundating the entire head—which you usually wind up doing anyway.

In order to provide the owners a valuable degree of privacy, the owner's stateroom and head should be in a separate suite aft rather than forward with guest or crew accommodations. When I visited with Bob and Eunice Stephens, who used to spend weeks at a time aboard their 58-footer *Moondancer* in the Gulf of California, the ship's complement included a total of eight people, which Eunice said was about average. When I asked her how she coped with constant entertaining she said her salvation was *Moondancer*'s aft owner's stateroom. "If I get a little rattled by all the activity aboard," she said, "I can spend half an hour down there by myself and I'm ready to handle whatever happens."

In some otherwise well-thought-out, well-constructed cruising vessels, the owner's stateroom is located in the bow, which is the area of the hull most subject to motion both under way and at anchor. I would recommend you think long and hard before buying a vessel with an owner's stateroom in that location. On an extended offshore passage in anything other than a flat calm, there is no way the off-watch is going to get proper rest in such a berth. As the bow falls off a wave, he or she will be lifted off the bunk, then slammed back down on it as the bow lifts to meet the next wave.

ENGINE-ROOM LAYOUT

In the next chapter, we'll get into the details of the specific systems you'll want your engine room to house; here we're looking only for a good layout. Your major concern should be accessibility to both the engine room itself and the main pieces of equipment in it.

If at all possible, select a boat whose engine space has standing headroom and is entered by a bulkhead passageway below-decks rather than a hatch in the salon sole. That arrangement often is impossible to find in cruising boats under 50 feet, but you normally will be in and out of the engine space at least twice a day, even at anchor or at the dock, and every couple of hours or so when you are under way. After weeks or months of moving furniture aside, lifting up a hatch, then crawling around on your hands and knees several times a day, you will be willing to sell one of your children to raise the money for a boat with an engine space that has a walk-in entrance and standing head-room.

Look for a boat with engine space that provides easy access to all sides of the power plants, generators, stuffing boxes, and batteries, especially for routine operations like checking oil and water levels, which you will be doing at least once a day. It also should be well lighted and have explosion-proof fixtures and space for any accessory equipment you might want to add. It should also be well sound-insulated from the boat's living spaces. The most effective soundproofing utilizes a material that has a lead backing.

Once you have a good idea of the type of layout that is best suited to your particular cruising needs, the next thing to figure out is what you will need in the way of basic systems to make your boat a comfortable floating home.

3

CHOOSE THE RIGHT BASIC SYSTEMS

As with layout, you also are going to be living every day
with the basic systems built into your cruising boat to handle
such necessary functions as generating and distributing electricity, keeping you cool when it's hot and warm when it's not,
preserving and preparing food, handling water and waste,
and—most important—keeping you safe. Once you have purchased a vessel, it can be impractical and expensive—in some

cases, virtually impossible—to correct deficiencies, so you want to select wisely at the outset. Here are some things I suggest you look for.

AUTOMATIC ENGINE-ROOM FIRE-EXTINGUISHING SYSTEM

I personally would not go to sea in a cruising vessel whose engine room was not protected by an automatic fire-extinguishing system (Fig. 3.1). These devices are cheap compared to the lives and property they protect, and you probably will recoup some of their cost through lower insurance premiums. If a vessel you consider does not have such a system installed, you can add it later, but if one is installed, it should meet certain minimum requirements. Systems that use Halon 1301, for instance, are preferable to those that use carbon dioxide (CO_2). Halon is more effective at lower concentrations, is lighter and more compact to

Fig. 3.1: *Every cruising powerboat should have a properly installed automatic fire extinguisher system in its engine room (left) which also can be manually activated by an above-decks discharge lever (right).*

carry, will not corrode electrical or electronic equipment, and will not asphyxiate you if you should be caught in the engine space when it discharges. The heat sensors that activate the system should be mounted just above and at the aft end of the engines and secured to a permanent bulkhead, not to a removable hatch or door that might be blown away in an explosion. The system should sound an alarm in the pilothouse and on the flying bridge if it is discharged; it also should be equipped with remote discharge levers at both locations.

When a CO_2 system discharges in an engine room, it normally chokes off diesel engines and generators by depriving them of air. Diesel engines and generators, however, will continue to run just fine on discharged Halon. (At one time, in fact, the Army considered using Halon to give its diesel-powered battle tanks an extra kick in the pants.) For that reason, if an installed engine-room fire-extinguisher system discharges Halon, its activation should also automatically shut down the vessel's electrical system and the fuel and air supplies to its engines and generators. For reasons we'll discuss in Chapter 12, on cruising safety, the engine room should also be equipped with a transparent, heat-resistant port through which you can see what is going on in the engine room without having to open the door or hatch. Once you're sure a fire is out, you should be able to manually override an automatic shutdown system to restart an undamaged engine. In a tight situation, you could need power to maneuver or reach shore.

ALARM SYSTEMS

At the very least, any cruising vessel you consider should have an audible alarm at both the lower steering station and on the flying bridge to alert you when the bilge pumps are working excessively, which could mean the bilge is taking on water. It also would be nice if the boat has alarms to warn of a drop in engine-oil pressure or a rise in the temperature of the engine cooling water, transmission-drive oil, or exhaust gases. Some yacht manufacturers offer a comprehensive monitoring system (Fig. 3.2) that contains these alarms and also warns if the engine-room fire extinguisher discharges or you lose AC power from your generator or shore lines.

Fig. 3.2: *A good alarm system will not only alert the helmsperson to a problem but quickly identify it and pinpoint its location.*

STEERING SYSTEMS

If at all possible, opt for a boat with hydraulic rather than mechanical steering. When the vessel is steered manually, hydraulic steering is far less tiring on the helmsperson, and it is easier to fit with a good autopilot.

ENGINE SYNCHRONIZERS

On twin-screw vessels, engines that are not in synch are not fuel-efficient. The electronic rpm gauges found on most vessels are prone to frequent interruptions and aren't particularly accurate even when they are working. The digital type are much more reliable. Mechanical rpm gauges are best, but the characteristics of their installation pretty well limit them to the engine room. Some skippers claim they can synchronize twin engines simply by their sound, but I'll wager if you put accurate tachometers on a pair of engines set by the best of them, you'd find they still vary by a hundred or so rpm. Engine synchronizers that match the rpm of the two power plants are not absolute necessities, but they are helpful.

ELECTRICAL SYSTEMS

Whether or not your vessel will have a 120/240-volt alternating-current (AC) electrical generator on board, the first thing you need is a good battery-powered direct-current (DC) system. Yacht manufacturers build cruising boats with 12-, 24-, or 32-volt DC electrical systems. In understanding the differences between them, bear in mind that the higher the voltage the more amps a DC system can push a greater distance through smaller-diameter wire with less voltage-drop.

On that basis, a 32-volt system would appear to be preferable, but little of the accessory equipment found on recreational vessels is available in that rather odd voltage. It originally entered the recreational marine industry, in fact, because for years Detroit Diesel offered its larger engines only with 32-volt starting motors. Now Detroit Diesel offers its larger engines with 24-volt starting motors, and most major yacht manufacturers are abandoning 32-volt systems in favor of the 24-volt alternative. The 12-volt systems are a spillover from the automotive industry. They are still used in most boats under about 50 feet because the wiring runs on smaller vessels are not long enough to make voltage-drop a serious concern.

The best choice for a DC electrical system aboard a cruising vessel over 50 feet is 24 volts. Many of the navigation and communications electronics you will want aboard your vessel are available in that voltage. For installing equipment that is available only in 12 volts, use a small, individual 12-to-24-volt power converter for each unit rather than a single larger unit so a failure will not mean complete loss of your 24-volt gear.

Whatever the voltage of the DC system aboard any vessel you consider, make certain the batteries are easy to reach and service. You'll be checking them frequently, and you don't want to have to stand on your head to top them off with water. Also make certain they are well secured, have a meter to indicate their condition (preferably as part of a DC distribution panel in the

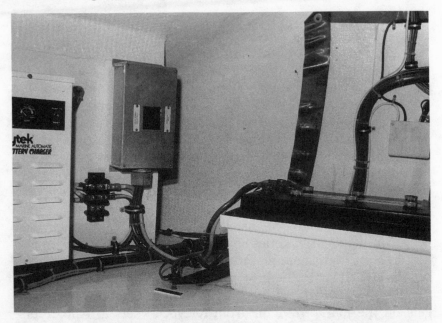

Fig. 3.3:   *A backup battery with its own charger installed as high as possible in a cruising powerboat (here placed beneath the flying bridge) can keep vital communications and navigation electronics functioning even after the primary batteries have been shorted out by flooding or their cables burned through by fire.*

pilothouse), and are equipped with an explosion-proof selector switch.

Most yacht builders install batteries in the engine room as low as possible to help lower the vessel's center of gravity. In that location, they probably will be quickly shorted out if the vessel takes on water, and an engine-room fire is likely to melt their cables in a matter of minutes. For those reasons, I'm a strong advocate of installing an extra battery as high in the vessel as possible—under the pilothouse or flying-bridge console, for instance—which in an emergency can be used to power essential communications and navigation electronics (Fig. 3.3). One of the new gel-cell batteries such as the Prevailer, which can't leak even if its case is ruptured, would be ideal for such an installation. It's a fairly simple matter to rig such a battery with a small voltage-regulated trickle charger to keep it up to its full-rated amps, a gauge to monitor its condition, and a switch to throw the vessel's electronics load over to it in an emergency.

BATTERIES-ONLY CRUISING

Like hundreds of other cruisers, Charlie and Nancy Bowen find on their cruises from Florida to Grenada and back that it's possible to cruise extensively and comfortably on a vessel that does not have a 120/240-volt AC generator but operates entirely on batteries—normally 12-volt. Under way the batteries are kept charged by a 12-volt generator or alternator driven by a belt off the main-engine flywheel. At the dock, they can be fed by a battery charger that transforms 120-volt current to 12 volts and converts AC to DC. If you go that route, carry along at least one spare generator or alternator and a couple of extra voltage regulators and know how to install and test them; be certain you have two banks of batteries so you will always have a fresh battery to start your main engine; and be very careful to keep the battery switch set in the proper position.

For this kind of cruising, there are all manner of 12-volt gadgets on the market ranging from television sets to hair dryers. For the times when you might really need 120-volt power you can tie up in a marina and plug in to shore power. For 120-volt power at anchor you can carry along a small portable generator driven by a gasoline engine that produces 500 to 2,000 watts. If you carry a portable generator, just be certain you are aware that gasoline and boats are one dangerous combination and electricity and water are a second. Operate it aboard your vessel with extreme caution and only in a well-ventilated area such as your aft deck or cruising cockpit.

With a batteries-only electrical system, you obviously will not have sufficient voltage for an electric range and oven and will need to use either liquefied petroleum gas (LPG) or compressed natural gas (CNG) for cooking. CNG is the safer of the two because it is lighter than air and in the event of a leak will tend to rise and dissipate into the atmosphere. LPG is heavier than air and can settle in your vessel's bilge where it could be ignited by an electrical or static spark. CNG might be a good choice if you will be cruising well-populated areas and are willing to go searching for a source to refill your tank—which may be hard to locate. For cruising remote areas, LPG is the better way to go because in the boondocks it's almost impossible to find CNG. If you use LPG, however, you must take proper precautions. In order to avoid its dangers, install your LPG tank in its own well-ventilated locker on deck and equip it and any appliances it will serve with a switch that closes a valve on the tank itself when the appliance is not in use. With battery power alone, you also will not have sufficient power for electrical refrigeration unless you run your main engine almost constantly. A better approach is to use a mechanical holding-plate refrigeration system whose compressor is driven by a belt off the main-engine flywheel rather than by DC current through the batteries.

You also won't be able to have an electric water heater on board. The units that utilize the heat in the main engine's cooling system through a heat exchanger work well but require rather adroit scheduling to ensure that all aboard get a hot shower.

ELECTRICAL GENERATORS

For most of us who want to take all our creature comforts with us when we go cruising, an on-board AC generator is a must. It's best to stick with the top names in the field such as Onan, Kohler, Alaska Diesel (manufacturer of the Northern Lights brand), and Westerbeke. Less well known products may be cheaper but may also lack an adequate service network.

The generators normally used on cruising vessels range in capacity from around 4 to 20 kilowatts (kw), and you need to size the unit you select carefully. Obviously, a generator with too little capacity will not give you adequate power. But installing one with capacity well in excess of the load you will put on it is needlessly expensive and can create problems as well. Generators operate most efficiently when loaded to about 80 percent of their rated capacity. If they are run consistently with significantly less load, their windings tend to burn out quickly. To size a generator for your vessel, add up the greatest load you are likely to put on it at any one time, then add a 20-percent margin and select a unit of appropriate kw output.

Wonderful as generators are, they can be the bane of the cruising man's existence. In hard cruising use, you will be lucky to get thirty days straight running out of your generator without having some kind of problem. Most of the difficulties occur not in their basic windings or engines but in their electronic controls such as relays and printed circuit boards, which fall victim to heat and vibration. "Installing a relay on a generator," an exasperated cruiser once told me, "is like installing it on a paint-mixing machine at the hardware store." He said he had found the best way to keep relays from being vibrated out of position was to seal the screws that attach them in place with epoxy glue.

For those reasons, you'd be wise to carry not one but two generators so you will have a backup unit to maintain essential loads when your main unit is not feeling well. To keep costs manageable, the backup unit can have about half the kilowatt output of your main unit. You'll have to do a little juggling to keep the loads within its limits, but that's better than being completely without a generator until you reach the next major port where you can get your main unit back in action. Even with a backup unit, carry extra relays and circuit boards in your spare-parts inventory.

A properly installed generator will be cooled by fresh water circulating inside a saltwater-cooled heat exchanger (but be sure the heat exchanger is made of copper or copper-nickel alloy, not cast iron). The saltwater intake should be equipped with a raw-water strainer, a water-lift muffler, and an hour meter. Its engine should also be fitted with a fuel filter. You should be able to start and shut down the generator remotely from the main salon or pilothouse electrical panel (Fig. 3.4) which has a positive-lock switch that makes it impossible for the vessel to receive shore power and generator power or the output from two generators at the same time. Electric fuel-priming and oil-changing systems on a generator are nice but not essential. Optional sound boxes do help muffle the noise a generator makes, but a number of cruisers I know wind up removing them and leaving them ashore because they can make servicing the unit unduly difficult. Any vessel you consider that will carry a generator should allow you to install it where you can get to all sides of it easily for service, especially for checking its oil and water levels, which you will need to do daily.

Many of us who love generators for the on-board amenities they provide also detest having their droning racket despoil the quiet of a peaceful anchorage. When I visited Carleton Mitchell aboard *Coyaba*, he showed me how you can have the best of both worlds by installing a good electric hold-plate refrigeration system and using LPG gas for cooking. "I can operate all the boat's electrical equipment and keep the batteries charged," he told me, "by running the generator only an hour each morning and night."

With such an arrangement, it also is helpful to install an inverter which, within limits, will allow you to operate small 120-

Fig. 3.4: *A well-designed electrical panel will allow all the electrical systems on a cruising vessel to operate on shore power, its own generator, or battery power as circumstances require.*

volt AC appliances off 12- or 24-volt DC battery power when the generator is not running. About the only thing this setup will not allow you to do is run your vessel's electrically powered heating and air-conditioning system at anchor. For that, you'll still have to crank up the generator.

SHORE-POWER INLETS

To safely accommodate the variety of docking situations you are likely to encounter in offshore cruising, the vessel you choose should have at least one adequately sized 120/140-volt shore-power inlet on both its port and starboard sides. It is even better if it has one set of inlets on either side forward and another set on either side aft, preferably in the cruising cockpit. If your vessel has only a single inlet and you must run a power cord across a foredeck or along a side deck to reach it, you could be issuing an open invitation to an accident.

Another handy device your shore-power system should include is a two-winding polarizing transformer which will eliminate any possible damage from reverse polarity of the shoreside power supply. Within limits, it will also allow you to operate 240-volt on-board equipment even though only a 120-volt power supply is available at the dock. Again within limits, in situations where only 240-volt shoreside power is available, it also allows you to split it and operate 120-volt on-board equipment off either of its two hot wires and ground.

ELECTRICAL WIRING

The manner in which electrical wiring is installed in a cruising vessel (Fig. 3.5) is a dead giveaway to the quality of its construction. If you encounter a vessel whose wiring looks like a pile of multicolored spaghetti, pass it by in favor of one whose wiring looks like it belongs in the space shuttle.

Under real-life conditions on the water, even the toughest-

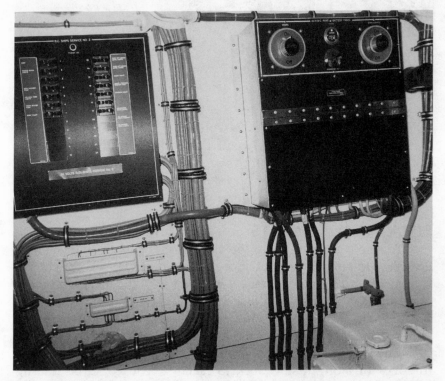

Fig. 3.5: One of the most readily-apparent hallmarks of a well-built cruising vessel is a neat electrical installation where all wiring is coded, tightly secured to the bulkheads, and protected from chafe.

built cruising boat is subjected to enormous straining and flexing which can chafe through improperly installed electrical wiring and create a significant fire hazard. In a well-laid-out electrical system, all circuits will be color-coded and numbered and the owner's manual will contain a detailed wiring schematic. All wiring bundles should be strapped with non-conductive bands every 18 inches and secured to a bulkhead at least every 36 inches by a nonconductive or insulated fastener. At every point where a wiring bundle passes through a bulkhead, it should be protected by a heavy rubber collar and cushioning to prevent chafe.

In order to protect the vessel's electrical wiring and equipment from electrolysis, all metal masses from the engine blocks to the hull fittings should be securely bonded together by at least #8 solid copper wire or 2-inch copper strapping which is connected to a heavy copper groundplate installed outside the hull. The electrical system of any vessel that has an aluminum hull or any aluminum parts below the waterline also should be equipped with an isolation transformer.

For Further Reading: The most comprehensive work I have seen on marine electrical systems is *Your Boat's Electrical System* by Conrad Miller and E. S. Maloney (New York: Hearst Marine Books, New York: 1988). It is available through many marine book stores or the Dolphin Book Club.

THROUGH-HULL FITTINGS

All underwater through-hull fittings should be of "noble" metals such as brass, bronze, or stainless steel—never plastic— and should be protected by a sea cock.

HEATING/AIR-CONDITIONING SYSTEMS

The most practical heating and air-conditioning system for cruising is a good water-source reverse-cycle unit (on shore often called a "heat pump"). You can't determine if an installation aboard a vessel you are considering is adequately sized without doing a complex heat-loss calculation, but do check that its distribution fans deliver an adequate volume of air to each area of the boat. The best of these installations will have separate compressors serving the main salon/pilothouse and the sleeping accommodations and will provide each stateroom with its own thermostat and fan control.

WATER SYSTEMS

If your cruising plans include an extensive foray into the boondocks, obtaining adequate supplies of potable water can be a major headache, especially during the dry season in areas like the Bahamas, the Virgin Islands, and Mexico's Baja Peninsula. If you do find an adequate supply, it is likely to be expensive. In those areas I've paid as much as a nickel a gallon for water, then found it had all manner of little squiggly things swimming around in it. Even worse are the invisible bacteria and viruses some water contains. They can cause a disconcerting case of the yucky tummy which can become serious if it leads to dehydration.

If you plan to rely on whatever water you can carry on board, your vessel should have a capacity of at least 300 gallons. Even then, if you have only two to four adults aboard and are careful with water use, you probably will be looking for a place to replenish your supply every week to ten days. If you go that route and will be cruising areas where the quality of the water is likely to be dubious, you can avoid at least some of the potential health problems by installing a kitchen-type filter on your galley faucet, then drawing water for drinking and cooking only from there. These filters are inexpensive and available at larger hardware stores and home-improvement centers. An even better approach would be to install a larger, commercial type charcoal filter in the line leading to that faucet from your water storage tank. Another way you can help prevent illness is by sanitizing your water supply with a product called Aqua-Tabs. Use one mega-tab per 100 gallons of water each time you fill your tanks. They will effervesce and produce a slightly chlorine taste, but it will disappear in a day or two. Over time, water tanks can build up scale and deposits which are a breeding ground for coliform bacteria and protozoa that can cause dysentery and a waterborne parasite called Giardia. To keep your tanks clean, about once a year you should fill them, add a product called Puriclean (142 ounces per 600 gallons of water), make a brief run so it can slosh around for several hours, drain the tanks (letting part of the water run through your vessel's plumbing system and faucets), refill them with clean water, and pump that out as a rinse before you take aboard your next supply.

The best way to make sure you have plenty of germ-free potable water is to install a watermaker that turns salt water into fresh. The units now on the market reduce salt and other contaminants from the 36,000 parts per million (ppm) typically found in seawater to around 500 ppm, well below the 1,500 ppm standard for drinking water established by major health organizations.

A watermaker's advantages are not limited to making certain the water consumed on board won't give you and your guests a case of Montezuma's revenge. It will also free you from having to plan your cruise around stops where you can refill your tanks. By eliminating the need for carrying the tremendous weight of several hundred gallons of water, it can also increase your vessel's range and fuel efficiency. Some cruisers who install watermakers aboard their vessels convert unneeded water tanks to fuel tanks, but that can be a risky practice as they are not really designed for the purpose. Installing a watermaker also gives you the option of considering the addition of such high-water-use appliances as a clothes washer (the stacked apartment-type washer/dryer units are compact and work well) and a dishwasher, which are really not practical to carry if you must rely only on the fresh water your vessel can carry.

If you consider adding a watermaker to your boat, there are a number of things to consider.

The units are of two basic types: evaporative and reverse-osmosis. At present, only one company (Riley-Beaird, Inc.) offers recreational boat owners an evaporative unit, which distills seawater through a process that utilizes engine heat. The rest of the industry has gone to the reverse-osmosis process, which forces seawater through a semipermeable membrane to filter out salt ions (Fig. 3.6).

The reverse-osmosis process requires a raw-water pump that delivers a minimum of 800 psi of pressure, and most units operate closer to 1,000 psi. In most systems, the raw-water pump is driven off the vessel's AC generator at 120 or 240 volts, with the higher voltage being the better choice. A typical 300-gallon-per-day (gpd) unit draws around 17 amps at 120 volts or 8.5 amps at 240 volts. There are, however, alternatives: Village Ma-

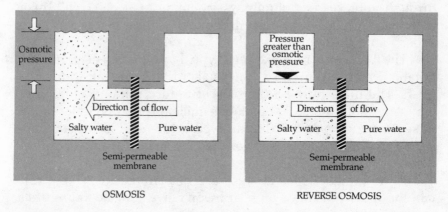

OSMOSIS   REVERSE OSMOSIS

Fig. 3.6: *The reverse osmosis process of making potable water works by forc-*
ing salt water through a semi-permeable membrane at pressures of around
1000 psi.

rine offers several units that operate off 12- or 24-volt battery
power; Galley Maid offers a pump driven by a separate diesel
engine; and Standard Communications, Inc., offers one driven
by a vessel's main engine through a magnetic clutch. An ideal
watermaker installation would drive the pump off the main engine while under way, then allow you to switch over to shore
power when tied to a dock or to generator power when you are
at anchor.

Watermakers come as single-unit cabinet models or as component systems. A typical cabinet unit producing 200 gpd requires about 4 cubic feet of space and weighs around 110 pounds.

Component units (Fig. 3.7) allow the membrane to be located outside the engine room. This can be a major advantage
since manufacturers recommend membranes not be subjected to
temperatures above 120 degrees Fahrenheit, which can easily be
exceeded in an engine room, especially when you are cruising
the tropics.

Watermaker prices vary widely. One company's 100-gpd unit,
for instance, lists at around $2,800, while another's is about $3,800.
In comparing prices, look closely at what is included as standard
and what is an extra-cost option. Most manufacturers, for instance, don't include the raw-water pump, which can add $250
to $300 to your cost. Others charge extra for mounting or instal-

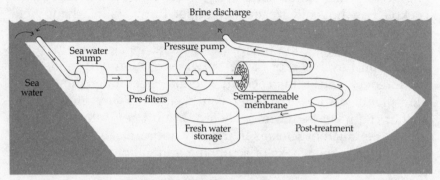

REVERSE OSMOSIS SYSTEM

Fig. 3.7: *A component watermaker system allows its heat-sensitive membrane to be installed outside the engine room where it will not be damaged by excessive heat.*

lation kits. Also look closely at each system's prefiltration setup. All include a basic raw-water strainer and should include an oil/water separator and a charcoal filter to remove chlorine, which the membrane will not take out. If the latter two accessories are not part of the basic system, you should plan on adding them as extras. Cruising acquaintances have given me good reports on Standard HRO, Sea Recovery, and Village watermakers.

One necessary feature that is standard on some units, an option on others, is an automatic salinity monitor which prevents water that has not been adequately purified from being pumped into the storage tank and contaminating fresh water already in the tank. Another worthwhile option is an ultraviolet sterilizer. Beware of a salesman who says you don't need a sterilizer because bacteria are larger than salt ions and his unit filters them out. What he says is true, as far as it goes. But you still need the sterilizer to kill viruses, which none of the membranes will filter out.

Whether you choose to carry all your fresh water with you or to install a watermaker, the vessel you select should have dockside water inlets both port and starboard and they should be fitted with a pressure-regulating valve. Also check the amount of pressure the on-board pumps can actually deliver to the galley, lavatories, and heads. There also should be a freshwater outlet in the engine room for topping off the cooling systems of your engines and generator. One nice touch you'll find useful in the cockpit is a hot/cold freshwater outlet fitted with a hand-held showerhead.

Aside from a good freshwater system, its also helpful if the vessel you buy has a pressure saltwater system with outlets on the foredeck and in the cockpit. The foredeck outlet should provide plenty of pressure to let you blast away any mud on the anchor chain before it comes aboard. If mud gets into your chain locker, the microorganisms in it decay and can cause a sickening odor which takes weeks of scrubbing and gallons of disinfectant to dispel.

WASTE MANAGEMENT

The laws of most nations now prohibit the discharge of un-treated waste into their coastal waters. Even though most na-tions—including the United States—don't adequately enforce such laws and don't provide the dockside pump-out stations neces-sary to make them practical, you should comply with them any-way in the name of protecting the environment. That means that any vessel you consider should have a sewage holding tank for use when you are in coastal waters. It should be plumbed for dockside pump-out and also should be equipped with a macer-ator pump for overboard discharge when you are well out to sea. Some cruisers fit their vessels' heads and galleys with Y-valves that permit them to discharge waste directly overboard. That may be all right for shower sumps, but operating marine heads that way allows the direct discharge of human solid waste overboard which is disgusting, not to mention inconsiderate. Any such waste should empty into the holding tank and be run through a macerator before it is discharged, and then only when the vessel is well offshore.

A number of cruisers simply dump their trash over the side, but I hope you will keep yours on board until you can properly dispose of it ashore. Be especially careful about properly dispos-ing of the plastic ring holders on beer and soft drink six-packs. Seabirds and turtles get tangled in them, and the encounter is almost always fatal. If you have room to install a trash compac-tor and the AC power to operate one, it will be useful for reduc-ing solid waste to a more stowable volume.

CRUISING REFRIGERATION

For cruising well off the marina circuit, the household-type refrigerator/freezers on most production yachts are totally unsatisfactory. These units have such skimpy insulation that they require almost constant power input. The "frost-free" type have internal heaters to dispell frost and condensation which draw about 2 amps even when the cooling coil's thermostat is not calling for power. Also, their freezer sections are too small to hold more than one or two weeks' worth of frozen provisions.

For extended cruising, the most practical approach to refrigeration is to install a holding-plate system which employs a eutectic solution of water-diluted ethylene glycol (the active ingredient in automotive antifreeze). This solution freezes solid at about zero degrees Fahrenheit and absorbs heat much more slowly than the freon gas used in household refrigerators. Holding-plate refrigeration compressors can be powered by a variety of sources: 12- or 24-volt DC battery current; 120- or 240-volt AC current from shorepower or an on-board generator; your vessel's main engine(s) through a 12-, 24-, or 120-volt alternator or a mechanical clutch; or some combination of these sources. The most desirable holding-plate system would employ two separate compressors: a mechanical unit that operates off the main engine through a clutch arrangement while your vessel is under way; and an electrical unit that operates off 120- or 240-volt shoreside power when your vessel is tied to a dock or its AC generator when it is at anchor. If a holding-plate system has two compressors, they usually must operate entirely separate eutectic circulating systems because manufacturers have not yet been able to develop a single system in which oil does not migrate between the compressors. Frigiboat, an Italian company, claims to have licked this problem, but I have not yet had an opportunity to see one of its installations in action.

A good holding-plate installation should allow you to keep food frozen solid by operating its compressor only about an hour in the morning and an hour in the evening. To operate the system that way, however, you need to incorporate in it a switch that allows you to force the compressor to come on when you fire up your vessel's generator. Due to the physical properties of something called the "heat of fusion," the thermostat will not call for the compressor to turn on until the eutectic solution is almost entirely melted. Without an override switch, the compressor's on/off cycle would not necessarily coincide with the times you are operating the generator.

To my knowledge, no major builder of cruising power yachts offers holding-plate refrigeration, even as an option. To get such a system, you probably will have to take your vessel to a marine refrigeration specialist. Several manufacturers of marine refrigeration systems advertise holding-plate systems which they claim are "off the shelf" units, but they normally require expert installation because they are not charged with eutectic solution until after the installation is completed. Sealing the system requires precise soldering of the copper tubes through which the eutectic solution is circulated. A good holding-plate installation on a 50- to 60-foot power yacht won't be cheap. It can easily cost from $4,000 to $6,000.

Some marine refrigeration companies will replace your boat's household-type refrigerator/freezer with an upright unit incorporating holding plates, but most will recommend that you go to a horizontal cabinet with a lid in the top. They are more difficult to retrieve food from, but they don't spill out great quantities of cold air every time they are opened.

The key to an effective holding-plate system is thorough insulation of the freezer cabinet with at least 4 inches of closed-cell polyurethane foam on all sides—including the lid or door. Closed-cell polyurethane insulation is available in slabs which can be cut to fit. Some custom installers feel they get more complete coverage by purchasing polyurethane's chemical ingredients, mixing them on site and pouring a slurry into the insulating cavity which, when it sets, fills all the nooks and crannies. If the installer you deal with follows that approach, make certain he's experienced. It he gets too little slurry in the cavity you will have gaps in your insulation coverage; if he gets too much, you can have problems of compressed, ineffective foam and even deformation of the cabinet. If the foam is in direct contact with your vessel's hull, the installation should also include a vapor barrier of heavy plastic between the two to prevent heat absorption and condensation outside the hull. The other critical area is a tight seal on the cabinet's door or lid. If the lid or door on a holding-plate system isn't at least a little difficult to open, its seal probably isn't tight enough.

At the minimum, a holding-plate system should have an easily readable thermometer on the outside of the cabinet to allow you to monitor the interior temperature without opening the unit. An even better safeguard is to install a visual and/or audible alarm that alerts you if the unit's temperature rises anywhere near the freezing point.

Now that you know the size and type of boat you want and what her layout and basic systems should include, you're ready to head for the boat show or the broker's dock, right?

Not quite. First, take time to get a good idea of what it's going to cost you to buy and operate the boat whose outline you are beginning to get fixed in your mind.

4

WHAT'S ALL THIS GOING TO COST?

Once you've figured out the basic specifications of the cruiser that's best for you, you still have several key questions to answer before you actually initiate your search for the vessel that will fulfill them. First, of course, you need to get a realistic idea of what it is going to cost you, not only to buy the boat you need and want but to operate it as well. Few things can spoil your cruising fun faster than worrying how the hell you are going to pay the bills. The answers you come up with to the money questions may well dictate your answers to two basic questions: whether you will look for a new or a used boat; and whether you will consider only vessels built in the United States or will also look at those manufactured abroad.

By this point you've probably begun to get a pretty good idea of the size and type of boat you want and what her basic systems should incorporate. As we go along, you will develop specific ideas about the accessory equipment she will need and will learn how to determine the cost of everything entailed in buying, rigging, and operating her. For now, all we want to do is construct rough buying and operating budgets to help narrow your search and make certain you don't forget any major necessary items. Once you have constructed those preliminary budgets, you can refine them as you progress deeper into the boat-buying process.

BOAT-BUYING BUDGET

Based on the ideas you have already developed about the type and size of boat you need, get an idea of your purchase price range by combing through the boating magazines and seeking recommendations from any cruising friends you might have. Try to come up with a list of boats that appear to meet your initial criteria.

BUDGETING FOR A NEW BOAT

As you come across appropriate new boats, contact their manufacturers or dealers to assemble all the literature you can, including a price list, so that you can begin to construct your boat-buying budget (Fig. 4.1). The prices boatbuilders quote for their products normally are simply "base-boat" figures which probably will be just the beginning of what it actually will cost you to buy a particular model. As you peruse the price lists, you may be surprised to find that a number of basic items like a flying bridge, bow pulpit, swim platform, aft deck enclosure, generator, and tender davits which you would expect to be included in the base-boat figure, are extra-cost "factory-installed"

NEW BOAT-BUYING BUDGET

Factory Charges:
    Base Boat Price $ _____
    Factory Installed Options   +   _____
    Factory Invoice Price $ _____

Dealer Charges:
    Transportation   +   _____
    Commissioning   +   _____
    Dealer Installed Options   +   _____
    Dealer List Price $ _____
      Less Discount   −   _____

    Sales Price $ _____
      State Sales Tax   +   _____

      Purchase Price $ _____

State Registration Fee   +   _____
Federal Documentation Fees   +   _____
Insurance   +   _____
Additional installed accessories:
    Navigation and communications
    electronics; tender and outboard;
    watermaker; life raft & safety
    equipment, etc.   +   _____

Miscellaneous Expenses   +   _____

      Actual Cost $ _____

Fig. 4.1

options which easily can increase the base-boat price by 15 to 30 percent or more. You'll have to include the costs of the essential "extras" in order to arrive at a more realistic "factory invoice price." In Chapter 6 we'll discuss in detail how to figure the discount you can expect to negotiate off the factory invoice price, but for your preliminary figures, estimate a 6- to 7-percent markdown. Even after you arrive at that figure, you can be certain a dealer will also charge you for the cost of transporting the boat from the factory to the point of delivery and will add on a commissioning fee to cover launching her and checking out her basic systems. And don't forget the cost of her initial fueling. Check with several dealers for any boat you are considering to get a rough idea of what those costs will run.

On top of the factory invoice price and minimum dealer charges, you can generally figure you will have another one-time expense of 25 to 35 percent of the base-boat price for outfitting her with everything from electronics and a tender with outboard to lifesaving equipment. Throughout this book, we'll discuss in detail the specifications of the equipment you'll need for safe and comfortable operation of your vessel, but lists of the basic items you'll want to include for both a coastal and an offshore cruising powerboat are given in Fig. 4.2. In addition to these items, don't forget to include the cost of interior furnishings, entertainment gear, and the like. And remember to take into account all the miscellaneous items you'll need from dock lines and fenders to foul weather gear. Again, check with retailers for that gear to get some idea of the list prices for the equipment you will need and want. At this early stage, figure you probably will be able to buy them on average for about 15 percent off list, including installation, and plug those rough numbers into your budget. By the time you get a new boat rigged and in the water, you probably will wind up actually spending on the order of 30 to 50 percent more than the base-boat price.

BUDGETING FOR A USED BOAT

If you run across a make and model on the used-boat market that might meet your specifications, begin to construct your preliminary budget (Fig. 4.3) by establishing a rough value for a boat about five years old equipped with a least your basic minimum equipment. Ads for boats of that type in the boating magazines are a starting place, though their asking prices are often

BASIC ACCESSORIES LISTS

Coastal Cruiser

Safety Equipment:

    Automatic engine-room fire-extinguishing system
    Portable fire extinguishers
    Coastal life raft
    Personal flotation devices (PFDs)
    Throwable PFDs
    Searchlight
    Visual distress signals
    Audible signaling devices
    Emergency Position-Indicating Radiobeacon (EPIRB)
    First aid kit

Navigation Electronics:

    Depth sounder
    Knot meter/distance log
    Autopilot
    Loran C receiver
    Radar

Communications Electronics:

    Installed marine VHF radio and antenna
    Hand-held marine VHF radio and charger

Ground Tackle:

    Primary anchor and rode
    Secondary anchor and rode
    Electric anchor windlass

Miscellaneous Equipment:
    Tender, outboard motor, battery, and fuel tank
    Tender davit system
    Spare parts
    Tool kit

Offshore Cruiser

Safety Equipment:

Automatic engine-room fire-extinguishing system
Portable fire extinguishers
Offshore life raft
Abandon ship bag
Personal floatation devices (PFDs)
Throwable PFDs
Searchlight
Visual distress signals
Audible signaling devices
Emergency Position-Indicating Radiobeacon (EPIRB)
First aid kit
Trauma kit

Navigation Electronics:

Depth sounder
Knot meter/distance log
Autopilot
Loran C receiver
Satellite navigation receiver
Radar

Communications Equipment:

Installed marine VHF radio with antenna
Hand-held marine VHF radio with charger
Single sideband marine radio with coupler and antenna

Ground Tackle:

Primary anchor and rode
Secondary anchor and rode
Electric anchor windlass

Miscellaneous Equipment:

Tender, outboard motor, battery, and fuel tank
Tender davits
Stabilizers (full-displacement hull vessels only)
Holding-plate refrigeration
Watermaker
Spare parts including spare shaft(s) and propeller(s)
Tool kit

Fig. 4.2

USED-BOAT-BUYING BUDGET

Asking Price	$	_____
Less Discount	−	_____
Negotiated Sales Price	$	_____
State Sales Tax	+	_____
Purchase Price	$	_____
Survey Fee	+	_____
State Registration Fee	+	_____
Federal Documentation Fees	+	_____
Insurance	+	_____
Delivery Expense	+	_____
Additional required accessories: Navigation and communications electronics; tender and outboard; watermaker; life raft & safety equipment, etc.	+	_____
Miscellaneous Expenses	+	_____
Actual Cost	$	_____

Fig. 4.3

from 10 to 30 percent higher than what the owner will actually accept. The most widely used reference in the marine industry on the value of used boats is *BUC Used Boat Price Guide* (normally just called the BUC Book) which gives the average wholesale and retail prices of a wide range of used pleasure boats. Ask a dealer, broker, marine insurance agent, or banker who deals in yacht financing to let you look through *his* copy and find the average retail figure for the model and year of boat you are interested in. But be aware that BUC Book figures are a starting place only as they are six to eight months out of date by the time they appear in print. In the case of popular boat models where there is a high level of sales activity, BUC Book valuations tend to be reasonably accurate. In the case of little-known boats where the figures may be based on only two or three sales, they can be well off the mark. The actual price of the boat in the area you are shopping can vary up or down by 20 percent or more. The best way to get closer to actual market values is to consult several brokers where you plan to shop and find out their most recent experiences with comparable boat sales.

Once you feel you have an approximate idea of what the used boat is worth, figure that you will have to add to that figure for a newer boat or one that has major extras and subtract from it for an older boat or one that has significant deficiencies. Before you buy any used boat, you should have it inspected by a good marine surveyor, and we'll show you how to figure what that is going to cost. For now, figure $10 to $12 per foot of boat length, which will include a haul-out. For a used boat, the cost of the accessory equipment needed to bring her up to your specifications can run anywhere from 5 to 15 percent or more of the purchase price, depending on how well she is equipped when you take delivery.

INCLUDE THE UNAVOIDABLES

Whether you are constructing a budget for buying a new or a used boat, there are a number of unavoidable expenditures you will need to include. We'll discuss them in greater detail in Chapter 6. Right now we're just trying to develop a ballpark figure.

Don't forget the tax man. In some states, you may have to pay a hefty sales tax on your boat's purchase price. As we'll discuss later, there may be some situations where you can save big money by buying or basing your boat in a state that levies lighter sales and/or use taxes on boats.

In addition to taxes, in some states you will have to figure in the cost of numbering or registering your boat. If you will be documenting it (which you do through the Federal Government), you'll have to add in those costs as well. (We'll cover the differences among those three procedures at length in Chapter 6.)

Check with a couple of marine insurance agents to get a rough idea of what your first year's hull, liability, and medical insurance is going to cost. On a $200,000 boat, insurance can run $2,000 to $3,000 a year or more for full coverage.

You'll need to figure in the cost of charts, medical supplies, and spare parts, which can add up to a tidy sum.

BOAT OPERATING BUDGET

Once you have a reasonably good fix on what it is going to cost you to buy the boat you want and rig her for extended cruising, the next step is to get an idea of what it is going to cost you to run her by constructing an annual operating budget (Fig. 4.4).

If you will be borrowing money to pay part of the cost of your boat, check typical boat loan rates and terms and carefully go over an amortization schedule for the amount you plan to borrow to be sure you can cover the payments comfortably. In many situations, boat loans can be considered in the category of second home mortgages, and the interest you pay may be deductible on your Federal and state income tax returns. Check your status with a good accountant.

In some states, boats are taxed as personal property and you could face a heavy outlay every year. You may also have to factor in the cost of annual renewal of your boat's state registration.

Add in your annual insurance cost, taking into account that it may increase as you extend your policy's cruising limits.

You generally can figure from about 10 to 15 percent of the boat's purchase price as its annual operating expense for fuel, oil, filters, hauling and bottom painting, repair, routine maintenance, replacing lost or damaged gear, and the other miscellaneous expenses involved in boat ownership, exclusive of insurance and taxes.

If you will be doing extended cruising, your expenses can vary all over the lot depending on your cruising area, your boat's fuel-consumption rate, how elaborately you like to live, and whether you will spend most of your cruising nights tied to a dock or swinging on the hook. For food—including dining out— you probably should figure about 15 to 20 percent more than you normally spend at home. On average, you will find food

ANNUAL BOAT OPERATING BUDGET

Fixed Expenses:

Loan Principal & Interest $ _____

Less savings on interest −
   deductible from Federal/
   State income taxes   _____

Property Taxes + _____
Insurance + _____
State Registration Renewal + _____

   Sub-total $ _____ $ _____

Cruising Expenses:

Fuel & Oil $ _____
Dockage + _____
Hauling & Bottom Painting + _____
Routine Maintenance + _____
Replace Broken/Damaged
   Gear + _____
Customs Fees + _____
Home/Boat Travel Expenses + _____
On Board Food & Beverage + _____
Dining Out/Entertainment + _____
Miscellaneous + _____

       Sub-Total $ _____ $ + _____

      Annual Operating
         Expense $ _____

Fig. 4.4

prices in other countries 10 to 15 percent higher than what you are used to paying in the United States for items of comparable quality—providing you can even find what you want. This is especially true in island communities where everything must be shipped in. Unless you are an extremely experienced fisherman or are practiced in the use of a spear gun, forget any idea of sharply reducing your food budget by "living off the sea." If you work at it, you may pick up the occasional grouper, amberjack, or lobster which can provide a welcome addition to the provisions you bring from home or purchase along the way, but don't count on them as staples of your cruising diet.

Also factor in the cost of traveling to and from your boat between cruises. Even if you will be living aboard during an extended cruise, you might want to include in your operating budget the cost of at least one trip home a year to tend to essential business.

In constructing a cruising budget, the experience of Charlie and Nancy Bowen on a thirteen-month cruise from their home in Delray Beach, Florida, to Grenada and back in 1985–86 may provide a helpful frame of reference. During the cruise, Nancy kept a meticulous daily diary that included every dime they spent, right down to the sixty-six cents they spent for bananas in St. Thomas and a twenty-five-franc tip they gave a waiter in Martinique. Their boat, *Takeabrake III*, is a 40-foot Marine Trader Sedan on which they had lived for two years before departing on the cruise. It has a single 120-horsepower Ford Lehman diesel and no generator. They used a rain catchment system on the flying bridge to keep their freshwater tanks full for most of the voyage. Refrigeration was provided by a standard refrigerator/freezer and a separate 3.5-cubic-foot freezer, both powered by an engine-driven holding-plate refrigeration system. For cooking, they used a four-burner LPG stove with oven. In cruising the Bahamas for two months every summer for fifteen years, Charlie and Nancy had become quite proficient undersea fishermen and could count on their skills to provide them with significant quantities of fresh seafood. They planned on buying most of their wine and liquor en route because of the generally lower prices for those items in the islands. Their tender was a 14-foot Boston Whaler with a 35-horsepower outboard. They had an average of two guests aboard for ten of the fifty-six weeks they were gone. Their expenses broke down this way:

Boat Expense:

Diesel Fuel	$ 2,573.74	
Maintenance	3,117.89	
Tender fuel	240.87	
Propane	62.40	
Water	45.95	
Dockage	269.45	
Customs Fees	104.53	
Subtotal	$ 6,414.83	$6,414.83

Provisions:

Initial Provisioning	$ 2,000.00	
Groceries purchased en route	1,731.75	
Beer, Wine, & Liquor purchased en route	593.97	
Meals ashore	2,006.99	
Subtotal	$ 6,332.71	6,332.71
Entertainment/Miscellaneous		1,930.86
Total		$ 14,678.40
Average per month		$ 1,129.11

Charlie and Nancy were aboard about the minimum vessel I would recommend for this kind of extensive cruising; it had only a single, low-horsepower main engine and no generator; they substantially supplemented their provisions by fishing, and they spent very few nights in marinas. Based on these factors, their net monthly outlay was probably low for a more typical cruising couple. I would say the minimum cost for a couple cruising the Bahamas and the lower Caribbean, exclusive of insurance, taxes, and any shoreside expenses, would be at least $1,200 per month, and $1,500 is probably a more realistic figure—and both those figures are based on the prices that prevailed in the mid-1980's.

After you have added up all your operating numbers—plus any expenses you still have to meet at home—that is the nut you are going to have to crack every year. If you have the slightest hesitation about being able to handle that comfortably, take another look at your previous decisions to see if you can get along with a less expensive boat.

NEW OR USED?

The figures you come up with in your boat-buying and operating budget probably will play a major role in whether you start your search for the vessel of your dreams on the new- or used-boat market, but it is not necessarily the only consideration.

Buying a new boat is something like buying a new car—it glitters and sparkles and you have the pride of knowing you are her first owner. In buying a new boat, you also can set up all her electronics and cruising accessories just the way you want. But buying a new boat has its disadvantages as well. First, of course, in buying a new boat you are likely to pay a significantly higher price than you would for the same model with comparable equipment but with a few years of age on her. You also have to go through the involved process of specifying, searching out, and purchasing all the accessory equipment she'll need for extended cruising, then make certain it is correctly installed. Some yachtsmen love the job of detailing exactly what they want in everything from radars and radios to tenders and safety gear. Others consider that process pure drudgery and prefer to buy a boat that is already fully rigged. In fact, one trend now among some manufacturers is to offer their boats as "sail away" packages that include at least what the builder considers the basic equipment and accessories most cruisers will want on board. If you consider one of these packages, even if you are satisfied the basic boat is the one you want, go over the equipment list carefully to make certain each item meets the specifications you develop after reading this book. In some cases, builders will include the cheapest accessory equipment they can find in order to keep the overall price of their package low. Also, be aware that the most extensive package is probably going to lack some items, anything from sophisticated electronic equipment to proper safety gear. You will have to purchase these separately and adjust your boat-buying budget accordingly.

If you elect to buy a new boat, take into account that all that new gear is not going to work exactly right the moment you flip the switch. You are almost certain to have to "work the bugs out" until you get all her systems operating properly.

There are always some excellent used boats on the market at prices substantially below what you would pay for the same models brand new. Also, a number of the most practical cruising boats ever designed (the Hatteras Long Range Cruisers, some models designed by Art Defever and Ed Monk, and the early Alaskans quickly come to mind) are no longer manufactured. To find them, you will have to turn to the used-boat market. A used boat may be a bit tired cosmetically but offer an excellent buy for the money. If she has been used for two or three years, chances are any serious defects in her basic systems already will have come to light and been dealt with, and if her previous owner was a knowledgeable yachtsman, any glitches will have been worked out. In buying a used boat, you may have to put up with some things the previous owner did that you would have done differently, but you may find you get more boat for the same or less money than buying new. There are some basic things you need to look for in buying a used boat, of course, which we will discuss in detail.

DOMESTIC OR IMPORT?

Whether you start out looking for a new or used boat, another basic question is whether you will select a boat built in the United States or one imported from abroad. If you consider comparable boats, as a general rule you will find very little difference in the price and construction quality among boats built in the United States, Canada, and Western Europe.

Most questions of significant differences in price and construction quality among boats of equal size involve vessels built in the Far East. Because of the markedly lower wage rates for workers in some Far Eastern countries compared to those in the United States, Canada, and Western Europe, boats built in Singapore, Taiwan, and Hong Kong, and more recently in South Korea, do tend to be somewhat less expensive than those of Western manufacture. While the gap is narrowing, the prices of these boats have put the cost of buying a fair-sized cruising boat within the reach of people who might not be able to afford a vessel of comparable size built in the United States. In addition, hundreds of people have cruised Far Eastern–built boats for years and love them.

For the most part, the well-known Far Eastern manufacturers have long done a creditable job in fiberglass hull lay-up, and their interior joinery tends to equal or exceed the best the West can produce. Their propulsion systems have not been much cause for concern because they generally use the same engines and gears as Western manufacturers. But for reasons peculiar to the ways of doing business in the Far East, even the most die-hard adherents of Far Eastern–built boats will admit that their electrical and plumbing systems have tended to be problem areas. For a number of years, the boatbuilding tradition in the Far East was for the primary builder to handle hull and superstructure construction, engine installation, and joinery with its own employees. The boat's plumbing and electrical system were subcontracted out to the lowest bidder. As a result internal systems the buyer could not readily see often were built with the cheapest materials and with slipshod or nonexistent quality control. The electrical systems of some of these yachts built from the 1960's to the late 1970's often were composed of two or three sizes and colors of wire in a single circuit and with the absolute minimum of fusing and circuit protection, and, of course, there was nothing approaching a wiring diagram.

John Matthews, a meticulous cruising friend and electrical engineer from Atlanta, told me a story while I was cruising with him and his wife Mary aboard their American-built 42-footer *Rigel* from Lucaya to Great Stirrup Cay in the Bahamas illustrates beautifully the potential pitfalls of buying one of these boats. "The first boat I bought was a thirty-six-foot displacement boat built in the Far East," John said. "I felt it was a good deal as the price was considerably below the cost of an American-built boat of comparable size. The hull was built like a tank and the propulsion system created no significant problems. But as we began to do extensive cruising, we found that the electrical system required a good deal of rework, as did the plumbing system. We also added a number of additional system components which were not included in the original boat such as a fire-suppression system and additional bilge pumps. By the time we did all of that, we found we had about as much money tied up in the boat as we would have had in a similar boat built in the United States. Of course, much of the money spent in reworking the boat's systems was lost at the time of resale. When we decided to buy a larger boat, I made up my mind that I would buy an American-built boat which would not have some of the problems we had previously encountered and would hold its resale value better." Eight years later, John still owns the same American-built 42-footer and says he has no plans to change any time soon.

Another potential problem to be on the lookout for in boats built in the Far East—particularly those built prior to the early 1980's—is deterioration in the decks and superstructure. In many of these boats, the decks and superstructure were made not of solid fiberglass or even cored fiberglass but of poor-grade plywood covered with only a thin veneer of fiberglass. They are subject to extensive rot and delamination, especially in the area of window, door, and hatch openings where moisture has been able to penetrate.

In the past decade, Far Eastern manufacturers have consolidated most of their manufacturing processes and have come a long way in bringing their electrical, plumbing, and superstructure construction standards up to those we are accustomed to in the United States. Even so, if I were to consider buying a used boat built in the Far East, particularly if it were built before 1980, I would make doubly certain that it was subjected to a rigorous inspection by a well-qualified marine surveyor.

If I were considering the purchase of a brand-new Far Eastern-built boat, I would stick with a well-known manufacturer and make certain I was working with a reputable, established dealer who would stand behind his product. The potential problems with buying one of these boats were vividly brought home to me recently when a yard manager showed me a Jefferson 46 barely a year old that he had hauled for a buyer's survey. When she came out of the water, he told me, her bottom looked fine. But when the surveyor began tapping the hull, he detected the dull sound that is characteristic of voids in a hull's lay-up. He insisted that a section of the hull be sandblasted so he could see what was underneath. The sandblasting removed the bottom paint and a thin layer of gel-coat which had hidden the voids that covered the hull's bottom. It was obvious that in laying up the hull the builder had not used sufficient resin to adequately penetrate the first layer of woven roving and had not rolled the layer by hand to squeeze out trapped air bubbles. The yard manager estimated it would cost a minimum of $4,000 to repair the obvious problems. Of course, finding that kind of problem in an almost new boat raises questions about other deficiencies which are not so readily apparent. Thanks to a competent, conscientious surveyor, the buyer was able to back out of the deal. Had he not gotten such a thorough survey, he could have wound up buying the boat and not discovering the problem until months later. The seller is not so fortunate. Unless he has a good dealer standing behind him, he is going to have to lay out a sizable chunk of cash to solve the osmosis problem and may have to spend thousands more if other difficulties are found in subsequent surveys.

Now that you have a basic fix on the type and size boat that will fit your needs and a general idea of how much you can afford to spend for her, the next questions are where you begin your search and how you will conduct it.

5

FINDING THE CRUISER OF YOUR DREAMS

The decision you make between buying a new boat and buying a used boat will pretty well determine whether you begin your search for the cruiser of your dreams at a boat show, a new-boat dealer's yard, or a used-boat broker's dock. They also will pretty well determine whether you limit your search to boats built in this country or include those built overseas as well. Wherever you start your quest, there are a few things it might be helpful for you to know.

SEARCHING FOR A NEW BOAT

If you're planning to buy a new boat, you can start by visiting dealers for the boats on your list or by scheduling a visit to one or more of the major boat shows. In either case, there are several things to consider.

STARTING WITH A DEALER

The drawbacks to starting your search with dealers are that they may be spread over a wide geographic area, they may not have at their docks the particular model you are interested in, and you may find yourself under pressure to make a decision before you have had a chance to check out everything that's available in the type of boat you're looking for. If you decide to start at the dealer level, take careful note of the physical setup as you visit each dealer's yard. If his yard, shops, and docks are busy and well maintained, chances are his business is too. When you bring your boat back to him for warranty service—as you are almost certain to do with a new boat—he's likely to tend to the work promptly and properly without a lot of hassle. If his yard shows little sign of activity or his housekeeping is sloppy, chances are his business is in the same shape. He may offer you a slightly better price, but when you bring your boat back to him for warranty service, you may encounter frustration and delay which won't be worth enduring for the amount of money you save. Or you may run into what's known in the industry as the "hatband" dealer. This is a guy who operates out of a small office and has no yard facilities at all. He'll probably tell you he has an agreement with a nearby yard to handle his launching and commissioning and attend to warranty repairs. Before you get into serious negotiations with him, insist that he give you the names of a fair number of his customers and check with them to see what kind of after-the-sale service they got. Unless he comes up spotless, I'd be extremely cautious about dealing with him.

The same warning is appropriate for boat manufacturers. In the past few years, an incredible number of new boats have been introduced to the cruising market, especially planing-hull motor yachts in the 40- to 50-foot range. While some of these boats offer introductory prices substantially below those of established manufacturers of the same size boat, you should be especially careful about checking the financial resources of the builder and the dealer. If you have serious problems with the engines or hull, you want to be sure you have a dealer and a manufacturer who are going to stand behind their product. Many of these companies will build and sell a dozen or so boats, then fold their tents and evaporate from the marketplace, often to pop up somewhere else offering the same or a slightly different boat under a new corporate name. If you are one of their unlucky victims and decide to sell your vessel, you could find that you own a boat virtually no one has ever heard of or, even worse, one that has acquired a bad reputation. Selling it can prove next to impossible. If you do finally find a buyer, its resale value may prove to be only a fraction of what you originally paid for it. I personally would hesitate to buy a boat from a manufacturer or dealer who has not been known around the industry for at least five years and couldn't give me the names of at least half a dozen customers who were pleased with his products and services.

Even if you buy a new boat built by a company that has been in business for years, be cautious about buying the first hull of a new model. Often the first boat in a series has defects that the manufacturer discovers and corrects in subsequent production. The exception to that general rule is when the manufacturer has commissioned and outfitted hull number one for use as a sales demonstrator. If the company has a good demo captain, chances are he has ironed out the wrinkles, and you are buying a well-proven commodity.

STARTING AT A BOAT SHOW

An even better place to start comparing individual vessels is at one or more of the major boat shows. Nowhere else will you be able to examine such a wide variety of boats in such a short time. But be aware that boat shows are designed to appeal to the widest possible audience, ranging from powerboat cruisers like yourself to sailboat racers, windsurfers, and bass fishermen. Only a fraction of the displays contain information that is really of value to you, and there is an art to getting the facts you came for.

In order to stay current on what's new in the boating industry, from new boat models to accessories, I visit at least six large boat shows a year. I have to cover a lot of territory, so I've developed a system for making sure I see what I need to see in the short time available. You may find some of the following tips helpful:

Never go to a show when it first opens to the public. That's when you get all the nonboaters with their sticky-fingered kids who are there for the spectacle. It's far better to visit a boat show on its "trade days"—normally the Thursday and Friday before the show is opened to the public. In order to be admitted on a trade day you will need a VIP pass from one of the exhibitors. There are a couple of ways to go about getting on some exhibitor's VIP list.

Call the sales department of the boatbuilders on your list and ask to speak to one of their dealer sales representatives. (This individual will not be a retail salesperson but one of the people on the manufacturer's staff who handles the company's relations with its dealers.) Tell him or her of your possible interest in their product, and ask them to send you all the available literature on the specific boat or boats in their line that interest you. Also ask at what upcoming boat shows they will display a representative model of the vessel you're interested in and whether it will be in or out of the water. Pick one of the shows you can fit into your schedule and ask for a trade-day or VIP pass. If the person you are talking to agrees to send you a pass, ask for the names of two or three company representatives who will be working there. Amid the show's confusion, you'll find it helpful to have a specific contact. On this initial call, some manufacturers' sales departments will try to shuffle you off to one of their dealers in your area. Tell them it's too early in the game for you to start talking with salespeople, and ask them to get the information you requested into the mail. If the person says his company can't supply you with a VIP pass, put that down as a black mark against their product and call the next company on your list.

At a major boat show, you probably will inspect a dozen or more vessels which at first glance appear to meet your basic criteria. As you attempt later to weigh them one against the other, you will find features of this boat and that boat tend to run together. To help solve this problem, make a brief list of the basic elements you are looking for in underbody configuration, exterior finish, and deck and accommodations layout (Fig. 5.1). Make a number of copies of your list and fill out one on each boat you inspect. Some people even take along a video or still camera to record salient features of the boats they view. If you do that, make sure it can take clear pictures in the low light levels you sometimes find belowdecks. If you don't take either of these suggestions, at least carry along a pad on which you can make notes.

Once you have a VIP pass, arrive early on trade day before the crowds build up. On the show directory's floor plan circle the location of each of the exhibits you want to visit, then draw yourself up a logical routing that will allow you to cover them all in turn.

When you arrive at a particular exhibitor's display, ask the person stationed at the exhibit entrance to introduce you to one of the factory representatives who is working the show. Hopefully you'll already have one or more names from your earlier call.

Even if you get a manufacturer's representative to show you the boat, he may try to steer you toward one of his company's dealers, who will have salespeople swarming around the display area. If possible, sidestep the maneuver. If the manufacturer's representative insists that a dealer show you the boat, make clear up front that you are at a very early stage in the search for the boat you want; you may be able to avoid a lot of heavy selling pressure this way.

If you are at a dry-land show, start your evaluation of a particular boat by examining its underbody to look for the characteristics we've been discussing. For esthetic reasons—or maybe to hide defects from people like you who know what to look for—some exhibitors conceal the underbody of a boat with a decorative skirt. In some cases you will be able to go around to the back of the display for the view you need. If not, don't hesitate to ask the factory representative to move portions of the skirt aside to give you a clear view.

If the boat is already in the water, you'll have to skip the underbody survey at this point, but see if the factory representative can arrange for you to see the same model out of the water at one of their dealers' yards near the show or close to your home.

After you've looked the underbody over or made arrange-

BOAT-BUYING CHECKLIST

Vessel: _____   New __ Used __ (Year __)
                                   Domestic __ Import ____
Engine(s): _____   Single _____ Twin ____
                                   HP _____ Turbos ____
                                   Est. Cruise Speed ____
                                   Est. Fuel Cons./Hr. ____
                                   Fuel Capacity ____
                                   Est. Cruising Range ____

Hull:

   Material: Fiberglass __ Wood __ Alum. __ Steel __
   Type: Planing __ Semidisp. __ Full-Disp. ____

   Keel Protects Props/Rudders   __   Hull-Form   __
   Obstructions Block Props/Rudders __   Hull Finish __
   Hull-to-Deck Joint   __   Bow Flare   __

Main Deck:

   Foredeck Area   __   Side decks   __
   Bulwarks   __   Cleat Placement   __
   Bow Pulpit   __   Lounge Area Forward   __
   Chain/Rope Lockers   __   Lounge Area Aft   __
   Stanchions   __   Cruising Cockpit   __
   Safety Rails   __   Transom Door
   Lifelines   __   Swim Platform
   Boarding Gates   __   Fresh/Saltwater
   Shorepower Inlets   __   Outlets   __

Flying bridge:

   Access   __   Helm Seating
   Visibility Forward   __   Companion Seating
   Visibility Side   __   Lounge Seating   __
   Console Space   __   Cruising Mast   __

Interior:

 Pilothouse

   Separation   __   Chart Flat   __
   Visibility   __   Chart Storage   __

| Alarm System | — | Helm Seating | — |
| Instrument Space | — | Companion Seating | — |

Main Salon

| Seating Space | — | Glass Expanse | — |
| Visibility | — | Traffic Flow | — |

Galley

| Appliance Placement | — | Storage Space | — |
| Countertop Space | — | Proximity to Dining | — |

Owner's Stateroom and Head

| Bed Width/Access | — | Hanging Lockers | — |
| Drawer Storage | — | Stall Shower | — |

Guest Stateroom(s) and Head(s)

| Bed Width/Access | — | Hanging Lockers | — |
| Drawer Storage | — | Stall Shower | — |

Engine Room

Standing Entry	—	Battery Access	—
Standing Headroom	—	Accessories Space	—
Fire-Ext. System	—	Through-Hull Fittings	—
Engine Access	—	Wiring Installation	—
Generator Access	—		

Notes: _____

_____

_____

_____

OVERALL RATING ____

_____

Fig. 5.1: *Completing a Boat Buying Checklist for each vessel you consider can help you remember which boat has which features and compare vessels to select the one most appropriate to your cruising plans and lifestyle.*

ments to do so later, go to the stern of the boat and, from a point about midway between the waterline and the sheer, sight down the length of the hull. At a dry-land show, you'll probably have to do this at the rear of the display since the crowd will block your view on the front side. You may have to get up on a chair or ladder to put your eye at its optimum viewing level. In the terrible lighting conditions at most enclosed shows, seeing what you're looking for here may be difficult, but give it your best shot. As you sight down the hull, you should see a clean, unbroken sweep without noticeable dips or bulges. If you do see dips or bulges in a fiberglass boat, this can mean any or all of the following: The hull lay-up was hurried or was not allowed to cure properly; the lay-up mold was what the engineers called "tired"; the interior bulkheads are not fitted properly which is putting stress on the hull. In time that boat is likely to have serious problems with hull flexing, bulkhead separation, delamination, and blistering, and you should not consider buying it, period. In the case of an aluminum or steel hull, dips and bulges in its exterior surface don't necessarily indicate structural or material problems, just poor workmanship in its weld-up. Again, I'd pass it by.

In the case of a boat built of fiberglass, back off from the hull amidships about 4 or 5 feet, select a section about a foot square, and study it from a number of different angles. It is best if the area is painted a dark color such as at a sheer stripe (but not covered by bottom paint). You should see a smooth surface unmarred by any discernible pattern. If you see a diagonal crosshatching pattern, you are looking at a boat that has an extremely thin layer of gel-coat and the pattern is the first layer of woven roving showing through it. At the least, that boat will be subject to excessive fading and crazing and attempts to restore it will quickly wear through the gel-coat down to the roving. Its bottom is more likely to be subject to damage from osmosis than a boat with a thicker gel-coat. Again, I'd strike it off my list.

Ask the sales representative to give you details on how the company joins the hull to the deck in the model you are considering. Some companies will have a sample or an engineering drawing of their joining method available (Fig. 5.2). Building a boat with a proper hull-to-deck joint is expensive. Since the joint is almost impossible to inspect after a vessel is completed, this is one place where a lot of lower-quality builders cut corners.

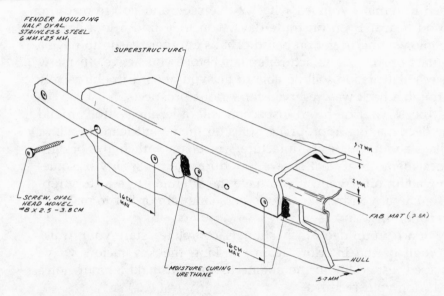

FENDER MOULDING
HALF OVAL
STAINLESS STEEL
6 MM X 25 MM

SUPERSTRUCTURE

SCREW, OVAL
HEAD MONEL
#8 X 2.5 - 3.8 CM

16 CM
MAX

16 CM
MAX

MOISTURE CURING
URETHANE

5-7 MM

2 MM

FAB MAT (2 EA)

HULL

5-7 MM

Fig. 5.2: *A look at an engineering drawing of a new vessel's hull-to-deck joint is the most reliable guide to making certain this vital area is properly constructed.*

The optimum hull-to-deck joint is composed of ⅜-inch or better stainless-steel bolts on 12-inch centers through-bolted to stainless-steel backing plates inside and outside the hull with stainless-steel lock washers and nuts. The hull and deck should overlap at least one inch, and the overlap should be sealed with a waterproof urethane compound. The inside of the joint should be sealed with a continuous 6-inch-wide strip of fiberglass mat soaked with resin and overlayed by a second strip of fiberglass mat 8 inches wide which also is soaked with resin. All air bubbles should be rolled out of both layers of resin by hand. A less desirable but still acceptable method of joining the hull and deck uses 1-inch #8 stainless steel screws in place of bolts. If screws are used, they should be on not less than 8-inch centers and the joint should be sealed as above. If you come across a builder who doesn't come pretty close to these specifications, pass up his products and look for a boat that won't come apart on you.

If the underbody, exterior finish, and hull-to-deck joint don't measure up to these criteria, don't waste your time with the interior, just move on to the next exhibit on your list. If those factors are within acceptable limits, make whatever notes you need to remind yourself what you've seen and you're ready to go on board. Even on trade days, you may find a long line of people waiting to get on board. That's another reason to have a contact on the manufacturer's staff before you arrive. In many cases, that person will be able to get you aboard unobtrusively through a back way reserved for serious prospects.

Begin your on-board inspection with a leisurely stroll around the deck making appropriate notes on the layout features we've talked about. Some manufacturers of boats with flying bridges block them off at boat shows to reduce the possibility of someone falling off. Again, if you have the attention of a factory representative, you may be able to persuade him or her to make an exception in your case.

Once your deck inspection is complete, start your walk-through of the interior, again checking the key factors we've covered, especially in the engine room, and making your notes or taking your pictures.

After completing this once-over-lightly inspection of a particular boat, go ahead and assign it a rating from one to ten based simply on your overall impression, not specific details. When you finally do an item-by-item analysis, you may be pleasantly surprised to find how well your initial reaction stands up.

Now check out the other boats on your list the same way. Once you've done that, find a quiet place where you can relax over lunch or a drink and go back over your notes. Eliminate those boats that seem to have major deficiencies and roughly rank in order the remaining boats that might be serious possibilities. You may want to organize your list for a second, closer inspection according to the logical walk-through of the show. At this point, however, I personally find it helps to start out with the lowest-rated boat on my list and work up to the one I've rated highest.

Before embarking on this more detailed inspection, revise your checklist to zero in on those areas that are really critical and be sure you cover any significant features of a particular boat you missed the first time around or failed to note.

Now go back for your closer look and take plenty of notes or pictures. On each boat mentally (if not physically) go through the motions of what you would actually do in each of its major areas. On the foredeck, imagine docking and anchoring the boat and note the positioning of deck cleats and hawsepipes. In the galley, mentally prepare a meal. That may be when you realize the refrigerator is positioned much too far from the sink or the sink is placed where it cannot be reached conveniently from the cooktop. In the engine room, go through the motions of checking the oil and water in the engines and generators and the acid level in the batteries. That may tip you off that the way the batteries are installed you'd have to be a contortionist to top them off.

SEARCHING FOR A USED BOAT

If you are interested primarily in buying a used boat, you can start your search by checking out the trade-in inventory of new-boat dealers, perusing the ads in boating magazines, or visiting brokers who deal only in used boats. I'd be hesitant to try to buy a vessel directly from an owner without having a competent broker involved in the transaction. As you will see later, the legal and financial intricacies of buying a sizable cruising vessel are at least as complicated as buying a house or condominium, which most of us would not attempt without the services of a qualified realtor.

If you start your search for a used boat with a new-boat dealer, bear in mind that his first interest may be in selling you the trade-ins or the boats he has on consignment at his dock, rather than scouring the used-boat market to help you locate the boat that best suits your needs.

I'd suggest that the best approach is to find a good used-boat broker. Look for a broker who has been in the industry for several years, seems knowledgeable about the particular type of boat you are looking for, and shows a sincere interest in helping you find the boat you have in mind, not simply getting your money and hustling you out the door. Ask him not only to help you find your boat but also to buy it on the best terms. Since his commission will be paid by the seller, his services should cost you nothing. But if he knows he is going to represent you no matter which boat you ultimately buy, he is more likely to put your interests first than if he were just trying to find a buyer for a boat on his own listing sheet.

In making your selection of a broker, be extremely cautious. The best of the brokers are highly knowledgeable, ethical people who have been in business for years and will go to great lengths to make you happy so you will come back to them if you decide later to buy another boat and will recommend them to your boat-buying friends. The worst brokers know little if anything about boats beyond how to talk a sharp line and are little more than skillful con artists who are in business strictly for the fast buck. Telling the difference between the two is difficult since many states have nothing in the way of licensing or qualification requirements for yacht salesmen or brokers and those that do don't have a lot of teeth in their laws. Under its so-called Sunshine Law passed in 1978, for instance, Florida eliminated state licensing for everything from yacht brokers to plumbers on the theory that the law cost more to administer than it produced in revenue. In 1988 the Florida Yacht Brokers Association did persuade the state's legislature to pass a law that requires yacht salesmen to post a $10,000 bond and brokers to post a $25,000 bond and to show they have at least two years' experience in yacht sales. California requires yacht salesmen to pass a written examination on the legal aspects of yacht sales transactions, then work for a broker for two years before being eligible to become a broker. Brokers in California must post a $10,000 bond. While these are steps in the right direction, most yacht brokerage contracts are so filled with disclaimers that it is difficult to collect damages for anything short of transparent fraud, and the size of the bond required provides little comfort for the cruising yachtsman who is planning to spend $100,000—or several times that—on his vessel.

Begin your search for a qualified broker by asking boating friends, marine insurance agents, and yacht financing sources for the names of brokers they have dealt with successfully. If you find a broker who seems to meet your requirements but you have no personal recommendations, ask for the names of a couple of satisfied customers and check with them. If a broker can't give you such names, or seems hesitant to do so, move on to someone else. It would be ideal if you could locate a competent broker reasonably close to your home, but if you live well inland you probably will do better to establish contact with a broker in one of the major boating centers, where there will be a wider range of choices to consider.

Because a good used-boat broker stays in touch with the full range of the market, he probably will know of any boat that comes close to meeting your requirements. The best of these people have a pretty smoothly working network, and any one broker can sell you virtually any boat on the market whether it is listed with his agency or with someone else.

Once you have found a broker you are comfortable with, give him a detailed list of your specifications and an accurate idea of your boat-buying budget. Within your specifications list, point out what is absolutely essential and what can be optional or negotiated. Then let him go to work. Chances are he quickly will come up with a list of boats that meet your requirements and your budget. That's when you get down to the tough job of sorting through the boats to find the one that's right for you. It's best to bring your broker with you when checking out a boat he recommends. If the inspection involves only a couple of hours and a drive of fifty miles or so, his presence should cost you nothing. If the trip involves airfares or overnight accommodations, have a clear understanding with him up front as to whether he expects you to cover his expenses or will take them out of his commission.

Your inspection of the hull, deck, and interior and engine-room layout of the used boat should follow roughly the same procedure recommended for new boats at a boat show. You can afford to concentrate most of your attention on the suitability of layout, accommodations, and appearance, since, before you buy any used boat, you are going to have it carefully inspected by a qualified marine surveyor. But even in your walk-through of a used boat take careful note of anything that is broken, missing, badly worn, or excessively dirty. If you get to the point of serious financial negotiations, those tics against the boat may be items you can use to get the price you want. During your inspection of the engine room, be on the lookout especially for any signs of excessive oil or water leakage. That's a dead giveaway to an engine that could require an expensive overhaul.

THE INITIAL SEA TRIAL

At some point in your search, you will find you are looking at a particular new or used boat and saying to yourself, "This may be the one!" The next step is to arrange for a sea trial.

If you are considering a new boat at an in-the-water boat show, some manufacturers can arrange a sea trial for you on the spot. If that's not possible, they should be able to arrange with one of their dealers or a cooperative owner for you to put one of its sister ships equipped with the same power package through a sea trial's procedures. If that is the case, make clear to the dealer that you reserve the right to repeat the process with your actual boat before you finalize any deal.

It would seem logical to subject a used boat to a sea trial before you go to the trouble of making a formal offer-to-purchase, but it often doesn't work that way. The owner normally bears any expense involved in sea trials to cover fuel and possibly an operator. In order to protect themselves from wasting time and money on tire-kickers and joyriders, most owners and brokers don't want to go to the trouble and expense of providing a sea trial until they have a signed offer-to-purchase contract on a boat. If you can convince the selling broker you are a genuine prospect, he might make an exception and arrange for you to take the boat out. If not, you will have to determine what your first offer should be (discussed in the next chapter). In any event, even if it involves significant travel, never buy a boat that you have not put through a rigorous sea trial first. If you do buy a boat without a sea trial and find it rolls too much to suit you or isn't as fast as you thought it would be, you have next to no chance of getting your money back.

In preparing to conduct a sea trial, make yourself a checklist of things to look for (Fig. 5.3) and be prepared to take comprehensive notes. I find it's easier to take sea trial notes with a small hand-held tape recorder than with a pad and pencil. There are a hundred things to look for in a sea trial, but something approaching the following routine will ensure that you at least cover the most critical areas:

Before the main engines are cranked, ask the person showing you the boat to crank up the generator; check its noise and vibration levels in the main salon and the staterooms, on the flying bridge, and, if the boat has one, on the aft deck. Are they levels at which you can comfortably carry on a conversation, dine, and sleep?

Make sure that the engines are completely cold at the outset of the sea trial. Beginning a sea trial with the engines already running, or restarting warm engines, is a good way for a less-than-scrupulous manufacturer, dealer, or broker to hide starting or smoking problems. Actually go into the engine room and put your hand on the block. If it is already warm, insist on the right to see the engines started when they are cold.

SEA TRIAL CHECKLIST

Vessel Sea Trialed _____

Noise/Vibration Levels at Dock,
Generator Only:
    Main Deck   —
    Belowdecks Forward   —
    Belowdecks Aft   —

Engine Smoking _____   Max. No-Load RPM _____

     Max. Load RPM   – _____

     Engine Droop   _____

Manueverability:
    Forward   _____
    Reverse   _____

Roll & Pitch:

	No Stabilizers	Stabilizers
Wind/Sea Forward	_____	_____
Wind/Sea Aft	_____	_____
Wind/Sea Abeam	_____	_____
Wind/Sea Forward Quarter	_____	_____
Wind/Sea Aft Quarter	_____	_____

Noise/Vibration Levels Under way:

Main Deck   _____
Belowdecks Forward   _____
Belowdecks Aft   _____

Notes: _____

_____

_____

                       OVERALL RATING _____

Fig. 5.3: Completing a check list on each vessel you sea trial helps insure you don't forget to inspect any vital aspects of its operation at anchor or the dock and its handling characteristics underway.

Before the engines are cranked, position yourself at the stern so you have a clear view of the exhaust. It's normal and acceptable for diesel engines to emit a brief belch of light gray smoke at start-up as they simply are burning off the bit of carbon residue and moisture condensation that builds up in any diesel engine after it has been idle long enough to cool off thoroughly. But if the boat emits heavy black smoke and continues to do so for more than about a minute, be alert to a potential problem. The salesman or broker may tell you the engines "just need a bit of tweaking." My attitude is, if the seller can't keep the engines from smoking excessively when a potential buyer is aboard, how anxious is he going to be to solve the problem after I have handed over my final payment? I'd be inclined to believe there was a significant problem with the engines or their installation and would mark it down as a major minus against the boat.

Here's how to get a quick feel for the basic condition of the engines and propellers of a boat. After the engines have been thoroughly warmed up at the dock, with the gear in neutral, run them up to their maximum rpm. Jot that down as their "no-load" reading. Once you are in open water with the gears engaged, again run them up to their maximum rpm. They should turn up to within about 150 to 200 rpm of their no-load reading. The difference is what diesel mechanics call "droop." If the droop from no-load to load readings in either engine is more than about 200 rpm, the engine or transmission has some internal problem or the prop it is driving is too large or has too much pitch. If the droop is less than about 150 rpm, the prop is probably too small or doesn't have enough pitch. A problem of prop size or pitch (as opposed to an internal problem with an engine or transmission) most likely will show up as too much droop in both engines at the same time.

Maneuverability around the dock is the next factor you need to check out. Many manufacturers, dealers, and brokers don't want anyone but their own employees or themselves to handle their boats around a dock because of the terms of their liability insurance or for fear an inexperienced helmsman will do some damage. If you find that is the case, at least insist that you be allowed to handle the boat you are considering for a few minutes in protected water away from the dock. Swinging her around in a few tight circles—using only her engines if she's a twin-screw boat—will tell you something of how she will handle in close quarters. Back her down to see how readily she answers her helm and tracks in reverse.

Insist that your sea trial include a run in open water, not just a few minutes in protected waters. You're considering buying this boat for safe, comfortable passages at her normal cruising speed. Merely running her across the calm waters of a harbor for a few minutes at half throttle is hardly going to tell you how she will handle in open water. If you get outside and are fortunate enough to have any sea at all running, ask to take her helm and make at least brief runs with the seas head-on, astern, abeam, and on the forward and stern quarters. If she is equipped with a flying bridge, make your runs from that helm station. To determine the ideal cruising speed of a planing-hull boat, bring her engines down to about 1,000 rpm, then run her throttles up slowly until her bow just falls over and she comes up on plane. A well-designed planing hull will nose over when her engines reach about 1,900 rpm. If you leave the throttle at that setting, the engine's governors will maintain it but will have to pump additional fuel through the injectors to do so. Also, a planing-hull boat operated at a speed that barely allows her to plane will tend to fall away from her track when she encounters the least bit of wave action. Instead of leaving her at that rpm setting, gently work the throttles up until you add about 2 knots of speed, which will probably put the engines at about 2,100 rpm. You will find she handles better at that speed, and if you check her fuel consumption over a measured course you should find that it is also her most efficient fuel-consumption setting. With those checks out of the way, note her degree of roll and pitch with wind and seas coming at her from various directions. If she's equipped with an autopilot, activate it for a few moments on each heading to see how well it keeps the boat on course.

If you are considering a full-displacement-hull boat, it would be ideal if the one you take out for a sea trial were equipped with the same brand and size of stabilizers you would plan to have, but you will probably have to make allowances. If stabilizers are installed, run the boat for a few minutes on each heading with the stabilizers off, then on, and note the degree to which they dampen her rolling.

With your handling test out of the way, let someone else take the helm and go below to position yourself on the main deck directly over the engines to assess vibration and noise while they are operating at normal cruising speed. Do the same thing well aft directly over the props and belowdecks in each of the staterooms. Are they levels you and your guests can live with comfortably for hours or perhaps days and nights on end during extended passages? If the boat is equipped with a generator, make sure it is running during this part of your inspection. While you're in the forward stateroom especially, note the degree of tossing about your crew will be subjected to in their off-watch hours.

Even after going through this orderly boat-searching process, you still may not find a boat that really measures up as the cruiser of your dreams. If so, don't be discouraged. Above all, don't let yourself be stampeded by a salesman's pitch into buying a boat you know deep in your heart is not the boat for you. Remember, you are going to be living with the boat you finally buy for a long time under a variety of circumstances. You may even wind up trusting your life and the lives of those you love to it. One cruising friend of mine who often waxes philosophical observes that buying a serious cruising boat is like choosing a wife. The blonde at the end of the bar may look great among the bright lights and glitter, but is she really the one you want to wake up to every morning for the rest of your life?

Let's suppose you have found the boat—new or used—that meets your specifications. Your next move is to negotiate a financial deal for her purchase at a price you can afford.

6

MATTERS OF MONEY

In negotiating with a salesman of new yachts or a broker of used boats, bear in mind that as a typical boat-buyer you might go through the boat-buying process once every three years or so. The guy across the table from you makes his living selling boats all day, every day, so don't be surprised if he's better at selling boats than you are at buying them. Except in rare and unusual circumstances, the chances of your getting the best of a yacht salesman or broker in a deal is pretty slim. The main thing you want to do is make sure you are treated fairly and not taken to the cleaners. Determining which is which will be a little easier if you know some of the cards the other guy is holding.

BUYING A NEW BOAT

In buying a new boat, one of the first decisions you need to make is whether you are going to allow the dealer to recommend, supply, and install the accessory equipment your vessel is going to need—everything from navigation and communications electronics to a tender and its outboard; whether you are going to handle that equipment's purchase and arrange for its installation yourself; or whether you want some combination of the two. We'll go into the matter of where to buy marine accessories in detail in the next chapter, and you'll have a much better basis for making your decision after reading that material. But because your answer has a lot to do with how you handle negotiations on the price of a new boat, we'll mention a few points here: First, there is no question that letting the dealer handle the details of accessorizing your vessel will mean a lot less wear and tear on you, but if he provides that service you may well find yourself paying a handsome price for it. Second, some new-boat dealers recommend good accessory equipment, provide it at a fair price, and install it properly. Others don't really know what you need for extended cruising, what does and doesn't work out in the real world, or how to correctly install the equipment they sell. Third, some of them charge unconscionable prices for anything they can persuade you to buy.

The key to deciding where you will buy the accessories your boat will need is making sure you know up front what you want and the fair price to pay for it. Hopefully, after reading this book you will have an excellent idea of what you do and don't need in the way of accessories and will have an idea of what it costs to buy that equipment and have it installed. When you sit down to talk dollars with a dealer, compare his price for accessories with the prices you've researched. If he can meet those prices with perhaps a few dollars more to pay for the convenience he can offer, it's fine to go with him. If his prices are out of line, present him with your own figures. If he won't come pretty close to your prices, you are better off taking care of that part of the boat-buying process yourself.

Any number of factors can influence a deal on a particular boat, but to illustrate some of the basic economics of the boat-selling business, let's construct a hypothetical but reasonably typical example. Let's say after going through the process described in the preceding chapters you've decided to buy a new boat and have chosen one in the mid-40-foot range. You find a dealer with the model in his new-boat inventory and it has the basic factory-installed options you want such as a flying bridge, bow pulpit, and the like. Its base-boat price as listed in the manufacturer's literature, including the factory-installed options, is $249,500. You don't have time to chase around after the accessories you would want, so you specify a list of options you will have the dealer install if you buy the boat from him. His list prices for those options seem in line with other figures you have seen for the same equipment and they will increase the boat's cost by roughly $48,000. Now the total list price of the boat is up to $297,500. The salesman does a little quick figuring, huddles with his boss and beams at you that he is willing to knock $15,000 right off the top and let you have that little jewel for only $282,500—a discount of about 5 percent off list. Is that a fair price to you, or are you funneling too much of your hard-earned money into the dealer's pocket?

To begin to answer that question, take 15 percent of the suggested list of $249,500 for the boat and its factory-installed options—that's $37,425. Most builders of sizable power yachts sell boats to their dealers at a discount of at least 15 percent off list. Some manufacturers offer dealer discounts up to about 18 percent off list, and some increase the discount even further if the dealer's annual orders pass certain volume levels. By taking 15 percent off the list price of a new boat, you can figure that if the dealer could sell the boat at list, that would be about his minimum potential gross profit on the boat alone. (If the boat you are considering is under 40 feet, figure the dealer's discount at 20 percent of the base boat price, including factory-installed options. As a general rule, the smaller the boat, the greater the dealer markup.)

Now take 40 percent of the $48,000 in options you would ask the dealer to install, which is a typical discount he's probably getting from the accessories manufacturers. That's another $19,200. Add that to his minimum potential gross profit of $37,425 on the boat itself and he stands to make at least $56,625 if he sells you the boat and the options at list price.

Of course he knows you aren't going to pay list, so he's authorized his salesman to offer you a $15,000 discount which brings his profit down to a minimum of $41,625. On a $282,500 deal, that's still a gross profit margin of almost 15 percent. Even after he pays his salesman the typical commission rate of 20 percent of the gross profit ($8,325), that leaves the dealer with $33,300—a profit after deducting the commission of almost 12 percent. Out of that he still has to pay his yard workers, his operating overhead, and such, but it's still not a bad day's work.

Now go back and work the deal your way. Take 7 percent of the manufacturer's $249,500 list price for the boat and its factory-installed options (10 percent if the boat is under 40 feet). That's $17,465, just a little less than half the dealer's minimum potential profit on the boat alone if he sold it at list. Now take 15 percent of the $48,000 in options you'd want him to install. That's $7,200—again a bit less than half the dealer's probable markup. Add the two figures together to get $24,665 and subtract that from the suggested list price of the boat and installed options of $297,500. The result—$272,835—is about the most you ought to pay for that boat with those options installed. With hard bargaining, you should be able to buy that boat for between $265,000 and $270,000. Offer no more than $250,000 for openers, then expect to be dragged kicking and screaming up to about the $265,000-to-$270,000 level before you make a deal. If you follow something approaching this scenario, eight out of ten times you'll have bought that boat on terms that are fair to both you and the dealer.

After you have worked out the numbers in a particular deal to arrive at what you feel is a realistic price, you can of course shop a number of dealers for the particular boat you want and play them off one against the other to get the absolute lowest price. If you do that, recognize that the dealer you finally buy the boat from has a very sharp pencil. That's worked to your advantage in the initial purchase, but it may well work against you when the time comes for warranty work to be done or for a trade up to a larger boat. Many boat-buyers find they are happier in the long run if they do all their boat-buying business with a single dealer. They may leave a few extra dollars on the table, but they build up a sense of trust and rapport that pays off in quick service on warranty work and a fair deal when they buy subsequent boats.

Of the factors that can influence a particular new-boat deal, the general state of America's economy and the particular model of boat you decide to buy are among the most important. If economic times are good and the boat you pick is a popular model in short supply, the dealer may have other potential buyers on the string and not be willing to make the concessions you want. On the other hand, if the nation is in the midst of an economic downturn and a dealer has had the boat you are considering in his inventory for several months, he may be getting desperate to unload it. In order to encourage dealers to order stock boats and thus keep their production lines busy, most yacht manufacturers agree to pay all or the lion's share of their dealers' floor-plan financing cost for the first four to six months they have a boat in inventory. If you know the dealer has had the boat you want for several months, the manufacturer's floor-plan support for it may be about to end. In that case, the dealer will be much more motivated to sell it to you at anything he can realize over his cost before interest charges begin to eat him alive. (In the example above, at a 15 percent discount, the dealer's cost in the boat would be about $212,000. Once the factory's support of his floor-plan financing runs out, at a 10-percent rate he would be looking at over $1,700 a month in interest charges.)

BUYING A USED BOAT

Shopping for a used cruising vessel is subject to so many variables it is difficult to make generalizations, but here are a few useful guidelines.

First, shop where the boats are. On the East Coast, that's the southeast coast of Florida. On the West Coast, it's the area from Los Angeles to San Diego. While you may find an outstanding buy in other areas, in general you will find a much wider range of boats to choose from at lower prices in those two areas than in any other part of the country. The time of year you shop can also be important. The used-boat business usually gets very slow in the heat of the summer—July and August—and from about Thanksgiving to the end of February. If you make an offer on a boat during those slow periods, you are more likely to have a hungry broker try to argue his seller into taking it than he would at the peak of the selling season in the spring and fall. In more northerly areas, an offer made in October or November is more likely to be accepted because the seller is looking at the cost of carrying the boat over a long winter until sales revive in the spring.

Most advertised prices for used boats listed with brokers are grossly inflated. It's human nature for an owner to list his boat with the broker who claims to be able to get him the highest price. Even if the owner is looking for a quick sale, most listing brokers will recommend that the owner set his "asking price" at least 10 to 15 percent higher than he is really willing to accept in order to leave some maneuvering room on the actual selling price and hopefully cover some of the broker's commission. If the owner is not pressed to get his money out of his boat, some brokers will recommend that he set an asking price of 20 to 30 percent above what he will actually accept. (Some wealthy owners, in fact, continuously keep their boats on the market just to see what kind of offers they bring. The owners have no real intention of selling and so set a ridiculously high price. But if some idiot comes along who is willing to buy at that price or at one that returns a 30- or 40-percent profit, they'll sell. That's why you see some bigger boats tagged in the classified section of the boating magazines as "seriously for sale.")

The discount off the asking price at which you can really buy a particular used boat, then, depends in large measure on the owner's motivation. If he is well fixed financially, he may have little reason to accept a price very much below what he is asking. But if he has listed the boat you are considering with the broker on consignment and is making payments on a newer boat, or has other personal or business situations that require immediate cash, he may be willing to slash his price considerably.

The used-boat brokerage business works this way: Brokerage contracts are either "open" or "central-agency" listings. In either case, the standard commission rate is 10 percent of the price the boat actually brings. In open listings, any number of brokers can list the boat and offer it for sale, deal directly with the owner, and collect the entire selling commission. In central-agency listings, the seller agrees that all offers to purchase will be channeled through a single broker. If the brokerage house holding a central-agency listing sells the boat, it keeps the entire 10 percent commission. If another brokerage house sells the boat, the listing broker gets 3 percent of the selling price and the selling broker gets 7 percent.

Since any broker's income is pegged to the boat's selling price, he has an interest in keeping the selling price as high as possible. At the same time, he makes nothing on a boat that is priced so unrealistically high that he cannot find a buyer for it, so a broker may be inclined to persuade an owner to accept a somewhat lower price in order to close a deal and move on to the next one.

Understanding how the brokerage business works is important to you in buying a used boat because—though it doesn't happen often—in cases where you and the seller get to within about 1 or 2 percent of the boat's value and neither of you will make the concessions necessary to bridge the gap, the broker may step in and agree to make up the difference, do some minor repair, or make other concessions in order to conclude the deal. Obviously, that is more likely to happen if the broker is both listing and selling the boat, since he doesn't have to split his commission.

Once you have found a specific used boat and a careful walk-through has convinced you it is worth pursuing, figure out approximately what that boat is really worth, which may have little to do with the owner's asking price. If you've followed the advice in the preceding chapter and involved a qualified broker of your own in your search for a good used boat, he is probably the best source of a reliable estimate of the true value of a specific used boat. If you are dealing directly with a listing broker, or want to check your own broker's recommendation, repeat the process you went through when you constructed your original boat-buying budget by checking the BUC book for its prices on boats of the make, model, and age you are considering and making inquiries of other brokers about recent selling prices of similar boats. Once you have a pretty good fix on the value of the boat in average condition, adjust it for pluses and/or minuses in the particular boat you are looking at.

One initial key to negotiating the purchase of a boat at a price you are satisfied with is not to be too anxious. Let the broker know you are willing to take your time and pass up several deals if necessary until you find one you feel is equitable. If you get into serious negotiation on a used boat, the broker often will suggest that you make an offer somewhat below the asking price. If the broker is one you have retained as your buying agent, you probably are safe to accept his recommendation. If you are dealing with the listing agent, the price he suggests you offer probably will be a bit higher than he is reasonably certain the owner will accept. If you are genuinely interested in the boat, you might do well to make an offer 10 to 15 percent below what the broker recommends. Make certain your offer is "subject to sea trial and survey," back it up with a deposit check made payable to the selling broker for 10 percent of your offer, and include a date a week or ten days in the future after which it will expire. The check makes yours a bona fide offer which the listing broker is legally obligated to present to the owner. The broker should hold your deposit check in escrow, and most will accept a personal check rather than insisting on certified funds. Some brokers go ahead and cash the deposit check, others simply hold it until the negotiations are concluded and return it if the deal falls through. The selling broker will want your offer-to-purchase to include a closing date and probably will try to get you to set it as early as possible, but don't let yourself be hurried. It may take a week or two to schedule a survey by a competent marine surveyor and another couple of weeks after receipt of his written report to finalize insurance and financing. Allowing a month between your offer-to-purchase and the closing date is not excessive.

If the owner is in a financial bind, he may accept your offer and the deal is done at a price somewhat below what the broker recommended. If the owner rejects your bid and comes back with a counteroffer, at least you are getting a little closer to what he will accept. If the owner's counteroffer indicates he is not willing to make enough of a concession below his asking price to keep you interested in the boat, you can retrieve your earnest-money deposit and walk away. If his counteroffer is at least in the direction of what you are willing to pay, you can then make a new offer at somewhat less than the owner's counteroffer and go through that process as many times as necessary until you agree on a formal "offer-to-purchase" and "offer-to-sell" contract at a price that is still subject to sea trial and survey. If you make a subsequent offer-to-purchase that is higher than your original or most recent offer, you may be asked to escrow additional funds to bring your deposits up to 10 percent of your offering price.

After you have signed a contract, if you have not had the opportunity for a sea trial, now is the proper time.

THE MARINE SURVEY

The next step is to arrange for a qualified marine surveyor to conduct a full prepurchase condition-and-valuation marine survey. In the case of a boat only a couple of years old, your insurer and financing source may be satisfied with a less complete survey, but you should have a complete "C-and-V" survey done anyway to make certain you know the boat's actual condition. You will be expected to bear the expenses the survey entails.

A qualified marine surveyor is a professional who inspects several hundred boats of all types every year. With that experience, he can spot a great many things the average boat buyer would miss or is simply not competent to evaluate. If a surveyor notes even one significant area of hull delamination, a serious electrolysis problem, or an engine in need of an extensive overhaul, he can save you many times his fee. At the least, he may uncover defects that should be corrected before you go to sea or that should properly affect the boat's selling price in your favor. Even if you wind up not buying a boat you have had surveyed, it may well be for defects the surveyor has pointed out to you, in which case he has helped prevent you from making an expensive mistake.

The key word where marine surveyors are concerned is "qualified." Employing one is largely a *caveat emptor* operation. Neither the Federal Government nor any state in the nation sets any standards or requires any examination or other proof of qualifications for anyone to hang out a shingle and call himself a marine surveyor. (Louisiana had a law regulating marine surveyors on its books for years but repealed it in 1988.) With that lack of regulation, anyone can get in the business for nothing more than the cost of a meaningless occupational license and a few dollars for business cards and an ad in the telephone book. Also, surveyors' reports usually contain disclaimers of responsibility for "concealed deficiencies and/or latent defects," which give you little recourse in case they fail to uncover problems that later prove serious. Since in most states surveyors do not have to be bonded, even if you proved gross negligence and won a judgment, your chances of collecting probably would be minimal.

Unfortunately, membership in a professional organization is not an infallible guide to finding a qualified surveyor. The leading organization of which some surveyors are members is the National Association of Marine Surveyors. NAMS requires applicants to have several years of practical experience and pass a rigorous examination before it certifies them, then requires them to periodically attend workshops and seminars to keep up their skills. The problem is that only a small percentage of those who call themselves marine surveyors are NAMS members, and some who are certified by NAMS survey only large commercial vessels. Also, a number of highly qualified marine surveyors for one reason or another choose not to join the organization. Membership in such organizations as the Society of Accredited Marine Surveyors, the American Boat and Yacht Council, the National Fire Protection Association, and the like is not a reliable guide in selecting a competent surveyor. These are largely advisory or informational organizations that require little if anything in the way of examinations or experience for membership and none polices its members or punishes violations of the lofty standards it professes to uphold. Just about anyone can join any of these groups for the price of a membership fee and the payment of annual dues.

Also be wary of choosing a surveyor based on the size of his ad in the telephone book. Some surveyors with the biggest ads are the most incompetent, and some of the best ones stay so busy with referrals from reputable brokers, yacht financing sources, insurance agents, and satisfied customers that they don't advertise at all.

The broker you are dealing with will almost invariably recommend a surveyor to you. If the broker is reliable, his recommendation may well be excellent, but check the surveyor's qualifications and reputation anyway. Some less-than-scrupulous brokers have a favorite surveyor or two whom they have found they can rely on to give the boats they are trying to sell a favorable "broker's survey" rather than performing their real job which is protecting the buyer's best interest.

Check with your insurance agent to make certain your insurer will accept the report of any surveyor you plan to hire. Some companies will accept only the reports of surveyors on their approved list. If you will be financing the boat, also check the acceptability of the surveyor with your financing source. If the broker, your insurance agent, and possibly your financing source all endorse a surveyor, you probably have someone who is competent. If any of these sources has doubts about a surveyor or is unfamiliar with surveyors in the area where the boat you are considering is berthed, check with several insurance agents, reputable brokers, yacht financing sources, and major full-service boatyards in that area until several mention the same name. That's probably your man.

Typical rates for a complete condition-and-valuation survey on a fiberglass-hull yacht run around $7 to $10 per foot of boat length. Rates for surveying wood-hull boats may be slightly higher, and rates for surveying a steel- or aluminum-hull vessel may be up to twice as high if the insurer or financing source insists that the hull be tested with an audio-gauge. Some surveyors base their charges on an hourly rate, which can vary from $40 to $60 per hour. Unless I was supersatisfied with a surveyor's credentials, I'd be reluctant to enter into an hourly-rate agreement because the surveyor can charge for waiting time and time spent writing his report and you have no idea how many hours he actually invested. Most surveyors will charge less if all you need is a survey to keep your insurance in force. In that case, they will check only those factors that affect the vessel's safety and seaworthiness and won't worry about how well the stereo or the microwave oven works.

When you find an appropriate surveyor, make certain up front you are getting a full condition-and-valuation survey. A few marine surveyors limit their work to checking the hull, and you will have to hire a separate technician to check the boat's electronics and a diesel mechanic to go over the engines, each of which could cost you anywhere from $250 to $400 in addition to the surveyor's fee. A good marine surveyor should be competent to give you an informed opinion on the entire vessel. Only if he finds serious problems and recommends separate checks by a specialized electronics technician or diesel-engine mechanic should you have to go to that added expense.

Make sure you know what the surveyor's rate is and what it does and does not include. If significant driving from the surveyor's home or office to the boat's location is involved (usually over about fifty miles), you may be asked to pay for mileage and travel time. If air travel, overnight accommodations, and meals away from home are involved, you will be expected to pick up the tab. Have a clear agreement with the surveyor about when he will be paid. Some surveyors will allow you to pay from an invoice that accompanies their written report. Others have been stiffed so many times by prospective buyers who decided not to buy a boat after receiving an unfavorable survey they will ask for their money as soon as they deliver their verbal report. To eliminate any possibility of confusion, settle up with your marine surveyor directly rather than paying him through any third party.

In negotiating some used-boat deals, you may be presented with a survey the seller has already had conducted. In other cases, you may be offered a copy of a survey a previous potential buyer had done on the boat at a cost of about half or less what he paid for it. Either survey may be quite legitimate. Some conscientious sellers have a survey conducted prior to putting their boats on the market so they can go ahead and correct any significant defects. A prior prospective buyer may have forgone purchase of the boat for reasons entirely unrelated to the survey's results. He paid for the survey and it is his property. If he wants to sell it to you to recoup some of his expense, that is his privilege, and most surveyors don't object to having their work resold. You might be safe in accepting it in lieu of paying for your own if, after checking the surveyor's qualifications and reputation and talking to him personally about the boat, you are convinced of his competence and integrity. Even in that case, his should be a full C-and-V survey and should be less than about three months old. Again, make certain your insurance company and, if necessary, your lender is willing to accept the report. Assuming the person who originally commissioned the survey agrees, most surveyors will supply a new cover sheet for the survey listing you as the buyer for a nominal fee. Before doing so, some very cautious surveyors may insist on making at least a brief recheck of the boat and charge you a hundred dollars or so. If any of the above conditions are not met or you have the slightest question about the surveyor's competence or integrity, spend the money to have your own survey conducted.

If at all possible, you should be present when the survey is conducted. If you are in attendance, the surveyor can give you an on-the-spot appreciation for the boat's true condition that might not come through as clearly in a written report. Give him room to do his work, but actually crawl down into the bilge with him and peer over his shoulder. Your broker should be along as well, and it would be ideal if the seller's broker can be present although staying in the background. If the surveyor finds a major problem area, you may be able to settle a lot of questions then and there and eliminate protracted negotiations.

Once you arrive at the boat, if your surveyor shows up for

the job in work clothes and spends several hours poking and prying into anchor lockers and hatches with a flashlight, crawls all through the engine room, pulls out drawers and looks behind them, and taps the decks and superstructure all over with a plastic mallet for signs of deterioration or delamination (Fig. 6.1), you're probably getting a thorough, competent survey. If he shows up in white slacks, gives a desultory glance at the boat's exterior, pokes his head into the engine room and pronounces her seaworthy, send him packing.

Once the surveyor has completed his initial in-water inspection and all is well, you should give the boat a second sea trial with the surveyor aboard. By scheduling this second sea trial prior to lifting the boat out of the water, if the surveyor turns up anything that convinces you it's not the boat you're looking for, you've saved the expense of the haul-out portion of the survey. Assuming you have already satisfied yourself about the boat's

Fig. 6.1: *Marine surveyor Dean Greger uses a rubber mallet to tap every inch of the hull and superstructure of a used vessel he has been hired to evaluate. A dull thud or hollow ring helps him spot areas of concealed deterioration.*

handling characteristics on an initial sea trial, in this one you need not worry about getting the boat into open water. If you've not had a chance to handle her in the open sea, now is the time to do it. You should, however, make certain the engines are run up to maximum speed to allow your surveyor to check them under full load.

During the final sea trial, spend most of your time with your surveyor as he climbs around the engine room checking all the systems while under way and gives the electronics a good going-over.

If everything still looks good after the in-water and sea trial portions of the survey, the surveyor should request that the boat be hauled so he can examine the underbody. This haul-out will be at your expense ($3 to $5 per foot of boat length is a typical charge, which includes both lifting and returning the boat to the water). Once the boat is out of the water, the surveyor should carefully check the condition and alignment of shaft, struts, props, and rudders, go over all through-hull fittings, and tap the entire exterior of the hull with his plastic mallet for signs of delamination, deterioration, or blistering. If you have not already done so, this is also the time for you to satisfy yourself that the boat's underbody configuration is appropriate to the kind of cruising you have in mind.

After his inspection is complete, the surveyor should be able to brief you immediately on any serious defects he has uncovered and give you a rough idea of what it will cost to repair them. If your broker and the seller's broker are both present, you may be able to hash out whether the seller will attend to the needed repairs or lower the price to offset the expense you will incur. You are probably better off if you can get the seller to undertake the repairs, since the boatyard may find additional problems after it gets into the job. You should reserve the right to have your surveyor check the boat again after the repairs are completed to see that they are done properly. Have a clear understanding with the surveyor as to whether his recheck of the repairs will cost you extra. If the seller is going to reduce his price and you are going to be responsible for the repairs, you should get a good boatyard to give you a quote on the work to make certain of the expense involved. Bear in mind that if you go that route and the yard finds other problems once it opens up the work, you are responsible for the added expense, not the seller.

Once the surveyor has completed his inspection, he should prepare a written report that details everything he found, down to missing clamps and light bulbs, and should give his estimate of the boat's present and replacement values. Most surveyors will present their written report within about forty-eight hours of the survey itself.

With his report in hand, you are now in position to finalize your offer.

IF YOU HAVE A TRADE-IN

If you have a boat you want to trade in on a newer or larger vessel, you need to get a realistic idea of what it's worth before you get into serious negotiations. Check the BUC Book's average wholesale price for a vessel of your boat's year and model in average condition with average equipment, and check brokers for typical selling prices, then adjust the figure to fit your boat's condition. Assuming your trade-in is in average condition with average equipment, you should expect a trade-in allowance from a new boat dealer which is about 10 percent less than similar boats have actually been retailing for. If your boat is exceptionally clean or well equipped, its value should be a bit higher. If a dealer offers you a trade-in price for your boat that is substantially above what your own research has indicated it is worth, go over his offer on the new boat with a fine-tooth comb. There ain't no free lunch, and there ain't no Santa Claus.

If your trade-in is a popular model in good condition which a dealer can turn quickly at a reasonable profit, you probably will encounter little resistance from him in taking it in trade. If it's a boat with a wood hull, is a brand few people have ever heard of, has an odd layout, or has serious mechanical problems, a dealer may refuse to take it in trade but agree to sell it for you on consignment. Most brokers would prefer to sell your old boat on consignment, which ties up *your* money, not theirs.

If you are going to sell your boat through a broker, choose one who deals in the type of vessel you want to sell. You will probably find that if you give him a central-agency listing, he will be more aggressive in trying to advertise and sell it since he knows he is going to get a commission of at least 3 percent of its sale price even if another broker finds you a buyer. All advertising expense should be borne by the broker. If he has slips at his brokerage, he should be willing to display your boat for a couple of months without charging you dockage. If it takes longer than that to sell the boat, you should only have to pay about half the going rate to keep your boat at his dock.

If you wind up listing your old boat on consignment, bear in mind that the dealer or broker probably is refusing to take it in trade precisely because his experience tells him it will not sell quickly. If you still owe money on it, or if you will have to borrow more money for the new boat to offset the loss of the trade-in allowance, don't fool yourself into thinking a buyer will come along and bail you out in a couple of weeks. Make certain you can carry the added cost for at least six months, or you could find that you have let your old boat go at far less than you counted on just to get some of the financial load off your back.

SALES TAXES

More and more states are beginning to realize what a financial bonanza booming boat sales represent and they are slapping sales taxes on both new and used yachts. The state of Florida, which is possibly the yacht sales capital of the nation, has been the trend-setter in this movement and its approach is being implemented or at least studied by a number of states. It's a fairly safe bet that most coastal states that don't already have machinery to enforce their sales taxes on boats will have something similar to the Florida program in place in the foreseeable future.

The Florida program works like this: The sales-tax rate for both new and used boats is 6 percent of the purchase price. In the example of the boat we discussed above, at a $265,000 sale price (assuming no trade-in was involved) the sales tax would be a whopping $15,900. If a dealer or broker takes a buyer's old boat in trade, the buyer pays sales tax only on the difference between the price of the new boat and the value of his trade-in. If the dealer takes the old boat on consignment and its sale is not closed at the same time the deal on the new boat is closed, the buyer pays sales tax on the full price of the boat he is purchasing. If the broker sells the buyer's old boat and the deals on both boats are closed simultaneously, the buyer of the new boat pays sales tax only on the difference in the sales prices of the two vessels.

Unfortunately, sales taxes are no longer deductible from Federal income tax returns.

Individuals who purchase boats in Florida are liable for Florida's sales tax regardless of whether or not they are residents of the state. The only way to buy a boat in Florida and legally avoid paying the Florida sales tax is to remove the boat from Florida within ten days of its purchase unless it requires repair or alteration, in which case it must be removed from the state within ten days of the completion of the repairs or alterations. In no case may it be kept in Florida more than ninety days from the date of purchase. In order to waive collection of the Florida sales tax, dealers and brokers in the state must require buyers who say they plan to remove their boat from Florida within the required time period to sign an affidavit to that effect and to send them the original of a fuel or dockage bill from another state as proof that the boat has left Florida's jurisdiction. The boat may not return to Florida within six months of its departure. Because so many East Coast owners keep their boats in the Bahamas for part of the year anyway, moving a boat there for the six months out-of-state period will not satisfy the requirement.

Even removing a boat purchased in Florida from the state within the required period and keeping it out for the stipulated length of time may not suffice to avoid the Florida sales tax. As one Florida revenue agent told me: "Say we run across an owner who bought a boat in Florida, avoided the Florida sales tax by taking it just across the state line into Georgia, then brought it back into Florida as soon as the six-months period was up. We'd look at that situation pretty carefully. If we found, for instance, that after having the boat in Georgia for a couple of months he had made a reservation for a slip in Florida beginning as soon as the six months waiting period was up, we'd probably rule his intent in moving it to Georgia was simply to avoid the Florida sales tax and would make him pay."

The penalty for illegally avoiding Florida's sales tax is severe: the tax, plus interest from the date it should have been paid, plus 100 percent of the tax as a penalty.

Florida and the other states that impose sales taxes on boats are getting a lot stricter in their enforcement. In 1983, for instance, the Florida Department of Revenue had three agents checking for boats still in the state on which Florida's sales tax was not collected because the purchaser signed an affidavit saying the boat would be taken out of the state. Today that section has eighty agents. The Miami Coast Guard office now routinely sends information on all the vessels it documents to the Florida Department of Revenue. If the Department of Revenue does not find evidence in its files that Florida sales tax has been paid on a particular boat within its borders, it contacts the purchaser to find out why. In addition, the Florida Marine Patrol is also on the lookout for vessels purchased and operating in the state on which the state's sales tax has not been paid. The crackdown has gotten so stringent that some new-boat dealers and used-boat brokers in Florida are now requiring purchasers who say they plan to remove their boats from the state to put the sales tax in escrow, then refund it only when they have proof from the owner that the vessel has actually been taken beyond Florida's borders.

Similar crackdowns are taking place in New York where the state sales-tax rate is 8 percent and in Connecticut where it is 7.5 percent. Those two states compare notes on vessels that are documented with the New York office of the Coast Guard and check to see if sales tax has been paid in either state. If not, they go looking for the owner.

Connecticut requires all vessels berthed in its waters for more than sixty days (rather than ninety days as in most states) to be state-registered, even if they are Federally documented. In order to register a vessel, the owner must present a bill of sale showing the date he bought it. If it was purchased within the preceding six months, he must also present proof of the price he paid for the boat and proof of the sales taxes he paid to any other state. If the sales tax paid to another state is less than Connecticut's 7.5 percent, he must pay the difference to Connecticut before they will register the vessel. (Most states will give credit for sales taxes paid to other states.) If the owner has no proof of sales tax paid to another state, he must pay the entire 7.5 percent. And the state is deadly serious about catching boat-owners who try to ignore its sales-tax regulations. "The revenue agents walk the dock," one Connecticut yacht-owner told me, "and take down information on the boats that are tied up. Sixty-one days later, they walk down the same dock. Any vessel that is still there and is not on their list as having had Connecticut sales taxes paid on it gets a note stuck on the windshield directing the owner to contact the state revenue department."

Any sales taxes that apply to a cruising vessel you buy will also apply to its tender.

If you buy a boat in a state with a high sales tax and want

to avoid paying that tax by removing it to a state with no sales tax or a tax that is lower, where do you take it? A few buyers of really expensive yachts go to the extreme of setting up a corporation in a no- or low-tax state, listing the vessel as a corporate asset, and either basing it in that state or keeping it on the move so that it is in no one state more than sixty or ninety days, depending on that state's regulations. Listing a yacht as a corporate asset also has the advantage of limiting the owner's personal liability in the event of an accident. For a fee of around $700, a number of yacht service firms will set up such a corporation in Rhode Island, which charges no sales tax, or in North Carolina, which limits sales taxes on boats to a maximum of $300 regardless of value. For that fee, you get a legal corporation, stock certificates, a corporate seal, and the address of a registered agent in the state which you can use as the corporation's own.

The upshot of this whole discussion of sales taxes is that you should be sure to include them in your boat-buying budget and check with your lawyer or accountant to make sure you know what sales taxes you will be liable for before you sign on the dotted line.

YACHT FINANCING

If you plan to finance your boat, the first question is where you will go to borrow the money.

The first place you should check is the bank with which you normally do your personal and/or business banking. Your contact there may be willing to make certain concessions in rate or terms because you are a good customer and he or she wants to keep your business. Also, your local bank is likely to retain your loan in its own portfolio. Should the time come when you need to make changes in your loan's terms and conditions, you'll probably be dealing with someone you know who has an interest in keeping you happy.

Some banks, of course, simply don't know anything about the peculiar intricacies of yacht financing and really aren't interested in lending money on a highly mobile piece of machinery that they can't keep an eye on. If you find your local bank is not interested in giving you a boat loan, check some of the well-established banks in the primary boating markets.

In many cases, a salesman or broker will offer to put you in touch with someone at a national finance company or a bank that offers yacht financing. Occasionally, the dealership or brokerage house may have an arrangement with the financing source which pays them a commission or some percentage of your interest in return for steering you to them and taking care of much of the paperwork. While some would call this a kickback, there is nothing illegal about the practice. But if that is the case, you should be aware of it and take the dealer's probable "side income" from the lending transaction (typically 1.5 to 3 percent of the amount you borrow) into account when you negotiate the price of a boat.

The national financing sources frequently will offer rates a quarter to half of a percentage point lower than you will get from a local bank. Saving interest expense is always nice, but there is a potential danger you should be aware of. Many of these yacht financing sources make the bulk of their income originating loans and/or servicing them (that is, collecting and processing payments for someone else), not from tying up their own funds for fifteen to twenty years and taking their profit from the interest you pay. In order to keep fresh funds coming in to lend to new customers, they sell the loans they originate to investors. Your loan might wind up being owned by a finance company, a bank, or even an individual halfway across the continent. If something happens down the road to make you want to modify the terms of the loan, you may find you must deal with someone you have never heard of who has no particular reason to want to accommodate your request. Again, there is nothing inherently wrong with this practice, but you should ask a potential lender about his policy on loan sales so you know all the ground rules before you sign the loan.

In any discussions about possible financing, insist on two things: that yours be a simple interest loan, not an "add-on" or "Rule of 78's" loan in which you actually wind up paying interest on interest. Also insist that you have the right to pay off the principal of the loan at any time without any prepayment penalty.

In considering your yacht loan, a lender is going to be looking primarily for two things: where your cash flow to repay the loan is going to come from; and how he can structure the deal so there is always more equity in the boat than what you owe on it. If he has to repossess it, he wants to make certain he can sell it for enough to cover both the outstanding principal and any expenses he might incur.

To determine how large a loan you can afford, the guidelines for analyzing your cash flow vary widely by institution. One usually reliable rule of thumb is to take 75 percent of your gross annual income as theoretically disposable after taxes. Most lenders don't want to see more than 40 percent of that figure committed to fixed payments such as your home mortgage and installment loans, or more than 60 percent committed to basic living expenses such as food, shelter, clothing, transportation, medical care, insurance, and the like. Even if you meet those criteria, most lenders will not make you a loan whose payments will eat up more than half of the 40 percent of your disposable income after meeting your basic expenses.

The primary way the lender will try to ensure that there is always adequate equity in the boat is to require a substantial down payment. In a typical case of a new cruising powerboat with a price tag of $100,000 or more, a lender will want a down payment of at least 20 percent of the purchase price and will finance the balance for up to twenty years. On a used boat, most lenders will want 25 percent down and will finance the balance over a maximum of fifteen years. There are, however, situations where a lender will take a smaller percentage for the down payment if you agree to a loan with a shorter term, say, seven to ten years rather than fifteen or twenty. In that case, you would be paying equity into the loan faster than the boat is depreciating.

It's difficult to determine the rate at which a particular yacht will depreciate. In boom times, some boats even appreciate in value. Check the BUC Book for the make and model of boat you are considering to see whether the average wholesale figures have gone up or down over several years. But remember that the figures themselves may not be all that accurate; also, they are based on past averages, which are not necessarily a reliable guide to what will happen in the future.

Having offered that *caveat*, however, it is possible to make a few general statements:

A boat built by a well-known, quality manufacturer will tend to depreciate less in bad times and appreciate more in good times than one from a manufacturer that is less well known and offers a lower level of construction quality. You might save a substantial sum up front by buying a lightly built boat from a little-known manufacturer, but when the time comes to trade or sell it, you probably will find that you have lost money over time.

New boats tend to depreciate at a faster rate than used boats in the first year or two of their operation. The minute you take delivery of a new boat and drive it away from the dealer's dock, it becomes a used boat and is valued accordingly.

"Character" boats, or boats to which the owner has added highly personal or unusual features, depreciate faster than more conventional models. That salty little cruiser with the lines of a New York Harbor tugboat may be exactly the boat you want, but be aware that if you decide to sell or trade it, you may have a tough time finding a buyer who shares your tastes and you may well take a sizable loss on your investment. Adding home-made bow pulpits, elaborate topside lounges, and the like to even a popular model may suit you perfectly but is likely to reduce the boat's value at resale or trade-in time.

Lastly, well-maintained boats retain a higher percentage of their value than boats that have been mistreated. Changing en-gine and generator oil at recommended intervals, keeping your vessel's engine room spotless, keeping your teak handrails pro-tected with oil or varnish, and all the other steps that go into proper boat maintenance may be tedious at the time but they will pay you back in significant dollars when you resell your boat.

In financing the purchase of a boat, many people go for the lowest possible down payment and longest term they can get. That route will hold down the cost of their monthly payments, but they will pay dearly in terms of interest cost, and when the time comes to sell or trade their boat they will have little if any equity in it.

Most yacht financing experts recommend exactly the oppo-site: pay down as much as you can and structure the loan over the shortest possible time consistent with the maximum monthly payments you can afford. Consider these figures on a $100,000 loan at 10 percent: If the term is twenty years, the payments will be about $965 dollars a month. Shorten the term to fifteen years and the payment increases only $110 to $1,075. Shorten it to twelve years and the payment goes up only another $120 to $1,195. But look what happens to your interest expense: Assuming you pay the loan to maturity, on the twenty-year loan you will have paid

$131,000 in interest; on the fifteen-year loan, $93,500; and on the twelve-year loan, $72,080. By shortening the term from twenty to twelve years and increasing your payments by $230 per month, over the life of the loan you will save $58,920 in interest expense—over half of what you borrowed in the first place.

Also look what happens to your equity: After making payments for three years, on the twenty-year loan you still owe a principle of $94,500; on the fifteen-year loan the balance is $89,900; and on the twelve-year loan it is $84,900. By reducing the term from twenty years to twelve at only slightly higher monthly payments, at the end of three years you have increased your equity in the vessel by almost $10,000. At the end of five years the difference is almost $18,000.

In summary, shop for your yacht loan as carefully as you shop for your yacht itself. As with the boat, the right loan can make your cruising experience a joy; the wrong loan can burden you with unnecessary expense.

MARINE INSURANCE

As a yacht owner, your potential for grief from improper or inadequate insurance ranks second only to that of dealing with paid crew. The waterfront is full of horror stories from yachtsmen who thought they were covered for a specific difficulty and found out they weren't, or had their insurance company refuse to pay a claim because of some alleged failure on the part of the owner to live up to his policy's terms and conditions.

In arranging insurance on your cruising vessel, get at least three detailed quotes on the coverage you need. Premiums for exactly the same coverage can vary 25 to 30 percent from company to company. All three probably can be supplied by a single agent since most marine insurance agents are independents and deal with several companies. Insist that your yacht insurance be written only by a company that is "A-rated." Lower-rated companies may offer cheaper premiums, but a couple of multimillion-dollar liability losses could quickly leave them insolvent. Under Murphy's Law, they will suffer all those losses in the two weeks before you file your claim.

Arrange your insurance with a company that has a separate marine division thoroughly knowledgeable in yacht insurance. Some companies write policies on yachts the same way they do on automobiles and take depreciation on losses, which good marine policies don't. On a new yacht, depreciation could cost you 20 to 25 percent the minute you take delivery. Also, make sure the company you go with will cover you in all the navigation areas you plan to cruise, even though you may not buy coverage for all those areas initially. You want to build up a history of trust with your insurer. You don't want to wind up in the Virgin Islands with plans to head for Martinique only to find that your present insurer won't extend your navigation limits and you have to negotiate the necessary coverage with a new company over a single sideband radio.

In filing your application for insurance, be completely truthful and comprehensive. In the event you suffer a loss, any overstatement of your experience and qualifications or understatement of previous losses could be used by your insurer to deny payment based on the policy's "fraud and misrepresentation" clause. Before you sign anything, read over the policy carefully to make certain it provides the coverage you need and says so in black and white. Verbal additions by the agent are not binding on the company.

Once you have bought a policy, read it again and make notes on what you must do to comply with its terms. Most policies, for instance, require that your vessel have an automatic fire-suppression system in the engine room and that it be checked and recertified by an approved technician annually. If you fail to have it recertified within the required time period and have an engine-room fire, you are giving the insurance company a perfect reason to deny coverage. Most policies protect against theft only if there are signs of forced entry or removal. Go ashore in your dinghy one evening, loop its rope painter over a piling, and have it disappear. When you file a claim, your insurer may deny payment by arguing that you should have used a wire painter and locked the dinghy securely to the dock. Goodbye to an uninsured $5,000 dinghy and outboard.

If you are about to embark on an extended voyage, make certain the address you list on the application is one through which you can and will be notified immediately of any changes in your policy or its cancellation. Most marine policies allow the company to cancel a policy simply by mailing a notice of cancellation to the most recent address they have for you at least ten days before the cancellation date. Some companies have been known to cancel all their marine policies arbitrarily for business reasons that have nothing to do with the policyholders themselves. Also make certain the person responsible for your mail knows who your insurer is, opens anything from the company as soon as it arrives, and notifies you immediately of any significant changes in coverage or cancellation.

The "standard yacht policy" offered by all the A-rated companies has substantially the same provisions, which are divided into sections for hull insurance, liability insurance, and medical payments.

Hull insurance covers your vessel and everything on it necessary to its operation or bought specifically for use on board. The amount of hull insurance normally will be based on "agreed valuation," which is what you and the insurance company mutually agree would be the cost of replacing the yacht in the event of its loss. There is no sense in insuring your yacht for more than its replacement cost. In the event of its loss, replacement cost is all the company will pay even though that total may not reach the limits of your policy.

From the base rate for the amount of hull insurance you buy, you will be given credits for such things as an automatic engine-room fire-suppression system (insurance companies prefer Halon over CO_2 systems), separate fuel shutoffs for each engine and separate shutoff switches for each bank of batteries, any boating courses you may have taken, and your boating experience. You normally will be charged a penalty above the base rate if your boat is more than five years old, even more if it is more than ten years old.

Before issuing a policy, the insurer will require a current survey on the boat (not more than six months old, in some cases not more than two months old). As we mentioned earlier, some insurers will accept only surveys conducted by marine surveyors on their approved lists. Most companies will require a new survey every couple of years or annually for boats more than five or ten years old. Some companies will refuse to issue insurance at all on wood-hull vessels. For steel- or aluminum-hull vessels, they often will require the thickness of the hull to be checked every square foot by an audio-gauge, which for a 40- to 50-foot boat can cost a thousand dollars or more and must be repeated every two or three years.

Most hull insurance covers losses while the vessel is being

operated by you or anyone who has your permission to operate it, except paid crew. If you will have paid crew operating the yacht you will have to purchase a separate endorsement to your basic policy. You should be covered for losses from any cause, even your own negligence (though repeated negligence will result in the company cancelling the policy or refusing to renew it). The policy should provide for replacing "new for old" with no allowance for depreciation. The exception in some policies is that the company will pay only "actual value"—replacement less depreciation—for outboard motors and canvas items. At the time you arrange for your insurance, you should make a complete inventory of everything on your vessel that is covered by your insurance policy, gather together any receipts or documents that will help establish values, and tuck the information away in a safe place—on shore, not aboard the vessel.

The normal deductible on standard yacht policies is 1 percent of the agreed valuation. In the case of extremely expensive yachts, some companies will negotiate the deductible down to 0.75 or 0.5 percent. If your cruising itinerary will take you well offshore or deep into the boondocks, some companies will insist on increasing the deductible to 2 percent or more. The deductible normally will not be applied in the case of total loss of the yacht.

Hull insurance will cover your dinghy and its outboard, but the sizable deductible it carries means you probably would collect little if anything in the event of loss. You may want to consider covering them with a separate policy or rider that has a smaller deductible—say, $250 to $500.

Carefully check the exclusions of any insurance policy you consider buying. Most will not cover losses incurred while the vessel is being used for any kind of commercial operation or those that result from "warlike operations," which include wars declared or undeclared, insurrections, rebellions, and the like. Nor will you be covered if your yacht is confiscated for any reason, whether the confiscation is legal or illegal.

For the cruising owner, the most important exclusions concern navigation limits. The policy will specify the area in which its coverage is valid. If you exceed those limits, your coverage automatically ceases. In some cases, companies will extend your policy's navigation limits if you pay additional premiums and, perhaps, agree to a higher deductible. The additional premium to allow a yacht to cruise the Bahamas might be no more than $50; to extend its navigation limits to the Virgin Islands might cost $500. Since you will have to renew your policy each year, buy only the extended navigation coverage you need for the duration of the policy. If you decide to venture beyond your policy's navigation limits prior to renewal, contact your insurance agent as far in advance as possible—a month is not too much. In order to request the extended coverage from your insurer's underwriter, your agent will need a detailed itinerary including your planned schedule, route, ports of call, and how far you will be venturing offshore, as well as a list of persons who will be aboard, including the boating experience of any of your guests.

Most policies also limit coverage to a certain distance offshore—ten to fifty miles—so make sure the offshore limits are adequate to cover your planned route.

Before most insurance companies will insure a yacht for offshore use, they usually require that there be at least two people aboard capable of operating it. In some cases, they will require three or four. Because of that requirement, it is not unusual for a couple who dream of extensive offshore cruising but have little boating experience to find that they can get insurance for coastal cruising but are unable to obtain insurance from any source for open-water passage-making. If you and your "significant other" have limited experience and ambitious plans, you may find you have to hire a professional captain acceptable to your insurer, cruise the boat under his supervision for several months, then hope to persuade the underwriter to issue you insurance based on the captain's recommendation.

Hull insurance normally will cover damage to your vessel while it is being transported on land, though some companies limit that protection to a certain number of miles from the vessel's home port. Transportation by water—shipping your yacht as deck cargo on a freighter, for instance—is not covered.

The hull insurance section of most policies specifically excludes coverage of personal property—clothing, cameras, sports equipment, and the like. Those few policies that do include personal property often have ridiculously low limits and/or high deductibles. Most companies will provide endorsements to their marine policies—at an additional premium, of course—to cover personal property, but even they normally cover only actual cash value and exclude coverage of cash or jewelry. If you have a homeowner's policy, you may find it covers your personal property while cruising. As with everything else aboard your vessel, you are wise to maintain on shore an inventory of personal property aboard along with any documents that will help establish its value.

Hull insurance also normally covers the cost of towing and assistance, but only if they are required to keep the yacht from suffering further damage. If you want coverage for towing and assistance in the event you simply run out of fuel, you will have to pay for a separate towing-and-assistance endorsement.

The liability insurance in most standard yacht policies (usually referred to as "protection and indemnity") pays for damage caused by you or your yacht while it is being operated by you or someone you have allowed to operate it, again with the exception of paid crew. Limits in the standard policy are normally $300,000 and $500,000. If you cause serious property damage, bodily injury, or death with your yacht, you can be sued for everything you own, so the best rule here is to buy enough liability insurance to cover your total personal assets.

Medical payments (including funeral expenses) under a standard yacht policy normally are limited to $5,000 or $10,000 per person per incident. With medical costs what they are today, that is likely to be totally inadequate. Buy all the extra coverage you can afford. Increments of $5,000 per person per incident usually cost only an additional $20 or so per year. Again, most standard yacht policies exclude medical payments to paid crew. To cover them, you must purchase a separate endorsement that meets the requirements of the Longshoremen's and Harbor Workers' Act, also called the Jones Act.

Standard yacht policies normally don't cover damages inflicted by uninsured boaters. You would be wise to add an endorsement for that coverage to your policy. There is always the possibility some yokel who has zero insurance might inadequately anchor his vessel upwind of you in a storm and sweep down on you in the dark of night.

If you have an accident, a standard yacht policy requires you to notify your insurer as soon as possible and take all reasonable actions to prevent further damage. Ideally, you will be able to reach your agent quickly and have your insurer's adjuster authorize you to have needed repairs done before the work is begun. If that proves impossible, use your best judgment. If you have to have repairs done before you get authorization from an adjuster, take pictures of the damage before it is repaired. Even better, if possible hire a local marine surveyor to check the damage and give you a complete report. Be certain you get good, detailed receipts for any expenses you incur.

DOCUMENTATION, NUMBERING, REGISTRATION, AND TITLING

There is a good deal of confusion among cruising yachtsmen as to the pros and cons, procedures, and legal distinctions involved in documentation, numbering, registration, and titling.

Documentation is a *Federal* process in which the United States Government, acting through the Coast Guard, issues a Certificate of Documentation that attests to a vessel's nationality. Documentation can also establish ownership of the vessel and allow for the legal recording of a "first preferred ship's mortgage" which protects a lender's lien against the vessel. (Because documentation is a Federal process—and *only* a Federal process—the terms "Federal documentation" or "documentation with the Federal government" are redundancies.)

If you finance your boat, the choice of whether or not you document your vessel may well be made for you. Since vessels are so mobile, lenders in most cases require documentation because it allows them to legally record a first preferred ship's mortgage which must be recognized in any state. Should the lender have to repossess the vessel in a distant state, he can have the process executed by Federal marshals rather than having to deal with individual state laws regarding repossession, which vary widely.

If you will be cruising the waters of other nations, I strongly recommend that you document your vessel even if documentation is not otherwise required. In my experience, the legal process of entering other nations is somewhat easier when you present your ship's papers to a foreign customs official in the form of a Certificate of Documentation issued by the United States Government rather than a wallet card from some state's Fish and Game Commission. If you should get into legal trouble in another country, the American embassy or consular official you call for help may have a bit more clout with the locals if he is representing the owner of a U.S.-documented vessel.

The basic drawback to documentation is its cost: $50 to $100 or more if you handle the process yourself; up to $500 or so (fees included) if you have a documentation service handle the paperwork for you.

Documenting a new boat is not particularly difficult. You can obtain the necessary forms from the Coast Guard district headquarters nearest your legal residence (or nearest the address of the corporation that owns the boat). Complete the forms and return them to the Coast Guard along with a bill of sale from the dealer, a Builder's Certificate (which the builder will supply), and a declaration (form supplied by the Coast Guard) that you are a United States citizen. In completing the forms, however, be very careful. The Coast Guard is supposed to reject any documentation application that does not contain all the required information or is defaced in any way including erasures, strikeovers, or white-outs. Some district offices are not quite as strict as the law allows them to be, but many will reject an application for the most minute of reasons. If the owner of the vessel is listed on the documentation application as Joseph A. Smith, for instance, but the bill of sale shows it was sold to J. A. Smith, the Coast Guard may send the application back.

In the case of a vessel that is already documented or a vessel whose documentation has been allowed to lapse, you must establish a legal chain of ownership from the most recent documentation. If the vessel has never been documented, you may either establish a complete chain of ownership or present a copy of its most recent state registration and evidence that establishes the chain of ownership from that registration to you.

In order to be documented, a vessel must be measured (technically the correct term is *admeasured*, but it is not used much today) to ensure that it is of at least five net tons. For documentation purposes, net tonnage has nothing to do with a vessel's weight or displacement but refers to the interior volume of its hull. The net tonnage of a typical cruising powerboat will be eight tenths of its gross tonnage. Gross tonnage is determined by the formula

$$\tfrac{2}{3} \; (length \times breadth \times depth \text{ divided by } 100)$$

where *length* is the vessel's overall length not including a bow pulpit or swim platform; *breadth* is the vessel's beam; and *depth* is the depth from the sheer to the keel measured on the center-line amidships.

In the case of pleasure vessels, the Coast Guard normally will use a "simplified measurement" process. For a new vessel, the Coast Guard normally will figure the vessel's net tonnage from the Builder's Certificate. In the case of a used vessel that has been previously documented, even though its documentation may have been allowed to lapse, the Coast Guard normally will accept the measurement from the previous documentation, provided the vessel has not been subjected to major alterations. In the case of a used vessel that has never been documented, if you can supply an original Builder's Certificate, the Coast Guard normally will take its measurements from that document. If you cannot submit a Builder's Certificate, apply for a simplified measurement by accompanying your application with a letter addressed to the Documentation Officer giving your name and address (or the name and address of the corporation that owns the vessel) and the vessel's name, type, builder, model, length, breadth, and depth.

Documentation must be renewed annually. The Coast Guard will send you a renewal form when your documentation is about to expire. If there have been no changes in the status of the vessel or its ownership, no fee is required. You will have to pay additional fees of $50 to $100, however, if you change your vessel's name, home port, or ownership, or allow your documentation to lapse.

A documented vessel must be marked in a fashion prescribed by the Coast Guard. Its official number, preceded by the abbreviation "No." must be permanently inscribed in block-type arabic numerals at least 3 inches high on the interior of the vessel forward of amidships. Its name and hailing port must be inscribed together on the exterior of the hull in clearly legible letters at least 4 inches high. For a hailing port on a documented vessel, you may use its port of documentation or its "home port" which normally will be the city and state of your legal residence or the legal address of the corporation in which it is held.

Numbering and *Registration* are processes carried out by the states, but the manner in which they are conducted are specified by Federal law and thus are relatively uniform nationwide. The distinction between them is primarily technical rather than practical, but you need to understand it in order to be aware of your options and responsibilities as a boat-owner.

The Federal Boat Safety Act of 1971 requires all boats owned by United States residents that are used on waters subject to Federal jurisdiction or on the high seas to be "numbered." That same law, however, specifically exempts documented vessels from being numbered. A boat must be numbered by the state in which it is most often used on the water, not the state in which the owner resides. All the states have agencies to handle vessel numbering with the exception of Alaska where it is handled by the Coast Guard. Numbering can best be understood as a specific type of state registration in which the state issues a Certificate of Number allowing a vessel to operate in waters under its jurisdiction. The number assigned must be displayed on each side of the forward half of the vessel. Most states also require numbered vessels to display adjacent to their number a validation sticker that indicates the payment of current fees. Federal law prohibits a Certificate of Number from being valid for more than three years. Many states require renewal annually. Renewal normally is evidenced by replacing the vessel's validation sticker with a new one for the current year.

Although FBSA/71 prohibits documented vessels from being numbered, it does allow the states to require documented vessels to be "registered" if they choose to do so. The process and the fees for registration are the same as for numbering. The only difference is that the documented vessel which is also registered will not display a number on its hull as a numbered vessel must but will be issued a decal that must be displayed on the port side window. Registration, like numbering, must be renewed periodically to remain valid. Renewal normally is evidenced by replacing the window decal with a new one for the current year. Fees vary widely, but as an example, the fee for registering a Class 3 vessel (40 to 65 feet LOA) in Florida is $82.00.

Under Federal law, numbering or registration by one state must be honored on a reciprocal basis in other states for at least sixty days. Some states recognize reciprocal numbering or registration for ninety days.

If you document that your vessel and your cruising plans will keep it outside United States waters or on the move so that you are not in the waters of any one state more than sixty days, you shouldn't have to worry about state registration. If you will be operating your vessel in a state longer than sixty days at a time (ninety days in some states), you probably will be required to register it in that state as well. Some states require documented vessels to be registered while others do not. The Outboard Boating Club of America, which is part of the National Marine Manufacturers Association, has put together a Boater's Guide, updated to 1989, which tells you which agency in each state is responsible for registration laws and whom to contact if you have questions. The booklet is available at no cost by writing to the Club at 1000 Thomas Jefferson Street, Suite 525, Washington, D.C. 20007.

Titling is a state process that establishes legal ownership of a vessel and also allows for the legal recording of liens against the vessel. In most cases, however, liens will be recognized only in the state in which the title was issued. At present, only nineteen states require or allow boats to be titled.

TENDER REGISTRATION

Under Federal law, the states have the option of exempting from the numbering regulations tenders that are used only for direct transportation between a larger vessel *which is numbered* and the shore and are powered by motors of less than 10 horsepower. Some states provide this exemption while others do not. In states which provide the exemption, such tenders must be identified by the number displayed by the larger vessel followed by a space or a hyphen and the numeral 1. A vessel used as a tender to a documented vessel must be numbered if it is propelled by a motor of any horsepower.

Now that you've learned how to decide what boat is best for you and how to find and buy it at a fair price, we can take a look at the accessory equipment she will need to allow you to cruise her in safety and comfort.

PART II

All the Bells and Whistles

7

WHERE TO BUY
MARINE ACCESSORIES

Whether the boat of your dreams is to be new or used, once you settle on the one you want, you are just beginning to create the vessel you really need. There is not a stock new boat on the market that does not require the addition of thousands of dollars' worth of accessory equipment to turn her into a safe, comfortable cruiser—everything from navigational and communications electronics to a tender and tender-handling system, ground tackle, safety equipment, and so on. If you decide to buy a boat that a previous owner has already outfitted for cruising, you are still going to have to decide which of the gear already aboard is what you need and want, what you need to replace, and what is missing and must be added.

In the case of a new boat, you can complete her rigging the easy way: by allowing the dealer to specify what you need, having it installed at the factory or after the boat arrives at his yard, and paying the bill. Now, I don't mean to knock competent boat dealers. There are a number of excellent ones around, and if you are fortunate enough to work with one who really knows his or her stuff, you can be spared a world of time and trouble, especially if you live well inland and are having your boat rigged at a considerable distance.

But allowing your dealer to supply all or most of your accessory gear can have its drawbacks. Bear in mind that if the dealer helps you specify all the accessory equipment you are going to require, makes arrangements to have it shipped in, and handles its installation, he is providing you a service—and it may well cost you dearly. Dealers in new boats often are not franchised dealers for the accessory equipment they sell. In many cases, they buy whatever they need through a local specialty retailer who does have a franchise. In that case, both the boatyard and the retailer will have a markup in the deal. Even worse, there are boat dealers who know little about real cruising and will load you up with every piece of equipment they can persuade you to buy at the best profit margin the market will allow.

One alternative is to buy the accessories you need directly from specialty retailers: a marine electronics retailer for your navigation and communications equipment; a small-boat dealer for your tender, outboard, and davits; a company that specializes in safety gear for your life raft, life jackets, and emergency signaling devices. Going that route requires a greater investment of time on your part, but you may find you get the advice of people who deal full time with specific items and know more than the people at the boat dealership. Since you are one step closer to the source of the equipment you are buying, you also should be able to save a few dollars. In the case of electronics, for instance, where a new boat dealer may offer you a 12- to 15-percent discount off the manufacturer's list prices (including installation), the specialty retailer should be able to offer close to 20 percent, again with installation included.

In the case of navigational and communications electronics in particular, if you rely on a single, competent source for your equipment—whether it's the dealer or a specialty retailer—and have him install it, he can help you work out the best placement of individual units and antennas to keep them from electrically interfering with each other as much as possible. Further, you know exactly whom to go back to if you have problems, and you may be able to negotiate a package price and have all the installation done at one time.

Even if you decide to let a dealer or specialty retailer supply most of a particular type of equipment, don't blindly accept everything he offers. If his price on an item seems out of line, or if the quality is questionable, keep talking and looking until you are sure you have what you really want and can buy it at a fair price. Especially in the case of marine electronics, there are a number of companies that manufacture very broad product lines—everything from VHF and single sideband radios to radar, navigation equipment, and the like. Be wary of a dealer who wants to sell you a single manufacturer's brand for everything you need. One company's radar may be the best value for the money, but its marine radios may be poorly designed or overpriced. Each of those pieces of gear is important, and you should consider each of them on its own merits and go for the best equipment rather than opting for the convenience—or even the price advantage—of working with a single supply source or manufacturer.

Still a third alternative is to buy the accessories you need through marine catalogs, which advertise prices substantially below what most new-boat dealers and specialty retailers charge. If you decide on this approach, a number of cautions are in order. First, in comparing prices between the catalogs and a boat dealer or specialty retailer, make certain you include all your costs. The price a marine catalog quotes for a single sideband radio, for instance, may be 40 percent or more off list but probably will include only the radio itself, not the mounting kit, coupler, antenna, and mounting brackets you'll also need. Make sure you're comparing apples to apples. Also be certain you include shipping costs. The equipment normally will be shipped to you via a parcel service or motor freight. Be sure to inspect the equipment before you sign for it, especially if the outside carton shows any sign of damage.

The biggest problem with buying accessories through a catalog, especially your key electronic navigation and communications equipment, is making certain it is installed properly. As you will see in the next two chapters, such installation factors as shielding from electrical interference, accurate calibration, proper grounding, and placement of antennas can be critical to the equipment's performance. In the case of single sideband radios, the law requires they be installed by or under the supervision of a technician licensed by the Federal Communications Commission. (The same used to apply to radar units, but in the case of voluntarily equipped vessels, the FCC dropped that requirement in 1987.) Since your safety could well depend on the correct functioning of such things as radar, Loran C and satellite navigation equipment, marine radios, and depth-sounders, you should be extremely hesitant to install those items yourself. Even if you decide to handle the installation, you probably should have your handiwork checked over by a qualified technician (include what you pay him in your overall costs).

Even if you do pay a local technician to install some of the equipment you need, you will still save significant chunks of money by purchasing from catalogs—in many cases up to 30 percent or more off list and 10 to 25 percent off the dealer's or specialty retailer's prices. But you will make that savings at the expense of your own time, especially if the equipment proves to be defective and has to be returned for service or replacement.

If you buy from a marine catalog, select one that is a franchised dealer for the equipment you buy and is authorized to service it with its own factory-trained technicians. There are several good marine catalog outfits around; some I have dealt with personally or have had consistently good reports on are Skipper Marine Electronics, Coast Navigation, International Marine Electronics, West Marine Products, Boat U.S., and E&B.

8

MARINE NAVIGATION ELECTRONICS

In the past decade or so, no aspect of recreational boating has seen more radical change than navigational electronics. The technological explosion in microprocessors, satellites, and digital electronics has produced an incredible array of new systems and devices to help the cruising yachtsman know precisely where he is and how to get safely to his destination. Today we routinely employ highly sophisticated on-board navigation systems that did not exist or were in their infancy just a few years ago. As systems like Loran C and Transit satellite navigation have come into wider use, we have seen vast improvements in equipment accuracy, reliability, compactness, weight reduction, and ease of operation. In the process, the cost of that equipment in many cases has dropped from the tens of thousands of dollars to no more than two or three thousand dollars. In the past five years particularly, even more dramatic advances have come as the marine electronics industry has developed the ability to interface the different systems and provide almost hands-off vessel operation.

Now we are on the verge of even more dramatic change.

The U.S. Department of Defense (DOD), whose dollars have long dictated many of the radionavigation systems available to recreational yachtsmen, is scheduled to have its new satellite-based Navstar Global Positioning System (GPS) operational in 1993. The DOD has announced that once GPS becomes operational, it will begin to phase out its financial support for several of the basic radionavigation systems in use today such as the Transit satellites, Loran C, and Omega. Once DOD support is withdrawn, these systems will be terminated or their operation significantly altered.

As a yachtsman trying to outfit a vessel for extended cruising, these impending changes present you with some perplexing questions. Among the systems currently operational, which ones will survive and which are on the verge of becoming obsolete? What is the best combination of systems? As for the emerging technologies, should you pay the high prices of the first-generation gear available now or wait until the equipment is further refined and prices drop to more reasonable levels? Not only are these choices difficult, but mistakes can be extremely expensive. You are likely to spend more money on navigational electronics than in any other area of outfitting.

This profusion of navigational goodies presents an even more profound question. We are beginning to see a new generation of boat-owners who are so bedazzled by the sophistication of the systems now on the market they feel they can purchase a vessel, equip it with a glittering array of electronic navigation aids, and embark for any destination they choose without learning basic coastwise piloting and offshore navigation. As long as all their elaborate equipment works, they can pinpoint their location down to minutes and seconds of latitude and longitude and read off their course headings to a single degree. But what happens when a storm sweeps away all their antennas or lightning zaps their circuitry? If they don't have a sound knowledge of basic piloting and navigation techniques and don't have the simple instruments required to perform them on board, they are as blind as the proverbial hog searching for an acorn. No matter how impressive your navigational electronics, make certain that if not one piece of it is working and you are caught off a lee shore in the midst of a terrible storm, you have aboard and know how to use a hand-bearing compass, a pair of dividers, and a parallel rule to guide your vessel to safe harbor.

Having said that, our job in this chapter will be to help you understand the electronic equipment and navigation systems that are currently available and suggest how they can be interconnected in the optimum configuration for your kind of cruising. Where a particular type of equipment is clearly required or strongly suggested, we will offer recommendations as to any specific units that experienced cruisers have found to be the most reliable, most useful, and best value for the money. We'll also tell you what's on the horizon and when to expect the various new technologies to become operational so you can decide what items of equipment you need now, what you might want to wait to purchase, and what at this point is merely expensive gadgetry and a waste of money.

Before we get into specifics we need to discuss some preliminary matters: the basic types of compasses used in both manual and electronic navigation; whether you should base your navigation on magnetic or true north headings; and when and how you should interconnect the different pieces of electronic navigation equipment you are likely to have on board.

COMPASSES

Standard magnetic compasses: For centuries, man has navigated his way across the seas with a standard magnetic compass—a profoundly important yet simple device that uses bar magnets to align itself relative to the earth's magnetic north pole, then reads out bearings on a compass card that is mounted on a pivot and suspended in a clear liquid. It requires no external source of mechanical or electrical energy.

Wonderful as they are, however, standard magnetic compasses do pose significant problems.

The first is that nearby masses of metal and strong electrical fields can cause significant deviation in the accuracy of its readings. In a cruising sailboat or a coastal-cruising powerboat, the problem of deviation usually can be managed without a lot of fuss. But as you equip a power cruiser to head for bluewater, you probably will wind up cramming the relatively tight confines of its pilothouse and flying bridge with powerful navigation and communications gear that contains a lot of metal and produces exactly the kind of strong electrical fields that make standard magnetic compasses go haywire. As you begin to plan the installation of your electronic equipment, one of your biggest headaches will be figuring out where to install everything you want within easy reach of your helm without having it play havoc with your standard magnetic compasses.

The deviation in the compass's headings caused by metal masses and electrical fields must be compensated for by physically manipulating magnets inside or outside the compass. Even after the standard magnetic compasses on your yacht are compensated for a specific environment, their readings can be distorted because the electrical fields in the pilothouse can change as you switch various pieces of electronic gear on and off. If you add electronic equipment to the environment around a standard magnetic compass—or take it away—you may have to repeat the compensation procedure. In some cases, it is simply impossible to completely compensate a compass and you have to use deviation tables for computing the course to steer in order to achieve the desired heading. Under certain conditions, even after you have had your compasses compensated you may find that the readings on your flying bridge compass differ significantly from those on an identical unit mounted in your pilothouse.

Another problem is that the earth's magnetic north pole does not coincide with its geographic north pole. In plotting your vessel's position on a standard nautical chart that is oriented to geographic north, you have to allow for magnetic variation. To make matters worse, magnetic variation not only changes from one area of the earth to another but increases or decreases from year to year.

As the marine electronics industry began to develop electronic navigation instruments that require some sort of heading input to perform their intended function, the problems with standard magnetic compasses multiplied. Initially the industry simply developed ways of reading the heading information produced by a standard magnetic compass either electrically or photoelectrically and fed that information to the navigational devices in the form of an electronic impulse. But as the card of a standard magnetic compass swings it develops inertia which can cause it to overshoot an intended heading, and the liquid in which it is suspended significantly lengthens the time it takes for the compass to settle down on a new heading.

Magnetic fluxgate compasses: In order to get a compass that reacts more rapidly and precisely to course changes, the industry developed the electronic fluxgate compass (Fig. 8.1). It is still a magnetic device, but rather than orienting itself to magnetic north with swinging bar magnets, it aligns itself by electronically reading the earth's magnetic flux with something called a toroidal fluxgate coil sensor. The technical details of exactly how a fluxgate compass works are not important here. The point is that it produces accurate magnetic bearing information much more rapidly and precisely than the floating card of a standard magnetic compass. Fluxgate compasses also have other advantages: Their sensing and display elements can be combined in a single unit, or they can be physically separated and the sensing element mounted in a remote location on a vessel which is relatively free of the electrical interference so often found in the pilothouse or on the flying bridge. If the remote location is selected carefully, the sensing element will not be significantly affected as electrical equipment aboard the vessel is switched on or off, added or removed. The sensing element's output then can be fed electrically to display units at one or more helm stations. Also, any compensation the sensing element requires can be accomplished electrically, which usually gives more accurate results than compensation by physically moving magnets around inside or outside a standard magnetic compass.

As a result of their speed, precision, and flexibility, magnetic fluxgate compasses commonly are used as heading sensors for autopilots and Transit satellite navigation receivers (but not for Loran C or GPS receivers which, as we will explain later,

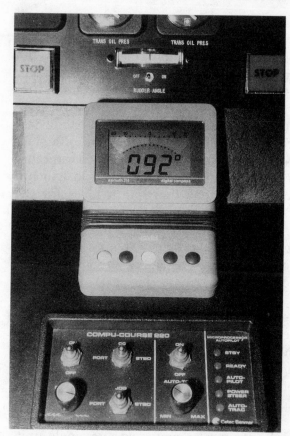

Fig. 8.1: An electronic fluxgate compass and autopilot make simple work of keeping this yacht on course. Neither, however, eliminates the need for a constant and attentive helm watch when she is underway.

operate differently and do not require heading input from an external source). Until recently, autopilots and Transit receivers usually had their own heading sensor. Now, however, a single multiport magnetic fluxgate compass such as the KVH Azimuth 314 (list price, $695) can feed heading information to as many as fifteen different displays or navigational instruments. The use of a single sensing element eliminates the possibility of confusion due to different readings from several sensors.

Because the standard heading readouts produced by a fluxgate compass are magnetic, variation must still be taken into account when using them to plot a position on a nautical chart. However, because these compasses are electronic, it is possible to match them with appropriate software to convert them to read out in true north.

Gyrocompasses: Still a third type of compass found aboard some larger cruising yachts is the gyrocompass. Because gyrocompasses are quite expensive ($8,000 and up), they are principally found on megayachts, so we won't take up a lot of time discussing them. Suffice it to say that they work on a totally different principle and read out in true degrees so that magnetic variation does not have to be taken into account when using their readings to plot a vessel's position on a chart.

SELECTING A NAVIGATION SYSTEM: MAGNETIC OR TRUE?

Our discussion of the problems with standard magnetic compasses and the alternatives now available in electronic fluxgate compasses leads us to the question of whether you will perform your navigation chores using traditional magnetic headings or shift to a new system using true north headings.

Following the traditional approach, you would: (1) install standard magnetic compasses in your pilothouse and on your flying bridge as your primary manual steering references, (2) install separate fluxgate heading sensors for your autopilot and Transit receiver, (3) instruct your Loran C and GPS receivers to produce magnetic heading information, then (4) allow for magnetic variation when you plot your vessel's course or position on navigational charts. As we discussed above, the problem with this approach is that, due to the difficulties of achieving absolute and consistent compensation in standard magnetic compasses, you may get several different readings from your various instruments while your boat is on a single heading.

If you replace your standard magnetic steering compasses with a single, remotely mounted magnetic fluxgate sensor, and also have it provide heading information to your autopilot and Transit receiver, they would all produce the same heading information (but your Loran C and GPS receivers might still have different readings). You also would eliminate the likelihood of changing deviation as you switch various pieces of electronic equipment on and off, and the arrangement would allow you greater flexibility in instrument placement. With this approach, you would still have to allow for magnetic variation in plotting your position or course on a chart.

A more radical alternative could also eliminate the problem of allowing for magnetic variation. With this approach, you would not only replace your standard magnetic compasses with digital displays from the same fluxgate sensor that provides heading input to your autopilot and Transit receiver, but you would also equip the fluxgate sensor with appropriate software to allow it to produce true rather than magnetic readings. You would then program your Loran C (and your GPS receiver if you have one on board) to work off true north headings and base all your navigation, both manual steering and chart plotting, on true north headings. Errors in computing magnetic variation or forgetting to take it into account would never arise.

The biggest argument against replacing magnetic compasses with electronic compasses is that if you have problems with the fluxgate sensor or lose electrical power, you don't even have a standard magnetic compass to help guide you to safety. There are several answers to that objection. One is to carry a spare fluxgate sensor as a backup to your installed unit. Another is to install an emergency battery as high as possible in your vessel, which at the minimum could power your electronic compass, your VHF radio, and your SSB radio. You could also have a good hand-held magnetic compass or one of the newer battery-powered hand-held electronic compasses aboard in the event you completely lost your electronics.

I realize the suggestion that magnetic compasses can be replaced as a primary steering reference will raise the hackles of the traditionalists, but it is a possibility worth considering.

INTERFACING ELECTRONIC NAVIGATION EQUIPMENT

It is virtually impossible to discuss modern electronic navigation gear without understanding a little about what is involved in interfacing various pieces of equipment. The actual mechanics are best left to a qualified electronics technician, but it might be helpful for you to understand what he is doing.

In order for two pieces of electronic equipment to exchange information, they must communicate through a structure in which a particular alphanumeric symbol or series of symbols means the same thing to both. Most of the manufacturers of this equipment are members of the National Marine Electronics Association (NMEA). In order to facilitate the interfacing of their equipment, they have cooperated to develop several standards that specify the data formats and information protocols that two or more marine electronic devices must have in common in order to communicate with each other. The standards you will encounter most often in evaluating specific pieces of marine electronic navigation equipment are NMEA 0180, 0182, and 0183. Standard 0180 is an older one used exclusively in autopilots that allows them to accept crosstrack error information from an external source such as a heading sensor or a navigation receiver. The 0182 standard is a newer and expanded variation of 0180 that also is used primarily by autopilots and allows them to accept not only crosstrack error information from an external source but also such information as the bearing to the next way point and present latitude and longitude position. Both 0180 and 0182 are used primarily to connect a single piece of sending equipment to a single piece of receiving equipment. Devices that utilize either of these standards are also limited in the rate at which they can exchange information to 1,200 baud (a baud being the smallest unit of data information).

The newer 0183 standard is far more versatile because far more types of data can be exchanged at a more rapid rate (4,800 baud) and shared between many more types of devices.

AUTOPILOTS

At its most basic, an autopilot is simply a device that receives instructions from the helmsperson on the desired course, recognizes any deviations from that course, and applies to the vessel's rudder enough force to cause the vessel to return to the intended track. Although a good autopilot is expensive (list prices for the equipment alone can run $5,000 or more), it is one of the most helpful and hardworking accessories you can have on a cruising boat. Not only will it relieve you from the tedious job of hand-steering on long passages, it will steer a straighter course than any human helmsperson could and waste less time and fuel in the bargain. If properly interfaced with an appropriate Loran C or satellite navigation receiver, it can automatically steer your vessel through course changes. Of course, none of an autopilot's abilities relieves you of the necessity for keeping an alert helm watch. Loran C receivers, in particular, can sometimes do strange things, especially in the vicinity of thunderstorms. If your Loran C unit hiccups while your autopilot is plugged into it, your vessel also will do strange things. If you do hook them together, keep a close eye on what is going on.

HOW AUTOPILOTS WORK

Autopilots are of two types—hunting and nonhunting. Older autopilots are of the hunting variety; they use a simple contact switch to close when the vessel moves to one side of its intended course and to open when it moves to the other. The chief drawback of the hunting type is that it works constantly and thus consumes a fair amount of power.

More modern autopilots are of the nonhunting variety. They employ two sets of contact switches that open and close as the vessel deviates from its intended track to port or starboard. So long as the vessel remains on course, the autopilot is in a "dead band" where no course correction is required. Because nonhunting autopilots are not working constantly, they consume less power.

Modern autopilots also make proportional-rate corrections, that is, they apply only slight pressure to the rudder to correct minor deviations from course but apply significant force to correct major deviations, just as you would if you were steering the vessel yourself.

An autopilot consists of three basic units: a control head through which you instruct it on what course to follow (you'll need two if your boat has dual helm stations); a sensor to track the intended course and your vessel's deviation from it; and a power unit to apply to the rudder the force needed to keep the vessel on track (Fig. 8.2).

Control heads vary greatly in the number of functions they allow you to select. Less expensive units limit you to steering manually or engaging the autopilot and entering a course to steer. More sophisticated units allow you to determine the sensitivity with which the autopilot reacts to course deviations, dodge around obstacles and return to your programmed heading, and instruct the autopilot whether to take its course from information you dial in or from data provided by a separate navigation receiver.

The heart of a good autopilot is its heading sensor which normally is mounted separately from the control unit in a location free of electrical interference and as near the vessel's center of gravity as possible. Some older units employ a magnetic compass as a heading sensor. On that type of autopilot, the compass normally will be separate from your vessel's steering compass

on one of Broward Marine's megayachts: mount
dge control in the armrest of your helm chair.)

RECOMMENDATIONS

power cruising yacht, I would recommend the
00DL coupled with the appropriate Robertson drive
ical or hydraulic steering. Robertson has been in
usiness since the early 1940's and developed the
essor-controlled autopilot, so it knows what it's
bertson design has an excellent rudder feedback
helps the vessel steer an extremely precise course.
ompasses supplied with Robertson's units are made
ch is a leader in its field. Another autopilot manu-
has been around almost as long is Cetec Benmar
ndix). Although its autopilots still use magnetic
they are very reliable and easy to use. I would rec-
Compu-Course 220 rather than its more complex
rse 2100 unit.

RADAR

is an acronym for *r*adio *d*etection *a*nd *r*anging. The
nology radar employs has been around since World
t the advent in recent years of digital signal processing
rated circuitry has allowed a number of improvements
y its information is displayed. Radar may well be the
ensive piece of radionavigation gear you buy (list prices
od serviceable unit will run anywhere from $2,000 to
,000). But it is an indispensable piece of equipment be-
its ability to detect the range and bearing of distant ob-
any weather.

RADAR WORKS

rotating antenna mounted as high as practical on a vessel
its a tightly focused beam of extremely-high-frequency ra-
ves that travel at the speed of light (186,000 statute miles
cond), bounce off obstacles in their path, and return back
antenna. By computing the time it takes the radio waves
diate outward and bounce back, the system measures the
nce between the antenna and objects in their path.
The bearing to a detected object is determined by the direc-

Fig. 8.2: *A typical autopilot installation includes control heads at both the pilothouse and flying-bridge steering stations, a magnetic compass or electronic fluxgate sensor located at the vessel's center and mounted as low as possible, and a rudder control unit.*

because it must be able to read degrees electrically or photo-electrically and feed the information to the control unit. A few units can, however, use your boat's steering compass as a heading sensor through the use of a course detector. You'll get more precise steering out of a unit that uses a magnetic fluxgate compass as a heading sensor.

The power unit you choose will depend on whether your vessel has mechanical or hydraulic steering. Some mechanical systems use a reversible electric motor to drive the rudder directly. Others work through a lead screw that exerts a push-pull motion on a tiller arm mounted to the rudder. Still others operate through a low-speed shaft coupled to the rudder with a chain-and-sprocket arrangement. For vessels with hydraulic steering, the autopilot should have a separate electric motor powering its own hydraulic pump which controls fluid flow in the vessel's hydraulic system with electric valves.

CHOOSING AN AUTOPILOT

You can purchase a basic autopilot, which is simply an "on-off" device, for around $500. The only thing it will do is maintain your vessel on the course you dial into it. Experienced cruisers recommend the more sophisticated autopilot which can, among other things, interface with a Loran C receiver—and with a satellite navigation receiver if you will have one aboard.

We'll discuss both Loran C and satellite navigation receivers in detail later in this chapter. Suffice it to say here that if you select a receiver of either type that has automatic way-point sequencing and interface your autopilot with it, your autopilot and navigation receiver (within limits) will not only work together to guide your vessel to any point you designate but will then automatically make course corrections to steer your vessel to the next point you choose. If you plan to use your autopilot this way, be sure to select one that interfaces with a navigation receiver utilizing the NMEA 0182 or 0183 protocol. A unit that uses only the NMEA 0180 protocol will accept input from your Loran C or satellite receiver to offset crosstrack error but not to make automatic course changes. You should also select a unit that sounds an alarm if it loses input from the navigation receiver. Also be aware that autopilots normally can handle only about a 15- to 40-degree deviation from a previous course. If a Loran instructs it to make a course change beyond the maximum deviation it can handle, it may go crazy and steer your vessel around in circles.

Select an autopilot whose control unit allows you to dial in the degree of sensitivity with which you want the autopilot to react to course deviations. In calm seas you can crank the sensitivity up to keep your vessel on a straighter line; in rough sea conditions you can dampen sensitivity to keep the autopilot and your steering system from having to work so hard. The control unit should also have a dodge function that allows you to swing the vessel to port or starboard to avoid an obstruction. The degree of deviation should depend on how long you hold down the dodge button. When you release the dodge button, the autopilot should automatically resume the course you have instructed it to follow.

Aside from these basic functions, there are several other autopilot features you'll find useful. The unit you select should display your deviation from a preset course either digitally or on a line or bar graph. It should also have a "manual steer" position in which it will continue to display crosstrack error even though you are steering your vessel with its wheel. (If you are manually steering toward a way point you have programmed into your

Loran C, this featu
Loran C also present
autopilot display it as
in front of the helm fo
within easy reach. If yo
can place your Loran C
but to one side rather t
autopilot unit should als
each time it swings your
ture will help you recogni
ing too hard and help y
sensitivity.

There are a number of
experienced cruisers find the
angle indicator. Theoretically
docking, but I can't recall eve
one else refer to it. Some units
exceed certain limits. This mig
but the helmsman should be ale
long before the alarm goes off.
chase (for an additional $500 to
remote unit with which you can
functions up to the limit of the h
cable. I've seen these things on hu
can't recall seeing one used more th
watching your budget, you might d
on something more practical. Some u
or "jog" function with which you can
a separate "joy stick" for push-button
standard in the unit you choose, fine,
for it.

AUTOPILOT INSTALLATION

Unless you are quite well versed in ele
installation of an autopilot to a qualified e
particularly if it will be interfaced with oth
The heading sensor should be mounted as
center of gravity as possible, and the contro
mounted directly in front of the helm within
helmsperson. (For the height of luxury, you

cently saw done
the autopilot's d

EQUIPMENT

For a new
Robertson AP 2
unit for mecha
the autopilot b
first microproc
doing. The R
system which
The fluxgate
by KVH whi
facturer that
(formerly B
compasses,
ommend its
Compu-Co

Radar
basic tech
War II, bu
and integ
in the w
most exp
for a go
over $10
cause o
jects in

HOW

A
transr
dio w
per s
to th
to ra
dista

tion in which the antenna is pointed when it transmits its radio-wave beam and receives a reflection (sometimes called an echo). The rotating motion of the antenna is not a factor in determining its position at the instant radio waves are sent and received because it makes only one revolution every two to four seconds but transmits radio waves at the rate of 400 to 6,000 pulses per second. Since it takes the radio waves only a fraction over 12 microseconds (millionths of a second) per nautical mile of range to make their round trip, the antenna can send and receive up to thirty pulses in the time it takes to rotate just one degree, which means that, electronically speaking, it is standing still.

Because the radio waves radar uses bend slightly to follow the earth's curvature, its horizon at any particular mounting height is about 7 percent further away than the horizon of the human eye at that same height. The maximum range at which a particular radar can detect an object depends on three factors: the strength of the signal it transmits, the height at which its antenna is mounted on the vessel, and the height of the object itself (Fig. 8.3).

As reflected radio waves are received, they are processed and displayed on some type of phosphor- or cathode-ray tube (CRT) which normally is mounted adjacent to the helm. The pattern of all reflected radio waves received on a single sweep of the antenna reveals the frontal outline of the objects it detects. This does not necessarily mean that the image displayed on the radar screen will match exactly what is seen with the human eye or on a navigation chart. Low-lying targets such as a beach along a coast will not show up as well as tall buildings several hundred yards inland. Radar can not "see" through a mountain to reveal the harbor entrance beyond, and the reflection from a large object such as a commercial ship can mask the reflection of a smaller vessel behind it.

CHOOSING A RADAR

For the crusing yachtsman, it's more important to be able to locate a harbor entrance between two mountains at a reasonable distance than it is to be able to detect the mountains themselves a hundred miles at sea. Therefore, the ability of a radar to discriminate objects (that is, draw the clearest outline) is more important than its range. Discrimination is a function of the

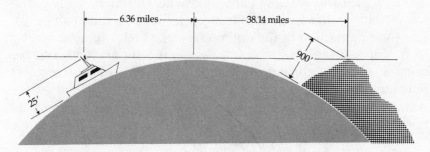

Fig. 8.3: *A radar's range is dependent on both the mounting height of its antenna and on the height of objects which reflect the radio waves it transmits.*

narrowness of the horizontal beam-width of the radio waves the antenna transmits (Fig. 8.4). In the radars normally found on recreational vessels, horizontal beam-width varies from about 1 to 4 degrees. Beam-width, in turn, is determined by the length of the radar's antenna. The antennas of radar units on the recreational marine market vary in length from around 30 inches to about 8 feet. The smallest antennas often are enclosed in a fiberglass dome, which is of value principally to sailboaters since the dome prevents the boat's running rigging from getting tangled in the antenna. The dome itself does not affect the efficiency of the antenna's signal. The drawback to these units is that the antenna itself is not long enough to give optimum discrimination.

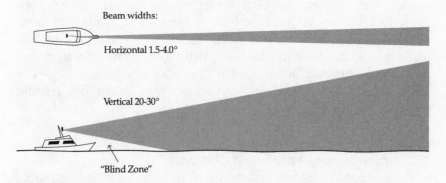

Fig. 8.4: *The narrower a radar's horizontal beam width, the more definitive will be its resolution of the targets which reflect its radio waves. Increasing the mounting height of a radar antenna affects its range only marginally but significantly extends its "blind zone."*

You will get better results with an open-array antenna. Look for a unit with the longest open-array antenna you can practically mount on your vessel, to give as narrow a beam-width as possible. But bear in mind that the larger the antenna, the larger the electric motor required to turn it. For a typical cruising vessel in the 50-to-60-foot range, a 4- to 6-foot antenna usually strikes a good balance between adequate target discrimination and acceptable weight and power consumption.

Pleasure-boat radars are available with maximum ranges of about twelve to seventy-two nautical miles. Many experienced cruisers find that a radar with a range of about thirty-six nautical miles (nm) is adequate for the situations they encounter. If you want to buy a unit with greater range, fine, but you will have to pay for it. The difference in list price between a 36-nm radar and a 48-nm radar can be $1,500 or more, and the difference between a 48-nm unit and a 72-nm unit can be as much as $6,000.

Range is a function of both the height at which the antenna is mounted and the level of output or peak power at which the unit transmits its signal. A unit with a peak power rating of 3 kw will have a range of about 36 nm; with a rating of 5 kw, about 48 nm; with a rating of 10 kw, about 72 nm. Bear in mind that a unit's peak power rating is a measure of signal strength, not the amount of power the unit will consume from your vessel's batteries. (Virtually all pleasure-boat radars operate on 12-, 24-, or 32-volt DC current.) The unit rated at 3 kw will draw only about 100 watts; the unit rated at 5 kw, about 120 watts; and the unit rated at 10 kw, about 150 to 225 watts.

The display portion of radar sets on the recreational marine market range from 6 to 16 inches measured diagonally. The larger the display the clearer the presentation of information, so buy a unit with the largest display you can afford and fit into the console of your primary steering station. In most power-cruising applications that will be a unit with a 9- to 12-inch display, with the 12-inch being the better choice.

Older radars display their information on phosphor tubes. Because the signal display has to be relatively weak to keep from burning an image into the phosphor, it fades rapidly and is replaced with updated signals from the next sweep. In daylight operation, the screen of a phosphor-tube radar display normally has to be covered with a viewing hood in order to increase the contrast between the screen and the signal. The newer "raster-scan" radar displays are a major improvement on the phosphor technique. They digitize signal information and display it on a CRT similar to the screen of a television set. The information does not fade but remains at full strength until it is replaced by updated information during the scanner's next sweep. The display can also be "frozen" to take precise bearings on a detected object. In daylight operation, raster-scan displays can also be seen clearly without a viewing hood.

The choice between a monochrome unit with either a green or amber display and a unit that presents its information in color is one of cost and personal preference. Units with color displays list for about 30 percent more than monochrome units with comparable peak power output and range. Monochrome displays provide slightly sharper image resolution, while color displays tend to square off signals received from nearby objects, giving them a blocky appearance. The primary advantage of a color display is that it uses a variety of colors to represent the relative strength of returned signals: red for the strongest, yellow for those of medium strength, and blue or green for the weakest. This can be an advantage when using radar to analyze weather clouds in the vicinity of your vessel. Light clouds that contain little moisture will show up as blue or green signals, while those that contain heavy rain will show up in yellow or red depending on their density. Some monochrome radars differentiate between the strength of returned signals with various levels of "quantization," with stronger signals presented in the deepest green or amber and weaker signals showing up in lighter shades.

Most of the radars now on the market incorporate one or more variable range markers (VRM) and electronic bearing lines (EBL), both of which are useful in the real world of cruising. With either of these features, you position an adjustable circle or radial line over a target on the display and the unit will read out the target's range or bearing in a digital presentation. (Unless a radar is interfaced with some sort of external heading sensor, EBLs will be relative to your vessel's position with the bow representing 0 degrees, not magnetic or true bearings.)

Many radars also allow you to establish a guard zone of varying dimensions around your vessel and sound an alarm if a target appears inside it. This can be useful both as an anticollision device while under way and as an anchor watch. It would be ideal to have an anchor-watch feature on both your radar and your Loran C and/or satellite navigator. The anchor watch on your radar would alert you if another vessel drifted down on you or tried to sneak up on you while you were at anchor—assuming, of course, the intruder gave off a readable echo and was not within your radar's "blind zone"—the area around your vessel that is passed over by the antenna's signals. It would also alert you if your anchor dragged and some obstacle not in the blind zone and capable of giving off a readable echo penetrated the guard zone. The anchor watch on the Loran C and/or satellite navigator would not alert you to physical hazards but would sound an alarm if your vessel drifted out of a preset circle, whether or not you were in danger of striking or being struck by another vessel or object.

Under the heading of "nice but not necessary" come such expensive radar features as the ability to interface with a heading sensor to change the orientation of the display from "course up" to "north up" in order to align it with most nautical charts; the ability to offset the display by as much as 75 percent or program in a 2X zoom on a portion of the display; and the ability to interface your radar with a Loran C and/or a track or chart plotter. (We will discuss electronic track- and chart-plotting equipment later in this chapter.)

RADAR EQUIPMENT INSTALLATION

You want to mount your radar's antenna as high as is practical on your vessel, but more to provide a clear, unobstructed path for its signals than to increase its range. Increasing its mounting height by only a few feet will not have a noticeable effect on its range. Of course, the higher you mount your antenna, the larger the blind zone around your vessel (Fig. 8.4).

The display unit should be mounted in reasonable proximity to your helm. Since it is not waterproof, it should be installed at the lower helm station where it will be protected from the weather. In some of the nicest radar display installations I have seen, the unit was mounted vertically in a pivoting cabinet to one side of the helm and below the centerline of the steering wheel. When not needed, it was out of the way; when needed, the helmsperson could simply pivot it forward into viewing position.

RADAR LICENSING REQUIREMENTS

The radar installation aboard your vessel must be covered by a valid Ship Radio Station License issued by the Federal Communications Commission. You apply by checking the box under item 13 on FCC Form 506 that is appropriate to your radar's frequency. Most radars found on pleasure vessels operate in the 9,300-to-9,500 MHz range and you would check box R.

No operator's permit is required.

On October 15, 1987, the Federal Communications Commission "authorized the installation of radar equipment on any voluntarily equipped ship by the station licensee or under the supervision of the station licensee." (PR Docket 87–10). Any internal adjustments that would affect the frequency at which a radar transmits signals, however, may be done only by the holder of a General Radiotelephone Permit or First- or Second-Class Radiotelegraph Permit, and it must have a ship radar endorsement.

RADAR EQUIPMENT RECOMMENDATIONS

For a typical cruising powerboat in the 50-to-60-foot range, the best monochrome radars on the market at the moment are Furuno's FR-8000D series. A good choice would be the FR-8050D which has a 5-kw peak power output, a 48-nm range, and a 12-inch display. It can accept a 6.5-foot antenna to provide a 1.23-degree horizontal beam-width for excellent target resolution.

If you are prepared to spend the extra money for a color radar, I would suggest you consider the Furuno FCR-1411 MkII, a 10-kw unit with a 72-nm range and a 14-inch display. I would also couple it with Furuno's 6.5-foot antenna.

(Either of these units could be matched to Furuno's 8-foot antenna whose 0.95-degree horizontal band-width provides even higher target resolution, but that's a pretty massive antenna to be mounting on a 50-to-60-foot vessel.)

LORAN C

Though the term *Loran* is an acronym for *long-range* navigation, it is actually a medium-range navigation system for both marine vessels and aircraft which covers only specific Coastal Confluence Zones around the world (Fig. 8.5). Despite the system's limited coverage, within the areas where you can receive usable signals a good Loran C receiver will prove to be one of your most versatile navigation instruments.

The Loran C system in use today was deployed during the late 1970's and is based on the earlier Loran A system which was developed during World War II for use by the U.S. military. This association with the military helps explain Loran C's somewhat

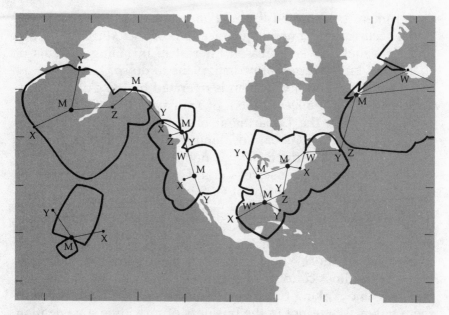

Fig. 8.5: *Loran C signals blanket virtually all coasts of the United States and Canada but do not cover such popular cruising areas as Mexico and the Caribbean.*

spotty coverage pattern. The Loran C system operated by the United States and in cooperation with its allies covers basically the East, West, and Gulf coasts of North America; the Great Lakes; the Labrador, Icelandic, and Norwegian seas; the Mediterranean Sea; and the Pacific Ocean west of Hawaii and around Japan and Korea. Systems operated by other governments include Saudi Arabia's coverage of parts of the Red Sea, the Persian Gulf, and the Gulf of Aden; systems operated by the Soviet Union covering portions of its east and west coasts; and a system recently installed by the People's Republic of China for the South China Sea. Norway is considering adding additional low-power (mini-Loran C) transmitters to extend existing coverage of the North Sea, and Australia is considering a system to cover its coastal waters.

There is no Loran C system covering such popular cruising areas as the coasts of Mexico (except for the Yucatán Peninsula) and Central America or the islands of the Caribbean, and there are no plans for the United States to extend coverage to include them. In the case of the Caribbean in particular, the United States

Government has studied the area and concluded there is no national security or economic justification for including it. Mexico and Venezuela have expressed interest in installing systems of their own, but have no immediate plans to do so.

The U.S.'s Loran C system is operated by the Coast Guard, which is part of the Department of Transportation (DOT), under a mandate from the Department of Defense (DOD). Based on the premise that its Global Positioning System will become fully operational in 1993, the DOD has notified the DOT that it plans to cease most military uses of Loran C overseas as of December 31, 1994. (If full deployment of GPS is delayed, the DOD's pullout from the Loran C system is likely to be pushed back accordingly.) In response to that notification, the DOT is now negotiating with the countries in which overseas Loran C transmitters are located to get those "host countries" to take over their operation. "If the host countries are not willing to take over the operation," one ranking Coast Guard officer told me, "we will shut them down. We're not in the business of providing a navigation system for Japanese fishermen."

Canada is almost certain to assume complete responsibility for the chains on its east and west coasts, which it now shares with the United States. Negotiations with Denmark, Norway, Iceland, and Germany to take over the Labrador, Icelandic, and Norwegian sea chains are proceeding nicely and an agreement for them to continue their operation is expected. In fact, the secondary transmitter at Sylt is already being phased over to German control. Negotiations have begun with Italy for that country to assume responsibility for the Mediterranean Sea chain. Japan and South Korea have made no commitment to take over the Northwest Pacific chain or the Commando Lion chain. Considering the importance of these chains to Japanese and Korean shipping and fishing interests, however, their eventual transfer is expected. The Soviet Union has shown interest in tying its systems into those operated by the United States and its allies through a procedure called "dual rating."

Because the DOD's 1994 pullout from Loran C involves only overseas stations, the outlook for the Loran C chains covering the coasts of the continental United States and Alaska is probably secure for a long time. The 1988 Federal Radionavigation Plan envisions continued operation of Loran C "for the forseeable future." A Coast Guard source told me that the system is likely to be supported for at least fifteen years past any DOD pullout. That pullout is expected to be announced once GPS becomes fully operational. In fact, the current Loran C system in the continental United States and Alaska is being expanded rather than contracted; because of its importance to the nation's domestic air travel, the Federal Aviation Administration has allocated $36 million to add four new transmitters covering the midcontinent gap, and coverage of south-central Alaska around Anchorage is being expanded. The exception to that positive outlook is the Central Pacific chain which covers the Pacific Ocean west of the Hawaiian Islands; because it has few users, that chain is likely to be shut down whenever the DOD terminates its funding.

In short, Loran C is likely to remain as a primary coastal radionavigation system in the Coastal Confluence Zones of the Northern Hemisphere for a long time. If I were planning to cruise the areas it covers, I would not hesitate to invest in a good receiver.

HOW LORAN C WORKS

Loran C utilizes a network of shore-based radio transmitters which in theory are designed to provide extremely accurate navigational fixes within fifty nautical miles from shore or out to the one hundred-fathom curve, whichever is greater.

A Loran C "chain" consists of one master transmitter (designated M) and two, three, or four secondary transmitters (designated W, X, Y, and Z) each of which sends out pulsed radio signals on 100 kHz. In order to enable Loran receivers to identify the source of these signals, the transmitters send out their pulses in sequence at precise intervals of an assigned number of microseconds (millionths of a second). The interval between transmissions from the master is referred to as the Group Repetition Interval (GRI), and each chain is assigned a distinctive GRI (Fig. 8.6).

Once a Loran receiver captures the signals from the master transmitter and one secondary transmitter in a chain whose positions are known, it measures the difference in time it took the two signals to reach it. Since speed, time, and distance are interrelated, that time difference (TD) locates the receiver on a hyperbolic Line-of-Position (LOP), a line along which that time difference would remain constant. As an example: If the TD establishes the distance from the vessel to the secondary as ten

Loran C Chain	GRI
United States and Canada	
Northeast U.S.	9960
Southeast U.S.	7980
Great Lakes	8970
U.S. West Coast	9940
Gulf of Alaska	7960
Canadian East Coast	5930
Canadian West Coast	5990
North Atlantic	
Labrador Sea	7930
Norwegian Sea	7970
Iceland	9980
Pacific Ocean	
North Pacific	9990
Northwest Pacific	9970
Central Pacific	4990
Commando Lion (Korea/Japan)	5970
Mediterranean Sea	
Mediterranean Sea	7990
Saudi Arabia	
South Saudi Arabia	7170
Northeast Saudi Arabia	8990
Northwest Saudi Arabia	38990

Fig. 8.6: Each Loran C chain is identified by its own distinctive Group Repetition Interval (GRI).

miles greater than the distance from the vessel to the master (Fig. 8.7A), the LOP will pass through all points at which the vessel-to-secondary distance continues to be ten miles greater than the vessel-to-master distance. The receiver then repeats the process with signals from the master and a different secondary to establish a second LOP (Fig. 8.7B). The point where the two LOP's intersect is the vessel's position (Fig. 8.7C). Using the two TD's, that position can be plotted on a chart overprinted with a grid of Loran C LOP's.

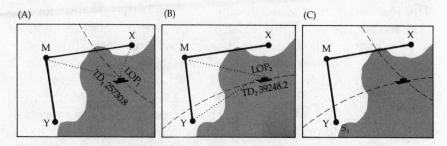

Fig. 8.7: In a typical sequence of fixing a vessel's position with Loran C: (A) the time difference (TD1) between signals received from the master transmitter (M) and one secondary transmitter (X) in the chain locates the vessel some-where along Line of Position 25730.8 (LOP1). (B) The time difference (TD2) between signals received from the master transmitter and a different secondary transmitter (Y) locates the vessel somewhere along Line of Position 39248.2 (LOP2). (C) The vessel's position is at the intersection of the two Lines of Position.

In addition to displaying position in terms of two TD's, most of the Loran C receivers now on the market are able to also translate TD's into latitude and longitude. They are able to do that because their memory has been programmed by the manu-facturer with the geographical coordinates of the transmitters they are receiving and they can then compute the vessel's position relative to the known position of the transmitters. Loran C units do not require input from any external heading sensor.

As we get further into this discussion of the different types of radionavigation systems, it's important to understand that the signals of the Loran C system we're discussing here don't tell you how far you are from a particular transmitter. They tell you only your *relative distance* from two transmitters, from which an LOP can be derived. A more advanced type of Loran C called a "rho rho" system does provide range from a single transmitter, but utilizing it requires that the transmitter and the receiver be synchronized with an extremely accurate atomic clock. The only such system currently in operation is one the French have in-stalled in the Mediterranean for use by their military forces.

Loran ground-wave transmissions have a maximum range of 1,000 to 1,200 miles from their transmitters. Within the ground-wave coverage areas of Loran C signals, the *absolute* accuracy of initial fixes normally is within 0.1 to 0.25 nautical miles. Under ideal conditions, absolute accuracy can be within 100 feet or less.

The reason Loran C is not totally accurate is that its functioning is based on the assumption that radio waves travel at a constant speed. That is true if they are passing over seawater, but where they must pass over land, they can be distorted slightly by soil conductivity and terrain features, which are referred to as Additional Secondary Factors (ASF). The LOP overlays on the first generation of Loran C charts were printed with no allowance for ASF. When field observation indicated the LOP's on some charts were off as much as two miles, those charts were reissued with a notation that their LOP's had been shifted to account for the theoretical effects of ASF. In recent years the Coast Guard has initiated a Chart Verification Program to correct Loran C LOP's on the basis of observed rather than theoretical data, and the latest National Oceanic Survey (NOS) charts contain a notice to that effect. The U.S. Defense Mapping Agency Hydrographic/Topographic Center publishes a series of *Loran C Correction Tables* based on actual field observations which also can be used to offset some of the effects of this "TD warping" and thus improve accuracy.

Even with these methods of ASF compensation, Loran C does not provide the degree of accuracy required for use in harbor approach and harbor navigation (25 to 65 feet for large commercial vessels) because the compensations are simply predictions of how the ASF are expected to affect signals in a specific area over time, not how they are actually affecting the signals at any particular moment. In order to do that, it would be necessary to set up monitoring stations to measure the observed effects of ASF in a particular area, then broadcast the necessary compensation information to receivers using the Loran C signals in that area. This concept, called *differential Loran C,* is being studied as a possible means of refining the accuracy of Loran C to the point where it could be used as a primary radionavigation aid in major harbors and for harbor approach.

The accuracy of Loran C's *repeatability*—its ability to reestablish a position it has fixed earlier—is even greater than the absolute accuracy of initial fixes. In ideal situations it can be 50 feet or less. The reason is that because the ASF in a particular area are more or less constant, the error rate is approximately the same when an earlier Loran fix is used to reestablish that same location.

Loran sky waves can be received at ranges up to 3,000 miles, but the margin of error for fixes based on sky waves can be up to eight times greater than that of ground-wave signals. They are thus virtually useless to the cruising yachtsman unless they can be verified by another position-fixing system.

CHOOSING A LORAN C RECEIVER

All a Loran C receiver really has to do is give you reliable TD's from which you can compute the remainder of your navigation tasks. It's possible to buy a basic or starter Loran C unit for around $500. Most experienced cruisers, however, would recommend a fairly sophisticated unit with a range of features you will find helpful on an extended voyage. Such a unit is likely to list for about $1,500 to $2,500. If your vessel has both lower and flying bridge steering stations, you can consider a component Loran C system in which a single remotely mounted processor unit runs control heads at both stations. For the sake of redundancy, however, a number of experienced cruisers prefer to install two completely separate Loran C receivers and their associated antennas.

Here's a rundown of the features available in Loran C receivers: those that a number of cruising yachtsmen have found to be important; those that are useful but not really necessary; and those that are basically marketing fluff.

Under the heading of "important" comes a Loran C receiver's ability not only to express position as TD's but to convert TD's into degrees of latitude and longitude. This feature is especially necessary for those whose cruise far off the beaten path, because for some cruising areas charts with Loran C overlays are only of large scale and thus virtually useless for pinpoint navigation inshore. For some of the more remote cruising areas, charts with Loran C overlays are not available at all.

Select a unit that also has ASF correction built into its latitude-longitude conversion program and allows you to input additional information manually from ASF correction tables. But even a unit with ASF correction will not be 100-percent accurate, and you should carefully monitor its performance. Wherever possible, buy charts with Loran C grids and double-check critical fixes based on lat/long readouts by also plotting them with TD's or other sources of navigation fixes. If your double-checking reveals substantial discrepancies, you may need to cancel out your unit's automatic ASF correction feature and manually input ASF correction from the tables or from your own observations. Also be aware that AFC correction can differ when you shift from one Loran C chain to a different one.

You can, of course, use a Loran C receiver simply to provide navigating information, then use that information to steer the desired course either manually or by entering the appropriate heading into your autopilot. If you select a Loran C unit that can interface directly with your autopilot, you will markedly increase the value of both pieces of equipment. But, as noted in our discussion of autopilots, be alert to anomalies in your Loran C receiver's performance that could dramatically affect where your vessel is actually going.

If you will be equipping your vessel with Transit satellite navigation equipment, your Loran C should interface with it as well to allow the Loran C to update the transit receiver's dead-reckoning function with speed, distance, and course information between satellite fixes whenever you are within Loran C's ground-wave coverage area. A setup in which a Loran C and a transit receiver are interfaced in this fashion is sometimes referred to as a LORSAT configuration.

If you are planning to buy a GPS receiver before the system becomes fully operational, you will want to interface your Loran C receiver with it, too, to allow it to input speed and heading information to the GPS receiver's dead-reckoning function between satellite fixes whenever your vessel is within Loran C coverage.

It is possible to interface a Loran C receiver with a radar and have vessel position displayed on the radar screen. Most of the cruisers I have talked to find this feature unnecessary since, unless the radar display is offset electronically, the vessel's position is already defined on the radar screen as the signal sweep's centerpoint.

Most Loran C units read out heading information as true north rather than magnetic north. If you will be using magnetic courses for navigation, select a Loran C unit that can be programmed to read out in magnetic bearings. Also select a unit that automatically compensates for magnetic variation once you input the current year. Having these features will save you considerable time and reduce the possibility of mixing up magnetic and true courses or bearings or of failing to allow for variation in a tight navigating situation. But again, compare your Loran C unit's magnetic variation compensation with what is printed on your chart and make certain it is not giving you unreliable information.

In long-distance cruising, you probably will find yourself in areas where it is possible to receive signals from two or more Loran chains. Select a receiver that will automatically select the chain providing the strongest signals rather than one that requires you to enter a new GRI manually as your route takes you from one chain's coverage area to the next. (In order to use this feature, you will have to use lat/long coordinates. Units will not shift from one chain to another if they are using TD's.) In chains that have more than two master-secondary combinations, units with this feature will monitor all available combinations and automatically select the two that provide the most reliable fix. You will still have the ability to override the automatic feature and enter a new GRI manually or enter master-secondary combinations that are different from the ones the receiver has selected. Even some of the most expensive Loran C units with automatic master and secondary signal acquisition require an initialization of approximate latitude and longitude when they are installed. Since this is a one-time process, it is not a drawback. Again, if you rely on lat/long readouts from your Loran C, periodically check your position with TD's or other sources of position information to make certain you are exactly where the lat/long information says you are.

If there is a problem with a Loran C signal at the transmitter source, it will contain a component that will cause the receiving unit's data display to blink as a type of alarm. In addition, the display of some receivers will blink if the ground-wave signals they are receiving are not strong enough to be used for reliable computations or if they are relying on sky waves. The unit you purchase should also display the signal-to-noise ratio of any transmitter it is receiving. It also should be capable of conducting its own check of its internal circuitry and display an alert if there is a short in its antenna circuit.

The Loran C receiver you select should have six to eight integral notch filters to screen out atmospheric and off-vessel interference.

Loran C receivers operate at 100 kHz, which is much lower than most of your other electronics. Because of that, they are more susceptible to radio frequency (RF) interference from on-board electrical sources. If you encounter problems with RF interference, you probably will require the services of a qualified electronics technician to filter them out.

Virtually all the Loran C units now on the market allow you to program into them the coordinates of "way points," which can be the location of navigational buoys, areas of special interest or potential hazards, points at which a course correction is necessary, and the like. On a lengthy voyage, you will find it helpful to have a unit that allows you to enter way points not only as TD's and lat/long coordinates but also in terms of bearing and distance from a previously entered way point.

If you enter *from* and *to* way points, the receiver will automatically compute the great-circle course between them; some units will also create a rhumb-line course. It is up to you, however, to make certain that the course the receiver computes is one that can be followed safely. If you give it the coordinates of a *from* way point on the south side of a shoal and those of a *to* way point on the north side, it will very obediently give you a course that runs right over the shoal. The unit should also display the bearing and course from your present position to any programmed way point and/or between any pair of way points. When you are running toward a way point, it should also give you not only your course-over-ground (COG) and speed-over-ground (SOG) but also your course-made-good (CMG), distance-made-good (DMG), and speed-of-advance (SOA) or velocity-made-good (VMG), which tells you how rapidly you are approaching the way point after allowing for current set and drift. If you will be using your Loran C as a primary or secondary steering reference, it should display your deviation from the intended course as crosstrack error (XTE, also sometimes referred to in the marine electronic community's alphabet soup of acronyms as CDX, or course deviation crosstrack) and indicate the correction needed to return to it. You will find a unit easier to use if it displays the required course correction with some type of steering indicator such as a shifting bar or tick marks rather than numerical degrees. As mentioned in the section on autopilots, if your autopilot also displays crosstrack error, you will have more flexibility in the placement of your Loran C.

Don't make the mistake of choosing a Loran C unit solely on the basis of its capacity for storing the greatest number of way points. The relationship between the total number of way points you can save and the total number of routes into which you can organize them is a more important criterion. One unit with capacity for storing 120 way points, for example, allows you to organize them into ninety-nine different routes with any number of way points per route (not exceeding a 120-way-point total). A second unit has capacity for storing 180 way points into routes but allows you to create only nine routes with a maximum of twenty way points per route. In practice, you will find that the unit with the capacity to store a greater number of routes with a greater flexibility as to their organization will be more useful than the unit with greater total way-point capacity.

Also make certain you understand what a unit's "way-point capacity" really means. Some units store all way points permanently and erase them only on instructions from the operator. Other units devote only a portion of their way-point capacity to permanent memory. Information entered into the remainder of their way-point memory will be overwritten once the capacity of that portion of the memory is reached.

Select a unit that has "automatic way-point sequencing" and allows you to run a route in either direction. With that arrangement, you can instruct the Loran in advance that as it reaches each way point it is to proceed to the next higher- or lower-numbered way point in the numerical sequence you have programmed. If you have it interfaced with an autopilot, it will instruct the autopilot to change course as necessary. With some units that have automatic way-point sequencing, you can instruct the unit to proceed from any one way point to any other way point, even though it is not necessarily the next higher or lower in the numerical sequence you have programmed. (If you purchase a Loran C receiver that has "nonautomatic way-point sequencing," upon arrival at each way point you have to manually ask it to display the course and distance to the next way point in the numerical sequence, then steer the course manually or enter it into your autopilot.) If you utilize automatic way-point sequencing, however, remember what we said in our discussion of autopilots about how much deviation from a previous course they can handle.

Experienced cruisers also recommend that you buy a unit with an integral timer. These units display current time in either a twelve-hour or twenty-four-hour clock mode; elapsed time from any programmed way point; time-to-go to the next way point;

and estimated time of arrival. With some of these units, you can save up to fifty positions en route and the time you arrived at each one.

Under the heading of "not really necessary" come alarms that sound as you approach a preprogrammed way point and allow you to designate the distance from the way point at which you want the alarm to sound. While such an alarm might be helpful if you are momentarily distracted or otherwise occupied, you should be maintaining a close enough watch over the helm to know you are approaching the way point long before the alarm ever sounds. Other features in this category include the ability to assign names to way points and the ability to interface a Loran receiver with a computer printer to create a ship's navigation log.

Features that come under "marketing fluff" are personal identification messages that must be entered before the unit can be operated and access codes to prevent unauthorized persons from accessing programmed way-point information (important primarily to fishermen who want to keep competitors or rivals from learning where they have been catching the big ones). Also in this category are units that allow you to enter information into the receiver or instruct it to modify its display with a remote-control unit. If your vessel is under way, you should be at the helm and in close proximity to your receiver anyway, so you can probably get along without such a device.

One word of caution: If the unit you purchase has a feature called "cycle-stepping," be certain you know what it involves and be careful about employing it. Loran receivers are phased to read only the initial part of the pulsed signal from each transmitter in order to capture that signal's ground wave before it has time to receive its sky wave. In fringe areas, this "tracking mark" may slip further into the signal. Cycle-stepping allows you to instruct the receiver to read a later portion of a transmitter's signal. When you employ cycle-stepping, you may be able to capture Loran C signals at a much greater distance from a transmitter, but you may be doing so by receiving its sky wave rather than its ground wave. The margin of error of TD's or lat/long coordinates based on sky waves can be far greater than those based on ground waves; they should be used only if they can be verified by another navigational system.

A number of manufacturers offer Loran C receivers that will

display your vessel's position, track, and other information on an integral or separate LCD or video display. We'll discuss track and chart plotters later, but at this point suffice it to say that all the companies that market these units warn they are intended as a convenience only and are not intended to take the place of standard navigation charts.

Several manufacturers now offer Loran C receivers that also incorporate some level of ability to receive signals from the Global Positioning System (GPS) which we will discuss in detail later in this chapter. The list prices of these combination units are on the order of $16,000 to $18,000. Unless you have money to burn or insist that your vessel be equipped with the absolute latest in electronics, my recommendation is that you hold off purchasing such equipment until GPS becomes fully operational in its two-dimensional mode and GPS receiver prices have dropped significantly. In the meantime, if I were going to cruise beyond the ground-wave coverage of Loran C, I would purchase a good Transit satellite navigation receiver and interface it with speed and heading inputs. You will find when we discuss the Transit system that it probably will be turned off at the end of 1996, but in the interim a Transit receiver will give you the most complete and reliable open-ocean navigating system available to the cruising yachtsman. By the time you decide to trash your Transit receiver and make the jump to GPS, the price of the GPS gear should have come down more than enough to offset the $3,500 or so you will have invested in a good installed Transit unit.

LORAN C ANTENNAS

All that is required in the way of an antenna for Loran C reception is good 8.5-foot whip. You can even use an 8.5-foot marine CB antenna, because the critical factor is its length. Its resonant frequency will be set by the small antenna coupler supplied with your receiver, which you will need to install at the antenna's base. Some manufacturers offer combination Loran C/VHF antennas, but you will get better operation from your Loran receiver if you connect it to its own antenna.

The antenna must be mounted clear of any large metal obstructions. It should not, however, be the highest metallic object on your vessel as it is subject to "precipitation static" which can occur during rain or snow. There are no restrictions on antenna-to-receiver distance. The antenna must be grounded to your vessel's RF grounding system which we will discuss in detail in the next chapter. The antenna-to-receiver connection should be made with GR58C/U coaxial cable.

LORAN C RECEIVER INSTALLATION

Unless you are extremely experienced with electronics, you should leave the installation of your Loran C receiver and antenna to a qualified marine electronics technician, preferably one with training in the particular unit you purchase. The most troublesome aspect of installation can be screening out on-board electrical interference. Some Loran C units may have to be tuned or calibrated after installation. In any event, the receiver must be firmly connected to your boat's RF grounding system, preferably by a heavy copper strap. If, in addition to using your Loran receiver for chart plotting, you will be using its crosstrack-error display for steering, the unit should be positioned so that its display can be viewed easily from both your navigation station and from the helm but at least 3 feet away from your magnetic compass. As suggested earlier, you will find that a more practical configuration is to choose an autopilot that displays course and crosstrack error clearly and use it as your primary steering reference. That arrangement will allow you to mount your Loran C receiver within reach of the helm but not directly in your line of vision.

LEGAL REQUIREMENTS

No licenses are required for either the installation or operation of Loran C receivers.

EQUIPMENT RECOMMENDATIONS

The Northstar 800 (Fig. 8.8) has proved to be the leader, primarily because the front-end design of its receiver provides superior signal acquisition. For an antenna I would recommend the Shakespeare 4208.

FOR FURTHER READING

The most useful book on Loran C operation is Bonnie Dahl's *The Loran C User's Guide* (1986). It is available through most marine bookstores or direct from Richardson's Marine Publishing, Inc., P.O. Box 23, Streamwood, IL 60103.

Fig. 8.8: *The accuracy and reliability of the Northstar 800 has made it a popular choice among cruising yachtsmen.*

TRANSIT SATELLITE NAVIGATION

When the Soviet Union launched Sputnik I in 1957, American scientists at the Applied Physics Laboratory of Johns Hopkins University noticed that the signals it emitted experienced a "Doppler effect" which was dependent on the relative velocity between the satellite and their receiver. "Doppler effect" is what you note in the shift in the sound-wave frequency of a train's whistle as it approaches, passes you, then recedes into the distance. After working out a complex series of algorithms based on this frequency shift, the scientists found they were able to accurately predict Sputnik's orbital pattern. They reasoned that if they could plot a satellite's orbit from a fixed point on earth, they could reverse the process to plot a fixed point on earth from the known orbit of a satellite.

During this same period, a major part of the United States' strategic defense system was the Polaris submarine. The Polaris employed an inertial navigation system which had to be reinitialized periodically with land bearings or celestial observations. When no land masses or celestial bodies were readily visible, the subs risked attack during long periods of exposure on the surface trying to get a fix. The Navy utilized what the APL scientists had learned about Doppler shift from the Sputnik signals to develop its Transit satellite system, which could provide fixes at sea on a predictable schedule and under any weather conditions. The system became operational for military use in 1964 and was made available to civilian users in 1967.

The Transit system is operated by the U.S. Navy for the Department of Defense. The DOD has announced that, based on the operational deployment of GPS in 1993, it will shut down the Transit satellites at the end of 1996 and that they will not be turned over to any other Government agency or to private interests. If GPS becomes operational on its present schedule, degradation of the Transit system could come before its scheduled 1996 termination date. The DOD has in inventory sufficient Transit satellites to support the program to 1996, but they would be put into orbit if necessary with U.S. Air Force Scout launch vehicles. The USAF was planning to shut down the Scout program in 1989 but may extend it to at least 1992. Once Scout is shut down, if additional Transit satellites are needed in orbit to replace failed units, the Navy may no longer have the ability to launch them.

HOW TRANSIT WORKS

Mariners often refer to the Transit system simply as "SatNav." With the advent of GPS, which is also a satellite navigation system, that shorthand designation could confuse the two. To make certain we properly distinguish between them, we'll call Transit by its proper name.

The system now utilizes a constellation of five active satellites in polar orbit at an altitude of some 600 nautical miles. Each satellite completes an orbit approximately every 107 minutes. These orbits are not constant but are subject to gradual changes due to a factor called "precession." Since the whole system is based on knowing exactly where the satellites are located in space when their signals are received, their orbit information must be updated periodically. This is accomplished by monitoring their signals at tracking stations located at Prospect Harbor, Maine; Rosemount, Minnesota; and Wahiawa, Hawaii. Data from the monitored signals are fed to a computing center at Point Magu, California, where new orbital data are computed and injected back into each satellite on a subsequent pass over one of the tracking stations. In practice, each satellite receives new orbital information about every twelve hours.

Each satellite then transmits its updated orbital information

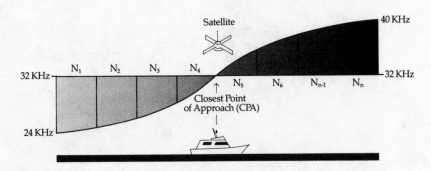

Fig. 8.9: *The Transit navigation system works by measuring the Doppler shift in the signal from a single satellite as it passes overhead.*

every two minutes as a navigational message on a precise frequency of 399.968 MHz. A Transit receiver on board a cruising vessel incorporates an oscillator which generates a reference frequency of 400.000 MHz, and the receiver measures the difference between the two frequencies. If both the satellite and the vessel were motionless, the difference would remain constant at 32 kHz. Because the satellite is moving, its signal experiences a Doppler shift, and the expected 32-kHz difference is received only at the satellite's Closest Point of Approach (CPA) to the receiver (Fig. 8.9). The receiver measures this frequency shift at the start of each two-minute message (T1, T2, T3, etc.) throughout the time the satellite is in view (Fig. 8.10) and uses the information in a complex computation to calculate a series of ranges from the satellite's known orbit. It then computes the point at which those ranges intersect, which is the vessel's position on the earth's surface, expressed as degrees of latitude and longitude. A Transit receiver will begin updating its position information as soon as it has captured information at two or three of the time intervals, but optimum accuracy is not achieved until it has captured all the signals received during a satellite pass, which can take about twenty minutes at the equator.

Because the measurements of the Doppler shift are sequential rather than instantaneous, the vessel's motion during the satellite pass must also be entered into the equation in terms of its speed and heading. Within the Loran C coverage area, speed and heading information can be supplied by interfacing the Transit receiver with a Loran C receiver. Outside the Loran C coverage

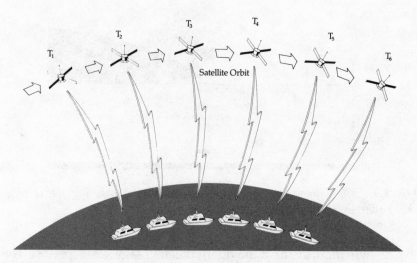

Fig. 8.10: *The Transit system has a relatively slow fix rate because a receiver must measure the Doppler shift in a satellite's signals over time (T1, T2, T3, etc.) before it can accurately compute the vessel's position. For maximum accuracy, the vessel's speed and heading during the time the measurements are taken must be known and included in the calculation.*

area, speed and heading information can be input most accurately by interfacing the Transit receiver with a knot meter and heading sensor. Transit manufacturers offer speed and heading sensors as optional, stand-alone accessories for their receivers. But if you select appropriate equipment, the Transit receiver can take speed input from your regular knot meter and heading information from the same magnetic fluxgate compass that serves your autopilot.

The design parameters of predictable accuracy of fixes based on Transit signals is 0.1 nm (roughly 300 feet) plus 0.2 nm (roughly 600 feet) per knot of error in vessel speed. (The satellites also transmit their signals just below 150 MHz, and Transit receivers capable of using both frequencies can achieve accuracies on the order of 75 to 100 feet. Due to the high cost of dual-frequency Transit receivers, they normally are not found on any but the most elaborately equipped cruising yachts.) In practice, fixes from single-channel Transit receivers are accurate to within 500 feet or less. This is more than adequate for offshore navigation.

Transit fixes should not be relied on for inshore navigation, however, since the system incorporates only a few satellites and their orbit is relatively low. Its "fix rate"—the time between satellite passes—can range from thirty minutes to as much as 110 minutes. You could wind up trying to run a nasty reef entrance in bad weather after a long delay between satellite fixes and find that significant dead-reckoning error has put you a quarter-mile or more from where the Transit receiver says you are.

CHOOSING A TRANSIT RECEIVER

Despite the limitations of its fix rate, until GPS becomes fully operational and the prices of GPS receivers become more reasonable, the Transit system should be your electronic navigation system of choice if you will be venturing beyond the ground-wave coverage area of Loran C. From the discussion above, you obviously should look for a Transit receiver that can be interfaced with your Loran C unit and accept speed input from your knot meter and heading input from your autopilot's heading sensor. It also should be capable of predicting the time of future satellite passes. As with a Loran C receiver, it should compensate automatically for magnetic variation and display your vessel's present course-over-ground and speed-over-ground, the bearing and distance to your next way point, speed-of-advance, crosstrack error, course-to-steer, and estimated time of arrival.

It should interface with your autopilot and provide automatic way-point sequencing. But since Transit is an offshore navigation system, the size of its capacity to store way-point coordinates is not as important as with your Loran C receiver.

You might want to look for a unit with an anchor-watch feature, which could be useful when you are anchored outside the Loran C coverage area. Units with all the features listed are available for around $3,500 to $4,000 installed.

As with Loran C, I would not buy one of the combined Transit-GPS units now on the market until GPS becomes fully operational and GPS equipment has been further refined and its price reduced. The same is true of Transit receivers that employ integral track plotters.

TRANSIT ANTENNAS

The antenna for your Transit receiver normally will be supplied with your receiver. It will only be about 24 inches long and should be mounted on your flying bridge in as unobstructed a position as possible.

TRANSIT RECEIVER INSTALLATION

You will want to install a Transit receiver in proximity to your navigation station where you plot position fixes on your charts. Most Transit receivers offer steering displays as one of their functions. As is the case with the steering display of a Loran C receiver, you will find you have more flexibility in equipment placement if you rely on the steering display of your autopilot and install your Transit receiver someplace other than in the line of sight of the helmsman.

LEGAL REQUIREMENTS

No license is required to install or operate a Transit satellite navigation receiver.

TRANSIT EQUIPMENT RECOMMENDATIONS

The top of the line in Transit receivers is the Magnavox MX4102 (Fig. 8.11). If your vessel will not be equipped with a knot meter and a fluxgate compass that are capable of NMEA 0183 interface to supply speed and heading inputs to the MX4102,

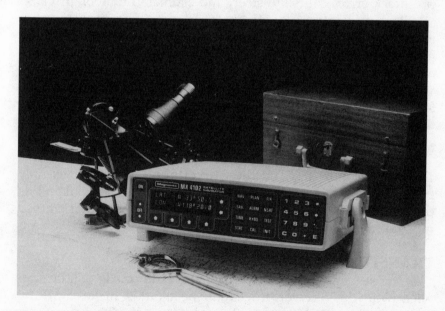

Fig. 8.11: *The Magnavox 4102 has proved to be a highly reliable Transit receiver which is quite easy to use.*

it should be interfaced with the Magnavox MX35 fluxgate compass and the Magnavox MX42 through-hull speed sensor.

NAVSTAR GLOBAL POSITIONING SYSTEM

The NavStar Global Positioning System (GPS) has been under development by the U.S. Department of Defense and its counterparts in NATO and Australia since 1973. As part of the program's development, a total of twelve test satellites have been launched since 1977. Five of those are operational today and provide GPS fix data in most areas of the world for about twelve hours a day. The DOD's early projections were to have GPS fully operational and providing twenty-four-hour coverage by 1989, but delays due primarily to the malfunction of launch vehicles and the Challenger shuttle disaster have pushed the schedule back about four years. The first operational GPS satellite was launched in February, 1989, with subsequent launches scheduled to follow every other month. Current projections are that the system will be operational for military use in three dimensions (latitude, longitude, and altitude) by mid-1993. Because recreational boaters do not require altitude fixes and because our accuracy requirements are less exacting than those of the military, we will be able to use GPS for reliable fixes twenty-four hours a day worldwide once twelve satellites are in orbit. The NavStar GPS Joint Program Office says that, barring further launching disasters, that should occur in September 1991.

The DOD expects GPS eventually to become the dominant—perhaps the "sole means"—radionavigation system for all land, sea and air forces of America and its allies. Equipment is under development to allow the system to be used by not only all military aircraft from transports to fighters and all naval vessels but even trucks, tanks, and as a backpack or hand-held unit for soldiers in the field. Users of GPS also will include commercial and general aviation, the land-surveying and oil-drilling industries, and such marine interests as commercial shipping, fishing and recreational boating.

The lure of the massive market potential for GPS equipment has already sparked development efforts by more than fifty companies in the United States, Canada, Western Europe, and Japan. Several manufacturers are already offering GPS receivers, either as stand-alone equipment or in conjunction with Loran C or Transit receivers. As the GPS activation date approaches, we can expect to see radical upgrading in equipment capabilities and major reductions in equipment prices.

HOW GPS WORKS

You must know the reason why GPS was developed in the first place in order to understand how it operates.

From a military standpoint, the drawbacks of the Transit system—its significant margin of position error, its thirty-to-110-minute fix rate, and the necessity to dead reckon between fixes—are obvious. But even if Transit's accuracy could be substantially increased and if it could be expanded to include enough satellites to provide fixes continuously, it has an even more profound inherent limitation: the length of time it takes to collect the data necessary to compute a fix once a satellite is in view. As we saw when we discussed Transit, its position-fixing dynamics are dependent on taking a number of measurements of Doppler effect in the signal of a single satellite over time, and maximum accuracy is not achieved until it has acquired all signals on a single satellite pass, which can take up to twenty minutes. Also, the speed and heading of whatever vehicle the receiver is mounted on during that time are critical to the system's accuracy rate and must be input from external sources. Those factors may not be much of a problem for the navigator of a naval destroyer proceeding along a straight course at 30 knots, but they are disastrous for the pilot of a fighter aircraft twisting through combat manuevers at better than 2,000 miles an hour. The fighter pilot must have a system that gives him a fix much quicker. GPS was designed to answer that need by receiving signals from several satellites almost simultaneously.

GPS will incorporate twenty-one active satellites and three operating spares in six orbital planes around the earth at an altitude of 10,900 nm (20,200 km) and an inclination angle to the equator of 55 degrees. Each satellite will take approximately twelve hours to complete a single orbit. A single satellite will follow the same ground pattern on each orbit but will be observable from a fixed position on earth approximately four minutes earlier each day due to the difference between its orbital speed and the speed of the earth's rotation.

As with Transit, the orbital precession of GPS satellites will be monitored, changes computed, and updated orbital information fed back to them (Fig. 8.12). This "control segment" of the system is already in place and operational.

Because of the altitude of the satellites and their staging pattern, at least five satellites will be observable by a ground-based GPS receiver at all times, which allows the system's fix rate to be continuous. Signals from any three satellites will be sufficient

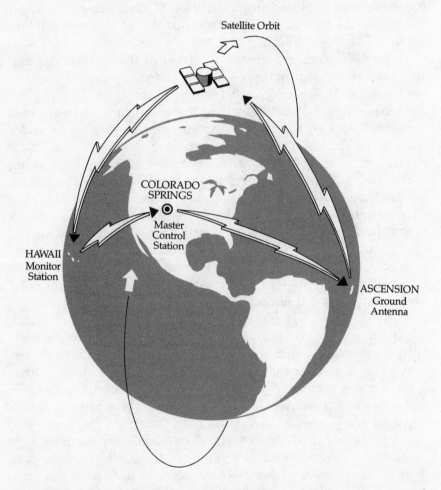

Fig. 8.12: Because physical forces cause the orbits of GPS satellites to gradually change, new orbit information must be computed periodically by the Master Control Station and fed back to the satellite to update the information it transmits.

to fix latitude and longitude. A signal from a fourth satellite is required only to determine altitude.

The signal transmitted from each satellite has two parts. One is a digital code unique to that particular satellite. Superimposed over that code will be a navigation message (NAVmsg) that contains updated information about that satellite's orbit (technically referred to as "ephemeris data"), what time it is as far as the satellite is concerned (GPS time), almanac data for all satellites in the constellation, and coefficients the receiver can plug into a computer model stored in its memory to calculate how the atmosphere is affecting the signal's transmission through the ionosphere (its propagation).

The GPS receivers already available in the recreational marine market are of three types. Single-channel sequential receivers have one hardware channel and read the code data and the NAVmsg from the satellites in view one at a time. Two-channel receivers have two hardware channels—one for reading the codes from up to four satellites in sequence and one for reading their navigation messages and searching for the next satellite coming into view. Multiplex receivers use a single channel but switch rapidly from one satellite to the other to collect code and NAVmsg data. When the system becomes fully operational, it will take a typical two-channel recreational marine receiver with a warm oscillator and almanac data regarding satellite passes already in its memory about a minute and a half to capture the required information and compute its first fix. After that, it will update position about every 1.2 seconds.

The satellite will tell the receiver the instant in GPS time that it transmitted its signal and the receiver will synchronize itself (approximately) to GPS time. By multiplying the difference between the time the satellite transmitted the signal and the time it was received by the signal's speed (186,000 statute miles per second), the receiver will be able to calculate its approximate distance (called a pseudorange) from the satellite. The receiver's computation of this distance could be absolutely accurate if it contained an atomic clock, but that would make the receiver prohibitively expensive. Instead, a GPS receiver uses for a time reference an affordable crystal oscillator that synchronizes it and the satellite with near but not total accuracy.

Once the receiver has computed its pseudorange from three satellites, it takes the navigation process one step further. It measures the frequency shift (Doppler effect) in the satellite's signal by comparing the satellite signal's frequency against that of a reference signal the receiver generates internally. This is also done in the Transit system, but there is a major difference: Transit compares the Doppler shift between the signals received from a single satellite over time (that is, at T1, T2, T3, etc.), while GPS compares the Doppler shift between signals it is receiving almost simultaneously from each of the three or four different satellites it is observing. From the Doppler effect, the receiver can compute its velocity relative to each of the satellites it is observing. (This ability to determine its own velocity during the time it takes the receiver to read the code signals from the satellites eliminates the need for inputs of vessel speed and heading from external sources, as the Transit system requires.)

Once the receiver has captured pseudoranges from the satellites it is observing, it uses them to solve three simultaneous equations with three unknowns and produce an estimate of its position. It then recalculates those same three equations using velocity rather than pseudoranges to compute its own velocity during signal acquisition and position computation. After making allowance in the earlier estimated position for its own velocity, it produces a position fix. In essence, what the GPS receiver has done is to measure the distance between itself and three satellites, use those differences as the radii of three spheres, each having one of the satellites as its center, then with spherical geometry determine its position as the intersection of those three spheres (Fig 8.13).

GPS actually will provide not one level of fix accuracy but two: a Standard Positioning Service (SPS) and a Precise Positioning Service (PPS). The SPS, which will be available to all users of GPS, is designed to yield fixes accurate to approximately 150 feet. The PPS, which will be available only to military users and an extremely limited number of nonmilitary Government agencies, is designed to yield fixes accurate to within 60 feet. (Actually both services probably will be even more accurate than the DOD is willing to state publicly. Based on their experience with SPS signals from the test satellites to date, United States companies that are already producing recreational marine GPS receivers claim accuracy rates of 45 to 90 feet. Published data indicate that in tests the PPS has proved under ideal conditions to be accurate to within 25 feet. Scuttlebutt says the military system

Fig. 8.13: *A GPS receiver determines vessel position by taking virtually in-stantaneous readings from at least three satellites, each of whose position be-comes the radius of a sphere. The receiver then calculates the vessel's position as the point at which those three spheres intersect.*

may be accurate within 2 to 3 feet. The DOD has said that once the system becomes operational, it will deliberately downgrade the accuracy of SPS to 150 feet. Pressures from lifesaving and commercial interests, however, may force the DOD to reverse that position.)

Discrimination between the two levels of accuracy will be achieved by having each satellite transmit signals on two fre-quencies—L1 at 1575.42 MHz, and L2 at 1227.6 MHz. Nonmili-tary users will be able to receive only the L1 signal which will carry a Course/Acquisition code (C/A-code). The 150-foot stated accuracy of fixes based on the C/A-code could be considerably greater except for the fact that the DOD will impose on its trans-mission a technique called Selective Availability (S/A) which is designed to deliberately degrade its accuracy rate. In addition, the C/A-code will contain only a predicted model of how the atmosphere is delaying the signal's propagation, not how it is affecting the signal in real time.

Transmissions on both the L1 and L2 frequencies will carry a Precise code (P-code) detectable only by military receivers and encrypted to prevent unauthorized use. The P-code will also employ the S/A technique, but military receivers will be able to offset it. By being able to receive the P-code on two frequencies, military receivers will be able to make a dual-frequency comparison to compensate for atmospheric propagation delay in real time. The two factors together will account for the PPS's greater accuracy.

One drawback to GPS that its designers have not yet been able to resolve is the "integrity issue." We mentioned that when the signals from a Loran C transmitter have a problem at their source, they can be transmitted in such a way as to cause the display of any equipment receiving them to blink. Such a system is not yet possible with GPS and may never be. The problem can be acute for high-velocity aircraft but is not likely to be a major problem for low-velocity marine users. But the integrity issue does point up again the truism that the prudent mariner will never rely on any single means of navigation but will employ and compare at least two to make certain his vessel is really where he thinks it is.

In the hope of refining the accuracy of GPS to allow it to be used for harbor approach, harbor operations, and possibly as an aircraft landing system, research is presently being conducted on *differential GPS*. Under differential GPS, a series of stations in specific areas will monitor GPS signals, determine the atmospheric effects on their propagation in real time, and transmit corrections to GPS receiver in the area. Special Committee 104 of the Radio Technical Commission for Maritime Services has recently developed a standard (RTCM SC-104) for the degree of accuracy a differential GPS system should provide and the electronic format in which it should be transmitted.

CHOOSING A GPS RECEIVER

As of this writing, several manufacturers offer two-channel sequential GPS receivers, either as stand-alone units or for use in conjunction with Loran C or Transit receivers, which list for $6,000 to $18,000. The only multiplex GPS receiver currently available is Shipmate Marine Electronics' RS5200 which, including the company's Transit satellite receiver to which it must be matched, lists for $15,000. Magellan Systems Corporation of

Monrovia, California, offers a hand-held GPS receiver with a suggested list price of $3,000. It is a single-channel sequential unit which cannot accept external speed and heading input for automatic dead reckoning until the system is fully operational, nor can it be interfaced with an autopilot, a Loran C unit, or a Transit receiver.

On a cost-effective basis, I do not recommend purchasing any of these first-generation GPS receivers. Instead, I would wait until the complete GPS system is operational in two dimensions and the equipment for receiving and utilizing its signals has been further refined and reduced in price.

The refinements in second-generation equipment are going to be primarily in the substitution of digital microprocessing for much of the analog signal processing in the first-generation gear. That is likely to produce only a minimal increase in fix accuracy but it should make the equipment considerably more reliable.

The reduction in GPS receiver prices from their current levels is going to at least equal what we saw in the price drop of Transit satellite navigation equipment as that system became operational. When Transit first became available to civilian users in 1967, receivers cost around $20,000. By the early 1970's, their prices were about a third that figure. The reduction in GPS equipment prices may be even more dramatic. Because of the worldwide nature of the system, such major electronics manufacturers as Panasonic, Sony, and Hitachi may well enter the GPS market and bring to it the savings of their massive production capabilities. My sources in the industry indicate that full-function two-channel GPS receivers will probably drop to the $5,000 range by early 1993.

Once the equipment is refined and its price drops, GPS will become the navigation system of choice for the cruising yachtsman who ventures outside the Loran C coverage area.

If you decide to purchase one of the units already on the market, it should meet certain minimum specifications: It should accept speed and heading inputs for dead reckoning between satellite fixes until the twelve satellites necessary for two-dimensional fixes are up. It should be capable of being interfaced with a Loran C or Transit receiver.

It should provide automatic selection of satellite signals. It should be either two-channel sequential or multiplexed rather than single-channel, since it will acquire signals quicker and thus provide fixes more rapidly. It should incorporate a Kalman filter, a data-processing algorithm that rejects information that is outside predetermined parameters (called "states") and applies a "weighting factor" to information it does accept to determine its relative importance in calculating the most accurate position fix possible. Lastly, it should be compatible with the RTCM SC-104 standard for differential GPS, since it is likely to quickly become a primary radionavigation system for harbors and harbor approach.

GPS EQUIPMENT RECOMMENDATIONS

The most promising unit on the market is the stand-alone Magnavox MX5400, a two-channel sequential receiver with an eight-state Kalman filter and the ability to accept speed and heading inputs to provide automatic dead reckoning until GPS becomes fully operational. It interfaces with a Transit satellite and/or a Loran C receiver using the NMEA 0183 protocol. In field trials the unit has demonstrated two-dimensional accuracy of better than 36 feet using the test satellites. Optional equipment will allow the MX5400 to accept differential GPS from an external monitor using the RTCM SC-104 format. It lists for $12,600.

DEPTH-SOUNDERS

"It's not the ocean that sinks ships," goes the old saying, "it's the hard stuff around the edges." While that statement may not be entirely accurate, one of the cruising yachtsman's most basic needs is a good depth-sounder that tells him where the "hard stuff" is located.

HOW A DEPTH-SOUNDER WORKS

At its simplest, a depth-sounder emits sound-wave pulses and measures the time it takes for them to be reflected back to its receiver. Since sound waves travel through water at 4,800 miles per second, the device performs a simple time-to-distance conversion and displays the result. A depth-sounder has four components: a transmitter that generates an electrical signal; a transducer that converts that electrical signal into acoustic pulses; a receiver that amplifies the returning echo and performs the necessary timing function and time-to-distance conversion; and a display that presents the computed information.

Depth-sounders come in three basic varieties which differ primarily in how they present their information. Flashing and paper or video recording depth-finders are primarily of interest to fishermen because they can not only indicate depth but can locate schools of fish and provide indications of bottom composition. For cruising, however, the most practical type are the digital units that read out depth on a liquid crystal display (LCD).

CHOOSING A DEPTH-SOUNDER

If your vessel has both lower and flying bridge steering stations, purchase a digital unit that offers both main and repeater display units that work off a single transducer. The unit should allow you to specify whether its readings will be in feet, fathoms, or meters, depending on the units in which depth is indicated on the chart you are using. You should also have the ability to set the unit's "zero depth" as the lowest point of your vessel.

Select a unit that allows you to have it set off an alarm if minimum water depth reaches about 5 feet beneath your keel or props. Some units offer multiple alarms for use as an anchor watch which sounds if water depth exceeds a maximum and minimum you set. Experienced cruising people find the anchor-watch function can be performed more effectively by a radar unit, Loran C, or a Transit or GPS receiver.

The more expensive depth-sounders on the recreational marine market will read to depths of 1,000 feet, but a unit that reads to about 400 feet or even 200 feet is more than adequate.

A number of manufacturers offer units that provide depth information in combination with a number of other factors such as speed, total distance and trip logs, sea temperature, and the like. These units have integral timers and are capable of being interfaced with electronic compasses or navigation receivers to provide course heading, crosstrack error, elapsed time, distance-to-go, time-to-go, estimated time of arrival, and the like. I personally don't see why you should spend $1,500 or so for one of these units, because all they do basically is duplicate navigation receiver display functions. You still need your navigation receiver in reasonable proximity to the helm in order to control its input function, so why duplicate information that is already close at hand?

Because a depth-sounder is such a critical piece of equipment on a cruising yacht, you might want to install two (Fig.

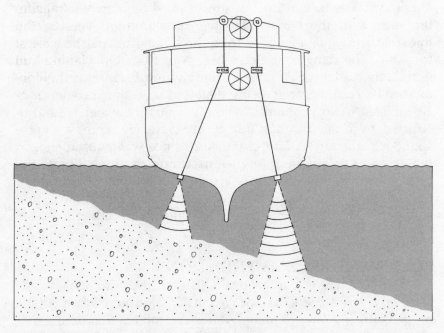

Fig. 8.14: *In a poorly-marked channel, dual depth-sounders installed with their transducers as widely separated as practical can help the helmsperson determine which way to steer to reach deep water.*

8.14) so you'll have a backup if one unit goes out. If you take that approach, you will need to select two different models that operate at different frequencies. If they both operate on the same frequency they will drive each other crazy. Frank Glindmeier installed two depth-sounders on *Summer Wind* and got an unexpected benefit. "I mounted the transducers about four feet to either side of the centerline of the boat," he says. "In a narrow channel which was poorly marked or not marked at all, I often got a significantly deeper reading off one unit than the other and knew in which direction the deeper water lay. I found I could use the difference in the two readings to kind of ping my way along and keep the boat over the deepest water."

EQUIPMENT INSTALLATION

The most important aspect of depth-sounder installation is correct placement of the transducer, which should be made of bronze, not nylon. It should be mounted through the hull rather than internally and should be positioned as nearly as possible to amidships. The face of the transducer must be exactly parallel to the surface of the water. On steel or aluminum vessels, the transducer must be insulated from the hull with a plastic washer to reduce the danger of electrolytic corrosion. On planing-hull vessels, be certain it is mounted far enough back from the bow to keep its readings from being distorted by water turbulence or air bubbles. Also position it where the flow of water is not obstructed by other through-hull fittings. Never mount a depth-sounder's transducer on the transom, since water turbulence in that location will cause it to give inaccurate readings. Locate the display unit so that it is easily visible from the helm and within reach. If you use a magnetic steering compass, position the depth-sounder so it does not contribute to compass deviation.

EQUIPMENT RECOMMENDATIONS

The Datamarine International Offshore 3000 (Fig. 8.15), which lists for around $850, has proved itself time and again in the rugged cruising environment. Almost as good is Standard Communications' DS20 model, which lists for around $300. Both companies offer matching digital knot meter/log units.

Fig. 8.15: *Many cruisers have found Datamarine's International Offshore 3000 depth-sounder and 3200 knot meter are both accurate and reliable.*

SONAR

Sonar is essentially underwater radar that uses sound waves rather than radio waves. It is primarily a fish-finding device and due to its cost (list prices run $2,000 to $6,000 or more) it is rarely found on any but the most elaborately equipped cruising yachts.

KNOT METERS

A knot meter/distance log records your vessel's speed through the water and distance traveled since your last fix. It is important that this essential navigational information be as accurate as possible. These units come in a variety of types which vary primarily in the way they measure speed through the water. Some high-performance boats utilize knot meters that employ a principle called the Hall effect to measure changes in the earth's magnetic field; another type measures changes in the magnetic field between two terminals installed as through-hull fittings. Still another type of knot meter measures the Doppler effect in transmitted and received sound waves. By far the most popular type of knot meter/distance log for recreational marine use employs a simple paddle-wheel impeller as its sensing device.

The paddle-wheel impeller is mounted as a through-hull fitting. As water flow causes the impeller to spin, magnets embedded in it rotate past a small coil which creates electrical pulses. These pulses are transmitted by cable to a receiver that translates the signal into a digital display of the vessel's speed through the water in knots.

CHOOSING A KNOT METER

Look for the knot meter that has the highest-quality signal processing and can translate the electrical current from the sensor into vessel speed most accurately. The best units will duplicate and double-check information—such as distance run since last fix and total distance run that is already provided by your navigation receiver.

If you have a Transit or a first-generation GPS receiver aboard, make certain you buy a knot meter that can interface with it to provide the speed input it needs for dead reckoning between satellite fixes.

If your vessel has two steering stations, select a knot meter that offers dual control heads. With a number of knot meters, a nylon through-hull impeller housing is standard and a bronze through-hull is offered as an option. Go for the bronze.

KNOT METER EQUIPMENT RECOMMENDATIONS

The Datamarine Navigator 3200 (Fig. 8.15), which lists for about $750, has excellent signal processing and stands up well in the cruising environment. Standard Communications' SL 20 is also a good unit and is less expensive, with a list price of $299.

SOUND-SIGNALING EQUIPMENT

Under the U.S. Inland Rules, certain vessels are required to carry sound-signaling devices with which to announce their intentions to other vessels in meeting and passing situations or to announce their presence in conditions of reduced visibility. Annex III of the Rules requires vessels 39.4 feet (12 meters) or more but less than 65.6 feet (20 meters) in length to carry a bell and a whistle capable of emitting a tone of 250 hertz to 525 hertz which is audible for at least half a mile or "other equipment" capable of producing a tone in the required frequency band which is audible over the same distance, provided the tone can be activated manually. (Vessels under 39.4 feet are not required to carry specific sound-signaling equipment, but if they do not, they must carry some other means of making an efficient sound signal, though no minimum range is defined.)

Under the "other equipment" clause in the Rules, many powerboat cruisers use an electronic loud-hailer/automatic fog horn to meet the requirement for sound-signaling capability. If you choose to exercise this option, your loud-hailer/automatic fog horn should be a separate piece of equipment with a 25-to-30-watt amplifier. In my opinion, the best value for the money in such gear is Standard Communications' 30-watt LH-10 unit which lists for $495 but sells through the marine catalogs for around $350. It requires a separate projection horn which adds about $60 to its price. With the addition of up to four speakers at around $50 each, it also can be used as a ship's intercom.

OMEGA

Omega is a land-based system that provides radionavigation fixes worldwide and continuously in all weather. However, I would not recommend that you consider Omega for offshore cruising for several reasons: It is subject to a number of anomalies that can cause its fixes to be unreliable unless they can be corroborated by another navigation system; its accuracy rate of 2 to 4 nautical miles is low; Omega receivers with the features required to make effective use of the system are expensive; and Transit satellite receivers—and GPS receivers when the system becomes fully operational—provide more reliable and more precise open-ocean navigation fixes at a comparable equipment cost.

TRACK AND VIDEO PLOTTERS

These are the newest marvels to hit the marine electronics scene—so new in fact that even their terminology is not yet clear. For our purposes: A *track plotter* is a unit that creates a graphic display of your vessel's course track, present position, and future dead-reckoning course based on information from an integral or external Loran C, Transit, or GPS satellite receiver without reference to an electronically generated representation of a nautical chart.

A *chart plotter* is a unit that creates a graphic display of the same information from the same sources but does so in reference to an electronically generated representation of a standard nautical chart.

TRACK PLOTTERS

These relatively simple gadgets can be thought of as a kind of electronic Etch-a-Sketch. Most of them combine both the screen required to present their graphic display and the source of the electronic navigation information required to create it in a single unit. The Furuno FSN-70, for example, combines a cathode-ray tube (CRT) with a Transit satellite navigation receiver. The Furuno GP-300 combines a CRT with a GPS receiver. The Furuno GD-2000 (Fig 8.16) carries the track-plotting idea a bit further by displaying track information on a color radar screen.

Basically, all that a track plotter does is accept fix information electronically from its associated navigation receiver and display it as a track across the display. Most units automatically update vessel position every few seconds and allow you to change the update interval based either on time or distance traveled.

If you want a visual display of your vessel's position as an adjunct to the electronic navigation equipment you decide to in-

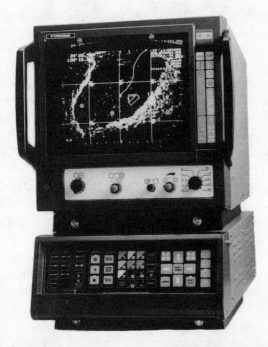

Fig. 8.16: *A track plotter indicates a vessel's position and movement without reference to a nautical chart.*

stall, fine. But a track plotter should never be used as any kind of substitute for old-fashioned position plotting on a standard nautical chart. I personally find them nothing more than amusing toys designed to appeal to the video generation.

CHART PLOTTERS

Chart plotters are considerably more sophisticated units that display your vessel's position and course track on an electronically generated represention of the appropriate nautical chart. Most of these electronic representations (they really shouldn't be referred to as "charts") are monochrome and are stored on microchips, read-only-memory (ROM) cards, various types of cartridges, and computer floppy or hard disks. Some units display their chart representations on an LCD screen, others use a CRT. In most cases the chart representations are quite large-scale and you can zoom in electronically and "blow up" the part you want to look at.

These units are only useful if they have chart representations for the areas you want to cruise in sufficient clarity, accuracy, and detail. Of the chart representation systems currently on the market, the C-Map system which is used by the Datamarine Chartlink plotter has the widest inventory, but it provides extremely limited detail. Through the use of a compact disk that is read by a laser, Laser Plot, Inc.'s ChartNav 20/20 unit (Fig. 8.17) presents its digitized chart representations in color, and its detail is as good as if not better than paper charts. The price tag for this degree of detail is stiff, however, as the unit lists for $12,000.

Considering television's dominant influence and our in-

Fig. 8.17: Video chart plotters like the Laser Plot ChartNav 20/20 plot vessel position and movement in reference to digitized nautical charts.

creasing dependence on computers, electronic chart plotting is likely to be the wave of the future. It will be a long time before traditional paper charts disappear completely, but I think more and more they will be relegated to a secondary role until in time they take their place in the maritime museums beside the pelorus and the astrolabe.

But we are not at that point yet. Electronic chart-plotting technology is making rapid strides; it is making available a wider selection of chart representations and is refining their detail and accuracy. For now, however, I would consider this segment of the marine electronics industry to be in its adolescence, and I would hold off acquiring any of these units until electronic chart plotting has matured.

9

CRUISING COMMUNICATIONS

In cruising, your marine radios have one overriding purpose: to protect your own life and well-being and that of the others aboard your vessel for whom, as its captain, you are legally and morally responsible. When it comes to freedom, those of us who have a passion for bashing around the boondocks in small boats get the best of it. But there is a cost. If we get in a jam, the hospital emergency room is a little farther away than the end of the block. When trouble strikes, more often than not the only link we've got with the outside world is our marine communications system and it had better work—right and the first time.

Imagine for the moment it's a black and violent night; you are far out at sea and have a fire on board, or your vessel strikes a submerged log and is seriously holed. Or pretend you are in a remote anchorage on the back side of beyond and a member of your party suffers a heart attack, a broken bone, or a nasty blow on the head. Then look at the radio you are about to purchase and ask yourself: Under those conditions, is this the piece of equipment I want to depend on to bring the cavalry running? It will help you cut through a lot of fancy salesman's talk about color-coordinated front panels and remotes in the master stateroom. In considering marine radios, we'll put our emphasis here on the two distinct types of radios you are going to need for serious cruising: a Very High Frequency (VHF) set for communicating with other vessels and coast stations within roughly ten to forty miles of your position, and a single sideband (SSB) unit for long-range communications. Some experienced long-distance cruisers also find amateur (or ham) radio useful, and we will cover it in enough detail to help you decide if it is an option you would like to explore further. There are three types of marine communications we will not cover. Citizens-band (CB) radio and cellular telephones have a limited range which makes them essentially useless in cruising. Nor will we cover satellite marine communication because the price, complexity, and weight of the equipment it requires put it out of reach for all but the mega-yachts.

In this section, we'll help you equip your boat with VHF and SSB marine radios and their associated equipment—properly installed so they provide maximum communications efficiency. We'll also offer some hints on getting the most out of your marine radios and review what you have to do to operate them legally—especially on the high seas and in the waters of other countries.

HOW MARINE RADIOS WORK

VHF and SSB in marine use have a number of factors in common. To understand those factors, we don't need to make you a radio engineer, but we do need to define a few technical terms you're going to run into.

Radio Waves, Frequency, Wavelength, and Amplitude: All radios operate through the use of radio waves, which are described by how rapidly (how frequently) they go up and down between a high point and a low point and back to their high point again. Think of frequency as a snake: If it's just ambling along, it moves like this: ∿∿∿ If it's in a hurry, it moves like this: ⌒⌒ The slow-moving snake illustrates low frequency: The rate at which its ups and downs pass a given point is low. The fast-moving snake, which undulates more, illustrates high frequency.

The distance from one midpoint of a radio wave to its next midpoint is its wavelength (Fig. 9.1). The lower a radio wave's frequency, the longer its wavelength. The higher its frequency, the shorter its wavelength.

The technical term for a radio wave's movement is *oscillation*. The technical term for the single movement of a radio wave from one midpoint to the next midpoint is a *hertz*, and the frequency of radio waves is most often measured in thousands of hertz per second, called *kilohertz* (kHz), or in millions of hertz per second, called *megahertz* (MHz). One megahertz equals a thousand kilohertz.

The term *amplitude* refers to how high or how low a radio wave swings to either side of its midpoint.

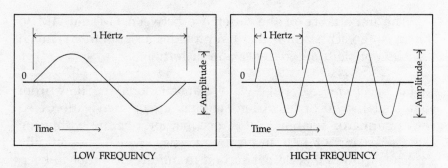

Fig. 9.1: *Radio waves are described by their frequency—the rate at which they go up and down from a high point to a low point and back to their high point again.*

Frequency Modulation versus Amplitude Modulation: Marine radios transmit human speech by distinguishing the pitch and resonance of the speaker's voice in one of two ways:

VHF radios use a technique called *frequency modulation* (FM) in which the radio wave's amplitude (its high points and low points) remains the same and speech is distinguished by minute variations in the signal's frequency. Graphically, an FM signal carrying human speech would look something like this:

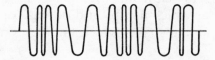

Single sideband marine radios use a technique called *amplitude modulation* (AM) in which the frequency remains constant and the radio distinguishes sound by minutely varying the radio wave's high points and low points. Graphically, an AM signal carrying human speech would look something like this:

The importance of the difference between FM and AM to the cruising yachtsman is that FM provides a signal that is much less susceptible to interference and distortion.

Radio Spectrum: All radio-wave transmissions, be they from commercial radio or television stations, aircraft navigation beacons, marine or aviation radios, or whatnot, operate within the same spectrum of radio-wave frequencies, which theoretically stretches from one cycle per second to infinity. In order to keep these various uses from overlapping and interfering with each other, most of the world's governments cooperate through the

International Telecommunication Union (ITU) to allocate group-ings or *bands* of frequencies for specific purposes—commercial broadcasting, marine communications, amateur radio, and so on. The bands reserved for marine use normally are referred to by their lower and upper limits in megahertz (often just called "megs"). We'll consider initially those bands of frequencies that are commonly used by cruising yachts (Fig. 9.2):

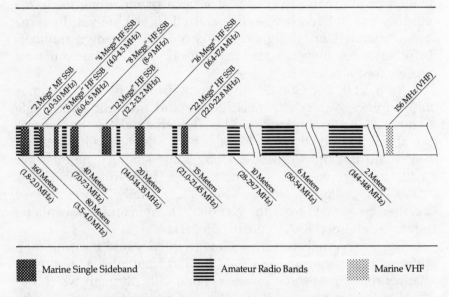

Fig. 9.2: *This presentation of a portion of the radio spectrum makes obvious the similarity of the frequencies used by marine single sideband radio and amateur radio operators.*

VHF marine radio operates in the single band between 156 and 163 MHz.

SSB marine radio breaks down into two subcategories which operate and are used in significantly different ways:

• *Medium-frequency* (MF) SSB operates in the 2–3-MHz band.

• *High-frequency* (HF) SSB currently operates in six bands: 4–4.5 MHz; 6–6.5 MHz; 8–9 MHz; 12.2–13.2 MHz; 16.4–17.4 MHz; and 22.0–22.8 MHz. In SSB jargon, these are referred to as the 2-meg, 4-meg, 6-meg, 8-meg, 12-meg, 16-meg, and 22-meg bands. (Because the 22-meg band runs all the way up to 22.8 MHz, it is also referred to as the 23-meg band, but don't let that throw you. Both references are to the same band of frequencies.) Proposals have been advanced which by 1991 would allocate additional frequencies for marine use in the 18- and 24-MHz bands.

Channels: In order for two radios to establish a communications link, they must be set to operate on the same frequency or pair of frequencies. Individual frequencies or frequencies that by regulation or international treaty have been paired—one for transmitting, one for receiving—are referred to as *channels*. In some cases, channels are designated by a one- to four-digit number. In other cases they are referred to only by their transmit and receive frequencies.

Both VHF and SSB channels come in two flavors—simplex and duplex. *Simplex* channels receive and transmit on a single frequency. An example would be VHF channel 16, the international calling and distress channel, over which a radio both receives and transmits on 156.8 MHz. Some simplex channels are "half" or "receive-only" channels. The VHF channel designated WX-1, for instance, allows "ship-receive-only" reception of weather broadcasts from the National Oceanic and Atmospheric Administrations (NOAA) on 162.55 MHz.

Duplex channels receive on one frequency and transmit on a different one. An example would be SSB channel 403, a popular channel for ship-to-shore radiotelephone calls, through which onboard radios receive on 4363.6 MHz and transmit on 4069.2 MHz. (Note: What we refer to throughout this book as "ship-receive" frequencies are sometimes referred to elsewhere as "coast-station-transmit" frequencies. Both terms refer to the frequency at which you receive transmissions on board your vessel.) Most duplex channels used by yachtsmen are not true duplex channels but are *semiduplex*. The practical difference between the two is that when you are communicating over a semiduplex channel, you have to push the microphone button down to talk and then release it to hear the person to whom you're talking. On a true duplex channel, this is not necessary.

In many—but not all—cases, the transmit and receive frequencies of both VHF and SSB duplex channels are covered by international treaties and are the same worldwide.

Crystals, diodes, and synthesizers: Making a radio operate on a particular frequency or pair of frequencies can be accomplished in three ways: by installing *crystals* that allow a radio to either transmit or receive on a single frequency; by using *diodes* that allow a radio to operate over a small group of perhaps a dozen frequencies; or by using a gadget called a *synthesizer* that allows the radio to transmit and receive on a great many different frequencies. Virtually all installed VHF and SSB marine radios sold in the United States now employ synthesizers. Crystals and diodes are used primarily in hand-held VHF radios that have limited channel capacity.

Propagation: This term refers to the manner in which radio waves of different frequencies react to the *ionosphere,* the naturally occurring layers of electrically charged (ionized) gas molecules that surround the earth.

Until a gas molecule in the earth's upper atmosphere is struck by the sun's radiation, it is electrically neutral—its positively charged nucleus is in balance with its negatively charged electrons. Ionization occurs when ultraviolet radiation released by solar storms on the surface of the sun strikes a gas molecule and knocks some of its negatively charged electrons free from its nucleus (Fig 9.3). What is left is a positively charged atom called an *ion.* So long as ions remain positively charged, they reflect radio waves back to earth like a mirror. As ions hurtle through the atmosphere, they in time will encounter electrons that have been

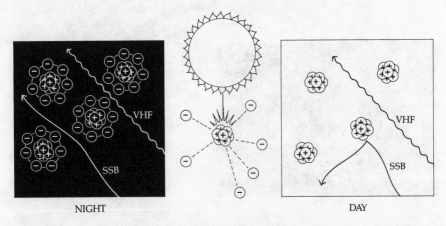

Fig. 9.3: *As the sun's rays strike gas molecules in the earth's atmosphere, they free negatively-charged electrons from the nucleus to create positively-charged ions. It is these ions which reflect radio waves in the marine single sideband frequencies back to earth.*

knocked loose from their nucleus and will combine with them to become electrically balanced or neutral again. After that happens, they will no longer reflect radio waves.

The ionization of the ionosphere has to be at a middle level for effective radio communication to take place. If there are too few ions floating around in the ionosphere, higher-frequency radio waves pass right through it and out into space. If the ionization level is too dense, it can actually absorb low-frequency radio waves.

Since the ionization process depends on the sun's radiation, it obviously is not constant. As the earth rotates on its axis presenting various parts of its surface to the sun, ionization above the area exposed to sunlight builds to a peak shortly after local noon, then gradually decreases until it is nonexistent after dark. In addition, the rate of occurrence of the solar storms that produce the ionizing radiation increases and decreases in a predictable eleven-year cycle. (The next peak during which global communications will be easiest will be in 1992.)

The ionosphere is divided into three layers (Fig. 9.4):

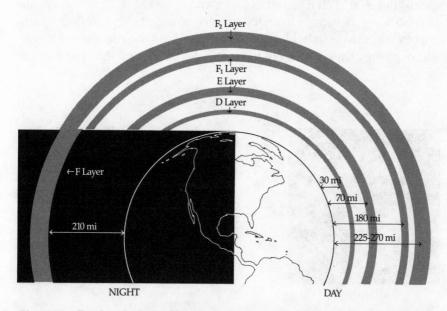

Fig. 9.4: *During daylight hours, ionization of the atmosphere creates the D, E, F1, and F2 layers at differing heights above the earth. At night, the D and E layers are not active, and the F1 and F2 layers combine into a single F layer.*

The D-layer is closest to the earth's surface—only about thirty to fifty miles up. Atmospheric gases are so dense at that level that ions quickly recombine with free electrons and lose their ability to reflect radio waves. The D-layer is only active about two hours before and two hours after local noon. It is so poorly defined and turbulent that when it is active it absorbs longer waves (2 and 4 MHz), making them useless for long-distance communication during those hours.

The E-layer is about seventy miles above the earth's surface. Its ionization gradually builds during the morning hours until it peaks shortly after local noon, then gradually dissipates during the afternoon, becoming nonexistent after dark. It reflects relatively low-frequency radio waves and is principally useful for short-range communications—from a few hundred to about 1,500 miles.

The F-layer is the highest, varying from about 180 miles to 270 miles above the earth's surface. Up that high, there are very few gas molecules. When an F-layer molecule has some of its electrons knocked free of its atom and becomes an ion, it tends to remain an ion for a fairly long time before it encounters free electrons, recombines with them, and loses its ability to reflect radio waves. For that reason, the F-layer does not lose all its ionization when the sun goes down but tends to remain ionized or "active" throughout the night.

The F-layer is actually composed of two sublayers—F1 and F2—which are separate during daylight hours but combine into a single layer at night.

During daylight hours, the F1 layer is about 180 miles above the earth's surface and is useful for reflecting higher-frequency radio waves over distances of about 2,000 miles.

Also during daylight hours, the F2 layer is from 225 to 270 miles above the earth and has the greatest density of ions. It reflects higher frequencies than any of the other layers and is useful for communicating over distances of 2,500 miles or more.

At night the F1 and F2 layers combine to form the single F-layer about 210 miles above the earth which is responsible for nighttime radio-wave propagation.

Ground Waves and Sky Waves: Depending on their frequency, radio waves have varying degrees of two components: ground waves, which for a certain distance follow the earth's curvature;

and sky waves, which are radiated into the atmosphere. Radio waves in the medium-frequency (MF) SSB 2–3-MHz band act almost exclusively as ground waves, which allows them to be used for communications up to about 200 miles in the daytime and about 500 miles at night. Beyond that distance, they are absorbed by the electrical interference that occurs close to the earth's surface. Ground waves are highly susceptible to static from thunderstorms. Radio waves in the 4-MHz band also have a significant ground-wave component although they act primarily as sky waves.

Radio waves in the high-frequency (HF) 6–22 MHz SSB bands and the VHF 156–163-MHz band act almost exclusively as sky waves. Those in the HF SSB bands bounce off one or more of the layers of the ionosphere, which allows them to be used for truly global communications. Radio waves in the VHF band pass right through the ionosphere, which limits their use to a "line of sight" between the antenna of the transmitting radio and that of the receiving radio.

Skip Zones and Windows: Because HF SSB radio waves reflect off the ionosphere, they pass entirely over an area between the point from which they leave the earth and the point at which they are reflected back to it (Fig. 9.5). In this area, called the *skip zone*, communications on that frequency under those conditions are impossible. The point at which the radio waves return to earth where they can again be received is called the *window*. Under certain conditions, HF SSB radio waves can be reflected between the earth and the ionosphere more than once. In each successive reflection, they create another skip zone in which communication is impossible and another window where communication can be achieved.

THE MARINE COMMUNICATIONS SYSTEM

A marine radio consists of a transmitter section and a receiver section (commonly combined into a single unit called a *transceiver*). The transmitter section has an amplifier that provides power for outgoing signals, and the receiver section has a second amplifier which increases the audio level of incoming signals to make them audible to the human ear. But the radio itself

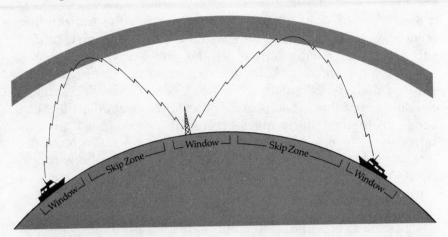

Fig. 9.5: *Depending on the state of the ionosphere and the characteristics of the marine single sideband frequency selected, radio-wave "skip" makes communications on that frequency impossible at certain distances but allows communication through "windows" which can be thousands of miles apart.*

is just one part of the total system. The other critical ingredients are the radio's antenna and power supply, your boat's radio-frequency-grounding system, and the proper installation of these various components. We'll consider each of these factors in detail as we discuss each of the types of marine radios.

VHF MARINE RADIO

VHF is the most common and widely used type of marine radio because—within its range limitations—it can be used for contacting lifesaving and rescue services such as the U.S. Coast Guard, other vessels, or a host of shoreside receiving stations ranging from bridge tenders and harbor masters to marinas and restaurants. VHF frequencies also carry official National Oceanic and Atmospheric Administration (NOAA) marine weather reports and navigational notices. You can also use it to contact shore-based marine radiotelephone operators who connect you with the land-based telephone system. These marine operators can also connect you with boats out of direct range of your VHF equipment.

We said that because VHF radio waves have no significant ground wave and are very-high-frequency "fast snakes" that wiggle right through the ionosphere they are useful only along a clear "line of sight" between the antenna of the transmitting station and that of the receiving station. Due to the curvature of the earth, the reliable range of VHF radio-wave ship-to-ship transmissions normally is limited to around ten to fifteen miles because the vessels' antennas are so close to the earth's surface. Reliable VHF transmissions in ship-to-shore communications can range up to about forty miles because the shore-based antenna normally is several hundred feet high (Fig. 9.6; 9.7). Note the term "reliable transmissions." Under certain atmospheric conditions, VHF radio waves can transmit considerably in excess of these approximate ranges, but those anomalies should not be depended on to provide consistent communications.

Marine use of the VHF band is divided up worldwide into more than a hundred working channels. In addition to the working channels, another eleven VHF channels (WX–1 through WX–9 and channels 15 and 70) are "receive-only" channels for weather and environmental information and other special purposes we'll discuss later. Of the worldwide total, fifty-four are allocated for marine use in the United States. Of these fifty-four, eleven are reserved for commercial users and five for the U.S. Government.

VHF radios on board vessels are limited to a maximum 25 watts of transmitter power and they are required to be able to reduce their power output to no more than 1 watt for short-range communications. Except in certain special instances, operations on VHF channels 13, 17, and 67 must be conducted on this 1-watt setting, and VHF marine radios manufactured after

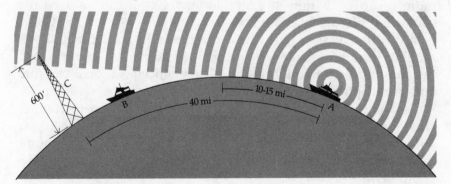

Fig. 9.6: *Because VHF radio waves travel in a straight line but the earth curves, vessel A can communicate with tower C but not with vessel B whose antenna is not high enough off the water.*

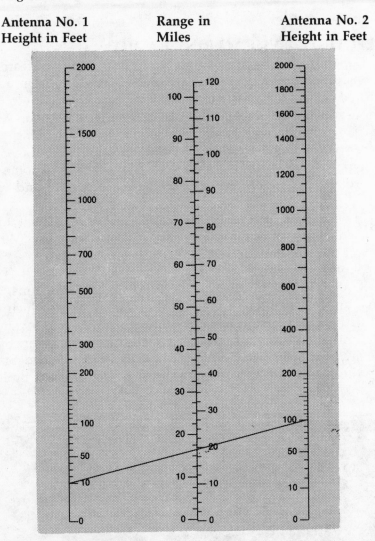

Fig. 9.7:   *Based on the installed height of your vessel's VHF antenna and that of the vessel or coast station with which you are attempting to communicate, you can use this chart to compute your VHF radio's approximate range.*

January 21, 1987, must automatically shift to this 1-watt mode when transmitting on channels 13, 17, and 67. They also must have a manual override to allow maximum transmitter power on channel 13 in emergencies.

SELECTING A VHF MARINE RADIO

Depending on how elaborate you get in terms of features, options, and accessories, you can spend anywhere from a few hundred dollars for a basic installed VHF radio (Fig. 9.8) to over a thousand dollars if you buy a unit with all the goodies and add remote units and hand-held equipment. In making your choices, you are going to have to wade through a lot of marketing hype. Here's a rundown on what's available and some advice from experienced cruisers on what is important and what isn't:

In deciding which particular brand and model of VHF radio to buy, the first question that comes to mind may be, "Which one will transmit the farthest?"

Wrong question.

If all other factors—such as atmospheric conditions, antenna, and installation—are equal, the distance over which one VHF radio will transmit a signal compared to that of a comparable unit is basically a function of its transmitter power. Since virtually all the installed VHF units sold in the United States have the maximum 25-watt transmitter power allowed by law,

Fig. 9.8: *The cruising console of this vessel provides a neat, convenient place to install both its marine single sideband and VHF radios.*

that can't be your basis for comparison. So the most important factor in selecting a VHF radio is its ability to *receive* signals. That ability can vary widely among units with vastly differing prices, and the most expensive unit is not always the best.

Reception ability is based primarily on two factors—selectivity and sensitivity. Probably the more important of the two is *selectivity* (also referred to as "adjacent channel rejection"), which indicates a radio receiver's ability to reject unwanted signals and accept only the signal you are trying to hear. It is usually expressed as a negative number of decibels ($-$db). The more negative the number, the better the adjacent channel rejection of the receiver. A receiver with an adjacent channel rejection of -70 db, for instance, will perform significantly better than one with an adjacent channel rejection of -50 db.

Sensitivity is the radio's ability to bring in weak signals over the background noise inherent in any radio transmission. It often is expressed as the number of microvolts (μV) required to produce 12 decibels SINAD. SINAD is a measure of signal strength relative to background noise and distortion. The lower or smaller that signal-strength number, the better the sensitivity of the receiver. For example, 0.3 μV for 12 db SINAD is better than 1.0 μV for 12 db SINAD.

In comparing the selectivity and sensitivity of competitive VHF radios from their manufacturers' specification sheets, bear in mind that the figures are not validated by any independent authority and should be viewed with some skepticism. Some marine radio manufacturers don't list the selectivity and/or sensitivity of their receivers in their consumer literature. I would insist that the dealer provide me with these figures so I could have a rough basis for comparison with those of other units I was considering.

In its new Infinity VHF receiver, Standard Communications uses a device called a "gallium arsenide field-effect transistor" (GASFET) which was developed by the company's SATCOM division, a primary supplier of broadcast satellite receivers. The company's claims about its GASFET technology are not just marketing hype. In situations where an incoming signal is exceptionally weak or there is a high level of background noise, GASFET really does give the Infinity unit the ability to receive signals other sets can't.

Virtually all installed VHF radios now sold in the United

States are synthesized sets that will operate on all the marine VHF frequencies. Most are programmed to access all U.S. and International marine VHF channels and have a switch that aligns their transmit and receive frequencies accordingly. The number of channels most manufacturers claim is inflated; they are counting U.S. and International channels twice and boasting of "ten weather channels" when only four actually carry weather broadcasts.

Several manufacturers have been marketing VHF radios which they advertise as having "access to 95 expansion or Private channels pending FCC approval." This is pure marketing baloney. The background to these claims is that there are some frequencies in the VHF band that the FCC has not authorized for use because of their potential for interfering with existing channels. In trying to develop a marketing advantage, some VHF manufacturers have included these frequencies in their equipment but blocked their access from the radio's normal operating controls. In order to activate them, it is necessary to go inside the radio and flip a switch or make minor adjustments to the radio's frequency programming. Even though it is strictly illegal, some individuals and a few electronics dealers have gone into these radios and made the necessary adjustments and are using these "private" frequencies. The FCC has no plans under consideration to allocate additional VHF channels for marine use. In October 1988, in fact, it proposed a new rule to prohibit the manufacture, importation, sale, or installation of VHF radios capable of operating on other than the authorized marine frequencies. Even if that proposal is adopted, however, it would allow the manufacture and importation of such radios for a year after the final order is issued, and the sale and installation of such radios for two years, so we will continue to see these units on dealers' shelves for the foreseeable future. Under a "grandfather" clause in the proposed rule, units with this capability sold prior to the cutoff date could still be used on authorized frequencies, but not, of course, on unauthorized frequencies.

Once you've found a VHF radio you are really interested in, try to get a look at that model in operation on a sunny day, preferably one that is installed on an open flying bridge with the sun shining directly on it; if you can read its display clearly, you'll be able to read it in just about any conditions you're likely to encounter. If you can't, look for another unit. Also make sure it provides for single-button selection of channel 16, which could be useful in an emergency.

Beyond those factors, you can buy VHF marine radios today with options to do just about everything but bring you a cold beer. You can get units that will scan all channels or scan only the channels you preprogram. Regency Electronics' Polaris models provide a visual display of the bearing from which a transmission is being received, and Apelco makes a separate unit that connects to a VHF to do the same thing. That might be of value to tournament sportsfishermen trying to find out where a less-than-generous competitor has raised a fish, but I don't really see its value in cruising. Pick and choose among these goodies to select whatever turns you on and fits your pocketbook.

One feature being built into several of the newer VHF radios on the market which I do think is valuable is the ability to sound an alarm when it picks up the alerting signal NOAA transmits just prior to broadcasting a severe weather alert.

In addition to a basic installed VHF radio, you can also buy remote VHF units for installation aboard your vessel in locations other than your primary operating station (for instance, on the flying bridge of a vessel normally operated from a pilothouse). My personal preference would be to install a completely separate VHF on the bridge, along with a separate antenna, as a backup in case my pilothouse unit went on the blink.

Some VHF manufacturers advertise that their radios can be made to do double duty as a ship's loud-hailer, and some also incorporate an automatic foghorn. A VHF radio is such an important piece of equipment on a cruising boat that I feel it should be dedicated exclusively to the job of communicating with other vessels and the shore. If you have a loud-hailer and automatic foghorn on your boat, it should be a separate piece of gear with a 25- to 30-watt amplifier. The speaker amplifiers in the receiver portion of VHF radios normally are only about 4 watts, which is not sufficient for communicating with a loud-hailer over any distance. As mentioned in Chapter 8, the best loud-hailer value on the market is Standard Communications' 30-watt LH-10 unit, which lists for $495 but is available through the marine catalogs for around $350. It requires a separate projection horn which adds about $60 to its price. With the addition of up to four speakers at around $50 each, it can also be used as a ship's intercom.

Some VHF radios can also be made to double as a ship's intercom system. If you will cruising shorthanded, an intercom can be valuable if, for example, you need to summon the off-watch without leaving the helm. But, again, if you install one, it should be a separate system or part of a loud-hailer and not involve one of your basic links with the outside world. For a reasonably priced stand-alone intercom, you might consider Newmar's Phone-Comm, which offers the equipment for a two-station setup for only about $260. (Unless you do it yourself, expect the installation of an intercom to be costly, because the power and audio cables the units require have to be snaked through the boat and this can be time-consuming.)

HAND-HELD VHF RADIOS

You will need a good hand-held VHF radio (Fig. 9.9) for communicating between your vessel and its tender, and you'll have to sort through about the same number of options on these as you do for the installed sets. Most of the units now available are about 6 inches high and weigh about a pound. Hand-helds may legally have up to 25 watts of transmitting power, but practical considerations of battery weight limit them to about 6 watts. Even with that low power, these units provide dependable communication over a three- to five-mile radius.

Most hand-held VHF's are powered by 13.2-volt rechargeable nickel cadmium (NiCd) battery packs with about 450 milliamp hours of capacity. With a current drain of around 1.5 amps when transmitting at 5 watts output and around 150 milliamps when receiving at maximum audio output, you can get five to ten hours of normal operation before the battery pack needs recharging. Transmitting range drops sharply as battery power runs low. You can purchase higher-powered battery packs with up to 900 milliamps of capacity, but they weigh more. Most hand-helds come with a plug-in transformer for recharging off an on-board 120-volt generator or shore power. You will find that the optional drop-in type charger is more convenient. The less hassle recharging is, the less likely you are to forget to do it. I would not rely on battery packs that use AA alkaline or nickel cadmium disposable batteries because they have a limited shelf life. On a lengthy cruise, the ones you brought from home may be almost dead by the time you need them, and there is no way to tell

Fig. 9.9: *A good hand-held VHF radio is a useful tool to meet a variety of cruising communications situations.*

how long the ones you can buy in the boondocks have been on the store's shelves.

Most hand-helds come with a standard flexible antenna which is handy but has limited range. If you find that range is a problem, an optional telescoping antenna will increase it up to 50 percent.

If you opt not to install a separate VHF as a backup, you can make your hand-held serve as a poor second choice by purchasing a linear amplifier that boosts its transmitter output to 25 watts. Also make certain it can be connected to your installed VHF antenna. Hand-helds with standard BNC-type antenna connectors will do that without modification. For hand-helds without a BNC connector, have a radio technician rig you an adapter. If you are going to rely on your hand-held for a backup and elect not to buy a linear amplifier, at least buy a DC regulator that will allow the hand-held to operate directly off your 12-volt ship's battery without going through its own batteries. If you get in a jam and need it, you may not have time to wait for the battery pack to recharge. If you get far enough down in your radio inventory to need the hand-held that is rigged that way and is putting out only 5 or 6 watts, it may not do much good, but you might as well cover yourself in every way possible.

Some manufacturers are coming out with micro hand-helds which are little bigger than an audio cassette tape and weigh only a few ounces. Because of their small size, they have only about 1 watt of transmitting power which limits their range to a mile or so, and their tiny batteries sharply limit the length of time they can be used before needing a recharge. They may be fine for use around the yacht club, but for serious cruising, get a serious hand-held.

VHF ANTENNAS

Even the best VHF marine radio is useless without an appropriate antenna. The antenna performs its function by resonating at the same frequency at which the radio to which it is attached is sending or receiving. The frequencies which the antenna is capable of resonating are a function of its length. Within limits, its length can be modified electrically. For technical reasons we won't go into here, the higher the frequency, the shorter the antenna; the lower the frequency, the longer the antenna. That's why a VHF antenna operating up in the 156-MHz band can be as short as 18 inches while a SSB antenna operating from 2 MHz to 23 MHz needs to be a minimum of 23 feet long.

Antenna gain: You'll see VHF antennas described by their *gain*, which refers to factors in their internal construction that determine their ability to radiate and receive a signal (Fig. 9.10). In signal transmission, think of gain in terms of a lighthouse. If you put a bare light bulb on top of a tall tower at the coast, its light would radiate with equal strength in all directions but would not reach out very far. But if you put a reflector behind the bulb that focused its light in a fairly narrow beam aimed at the horizon, the light would cover a smaller area but would be much stronger and would extend much farther away from the tower. In the receiving mode, think of gain as cupping your hand behind your ear. Both kinds of focusing are analogous to what gain does to a VHF antenna's ability to radiate and receive radio signals, except of course that the focusing occurs through 360 degrees continuously, in a kind of doughnut pattern, rather than sweeping a beam around the horizon like a lighthouse.

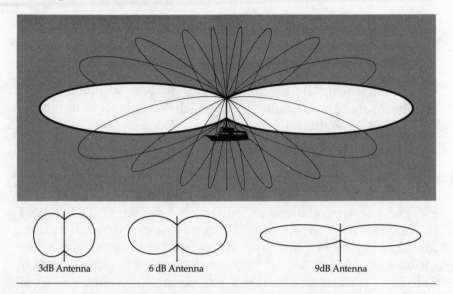

Fig. 9.10: This drawing dramatically illustrates the difference in gain between 3 db, 6 db and 9 db VHF antennas.

The illustration above makes the point that gain affects the strength of signals the antenna can send and receive over specific distances, not simply the distance itself.

Gain is expressed in decibels (db) and refers to the increase in the relative strength at which the antenna will radiate or accept a signal compared to a standard reference. Just what that standard reference consists of is something the engineers are still arguing about and gets too technical for us to deal with here. It will be sufficient for our purposes to say that a 0db-gain antenna—like the bare light bulb at the coast—radiates its signal equally in all directions. Every time you increase an antenna's gain by 3db, you double its effective transmitting and receiving ability.

3db gain = 2X increase (the effect of doubling your transmitting and receiving ability)

6db gain = 4X increase (the effect of quadrupling your transmitting and receiving ability)

9db gain = 8X increase (an eightfold boosting of your transmitting and receiving ability)

Note, however, that here we are talking about "transmitting and receiving ability," which refers to signal strength and clarity and does not mean you get a one-to-one increase in actual range. For a theoretical VHF radio with a 0db-gain antenna, for instance, increasing its signal strength by 9db would approximately double the distance over which it could communicate, not increase it eightfold.

The VHF antennas commonly sold for use on power cruising yachts usually have gain ratings of 3db, 6db, 9db, or 10db. Some experts recommend either a 3db or 6db antenna on the theory that the beam of a 9db or 10db antenna is so narrowly focused it can overshoot or undershoot its target as the boat pitches and rolls. A substantial majority of experienced cruisers find that beam overshoot and undershoot is not normally a factor on a sizable powerboat because the angle of pitch and roll is not nearly as great as that of a sailboat and the antenna is not mounted nearly as far off the water.

I'd equip my VHF radio with the highest-gain antenna I could afford (price increases significantly as gain increases) and one that I could securely install aboard my vessel with confidence that it wouldn't be swept away in rough weather. Length and weight, like price, increase dramatically as gain increases. Where a 3db-gain VHF antenna is normally 8 feet in length and weighs around 5 pounds, a 9db or 10db antenna can be up to 23 feet long and weigh up to 12 pounds.

In choosing a specific VHF antenna, look for rugged construction. Antennas that employ hollow copper or brass tubes for their radiating element hold up better than less expensive ones which use wire or coaxial cable. The unit should also incorporate a choking sleeve or stub that confines all its radiating effect to the antenna itself. Without a choking sleeve, the cable that connects the antenna to the radio may also radiate a signal and dilute the antenna's effectiveness.

VHF RADIO INSTALLATION

If your vessel has a valid ship station license, you may install VHF radio equipment yourself provided it has been pretested to ensure that it will operate only on its assigned frequencies. The manufacturers of all VHF radios legal for sale in the United States pretest their products before they ship them from the factory and certify that they operate only on the appropriate frequencies. Modifications that will change the operating frequencies, however, may be done only by or under the direct supervision of the holder of a General Radiotelephone Operator License.

You'll want a VHF transceiver within easy reach of your helm station—two if your vessel has a flying bridge. All your cruising radios should be installed in a location that protects them from rain and salt spray and allows ample room for air to circulate around them to dissipate the heat they produce.

Marine radios can be susceptible to interference from other on-board communications and navigational electronics and vice versa. Plan your installation carefully to keep your radios and their antennas separated as far as possible from each other and from other electronics and their antennas. In extreme cases, it may be necessary to install electronic filters on some of your on-board units in order to keep them from interfering with each other. That is a job for a qualified marine electronics technician.

Some VHF radios, particularly those with all-plastic cases, can be subject to feedback from their antenna's signal resulting in a high-pitched squeal or howl. Feedback can also play havoc with the memory of a VHF's channel programming and scanning functions. To prevent feedback, the radio and antenna should be installed so they are at least 6 feet apart.

Electrical ground for the radio is provided through its negative wire connection to the battery, but it should also be connected to your vessel's radio frequency ground (which we'll discuss later in this chapter). Ground for the antenna is provided by the coaxial cable connecting it to the radio. The key to assuring a good ground is that connections are made only between surfaces that are scraped down to bare metal and are kept tight and clean of corrosion.

Marine radios normally operate off 12-volt direct-current (DC) battery power and are extremely sensitive to inadequate voltage or amperage. The power cable should be as large in diameter as practical and should be run from the battery to the radio as directly as possible, avoiding kinks and crimps. Leave only enough excess power cable to allow a technician to remove the radio from the bulkhead and service the set without having to disconnect it.

The channel programming and scanning features offered in a number of VHF units can be highly susceptible to interference from main-engine and generator-engine starting loads. In extreme cases, it may be necessary to power your radios from a separate bank of batteries that is isolated from the batteries used for cranking your main engines and generators.

As discussed in Chapter 3, it's a wise precaution to install a backup DC power source for your essential electronics at the highest practical point in the vessel.

You should also mount your antenna as high on your vessel as you can, since the reception and transmission performance of your VHF marine radio will be directly affected. But increasing its height by only 4 or 5 feet with an extension will increase its effective operating range by only about a mile or so. Since your VHF antenna presents an attractive target for lightning to strike, you should also install it in a manner that will allow you to lay it down horizontally when you are in the vicinity of thunderstorms.

VHF LEGAL REQUIREMENTS

In order to operate a VHF radio aboard your vessel, you must have at least a Ship Radio Station License (often just called a "ship station license" or "ship license"). For operation in the waters of other countries, and in United States waters under certain circumstances, you will also need a Restricted Radiotelephone Operator Permit.

Ship Station License: Installed VHF radio equipment aboard your vessel must be authorized by the Federal Communications Commission under a valid ship station license which also assigns your vessel's call sign, which you are required to use to identify the source of your transmissions. You apply for a station license on FCC Form 506 which is available from most marine electronics dealers or the nearest FCC field office. All the devices on your vessel that emit radio waves—VHF and SSB radios, radar, and your Emergency Position-Indicating Radiobeacon (EPIRB)—require a station license. If you check the appropriate boxes on the application, a single station license will cover them all. No fee is required for a ship station license.

The FCC will license only marine radio equipment that it has "type-accepted." It is illegal to sell radio equipment in the United States for use on the commercial services that is not type-accepted. Do not buy some oddball brand radio on the black market or in another country that is not identified as "FCC type-accepted." The nearest FCC field office can tell you whether or not it is accepted; if it's not, you won't be able to get it licensed.

Before you apply, your vessel must be documented or numbered. If you will be living aboard your boat for extensive cruising, you may not have a permanent home address and wonder what to do with the "home address" line common to all FCC station and operator's license applications. You may list the address of an individual or company that will be taking care of mail for you, but you will be responsible for mail received at this address as if it were your permanent residence.

When you complete Form 506, you tear off a portion of it called Form 506-A and post it aboard your vessel. That gives you temporary authority to operate the radio equipment on board your vessel for ninety days from the date you mailed in the application. Until you receive your station license and call sign, on a documented vessel you use as a temporary call sign the letters "KUS" followed by your vessel's six-digit documentation number. On a numbered vessel you use as a temporary call sign the letter "K" followed by your vessel's number.

Once you receive your ship station license, you are required to keep it on board, preferably posted next to your radio equipment. Your station license will assign your vessel a permanent call sign of three letters and four digits in your name. Call signs may not be transferred from one boat to another or from one owner to another. If you sell a vessel that has been assigned a call sign, whether or not you leave its radios aboard, you should promptly return your station license to Secretary, Federal Communications Commission, Washington, DC 20554, and request its cancellation. If you fail to do that and the station is improperly used, you can be held liable for any penalties involved. The new owner will have to file a Form 506 application for a ship station license and a new call sign in his or her own name.

Changing your own name, your permanent address, or the name of your vessel does not invalidate a station license, but you are required to notify the FCC promptly of the changes in writing at P.O. Box 1040, Gettysburg, PA 17325, and to post a copy of the letter along with the station license.

Ship station licenses must be renewed every five years. Normally the FCC will mail the necessary renewal application (Form 405-B) to your address 120 days prior to the expiration date of

the license. If you don't receive a renewal form at least thirty
days before your station license expires, you should request one
from the nearest FCC field office since you must complete and
return it to them prior to the expiration date in order to stay
legal. If you get it to the FCC by the renewal date, you can continue to operate until you receive your renewed license.

Restricted Radiotelephone Operator Permit: In some cases the
operation of a VHF marine radio also requires a Restricted Radiotelephone Operator Permit (often referred to as an RP), which
is also issued by the FCC. In 1985 the FCC eliminated its requirement for an RP to operate VHF marine radios in "domestic waters"
(that is, within twelve miles of the United States coastline, which
includes the coasts of Alaska, Hawaii, Puerto Rico, and all other
U.S. possessions and trust territories). However, because of an
international treaty with Canada, an RP is required to operate
VHF marine radios in the Great Lakes on pleasure vessels over
65 feet in length. If you sail out of U.S. domestic waters into
international waters, you are not required to have an RP unless
you dock in a foreign port. In all cases you are required to have
a RP if you operate a VHF marine radio in the waters of another
country.

    You should go ahead and get an RP so that you can operate
your VHF in the waters of other countries. You will need one
anyway to operate an SSB radio, even in United States waters.
If you are eligible for employment in the United States, you apply for it on FCC Form 753. If you are not eligible for employment in the United States, you apply on Form 755. Form 753
applications normally come packed with new radios or are available from most marine electronics dealers. Both forms are available from the nearest FCC field office. The minimum age limit is
fourteen, and no fee or test is required. For temporary operating
authority while your application is being processed, fill out Part
3 of Form 753 or 755 and keep it with you. It is valid for sixty
days from the date you mailed your application. RP's normally
are valid for the lifetime of the licensee. In operating situations
where it is required, you must have the *original* of your RP with
you any time you transmit.

    In situations where an RP is required, you may allow per-
sons who do not have an RP to speak over the microphone of a
marine radio under your supervision, switch frequencies, and

the like, but you must begin and end the transmission with the appropriate identifications and operating procedures, and you are liable for any violations that occur during the transmission.

The FCC no longer requires you to maintain a radio traffic log, however the agency does recommend that you keep a record of any emergency transmissions in which you participate. (Enter that information as a part of your normal ship's log.)

The FCC does require you to keep a log regarding your radio equipment's installation, maintenance, and service history. Forms for this purpose are available through marine electronics dealers, but you can just as easily keep the information in your regular ship's log.

The ship station license that covers your installed VHF radio will also cover your hand-held VHF as an "associated ship unit." However, legally (except in emergencies) you may use your handheld only to communicate with your main vessel; you may not operate it from shore; you may transmit at only 1 watt of output power; and you must identify transmissions using the call sign of your main vessel and the appropriate "associated unit designator" (for example, "WXY 1234, mobile one"). Every cruiser I know blithely ignores all the foregoing.

Where necessary, your operation of a hand-held VHF is also covered by your RP.

VHF EQUIPMENT RECOMMENDATIONS

While there are a number of good VHF marine radios currently on the market, several of my cruising friends have found they get excellent service out of the ICOM M120, which lists for around $990. Because of its GASFET feature, superior water resistance, and reliability, you might also consider Standard Communications' Infinity unit, which lists at $995. In VHF antennas, the best units are from Shakespeare and Morad. I would go with at least a 6db-gain antenna in the form of Shakespeare's 8-foot model 5225 or Morad's 7-foot 156FG. In higher-gain units you might consider Shakespeare's 8db, 14-foot model 5230 or its 9db, 23-foot model 5208. Morad's 10db, 18-foot antenna is also an outstanding performer. In hand-held VHF equipment, I'd suggest you look at the 6-watt ICOM IC-M11 or the 6-watt Standard Horizon HX-220S. Both list for just over $650 but are available through the marine catalogs for under $400.

VHF MARINE OPERATOR RADIOTELEPHONE CALLS

Once you have a good VHF radio properly installed and licensed, you can use it to contact not only other vessels and shoreside facilities but VHF marine telephone operators who can connect you to the worldwide land-based telephone system. The rates for their services vary from company to company but generally run around $2.50 to $3.00 for the first three minutes and about a dollar for each additional minute. In addition, you will be charged the applicable long-distance rate from the marine operator's location to the number you are calling. You can place calls either station-to-station or person-to-person.

The billing procedures for VHF marine calls can be a bit of a hassle. The VHF marine operators owned by companies that also provide regular land-based telephone service (the Baby Bells and GTE, for example, issue a Marine Identification Number (MIN) which allows you to charge calls to your vessel. Contact the business office of the VHF marine operator nearest you and it will either send you an application or tell you where to get one. Some—but not all—privately owned VHF marine operating companies also honor MIN numbers. Some companies that don't honor MIN numbers allow you to charge a call to a regular telephone company credit card, your home phone, or a third number. Others won't allow charges to home or third numbers unless they can call and verify the billing information. When you bill calls in any of those ways, you are broadcasting information that anyone listening on the working channel could use to charge calls without your authorization. The best way to handle billing, providing the party you call agrees to accept the charges, is to call collect.

If you expect family, friends, or business associates to contact you from shore via VHF, it will be a great help if you give them your vessel's name, your call sign, and an itinerary. Also give them a listing of VHF marine operators in the area you will be cruising. To reach you, they simply dial 0 and ask for the VHF marine operator in the town closest to where you are expected to be at that point in your cruise.

To receive a shore-based call on board, monitor channel 16. If you are expecting a call and don't hear your call sign on 16, call the VHF marine operator in the area on their appropriate working channel and ask if they are holding traffic for you. The companies don't charge for traffic inquiry calls, but some of their operators get a bit testy if you bug them too often.

FOR FURTHER INFORMATION

The best publication on VHF radio operation is a small book produced by the Radio Technical Commission for Maritime Services called *Marine Radiotelephone Users' Handbook.* It covers licensing requirements and operational procedures in detail and contains a complete listing of VHF marine operators in the continental United States, Alaska, Hawaii, Puerto Rico, and the U.S. Virgin Islands. Its price is $7.95 and it is available from RTCM, P.O. Box 19087, Washington, DC 20036.

SINGLE SIDEBAND MARINE RADIO

Single sideband marine radio is completely different from VHF. Its range is much greater and its equipment (Fig. 9.8) is much more expensive and complex requiring a somewhat higher level of operator sophistication. SSB marine frequencies carry valuable official weather and Notices to Mariners information and can be used to contact other vessels and place distress or information calls to the U.S. Coast Guard and its counterparts in other nations. SSB radios can serve as the receiver for weather facsimile machines, and some models can be used for both voice and radiotelex transmissions. SSB is used most often in cruising by yachtsmen who are beyond the range of VHF to contact shore-based High Seas Radiotelephone coast stations and, through them, the land-based telephone system.

HOW SINGLE SIDEBAND RADIO WORKS

Medium-frequency (MF) SSB in the 2–3-MHz band functions through ground waves that can follow the earth's curvature for a certain distance. They can be used to communicate as far as 200 miles or so during the day and 500 miles at night if conditions are good. They are, however, extremely susceptible to interference from static during thunderstorms.

High-frequency (HF) radio waves in the 4–23-MHz SSB bands can be bounced off the ionosphere to produce truly long-range communications, in some cases virtually worldwide. As we mentioned in our discussion of radio-wave propagation, because ionization of the ionosphere is affected daily by the rising and setting of the sun, the range of the various HF SSB bands varies greatly according to time of day. We'll get into a more detailed discussion of the ranges and the best time of day to use particular SSB channels later in this section.

As with VHF, SSB has both simplex and duplex channels. Because of significant differences in their ranges and operating modes, the designations and use allocations of channels and frequencies in the MF SSB 2–3-MHz band and those of HF SSB in the 4–23-MHz bands are treated somewhat differently:

• Most frequencies in the 2–3-MHz MF SSB band are not covered by international treaties. Both the purposes for which these frequencies are used and the pairing of transmit and receive frequencies of duplex channels vary from country to country. Though there are exceptions (which we will cover later), most channels in the 2–3-MHz band are designated by their transmit and receive frequencies rather than by channel number.

• Most frequencies in the 4–23-MHz HF SSB bands are covered by International Telecommunication Union (ITU) agreements. The purposes for which these channels are used and the pairing of transmit and receive frequencies of duplex channels are essentially the same in ITU-member countries throughout the world. ITU channels are designated by three- or four-digit numbers. In three-digit channel designators, the first digit identifies the meg band in which it is located (for example, channel 401 is in the 4-meg band). In four-digit channel designators, the meg band is identified by the first two digits (for example, channel 2236 is in the 22-meg band).

Channel 2.182 MHz (almost always referred to by its kilohertz designation simply as "twenty-one-eighty-two") is reserved internationally as a calling and distress frequency and is used much the same way as VHF channel 16.

SSB radios licensed in the United States are allowed a maximum transmit power of 150 watts when operating on the 2–3-MHz band and 1,000 watts when operating on the 4–23 MHz frequencies. To be type-accepted by the FCC, units with more than 150 watts of transmitter power must shift automatically to 150-watt output when they are operated on 2–3 MHz.

SSB BAND SELECTION

One of the most important factors in achieving optimum SSB communication is selecting the right band. A good way to learn band selection is to listen to your SSB and make notes on what you hear in a logbook. In a loose-leaf notebook, assemble separate pages for distance groupings of under 500 miles, 500 to 1,000 miles, 1,000 to 2,000 miles, and over 2,000 miles. Down the left side of each sheet, space out the hours of the twenty-four-hour clock. At their scheduled times, listen to the traffic-list broadcasts of the High Seas coast stations and the U.S. Coast Guard's Notices to Mariners broadcasts. Try each of the channels on which each broadcast is made. When you hear a station clearly, identify its location and compute its distance from you. On the sheet in your listening log for that distance, make a note of the station received and the channel under the appropriate hour heading.

Once you have twenty or thirty entries in your log and are ready to make a call, compute the distance over which you wish to communicate. On your log sheet for that distance, alongside the hour you wish to make the call will be the channels over which you are most likely to make contact over that distance at that time of day. After a month or so of this kind of practice, you'll find it becomes almost automatic to make the calculations in your head. Where your log indicates you have a choice between two or more bands, try the higher one first since it is more likely to provide the greatest signal strength and the lowest atmospheric noise.

After you've worked with your SSB for a while, you'll find that the various SSB bands tend to have certain predictable characteristics:

The reliable range of frequencies in the 2–3-MHz bands is about 200 miles during the day, around 500 miles at night. The band is susceptible to static from thunderstorms but since it is ground-wave, it has no significant skip zone.

Channels in the 4-MHz band can be virtually useless from sunrise to late afternoon. In early evening, range increases to around 600 miles. At night, its skip zone makes contact difficult within 100 to 200 miles, but maximum range stretches up to 2,000 miles or more.

Channels in the 6-MHz band have a range of about 500 miles in daylight hours and stretch out to about 2,000 miles at night. However, because the 6-MHz band is subject to a number of anomalies, it is the least used of the HF SSB bands. A few 6-MHz channels are used by the Coast Guard, and High Seas station WHA operates over two, but they are not used by the AT&T High Seas stations or by WLO.

Channels in the 8-MHz band have a reliable range of around

700 miles all day with minimal skip zone. At night, skip zone is about 500 miles but beyond that, range can be 3,000 miles or more.

The 12-MHz band is inactive or weak until midmorning. Around noon skip zone begins to stretch out to around 500 miles and range to 2,000 to 3,500 miles. After sunset, skip zone gradually widens to about 2,000 miles and range to about 4,000 miles.

The 16-MHz band is inactive or weak until late morning. Around noon skip zone widens to around 750 miles and range increases to 4,000 to 6,000 miles. The band fades sharply about three hours after local sunset.

The 22-MHz band is inactive or weak until around noon, then strengthens, with skip zone widening to 1,500 miles and range up to 7,000 miles. It fades shortly after sunset.

Bear in mind that these are averages. Any of the SSB bands can be rendered temporarily unusable by atmospheric conditions or ionospheric disturbances for periods ranging from a few hours to several days.

SELECTING A MARINE SSB RADIO

Fortunately for the buyer, all the companies now marketing marine SSB radios in the United States make good equipment. Choosing among them comes down to a matter of what you want in the way of transmitter power and features—and the size of your budget.

Although SSB radios may legally have up to 1,000 watts of transmit power—technically referred to as "peak envelope power" (PEP)—when operating in the HF SSB bands, the choices are among units with 125, 150, 300, and 400 watts of output power. (It is technically possible to boost the transmitter power of any of these units up to the maximum allowable 1,000 watts with a linear amplifier. But, to be legal, the linear amp would have to be FCC type-accepted for use on the marine SSB frequencies. The linear amps sold through ham radio shops are not type-accepted, therefore would be illegal if used to boost the output of a marine SSB radio. Harris Corporation's RF-3230 linear amplifier is FCC type-accepted for use on the marine SSB frequencies, but its cost and weight makes it impractical for most pleasure yachts.)

Except in rare instances, 125 to 150 watts of output power is quite adequate to establish worldwide SSB communication. In an interesting experiment, for instance, Harris Corporation (using an optimally located, very tall transmission tower and waiting for just the right atmospheric conditions) established a clear SSB communications link between Rochester, New York, and Cairo, Egypt, using only a quarter-watt of transmitter power. Higher transmitter power does not necessarily guarantee greater range because optimum SSB performance is much more a function of antenna design, a good radio-frequency (RF) ground, favorable atmospheric conditions, and proper channel selection than is it of output power. The major benefit of higher power output is that it gives the user the ability to punch through electrical interference or literally overpower competing traffic on the frequencies he is trying to use.

Increases in transmitter power cost dearly. The units with 125 to 150 watts list for around $2,000 to $3,200, while 300-watt units sell for around $8,000 and those with 400 watts cost over $15,000. And those figures cover only the radio itself. All SSB radios require in addition a separate antenna coupler which adds at least another $1,000 to $1,500 or more to the price.

All SSB marine radios sold in the United States are synthesized to transmit and receive on all assigned frequencies from 2 MHz to 23 MHz, and most receive over an even wider spectrum, so there's not much choice to be made regarding frequency coverage. Aside from transmitter power, the differences among marine SSB radios lie in their capacity to store transmit-and-receive frequency pairs. SSB manufacturers ship their units with the paired frequencies of anywhere from fifty to more than six hundred ITU channels already programmed into their radio's memory, then allow the user to program additional channel frequencies into a "scratchpad memory" in the field. Field-programming ability is necessary because frequency-pairing in the 2–3 MHz band is not controlled under ITU agreements and varies from country to country. Field programming allows you to program appropriate 2–3 MHz transmission-and-reception frequency pairs into memory for recall as you move from country to country.

(Note: In order to create more channels, the World Radio Administrative Conference in the fall of 1987 voted to reduce the frequency spread for HF SSB voice transmissions from 1.3 kHz to 1.0 kHz. This means that the transmit-and-receive frequencies for most ITU channels will change by about 100 kHz. The date scheduled for the changeover is July 1, 1991, at 0000 hours Universal Time Coordinated (UTC). At such receiving stations as

Coast Guard facilities and High Seas coast stations, the change-over will occur in a matter of a few minutes, after which the frequency pairs of ITU channels that have been factory-pro-grammed into marine SSB sets will no longer be correct and can-not be used. The sets will have to be taken to an appropriately licensed FCC technician for reprogramming. At that time, ma-rine interests will be allocated frequencies in the 18-MHz and 24-MHz bands to which we currently do not have access.)

Most SSB radios house all their internal parts (except the antenna coupler) in a single case. Others have their transmitting amplifier and transceiver in a separate box that can be mounted out of sight, requiring only the controller to be mounted in an accessible location. These split units normally can accommodate two to four remote controllers that can be mounted in various locations around the vessel and can be used to both receive and transmit. In practice, a single controller properly located in your lower steering station will be sufficient. If you have money to burn, a second control unit on the flying bridge or next to your easy chair in the salon might be nice, but you don't really need either one.

One feature worth having which some SSB radios incorpo-rate is an internal International alarm. In an emergency, it can be used to alternately transmit two frequency tones on 2182 kHz at the touch of a button on the front of the unit. The signal sounds something like an ambulance siren and is intended to alert re-ceiving locations such as U.S. Coast Guard and High Seas coast stations that you are about to transmit an emergency message. Some receiving stations are equipped with detectors that ring a bell or sound a horn when the International alarm signal is re-ceived to get the attention of an operator. Under International agreements, you may transmit this alarm only if you follow it up with the Mayday distress or Pan urgency signal and then only for thirty seconds to one minute.

FIBERGLASS STICKS AND ANTENNA COUPLERS

In order to achieve optimum communications throughout the 2–23-MHz SSB bands, you will need a white fiberglass stick with a hollow copper tube inside it that is at least 23 feet long. (For reasons we'll get to shortly, don't think of this stick as an "an-tenna," just think of it as a white fiberglass stick with a hollow copper tube inside of it.) Larger vessels that can support the added weight can get even better performance from the same kind of fiberglass stick that is 28 feet long.

Because you will be operating your marine SSB radio on more than one band of frequencies, you will also need a coupler which automatically tunes the resonance of your antenna (here, as you'll see, it's okay to use the word "antenna") to match the frequency on which the radio is operating. All SSB manufacturers offer their own couplers which they suggest be used with their equipment. On the ICOM IC-700 and IC-700TY connected to the company's AT-120 coupler, you must push a button on the front of the transceiver to activate the tuning process, which takes two to three seconds. The SEA 222 and 322 connected to Stephens Engineering's SEA 1612 coupler activate tuning with the first voice syllable. The first time a frequency is used, the tuning process takes about five seconds. Once a frequency is tuned, it is retained in the 1612's memory. The next time it is needed, tuning takes only about 20 milliseconds. The Harris RF-3200 connected to the company's RF-3281 digital antenna coupler activates tuning when the microphone is keyed. The first time a frequency is used, tuning takes about a second. In subsequent uses of that same frequency, tuning takes only 30 milliseconds.

All but the Harris unit require the radio and the antenna to be connected by both a coaxial cable to carry the signal itself and a control cable to handle the coupler's tuning functions. Harris has multiplexed the tuning information inside the radio, which allows the tuning signal to be transmitted over the co-ax and eliminates the need for a separate control cable.

A frequently overlooked advantage of fully automatic antenna couplers is that in an emergency they can be used to tune practically any jury-rigged wire to a frequency you can use to get help.

SSB INSTALLATION

In this section, I'm going to say some things about marine SSB radios, antennas, antenna couplers, and installation that will run counter to just about everything you've ever heard on the topic. I assure you it is based on solid information from some of the best technical experts in the field.

When someone says "marine SSB antenna," you probably think of that white 23- or 28-foot long fiberglass stick we mentioned. Actually, that fiberglass stick is only half of the true antenna on your boat that radiates and receives SSB radio waves. The other half is your vessel's *radio-frequency* (RF) *ground* (sometimes referred to as capacitive ground, ground plane, or counterpoise). On a typical cruising boat, that true antenna doesn't really care where on your vessel you choose to install that fiberglass stick; it is going to start at the RF ground on your vessel, run up through the metallic strap that connects the RF ground to the fiberglass stick, and end at the top of the fiberglass stick—and there's not really anything you can do to change that. But you can take advantage of it rather than—as most marine SSB installations do—try to fight it. (Since the fiberglass stick portion of your true SSB antenna contains a hollow copper tube, it will be an inviting target for lightning. Install it as you do your VHF antenna in a manner that will allow you to lay it down horizontally when you are in the vicinity of thunderstorms.)

Because of this true antenna's obdurate insistence on obeying the laws of physics, its performance is not nearly as affected by how high you choose to install that white fiberglass stick as it is by how effective an RF ground you construct aboard your vessel. For effective marine SSB communications, this RF ground is absolutely, totally and completely critical. Without it you will never achieve optimum communications with HF SSB regardless of the quality or the transmitter power of your radio or the length of your fiberglass stick.

In addition to critically affecting your SSB radio's performance, a poor RF ground, or improper connection of your SSB radio and antenna tuner to it, can make your autopilot and analog electronic instruments go crazy when you transmit over the radio, can burn out tiny integrated circuits in your electronic equipment, and even give you a tiny RF shock when you place the microphone close to your mouth.

(Don't worry about gain in connection with SSB antennas. Because a marine SSB antenna directs its signal upward toward the ionosphere rather than toward the horizon as a VHF antenna does, the term *gain* does not properly apply.)

Creating an RF Ground: The key to creating an effective radio-frequency ground is making a good RF connection between your vessel and the water surrounding it. Because this RF connection shares some principles and terminology with the grounding needed for DC or AC electrical systems and lightning protection which we discussed in Chapter 3 people often get them confused. In fact, the two are quite different and must be thought of separately (and as nearly as possible, kept physically separate). In electrical grounding, for instance, a wire conductor's ability to carry current is analogous to a water pipe's ability to carry water: The critical measurement is its diameter. In RF grounding, the critical factor (due to something called "skin effect") is the conductor's surface area. An SSB antenna actually works by exciting electrons. The more surface area it has, the more electrons it can excite. For that reason, a copper strap only a few mils thick will not provide much of an electrical ground but it is an ideal RF ground because of its expansive surface area. Actually, copper or brass mesh screen provides a better RF ground than strap because in equal dimensions it has greater surface area. However, it is much more susceptible to corrosion and should be used only where it can be encapsulated in fiberglass (as in a vessel's cabintop or hull). Don't use flat braided battery cable for an RF ground as it corrodes much too rapidly.

As another example: Your vessel should have a bonding system that ties its engines, generators, and all other metal masses together with round wires. That's fine and necessary for electrical grounding and lightning protection, but it does not create an effective RF ground. For effective SSB performance, your bonding system must be duplicated (not replaced) with a separate RF grounding system composed of metal strap. The two systems will be interconnected in that they are both tied to the same metal masses, but they should not be deliberately interconnected at other points.

For effective SSB communication, you need to have an absolute minimum of 100 square feet of metal surface tied into your vessel's RF grounding system. Even more is better. On nonconducting hulls such as wood or fiberglass you want to get as much of that metal surface as possible below your vessel's waterline. In the following paragraphs I'm going to describe the optimum RF ground installation. While you will probably wind up doing something less expensive and time-consuming, at least you'll know what the experts recommend:

RF Grounding of Metal Hulls: Steel- or aluminum-hull vessels make an ideal RF ground. To take advantage of their RF grounding characteristics, their engines, batteries, metal through-hull fittings, metal water and fuel tanks, stainless steel or aluminum railings, copper water, fuel, and hydraulic lines, and any other masses of metal should be firmly connected directly to the hull—with copper strap, not round wires. If such a vessel's engines rest on insulating rubber mounts, for instance, they should be RF grounded to the hull. The large propellers on displacement-hull boats can also contribute to a good RF ground. To incorporate them, you will need a metal wiper brush that rests against the shaft and is RF grounded to the hull itself.

Once you have all the vessel's metal masses interconnected, you need to carry their grounding potential up to your electronics. To do that, drill a 3/8-inch hole in a stringer or other mass of metal that is below the waterline and is securely welded to the hull itself. The hole should be directly below where most of the vessel's communications and navigation electronics will be installed. Sand a 4-inch by 4-inch area around it down to bare metal. Double the end of a long 4-inch-wide copper strap over itself several times, drill a hole through the folded sections, and affix it securely into the stringer with a stainless-steel bolt and nut. (Anywhere you attach copper strap to a metal hull, put a stainless-steel washer between the two to help retard electrolysis.) Coat the area of attachment with several layers of paint to exclude water and help prevent corrosion. Run the strap up the inside of the hull to the vessel's uppermost deck. It may be painted or covered with fiberglass or interior paneling without affecting its RF grounding capability. We'll talk later about tying your electronic equipment into it.

RF Grounding of Nonconducting Hulls: For vessels with nonconducting hulls such as wood or fiberglass, RF grounding is considerably more difficult. If you should have the luxury of building your dream cruiser from scratch, you could create an ideal RF ground by having the builder laminate a minimum of 100 square feet of copper or brass mesh screen (remember, the more the better) inside the hull below the waterline. Again, the fact that the screen is not in direct contact with the water is no problem since RF energy passes through wood and fiberglass quite easily.

On an existing boat with a nonconducting hull, create an RF ground by running a minimum of 100 square feet of copper strap around the entire inside circumference of the hull below the waterline and connecting it to all metal masses inside the hull.

Connect it to round through-hull fittings with stainless-steel hose clamps, but keep it as flat as possible. Where the strap must be run through a small hole, loosely roll it lengthwise, pass it through, then flatten it out on either side of the obstruction. Bring the strap to a point where you will connect it to a second strap going from the inside of the hull to your pilothouse and flying bridge electronics. If your vessel will not have metal mesh in its cabin top (as we'll discuss just a bit further on), you should locate that point somewhere other than in the engine space.

Once you have a good RF grounding system installed inside the hull, connect it to a strap and run it up the inside of the hull in as direct a line as possible to the boat's electronics.

Whether the vessel is one with a conducting or a nonconducting hull, when you get this grounding strap up to your pilothouse, run a separate grounding strap from it to each piece of electronics on your vessel; the straps should be like the spokes of a wheel, not strung together one after another like Christmas tree lights. Every single piece of equipment in your pilothouse and on your flying bridge should be tied into the grounding strap from the bilge.

Don't weaken your RF grounding system by using round wires to connect the ground strap from the bilge to the equipment. If the electronic equipment has a ground-post stud with a nut and washer, fold the strap back on itself, drill a hole in it, and make your connection there. If no ground stud is provided, fold the strap, drill aligning holes and attach it to the sheet metal screws in the equipment chassis. Accordion-fold enough excess into the strap to allow the equipment to be removed from the bulkhead for "live" checks of its tuning.

You can also increase the area of an RF grounding system by installing copper or bronze mesh screen in a vessel's cabin-top. This screening can be installed beneath the headliner or laminated into the cabintop itself, but it also must be tied into your below-waterline RF ground with straps. It's better if that connection is made with straps at each corner of the screen rather than at a single point. Some cruising yacht manufacturers install an RF screen in their boats' superstructures at the factory. If that mesh is at least 100 square feet in area and is well connected to all the vessel's below-waterline metal masses, it probably will give you an adequate RF ground, and metal strapping in the bilge will not be necessary.

As I said, this kind of RF grounding system is the optimum and should be installed even if it involves a good deal of effort and expense. If you want more of the technical reasoning behind this kind of an installation, try to locate an article by Charles S. Carney, editor of the National Marine Electronics Association's *NMEA News*, which appeared in that publication's July 1975 issue and again in the November/December 1988 number.

If installing the system described above is simply impossible, you can do what most owners do to create an RF ground—install a couple of brass or copper plates at least a foot square outside the hull below the waterline and ground them firmly to all metal masses inside the boat. Use solid copper plates rather than the porous type, which, like round wires, are suitable for grounding DC and low-frequency AC electrical currents but not for RF grounding. Grounding plates won't work nearly as well as the system I've described, but they are better than no RF ground at all.

Coupler Installation: Your coupler should be installed at the base of your vessel's true antenna, not necessarily—as you have probably been led to believe—at the base of your fiberglass stick.

On properly RF-grounded metal-hulled vessels and vessels that have at least 100 square feet of properly installed metal mesh in their cabintops, the RF ground is in the uppermost deck and the true SSB antenna starts at the point where the ground and the fiberglass stick are connected (Fig. 9.11). You want to install your antenna coupler as close as possible to that point and ground the coupler to it with a metal strap that is as short as possible and at least 2 inches wide. The best location normally is in the cavity below the flying bridge console, which keeps the coupler out of the weather.

On wood- or fiberglass-hulled boats that do not have at least 100 square feet of properly installed metal mesh in their cabintops, your true SSB antenna starts at the point where you connected the below-water-level RF ground to the strap going to the pilothouse (Fig. 9.12). Your antenna coupler should be installed as close to that point as possible, which means belowdecks. Avoid making the connection in the engine room, where the coupler would be subjected to high temperatures.

If you disregard this recommended location and install your coupler—as most people do—in the pilothouse overhead, or be-

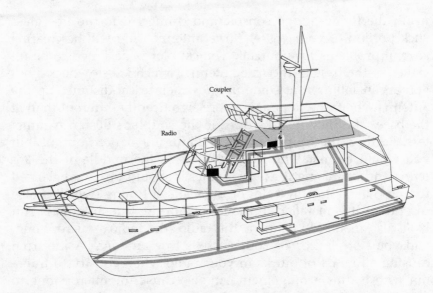

Fig. 9.11: *On a fiberglass or wooden cruising vessel with at least 100 square feet of radio-frequency ground screen in its cabintop, the SSB antenna coupler can be mounted beneath the flybridge at the base of the fiberglass stick.*

Fig. 9.12: *On a fiberglass or wooden cruising vessel which has no radio-frequency ground in its cabintop but only in its hull, the SSB antenna coupler should be mounted at the connection between the RF ground and the grounding strip which runs up to the fiberglass stick.*

neath the flying-bridge console and connect it to the fiberglass stick portion of your vessel's true antenna, you will be creating several problems for yourself. The coupler is designed to be installed at the base of the true antenna, which is belowdecks, but you are installing it at some unknown electrical distance up the antenna where the impedances are significantly different than at the base, and they may be outside the coupler's design parameters. Further, the coupler is designed for unbalanced output, but you would be installing it somewhere in the middle of the antenna and confusing it as to whether it should provide balanced tuning (which it cannot do) or unbalanced tuning (which it also can't do if it is installed in the middle of the true antenna). You have also made the coupler, the radio, the radio's microphone, and yourself all part of your vessel's true antenna. Aside from causing all kinds of quirks in your radio when you try to transmit with it, this arrangement can also cause the microphone to give you a tiny RF shock when you key its microphone.

Transceiver Installation: As with any piece of marine electronic equipment, an SSB transceiver should be protected from spray. Most cruisers install their SSB radios in the pilothouse. While the unit should be installed in a location that's handy to the helm, I don't recommend installing it in an overhead console. Selecting the proper band, finding a channel on which you can get the attention of a High Seas coast station, and switching channels to offset atmospheric interference can tie up a lot of time. It's much better to install your unit where you can reach all of its controls from a comfortable sitting position.

All the SSB units now on the market operate off 13.6-volt DC power. Current drain in voice transmission averages about 12 amps and in transmitting the International alarm about 17 to 20 amps. You can also buy an optional power converter to operate the unit off 120-volt AC.

SSB LEGAL REQUIREMENTS

Because SSB in the 2-MHz band overlaps that of VHF, your vessel must be equipped with a VHF marine radio before you add a marine SSB radio. The SSB radio can be installed only by or under the direct supervision of someone who holds an FCC General Radiotelephone Operator License or a First- or Second-

Class Radiotelegraph License. I continue to see statements in print to the contrary, but they are inaccurate. The FCC most recently reaffirmed its stance against owner installation of SSB radios on May 6, 1986, when, by its Order 86-234, it denied such a request by the Boat Owner's Association of the United States.

The vessel on which an SSB radio is operated must have a valid Ship Radio Station License and the operator must have a Restricted Radiotelephone Operator Permit.

SSB EQUIPMENT RECOMMENDATIONS

Before you make any decisions on an SSB marine radio, you should read through the sections on the use of amateur radio and telex in cruising, the discussion of weather-facsimile receivers and the NAVTEX system, all of which follow later in this chapter, because the decisions you make regarding those options will affect your choice of an SSB radio.

For SSB voice communications only, most of my cruising friends who are on a budget give high marks to Stephens Engineering Associates' SEA Model 222 and ICOM's M700, both of which are 150-watt units. The SEA unit with the company's 1612B antenna coupler lists for just under $3,000. The ICOM M700 matched to ICOM's AT-120 antenna tuner is priced at just under $3,500. I have not yet had an opportunity to see the 125-watt Harris RF-3200 in action, but based on past experience with Harris equipment, I would expect it to be an outstanding unit. The RF-3200 with an RF-3281 digital antenna coupler lists for just over $4,500. My friends with more elaborate resources report excellent results from the 300-watt Furuno FS-4001 and its antenna coupler, which lists for just under $10,000. If you want to really go first class, you can spring for Radio Holland's 400-watt Sailor Programme 1000B which, with its antenna tuner, lists for just over $17,500.

As a good 23-foot fiberglass stick for your SSB antenna, I'd suggest Shakespeare's 390 which lists for just under $150. If your choice of a VHF antenna is Shakespeare's 9db, 23-foot 5208 model, the company's 23-foot model 5308 stick will match it cosmetically. Another good choice in a 23-foot whip would be Morad's WH23W which lists for around $185. If your vessel will support a 28-foot fiberglass stick, look at Shakespeare's 5300 or Morad's WH28W, both of which will cost you around $225.

SSB MARINE OPERATOR RADIOTELEPHONE CALLS

Since your main use of marine SSB is likely to be for radio-telephone calls, we'll take a closer look at that subject.

There are two types of marine radiotelephone services that handle SSB calls to and from your vessel—the Coastal Harbor Service and the High Seas Service. Coastal Harbor Service stations handle SSB calls only on the medium-frequency 2–3-MHz band and are used primarily by marine interests on the nation's inland waterway system. Most yachtsmen who cruise offshore place ship-to-shore calls and receive shore-to-ship calls through coast stations in the High Seas Service, which handle calls on both the MF 2–3-MHz band and the high-frequency 4-, 8-, 12-, 16-, and 22-MHz bands.

There are four High Seas stations in the continental United States and one in the U.S. Virgin Islands. AT&T operates what experienced cruisers call the "big three"—WOM in Ft. Lauderdale, Florida; WOO in Manahawkin, New Jersey; and KMI in Point Reyes, California. Mobile Marine Radio, Inc., operates WLO in Mobile, Alabama. Global Communications Corporation operates WAH in St. Thomas, U.S. Virgin Islands.

Placing High Seas Radiotelephone Calls: While any High Seas coast station can handle calls to and from vessels anywhere in the world, each does tend to concentrate its directional antennas toward particular parts of the world (Fig. 9.13). If you are in the Pacific, it makes sense to try KMI first; if in the Caribbean or Gulf, WOM should be your first choice; if in the North Atlantic, try WOO first. The proximity of your vessel to a particular High Seas station, however, is less important than propagation factors. After placing a few High Seas calls, you'll get a feel for which stations you can reach most easily at different times of day.

Each station broadcasts "traffic lists"—the names of vessels for which they are holding calls—on specific channels at designated times. One way to place a call through a High Seas station is to listen to its scheduled traffic-list broadcasts and try to make contact on the clearest channel as soon as the traffic list is over. A dozen or more vessels may be trying the same tactic, so you may have to wait an hour or more to get through.

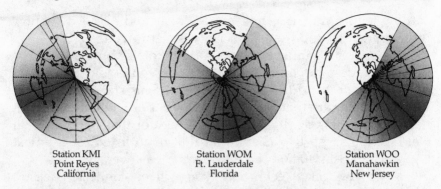

Station KMI
Point Reyes
California

Station WOM
Ft. Lauderdale
Florida

Station WOO
Manahawkin
New Jersey

Fig. 9.13: *Frequency selection and the state of the ionosphere are more important in determining which of the AT&T High Seas Coast Stations you can reach most easily. Each of the stations does, however, focus its directional antennas toward differing parts of the world.*

To relieve congestion, the High Seas stations urge customers to place calls at times other than the hour or so following the traffic-list broadcasts. To do that, figure the approximate distance from your vessel to the High Seas station you want to use. From your listening log (see page 256), select the most likely band to accommodate the hour and distance of your call. Tune your radio to one of the channels in that band listed for the High Seas station you want to call and listen to it for about three minutes. Remember that you are listening only to the channel's station-transmit frequency. If someone on another vessel is talking to the High Seas station, he'll be on the channel's ship-transmit frequency and you won't be able to hear him. If after about three minutes you don't hear any traffic on the channel, go ahead and make your call. A typical call to WOM might sound like this: "Whiskey, Oscar, Mike . . . Whiskey, Oscar, Mike . . . Whiskey, Oscar, Mike. This is the motor yacht Mad Hatter, Whiskey, X-Ray, Yankee 1234, calling from offshore St. Lucia on channel eight thirty-one." Giving the channel number you are using in your initial call helps the technician at the High Seas station to select it from among the twenty or more channels he or she is monitoring to respond to your call. Giving your vessel's position in your initial call helps the technician know where to point the station's directional antennas for the best connection. After making your initial call, wait about a minute before trying it again. If your call is heard, it probably will take the technician that long to select and tune the station's equipment. You may get a recording telling you all technicians are busy and to stand by. Stay on that channel and the technician will get to you.

If the first channel you try is busy, or if you can't raise a technician after three or four calls, shift your radio to another channel in the band listed for that High Seas station and listen there. Chances are that after two or three tries you'll find a channel that is not in use. If all channels listed for that station in that band are busy, go to a channel in that band listed for the next logical High Seas station, based on antenna coverage.

Once you get a technician, you will be connected with a telephone operator who will take the calling details and billing information and connect you with your party. If you want time and charges on the call, say so before the telephone operator makes the connection; operators will not honor time-and-charge requests after the call is completed. All High Seas calls are handled as person-to-person calls, even if you agree to speak with anyone who answers, and charges do not begin until the individual you call answers. Once you get your party on the line, if the person is not familiar with radiotelephone calls, briefly explain that you both need to say "over" after you have finished a segment of the conversation and the listener should not speak until he hears the speaker say "over." If you don't, you'll probably find you have to repeat a lot of missed conversation. If you encounter difficulties during a marine radiotelephone call, have the person you are talking to momentarily depress the switchhook on his or her telephone. This will stop billing time on the call and signal the operator. The telephone operator can then try the call again or bring in the High Seas technician if necessary to try another frequency.

When your land party hangs up, stay on the channel until the telephone operator comes back on the line. If you have another call, give the details and proceed as before. When you are through with your last call, again wait until the telephone operator comes on the line, have him or her reconnect you with the High Seas technician, and sign off the channel with the High Seas station.

As far as the AT&T High Seas stations (WOM, WOO, and KMI) and WLO are concerned, so long as the final destination of your call is in the United States (including Alaska and Hawaii), Canada, Mexico, Puerto Rico, or the U.S. Virgin Islands, the charges will be a flat rate no matter which of the coast stations you place the call through or the position of your vessel. (At this writing, the rate is $14.93 for the first three minutes and $4.98 for each additional minute.) If you are calling a country other than those listed, you will also be charged the person-to-person rate from the High Seas coast station to the call's destination.

You can place calls through the High Seas stations collect or have them billed to your home or office phone. But you will save yourself a lot of time if you preregister your vessel with the High Seas stations before you leave on your cruise. You can preregister with all three AT&T High Seas stations by calling toll-free 1-800-SEA-CALL, but you will have to preregister separately with the owners of WLO and WAH. Once your vessel is preregistered, all you have to do is instruct the operator to "bill the vessel calling." You also won't be giving out information that someone else might overhear and use to charge calls without your authorization.

Receiving High Seas Radiotelephone Calls: The normal way to receive a SSB radiotelephone call from shore is to periodically monitor the scheduled traffic-list broadcast over any of the High Seas stations to see if you have a call. All three AT&T stations broadcast the same traffic list, and you may return a call to the station of your choice. You can call a High Seas station to see if they are holding traffic for you without charge, but it's best to limit inquiry calls to other than the peak traffic hours during the midmorning, late morning, and early evening.

If your family, friends, or business associates want to reach you on board your vessel, and if you will be monitoring the traffic list of one of the AT&T coast stations, instruct them to call 1-800-SEA-CALL which will connect them with AT&T's central High Seas operator 11362 in Pittsburgh, Pennsylvania, where traffic lists for all three of the company's High Seas coast stations are coordinated. If you will be monitoring WLO's traffic list, instruct them to call 1-800-633-1634 and ask for the High Seas operator. Be sure they know the name of your vessel, its call sign, and its approximate location. Your vessel will be listed on the coast stations' next traffic list and will stay on the list until you answer or the shore party cancels the call. In cases where the call is not answered and the coast station cannot contact the calling party for instructions, the vessel normally will be removed from the traffic list after twenty-four hours.

Few cruising yachtsmen are aware of it, but if you equip your vessel with an SSB radio capable of receiving continuous-wave (CW) transmissions, which are the basis of Morse code, you can add peripheral equipment to it that will alert you when an AT&T High Seas coast station is holding traffic for you.

AT&T now has in place its Data Information System (DIS) through which all three of its stations broadcast the call signs of vessels for which they are holding traffic in Morse code twenty-four hours a day over selected channels. As with their voice communications, the traffic list is the same for all three stations. WOM broadcasts these signals on ITU channels 423 (4425.6 kHz) and 810 (8746.8 kHz); WOO on channels 811 (8749.9 kHz) and 1210 (13128.7 kHz); KMI on channel 416 (4403.9 kHz) during nighttime hours and on channels 804 (8728.2 kHz) and 1229 (13187.6 kHz) during the day. These frequencies also carry normal voice transmissions, but a bit of electronic wizardry called "data-under-voice" allows them to carry the Morse signal at the same time the channel is being used for voice communications. To pick up the signals, you would tune your SSB to receive at 700 hertz (note that's hertz, not kilohertz) below the listed frequency.

AT&T has already developed a prototype device that will decode Morse and flash a light or sound a bell when it recognizes a preprogrammed string of letters and numbers such as a particular vessel's call sign or its Selective Calling Number. No such device is commercially available yet, but AT&T is trying to interest SSB radio and accessory manufacturers in offering such a unit either as an integral part of their radios or as a plug-in option. Such units probably will be on the market by the early 1990's.

In the meantime, a number of multimode data controllers, such as the AEA PK232 or the MFJ1278 are available from ham radio dealers for about $250 to $350. These will decode the Morse code, but none can be programmed to recognize a particular string of letters and numbers and activate an alarm. If you have a personal computer aboard, you cold take advantage of the CW-DIS system by hooking a multimode controller to your SSB and letting it decode all the information on one of the CW-DIS channels for half an hour or so to capture the traffic list and have it feed the decoded data to your computer. You could then use the "Find" function of just about any word-processor software package to sort through the data and search for your vessel's call sign.

FOR FURTHER INFORMATION

Stephens Engineering Associates, Inc., has published an excellent book by Fredrick Graves called *Mariner's Guide to Single Sideband*. It is available through marine bookstores and catalog houses or from the company at 7030 220th S.W., Mountlake Terrace, WA 98043. It is especially valuable for its information on worldwide SSB channels and frequencies.

AT&T offers a very useful *Fingertip Guide* which gives the frequencies and traffic-list and weather-broadcast schedules for all its stations. You can get one free by calling 1-800-SEA-CALL. WLO offers a guide to its marine communications services which is available by writing to Mobile Marine Radio, Inc., 7700 Rinla Avenue, Mobile, AL 36619-5110.

SHIPBOARD TELEX

While most communication over SSB is by way of voice transmissions, with a properly equipped marine SSB radio and the necessary associated equipment, it is possible to send and receive telex messages aboard your vessel from and to virtually any telex machine in the world through something called *SIm*plex *T*eleprinting *O*ver *R*adio (SITOR). The service is not cheap: Equipping a vessel with SITOR can cost from $5,000 to $10,000. Having telex capabilities aboard will appeal primarily to the cruising businessman who needs to stay in relatively private contact with his office or clients no matter where in the world he might choose to roam.

Telex can be considered (roughly speaking) a complex form of continuous-wave (CW) transmission using Morse code. Communicating over SSB with CW signals has several advantages. Remember we said that in SSB voice transmission, the signal is amplitude-modulated, which means that the transmitter puts out its full power only when the person transmitting is actually speaking. Because CW radio waves are of constant amplitude rather than modulated, the transmitter is always operating at full power which allows CW signals to punch through atmospheric interference when voice transmissions can't. With the addition of an appropriate decoder and printer, telex messages can be printed out on board your vessel as hard-copy. If you structure a SITOR system properly and let the coast station you are likely to work through know which channel you will monitor, your SITOR equipment can send and receive messages automatically, even when you are asleep or otherwise occupied. Whereas voice transmissions over SSB can be overheard, telex communications are more difficult to intercept. And SITOR transmissions cost about $3 per minute, whereas High Seas radiotelephone calls run around $5 per minute.

If you can stand the financial bite for the equipment, you can open up a whole new world of marine communications with a SITOR system. Through a coast station that handles SITOR you can access the land-based telex system and communicate with any telex machine in the world, or you can establish contact with other shipboard telex machines. You can reach another telex machine directly and conduct real-time conversations, or you can send and receive telex messages at your leisure through a service of SITOR-equipped coast stations called "store-and-forward."

With SITOR you can also receive and print out weather broadcasts and—if your printer is of the ink-jet or dot-matrix type—weather facsimile charts as well. If your SSB radio can be tuned down to 518 kHz, you can receive worldwide Navigational Telex (NAVTEX) broadcasts without needing a separate NAVTEX receiver on board. If you are willing to spend about $375 a month, you can even subscribe through a SITOR-equipped coast station to the Associated Press news, sports, and financial services and in effect have a newspaper printed out on your vessel every morning.

At WOO and KMI, AT&T is using a refinement and extension of its Data Information System which is based on SITOR— that is, it is in plain English rather than Morse code dots and dashes. In addition to the call sign of vessels for which the station is holding traffic, SITOR-DIS transmits the vessel's Selective Calling Number and in some cases even the name of the person being called. It also carries weather information. WOO now broadcasts SITOR-DIS twenty-four hours a day on 8051.5 kHz and KMI broadcasts it on 8087.0 kHz. WOM is not yet broadcasting SITOR-DIS but is likely to begin doing so by early 1990. Even after SITOR-DIS becomes fully activated, AT&T plans to continue CW-DIS because it can be read by Morse-trained radio operators on commercial vessels that are not equipped with SITOR.

HOW SITOR WORKS

In order to use SITOR, you must have several things. First is a marine SSB radio capable of receiving Frequency Shift Keying (FSK) telex transmissions, and it must be capable of switching back and forth between its send and receive modes within 20 milliseconds. It also should have a 300-hertz narrow-band filter. A marine SSB radio with these features can be used for voice as well as SITOR communication.

The heart of a SITOR system is an Automatic Repeat Requested (ARQ) error-corrected modem. Just as with SSB voice transmissions, SITOR transmissions bounce off the ionosphere where they are subject to something called multipath transmission. This phenomenon in some situations splits the signal and a portion of it that is reflected off the lower levels of the ionosphere reaches a receiver several milliseconds before the portion that reflects off a higher ionospheric level. In some cases, the portion of the signal that reaches the receiver first might actually have been sent after the portion which arrives later. In voice transmissions this factor often causes fading; in telex transmission it creates a jolly mess.

In simple terms, SITOR offsets this problem by transmitting in bursts of only three characters of text at a time with each character being composed of a distinctive grouping of four data 1's and three data 0's. If the receiving station doesn't get characters with the correct four-1's/three-0's pattern, it assumes it got an error and the ARQ modem requests the transmitter to send the same three characters again. It keeps doing this until the receiver gets all three characters with a correct pattern of four 1's and three 0's. Only then does it tell the transmitter to send the next three characters of text.

Next you will need a keyboard, a central processor unit and an LCD or video display unit (VDU) and a word-processing software package with which you will compose and format your telex messages prior to transmission. This portion of the SITOR system can be equipment dedicated strictly to SITOR, or a personal computer that can be used for other on-board chores. You will need a telecommunications software program on a standard floppy disk which comes with the modem you select. You will also need a computer printer to print out incoming messages. If you choose a dot-matrix or ink-jet printer, it can be used to print out both standard telex messages and weathermaps received over SITOR.

Aside from the hardware involved, you must request the assignment of a five-digit (soon to be nine-digit) Selective Calling Number (often referred to as a "sel-call" number) for your vessel from the FCC. The FCC does not automatically assign sel-call numbers to just anybody, and you must go through the following special procedure to get yours:

If your vessel has already been assigned a ship station license, request a modification of it to include SITOR by filing FCC Form 506 and be sure you give your vessel's existing call sign and its name exactly as it is listed on your station license. Under item 8 on the application labeled "International Selective Calling Number (if any)," pencil in "Requesting." In item 13 of the application, check category N, "Radiotelegraph (2000–26,000 kHz) Direct Printing." On the back of the application form under "Additional Answer Space," explain that you are requesting a sel-call number because you are adding SITOR equipment to your vessel. If you do not have a ship station license, when you file Form 506, in addition to checking the boxes for the other radio equipment you will have aboard, do the same as above. If you just check the N box in item 13 and don't explain on the back of the application that you are actually installing or planning to install SITOR equipment on your vessel, the FCC won't assign you a sel-call number. As of this writing, there is no charge for securing a new station license or modifying an existing one.

We said earlier that if you retain part 506-A of your FCC application, you can engage in voice operation of your SSB under temporary authority while you are waiting for your station license to be issued. Because of the procedures SITOR employs, you can't use it without a sell-call number. Whether you file Form 506 to modify an existing station license to include SITOR or to get a new station license, put a note on it in the "Additional Answer Space" on the back requesting the FCC to call you with your vessel's sel-call number as soon as it is awarded. The FCC will do so without charge, and you won't have to wait until you get your station license in the mail to start using your SITOR equipment. Once you have a sel-call number, you can program your SITOR modem to respond automatically to it and print out any messages addressed to your vessel without attention from you.

Once you have your sel-call number, you create your vessel's "answerback" which consists of your sel-call number, a space, the first four letters of your vessel's name as it is documented with the Federal Government or registered with a state, another space, then the letter "X."

You must also have an "accounting authority"—some recognized organization that agrees to handle payments for telex messages you transmit from your vessel. If your vessel is documented or registered in the United States and you transmit your SITOR messages through a coast station outside the United States that handles SITOR, you can use as an accounting authority the code number US01 which is the FCC. The coast station will bill the FCC and the FCC, which has your name and address from your Form 506 application, will bill you. You do not need to make previous arrangement with the FCC for this service and it costs nothing. You may not, however, use US01 as an accounting authority with SITOR coast stations in the United States. To send telex messages through a U.S. coast station that handles SITOR (there are several of them but WLO in Mobile, Alabama, handles the largest percentage of pleasure yacht traffic) you must have an arrangement with a private accounting authority. There are a number of such companies, but the largest in the United States is Mackie Communications, Inc., P.O. Box 331, Elizabeth, NJ 07207-0331. It charges a flat rate of $40 per year plus 12 percent of any bills they settle for you. They also can settle your bills with foreign SITOR coast stations and, if you choose, those for radiotelephone calls with High Seas coast stations as well.

SITOR EQUIPMENT RECOMMENDATIONS

In moderately priced equipment you might look at Hal Communications Corp.'s ARQ200 modem which lists for $1,795, matched to a SEA 322 or ICOM M700TY SSB radio which, with their antenna couplers, list at around $4,000 and $5,000, respectively. If you can afford to go a bit higher, consider the Thrane & Thrane TT-3210A modem, which lists at $3,675, matched to a Harris RF-3200 radio and RF-3281 antenna coupler, which together list for $4,500. To go really first class, match the Thrane & Thrane modem to a $10,000 Furuno FS-4001 radio and its antenna coupler, or to Radio Holland's Sailor Programme 1000B which, with the telex option and antenna coupler, is priced at just over $23,000.

If you plan to use SITOR extensively, you probably should go with a keyboard/VDU/printer setup that is dedicated strictly to SITOR such as Hal Communication's MX-10 (Fig. 9.14). It includes a modem and the necessary telecommunications software and lists for $4,400. For only occasional telex use, you will get more flexibility by connecting your SSB and a telex modem to an IBM-compatible personal computer and its printer which you can use for other on-board chores.

WEATHER RECEIVERS

While you will be able to receive regular voice marine weather broadcasts through the VHF and marine SSB radios aboard your vessel, there are two types of equipment especially devoted to receiving more detailed marine weather information. One is a weather-facsimile recorder (usually just called a weatherfax), which receives actual weather maps from the National Oceanic and At-

Fig. 9.14: *When connected to a SITOR-compatible marine SSB radio, Hal Communications Corp.'s MTX-10 and Microline printer create a dedicated marine radiotelex system for under $5,000.*

mospheric Administration's (NOAA) National Weather Service (NWS) and its counterpart services worldwide. The other is a Navigational Telex (NAVTEX) receiver which receives, stores, and prints out telexed weather forecasts, warnings, and Local Notices to Mariners worldwide. While I would not say that either of these units is really required equipment on a cruising boat, I would say that the more you can know about the weather the better.

WEATHERFAX

A weatherfax receives and prints a variety of charts and maps of current and predicted weather conditions which are transmitted from fifty different transmitters worldwide. While a reasonable degree of proficiency in interpreting weather data and symbols is needed to get the most out of them, these charts present both a more comprehensive and a more detailed picture of weather conditions than you can get from voice weather broadcasts. They cover such topics as the existing and forecast position of weather highs and lows along with the speed and direction of their movement; satellite weather pictures that show cloud patterns and storm development; the direction and intensity of surface winds; wave analysis; and ocean-current analysis. The worldwide schedule of the types of charts and the times and frequencies over which they are transmitted is contained in *Worldwide Weather Broadcasts*, published by NOAA.

Weatherfax units have three component parts: a signal receiver, a signal processor, and a printer. Because the majority of weather charts are transmitted over the same 2–22-MHz bands received by a SSB marine radio or HF ham radio, weatherfax setups can be configured in three different ways: with a signal processor only that must be connected to both an external radio receiver and a printer; with a combined signal processor-printer that requires only connection to an appropriate receiver; and as a stand-alone unit that combines all three components in a single cabinet.

CHOOSING WEATHERFAX EQUIPMENT

Since you should have a good SSB radio on board anyway, the most economical way to go would be with a unit like the Alden Electronics Faxmate, which has its own integral printer but must be connected to a SSB or HF ham receiver. The printer can also be connected to a personal computer and put to other uses. For facsimile recording it uses thermal paper but it can be changed over to plain paper when used as a computer printer. Another alternative would be to select the Stephens Engineering Associates' Seafax, a digital signal processor that must be connected to both an external SSB radio or an HF ham receiver and an ink-jet or dot-matrix plain-paper printer. Both units list for around $1,000, but with the SEA unit you still have the additional cost of a printer. With both the Seafax and Faxmate units you must manually tune your SSB or ham radio to the frequency over which the desired chart will be transmitted. Both units incorporate integral timers that allow you to program in the time of chart transmission, and the units will turn themselves on at the appropriate hour. They also will automatically record more than one chart on the same frequency sequentially, but since they do not control your radio's tuning, they cannot change frequency.

Alden, Furuno, and Raytheon offer stand-alone weatherfax units which house a fully synthesized SSB receiver, a signal processor, and a printer in a single unit and carry list prices ranging from around $1,700 to almost $3,700. These units allow you to program in the time and frequency of any chart you wish to receive; they turn themselves on and tune to the appropriate frequency automatically, then turn themselves off. They also cover slightly more of the radio spectrum, usually 80 kHz to 30 MHz, and can be used for voice as well as facsimile reception. They cannot however, be used to transmit. (As you will see when we discuss NAVTEX, because these radios are capable of being tuned to 518 kHz, they can also be used to receive NAVTEX weather information.) If you can stand the price difference, you will be much happier with one of these stand-alone units because of their programming and unattended operation features.

You will also find that the wider the chart a unit is capable of producing, the easier it will be to use.

WEATHERFAX EQUIPMENT RECOMMENDATIONS

In a stand-alone unit the Alden Marinefax TR1 is the best choice. The company's founder, Milton Alden, was a pioneer in facsimile communication going back to the 1930's, and the company he founded is a major supplier of weather facsimile recorders to NOAA, NWS, and other national weather services worldwide. For a unit you will connect with your existing SSB or ham radio as a receiver, I would suggest Alden's Faxmate if you don't plan to have a printer aboard for other uses. If you will use a computer printer for a variety of functions, I would go with the Seafax to avoid having to switch from thermal to plain paper.

FOR FURTHER READING

Alden has published an excellent volume, *A Mariner's Guide to Radiofacsimile Weather Charts*, written by Dr. Joseph Bishop. It's carried by many electronics dealers, marine bookstores, and catalogs, and is available directly from Alden at Washington Street, Westborough, MA 01581. Its list price is $19.95.

The publication *Worldwide Weather Broadcasts* is available from the Superintendent of Documents, U.S. Government Printing Office, Washington, D.C. 20402. Ask for NOAA–S/T 81-184.

NAVTEX

With VHF and SSB marine radios, you already have access on your boat to a wide range of broadcast weather information from such agencies as the U.S. Coast Guard and the National Weather Service and their counterparts in other countries. As mentioned earlier, information as to the times and frequencies of these broadcasts is available through the NOAA publication *Worldwide Weather Broadcasts.* The only problem is that in order to receive the information, you have to discipline yourself to note the times and frequencies of the broadcasts covering the area you will be cruising, then tune your radio to the appropriate frequency at the appropriate time. Even doing all that doesn't guarantee you will receive special unscheduled warnings and emergency broadcasts. Also, poor reception caused by weather or atmospheric disturbances can make voice broadcasts unintelligible. Even if the signal is clear, unless you record the broadcasts or take good notes, you can quickly forget important information, or you may simply be occupied with other chores or on shore when an important broadcast comes through.

Those difficulties are some of the reasons the International Maritime Organization (IMO), the London-based United Nations agency responsible for safety at sea, has instituted its new Global Maritime Distress and Safety System. As a part of this system, the IMO gathers together weather forecasts and warnings; information regarding vessels in distress and search-and-rescue operations; Local Notices to Mariners; and signal propagation correction information for Loran C, the Transit and GPS satellite navigation systems, and Omega; it then rebroadcasts this information at specific times for specific areas on a single frequency—518 kHz. These transmissions are in English and like SITOR they are in the form of continuous wave (CW) telex which is better able to penetrate weather and atmospheric disturbances than are voice broadcasts. The system, called NAVTEX (for Navigational Telex), is already operational along the East and Gulf coasts of the United States, around Puerto Rico, and in much of Europe and is being phased in along the U.S. West Coast. It is expected to offer worldwide coverage by the early 1990's. NAVTEX signals will reach approximately 200 miles offshore.

A dedicated NAVTEX receiver is designed to operate only on 518 kHz, and you can program it to receive only the type of messages you want and only those that cover the cruising area or areas you are interested in. The receiver also has the ability to accept a particular message once and reject it when it is rebroadcast. The information is then printed out on a narrow roll of thermal paper.

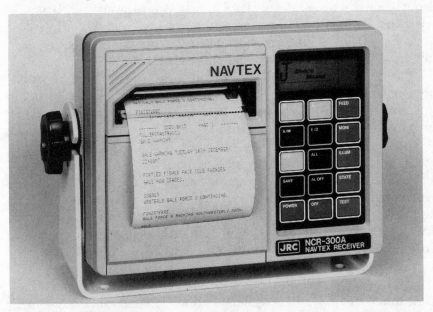

Fig. 9.15: *The Raytheon NCR-300A is dedicated solely to receiving NAVFAX weather broadcasts and warnings.*

CHOOSING A NAVTEX RECEIVER

You can purchase a receiver devoted exclusively to NAV-TEX such as the Raytheon NCR-300A (Fig. 9.15) which lists for about $1,400. That unit is offered with its own active antenna which lists for about $250. If your vessel is equipped with SITOR, and if the SSB or ham receiver it includes is capable of being tuned as low as 518 kHz, you can use it to receive NAVTEX broadcasts. You can also pickup NAVTEX broadcasts through a stand-alone weatherfax receiver.

HAM RADIO IN CRUISING

We're not going to try to qualify you here for a ham radio operator's license. All we want to do is quickly give you an idea of what ham radio equipment can and can't do for you in cruising situations and what is involved in properly utilizing it so you can decide if it's a subject you'd like to pursue further.

Amateur or ham radio (nobody seems to know where the nickname came from) is both similar to, and significantly different from, the types of marine radios we have discussed so far. Marine VHF and SSB operations are regarded by the FCC as commercial services. Ham is an amateur service, and there is a world of difference. In fact, ham radio is not, strictly speaking, marine radio at all. A ham radio on a cruising vessel operates over the same frequencies, uses the same equipment, and is covered by the same FCC regulations as a ham radio being operated on shore. The only difference is that when a ham is operating aboard ship, he is regarded as being "mobile," just as he would be if he were operating from a vehicle or a temporary location on land, and the FCC has very specific rules covering a ham radio in mobile operation.

Ham equipment normally is less expensive than SSB gear, but *it should never be considered as a substitute for VHF and SSB marine radios* because the Coast Guard does not continuously monitor ham frequencies. Many Coast Guard stations have ham capability and will employ it in an emergency, but you shouldn't bet your life they'll be listening when you might need them most.

Cruisers like Carleton Mitchell who are also licensed ham operators (Fig. 9.16) use their on-board equipment to chat with other land-based and seagoing hams on all manner of topics.

Fig. 9.16: *During a lifetime of cruising, ham radio has allowed Blue Water Cruising Medal winner Carleton Mitchell to keep in touch with a worldwide circle of friends.*

Some of the most interesting bull sessions around are the Maritime Service Nets, in which cruising ham operators all over the world "chew the rag" at agreed days, times, and frequencies about everything from where to anchor in Fiji to where to find fresh seafood in St. Thomas. Like SSB marine radios, ham radios can also be used as multiband receivers to pick up worldwide weather information and such news and entertainment services as the British Broadcasting Company (BBC) on frequencies ranging from 0.1 MHz to 30 MHz.

One reason many cruisers carry ham gear is that they can get hams ashore to patch them through to land-based telephone lines, which allow them to talk to the folks back home without paying the fairly stiff rates charged by High Seas marine coast stations. A number of ham operators in the United States are quite happy to provide that service, but others strenuously object to it on the basis that their frequencies should not be tied up by a cruising yachtsman who is only interested in using their service to save money on marine telephone calls.

In some quarters of the ham operators' fraternity there is quite a bit of antagonism toward the use of ham radio by cruising yachtsmen—and not without reason. In the past, a number of cruisers have put ham rigs on their boats but not gone to the trouble of getting a license. Since they don't know the proper procedures, they are easily spotted. These "bootleggers" routinely violate the law and play havoc with the operations of licensed hams. The most frequent violation they commit is using the ham bands to conduct conversations that can result in financial gain (such as establishing a phone patch to order parts), which is quite illegal. They also transmit from the territorial waters of other countries without getting a Reciprocal Operator's Permit, and they establish phone patches from the territorial waters of countries with which the United States does not have formal third-party traffic agreements. As long as you get an appropriate ham license and conduct your operations with the proper protocols, you will be welcomed to participate in ham operations from your vessel. But if you try to operate without a license and without knowledge of proper procedures, some hams will quite happily help the FCC track you down. If you decide that having a ham radio aboard is worth the effort of getting a license, and you plan to transmit over the ham frequencies from the waters of other nations, request your Reciprocal Operator's Permit from the countries you plan to visit well in advance of your departure. In some instances, processing your application can take up to six months.

HOW HAM RADIO WORKS

The most popular bands are: 1.8–2 MHz; 3.5–4 MHz; 7–7.3 MHz; 14–14.35 MHz; 21–21.45 MHz; 28–29.7 MHz; 50–54 MHz; and 144–148 MHz. A check back at the radio spectrum in Fig. 9.2 shows that the first six of these are fairly close to the bands used by marine SSB. Since ham transmissions in those bands are "slow snakes," they can be bounced off the ionosphere just like the SSB frequencies to provide truly globe-girdling communications. Notice also that the 144–148-MHz ham band is quite close to the 156–163-MHz band used by marine VHF. Just like marine VHF, transmissions on that band are essentially "line of sight" which limits their range, but they can be useful to cruisers who are in coastal waters.

Ham operators don't use the word *"channels."* Instead, they say they are "working 40 meters" or "20 meters" or "15 meters." Now what's that all about? Rather than just learn by rote that

"40 meters equals 7–7.3 MHz," take a moment to understand what hams are talking about and why.

Remember about our slow snakes and fast snakes? Well, actually, both snakes are moving through space at the speed of light—186,000 miles per second, which translates to 300 million meters per second. The difference, as we said, is their frequency—the rate at which their ups and downs pass a given point. The guys who are into this sort of thing have figured out that if a radio wave is going up and down (oscillating) at 7 MHz (7 million cycles per second), the length of one complete undulation (high point to low point and back to high point again) would be about 40 meters. If that radio wave is oscillating at 21 MHz, the length of one oscillation would be only about 15 meters. Therefore, as we also said earlier, the higher the frequency, the shorter the wavelength. That's why in ham jargon, there is an inverse ratio between frequency (7 MHz, 14 MHz, etc.) and band designation (40-meter band, 20-meter band, etc.). If that gets past you, just divide frequency in MHz into 300 which will put you close to the band designation in meters.

The relationship between megahertz and meters for each of the ham bands is as follows:

Band Frequency in MHz	Band Frequency in Meters
1.8–2.0 MHz	160 meters
3.5–4.0 MHz	80 meters
7.0–7.3 MHz	40 meters
14.0–14.35 MHz	20 meters
21.0–21.45 MHz	15 meters
28.0–29.7 MHz	10 meters
50.0–54.0 MHz	6 meters
144.0–148.0 MHz	2 meters

Radio waves in all but the 6-meter and 2-meter ham bands bounce off the ionosphere, so they can be used for long-distance communication. Since they do bounce off the ionosphere, their propagation—and thus their range—is affected by the rising and setting of the sun just like those in the SSB bands.

Radio waves in the 2-meter ham band (144–148 MHz), like marine VHF, go right through the ionosphere and thus are useful only for line-of-sight communication at typical ranges of fifty to seventy-five miles. Because of their limited range, most hams who cruise primarily offshore don't even bother having 2-meter equipment on board. The 2-meter ham band is used by some coastal cruisers, especially when they are within range of land-based repeaters that receive a 2-meter signal and retransmit it at much greater power. Repeaters normally are positioned on hilltops or towers to increase their range. On 2 meters, a ham can talk to other hams with 2-meter equipment, much of which they operate "mobile" in their automobiles.

HAM RADIO EQUIPMENT

Ham transceivers normally cover either 1.8 MHz to 30 MHz (the 160- to 6-meter bands) or 144 MHz to 148 MHz (the 2-meter band) but not both. (A single ham radio that covered all the ham frequencies from 160 meters to 2 meters would be sort of like having a marine SSB radio and a marine VHF radio in a single unit.) A transceiver that covers from 10 to 160 meters lists for about $1,100. If you want to operate on 2 meters you will have to buy a completely separate 2-meter transceiver (they cost anywhere from $300 to over $700).

Classes for a ham radio operator's license will tell you how to set up your "shack" and give you far more information about the equipment you'll need and where to get the best deals than we can cover here, but three general comments are in order. Stick with quality gear and choose transistorized, solid-state units, which produce less heat and perform better in the tough marine environment. Since ham equipment is not really designed for shipboard use, a little extra care is needed to protect it. Insist on digital readout of the frequencies you are tuning (trying to tune in a ham radio without digital readout on a boat that is rocking at anchor or pitching through a head sea will make you say things not considered proper in polite society).

You will find that ham radios and their antenna tuners look very similar to and operate on almost the same frequencies as marine SSB radios, and both types of radios are made by the same companies. You may wonder why you can't buy just one radio, one antenna tuner, and one antenna that would allow you to operate on both the marine SSB bands and the ham bands.

Actually you can.

The companies that manufacture marine SSB radios don't mention it very prominently in their advertising or literature, but their radios are quite capable of receiving and transmitting on all the bands between 2 MHz and 23 MHz, which include the 80-, 40-, 20-, and 15-meter ham bands of primary interest to the cruising yachtsman. Some marine SSB radios transmit and receive on all frequencies from 1.6 MHz to 30 MHz, which take in the 160- and 10-meter ham bands as well.

This may appear to be in violation of 47 CFR 97.101(b), the section of the FCC rules governing the amateur radio service, which states specifically that "the amateur mobile station shall be separate from and independent of all other radio equipment, if any, installed on board the same ship." This provision was written into the FCC rules to eliminate the possibility of ham radio equipment interfering with the SSB radio on the same ship, which is used for emergency situations.

In trying to determine whether it is legal for a cruising yachtsman with an appropriate ham license to transmit on the ham bands with such a radio, I figured it must be or the FCC wouldn't let the marine SSB radio manufacturers sell such equipment in the first place. I discussed the matter with the chief of the FCC's Aviation and Marine Radio Branch, which regulates SSB marine radios. He told me there is nothing in the sections of FCC rules his branch enforces that prohibits the manufacturer of a radio that is type-accepted for use on the commercial marine frequencies from including in it the ability to operate on other frequencies. He further told me that his office has no role in enforcing 47 CFR 97.101(b) because it governs the amateur radio service, not the commercial marine or aviation services for which his office is responsible.

I then spoke to the chief of the Personal Radio Branch, which regulates the amateur radio service and is responsible for enforcing 47 CFR 97.101. He reminded me that ham radios don't have to be FCC type-accepted and said his office is concerned with regulating ham radio operators, not radio equipment manufacturers. He said it would be illegal for a seagoing ham to transmit over the ham frequencies using a radio that was not "separate from and independent of all other radio equipment, if any, installed on board the same ship." He said that Gordon West, a ham operator, yachtsman, and writer on marine electronics, had petitioned the FCC to allow ham operators to transmit maritime mobile using a marine SSB radio, and that the FCC had rejected his petition on September 16, 1985.

The upshot of all this is that it is not illegal for the manufacturer of a SSB marine radio to build into that radio the ability to transmit over the ham bands, but it is illegal for even an appropriately licensed ham operating maritime mobile to use it for transmitting on *both* the ham bands and the marine bands.

While it is apparently illegal to transmit on the ham bands using an SSB marine radio, receiving on those bands is not illegal. To find the frequencies on which hams are operating, however, you need to know that by mutual agreement, when working frequencies of 14 MHz and higher (that is, 20, 15 and 10 meters), ham operators generally operate in the upper sideband mode which is the same used by the marine SSB bands. On frequencies of 7 MHz and below (that is, 40 and 80 meters), hams operate on the lower sideband. Most of the marine SSB radios now on the market have a marked switch on their front panel that allows you to select upper or lower sideband mode. On the ICOM M700 and M700TY, the lower sideband mode is not marked, but you can switch either of them to it by turning the mode selection switch to the unmarked position all the way to the left.

HAM RADIO ANTENNAS

Until the fairly recent development of sophisticated electronic antenna couplers, about the only way to operate on the lower ham frequencies was to rig an unsightly and cumbersome "long wire" antenna which needed to be at least 12 meters (39.36 feet) long. With today's high-quality digital antenna tuners and a good RF ground, in most situations you can get excellent results with a 23-foot whip antenna.

As of this writing, under 47 CFR 97.101, an antenna and antenna coupler used for transmitting on the ham bands have to be "separate from and independent of" similar equipment used to transmit over the marine SSB bands. However, the FCC has requested comment on a proposed new rule that would allow a maritime mobile ham transceiver and a marine SSB radio installed on the same vessel to share a single antenna and antenna coupler.

HAM RADIO LEGAL REQUIREMENTS

Ham radio operation requires a combined station/operator license, but it has no relation to the ship station license or the Restricted Radiotelephone Operator Permit we discussed under marine VHF and SSB radio. Unlike them, the ham license re-

quires a written examination on which the applicant must dem-
onstrate a knowledge of basic radio theory, proper operating
procedures, and the ability to receive Morse code at certain minimum speeds.

Passing the exam is relatively simple. The best approach is
to enroll in a class sponsored by a local ham club or community
college in your area. It probably will meet one night a week for
six weeks leading up to the Novice License exam. Once you've
got your Novice ticket, another four-week class will get you ready
for the General Class exam. The radio theory part of the course
isn't very difficult—nor is learning Morse code if you get yourself a set of audio teaching tapes and practice about twenty minutes a night. The General Class License, which is the one you'll
need to operate by voice over the frequencies most useful in
cruising, requires the ability to receive Morse at thirteen words
per minute. The easiest way to find out when and where classes
are held is to call the nearest electronics shop which sells amateur radio equipment. If there is no ham equipment dealer in
your area, write to the American Radio Relay League, 225 Main
St., Newington, CT 06111, and request the name of the secretary
of their nearest chapter.

Don't make the mistake of trying to "bootleg," that is, operate ham radio equipment without a license. It is illegal, and if
you get caught you can have your equipment confiscated, and
you can be fined and barred from ever getting a ham license.
The biggest drawback is that without going through the study
that leads up to a license, you will never fully understand the
equipment and therefore will never be able to utilize it to its best
advantage. You should also be aware that because of the Government's attempts to stem the flood of illegal drugs into this
country, the FCC is much more active than it has been in tracking down all kinds of illegal radio operations aboard boats, especially those operating in the Bahamas, the Caribbean, South
and Central America, and Mexico.

HAM RADIO EQUIPMENT RECOMMENDATIONS

Until and unless the FCC starts enforcing its "separate and
independent" rule, I wouldn't lose a great deal of sleep over
buying a marine SSB radio capable of transmitting over the ham
bands and using it for that purpose (but only with the appropriate ham license). If you decide to go that route, you'll find it

best to select a radio that allows you the option of changing frequencies quickly with a thumbwheel rather than having to keypunch them into the radio's memory, then recall them. The reason is that the frequencies listed for the various maritime nets you will be interested in are for contact only. To carry on a conversation, you'll need the ability to quickly shift frequencies up or down in whatever band you are working. One marine SSB that offers this option is the Harris RF-3200.

In view of the pending rule modification regarding antenna sharing, even if I added a separate ham transceiver, I'd hook it up to my marine SSB antenna coupler and antenna with a coaxial switch to shift from one to the other.

If you want to be super cautious and buy a completely standalone ham rig, I suggest the ICOM M735, which lists for $1,090, matched with the ICOM AH-2a antenna tuner and controller unit, which lists for about $500. In most cases, this setup will work well with any of the 23- or 28-foot fiberglass sticks I recommended for use with your marine SSB radio. Since the AH-2a antenna tuner is not quite as electronically advanced as the antenna coupler used with most marine SSB radios, you may find you have to go to at least a 12-meter long-wire antenna to get maximum use out of the 160- and 80-meter bands (because of their low frequency) and out of the 15-meter band because a 23-foot whip is close to that band's half-wavelength.

WHAT'S ON THE HORIZON?

In addition to the sophisticated communications technology already available, there are some interesting new services and technologies that are not really available yet but will be on the market by the mid-1990's.

DIGITAL SELECTIVE CALLING

A basic problem with existing VHF and SSB marine communications is that in order for a vessel to receive a call from another vessel or from a coast station or be made aware of critical weather and distress information, the radio on board must be turned on and tuned to an appropriate channel.

Member nations of the International Radio Consultative Committee (CCIR) have recently set aside VHF channel 70 for a new type of communication called Digital Selective Calling (DSC) and are now finalizing designations of channels in each of the marine SSB bands for the same purpose. These channels will not be used for normal communications but only for the transmission of alerting messages. The system is expected to become operative for commercial vessels in the early 1990's and for recreational vessels later in that decade.

As to how DSC will work in practice: If your vessel is equipped for DSC, you will no longer need to monitor VHF channel 16 or the traffic lists of the SSB High Seas coast stations to find out if a marine operator is holding a call for you. If you have registered your vessel's DSC number with the marine operator, you will have your VHF radio monitor channel 70 and your SSB radio monitor one of the channels designated for DSC and the operator will send you a data message telling you to call back on an appropriate working channel. Likewise, a cruising buddy equipped for DSC will be able to punch in your vessel's DSC number and send you a message telling you to call him on an appropriate working channel.

DSC will also have important safety functions because it will be tied into the Global Maritime Distress and Safety System (GMDSS), which will become operative during the same time period. Under GMDSS, appropriate authorities in each member nation will be able to transmit sel-call messages to all vessels in any one or all of seven areas of the world. Messages to DSC-equipped vessels in A-1 zones—within forty to fifty miles of each member nation's coastline—will be transmitted via VHF channel 70. Messages to DSC-equipped vessels in A2 areas—within 150 miles of each nation's coastline—will be transmitted over designated MF SSB frequencies in the 2–3-MHz band. Messages to DSC-equipped vessels in A3 zones—deep-ocean areas—will be transmitted over channels to be designated in each of the HF SSB bands.

STANDARD-C SATELLITE COMMUNICATIONS

Standard-C will be similar to SITOR in that it will be a data-only form of transmission (no voice) that will bounce its signals off a network of satellites rather than the ionosphere and will connect with the international telex system. Since Standard-C signals will be propagated by satellites rather than the ionosphere, they will be totally unaffected by atmospheric interference. Standard-C transmissions also will be private, since they will be coded for receipt only by the specific vessel or land-based station to which they are addressed.

Under the name Standard-A, this technology has been in use for several years by some 6,500 commercial vessels worldwide for receiving and transmitting operational, safety, and distress messages and receiving weather information. The equipment required for on-board use of Standard-A is so heavy and expensive and the antenna it requires so large that it is impractical for most pleasure boats. Now, however, the International Maritime Satellite Organization (INMARSAT) has developed prototype equipment for the Standard-C version of the technology which is inexpensive and small enough to be useful to the owner of a cruising vessel of moderate-size. The prototype transceiver, which can be mounted out of sight, is about $12'' \times 12'' \times 3''$ and weighs only about 6 pounds. For data entry and printout functions, the transceiver can be hooked to a personal computer of the same type used in a SITOR system. The prototype Standard-C antenna is cone-shaped and measures about 10 inches high and about 6 inches in diameter at its base. It weighs around 10 pounds. Standard-C's data-transmission rate will be 600 bits per second. So far, only one company, Thrane & Thrane, has announced plans to manufacture and sell Standard-C equipment, but you may be certain that other manufacturers in the marine communications field eventually will be announcing their own versions.

Comsat Corporation, the U.S. member of INMARSAT, now has a new maritime safety broadcast system using Standard-C. The system, called SafetyNet, will allow the broadcast of weather information to all Standard-C-equipped vessels.

Aside from the ability to receive weather information without worrying about atmospheric interference, Standard-C should be of major interest to cruisers who need to stay in contact with their offices through a dependable, secure, printed-medium communications system whose satellite-transmitted signals will be less prone to interference than SITOR is.

10

ANCHOR OPTIONS

Some people own beautiful boats that are capable of extended cruising and operate them for years without ever setting an anchor. Instead, they plan all their runs so that every night they can securely lash their vessels to the dock of some marina. In the process, of course, they severely limit their cruising options and rob themselves of one of the most rewarding aspects of cruising—luxuriating in the stillness of a beautiful anchorage with no traces of distracting civilization buzzing in their ears.

You, or course, aren't one of those people. But even if you anchor out only occasionally, you quickly will find that not all your anchorages are going to be roomy, placid, and protected. Some will be subject to heavy surge and vicious currents. Some will be so congested you will find the scope you can put out will be limited. The bottom into which you are trying to set an anchor is not always going to be hard sand. Sometimes it will be soft mud with the consistency of oatmeal, other times it will be coral, and still others it may be impenetrable granite. And the winds will not always be gentle. Sooner or later, you are likely to find yourself anchored out in at least half a gale if not in an actual hurricane, and the safety of your vessel and all aboard it will be dependent on the holding power of one or two chunks of metal and a couple of lengths of chain or nylon line. It makes sense, then, to devote a good deal of thought to the equipment you need for anchoring your vessel securely. At a cost of up to $5,000 or more, good anchoring equipment can seem terribly expensive until you realize that the entire value of your vessel— and possibly the lives or safety of all aboard—may depend on it.

But good equipment is not the whole story.

If you cruise for a while, you're bound to witness a situation in which a cruising couple pull into a lovely cove where you are already settled and go through an anchoring routine worthy of the Keystone Kops. Papa will be on the flying bridge waving frantically and yelling orders to his frustrated and perplexed spouse who will be scurrying around the foredeck. Their anchor will not hold on the first try, and probably not on the second. A few choice expletives will waft across the water. If they finally get an anchor to hold, it probably will be in a position where their vessel's swinging room makes them a danger to you, and you will have to up anchor and move to a safer location. As the tide rises or the wind gets up in the night, you'll probably hear them repeat the whole routine at about two or three in the morning because they failed to set the anchor properly, were using the wrong kind of anchor or rode, or failed to put out sufficient scope to allow for changing conditions. Sadly, some people who cruise for years never learn from their mistakes.

To help you avoid doing that yourself, in this chapter we'll show you how to devise a complete anchoring system and an anchoring technique that will allow you to get the right anchor down in the right place on the first try, tie it off securely, then relax and enjoy a chuckle or two as you watch others in the harbor go through their anchoring antics.

BOW PULPITS

When we discussed a cruising vessel's main-deck layout in Chapter 2, we mentioned the advisability of selecting a boat with a good stout bow pulpit that projects about 3 feet beyond the bow, has a sturdy railing around it, and accommodates at least your primary anchor in a self-deploying bow roller. We suggested that it would be even better if it could accommodate your secondary anchor as well (Fig. 10.1). We also mentioned the need for space just aft of the bow pulpit for mounting a hefty electric windlass; plenty of unobstructed working space on the foredeck; and roomy, vee-bottomed lockers for both rope and chain in the forepeak. When we discussed water systems in Chapter 3, we also mentioned why it's a good idea to have a high-pressure saltwater outlet on the foredeck to wash off any mud which might be brought up on your anchor chain.

Our focus in this section will be on the equipment you need

Fig. 10.1: *This double-roller bow pulpit installed on a full-displacement power cruiser is equipped with a plow-type primary anchor to starboard, a Bruce secondary anchor to port, and a horizontal windlass.*

to put on and around that bow pulpit to ensure that anytime you drop the hook, you can be reasonably certain your vessel will stay where you anchor her.

CRUISING ANCHORS

Most boating books that cover anchoring refer to three anchors: a working anchor, a storm anchor, and a lunch hook. This terminology relates most accurately to sailboats whose anchor rodes usually are rope rather than chain and whose owners often handle their anchors manually rather than with an electric windlass. In selecting anchors for a cruising powerboat that is large enough to carry the substantial weight of an all-chain rode and has the battery capacity to power an electric windlass, I suggest it's more practical to think in terms of a somewhat oversized primary anchor that combines the functions of both working and storm anchors, and a slightly smaller secondary anchor. For those situations when a stern anchor would be useful, or when you lose either your primary or secondary anchor, carry a third one; this anchor can be lighter than your secondary one but heavier than what a sailor would call a lunch hook.

While there are several different types of anchors on the market, there are three basic types for serious cruising: the plow, the fluke, and the Bruce (Fig. 10.2).

Primary Anchors: You can get into some lively arguments with cruising people on the topic of which anchor works best in which anchoring circumstance. The debate swirls around which type has the greatest "holding power" or "drag value." Actually both terms are meaningless unless you take into consideration the type of bottom in which the anchor is set. Simpson-Lawrence's Technical and Development Department, for example, compiled and published the results of three tests of the company's 25-pound CQR anchor (the initials are a play on the word *secure*) under actual anchoring situations. The tests were carried out by three independent groups in three different locations and were witnessed respectively by Lloyd's of France, Lloyd's of the U.K., and France's Bureau Veritas. In each test, measuring instruments were used to determine the amount of load that caused the anchor to break out of the bottom, which was designated as its "maximum drag value." In sand off the beach at Beg-Rohu,

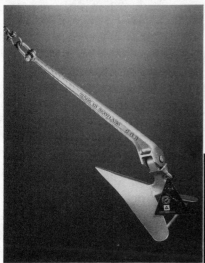

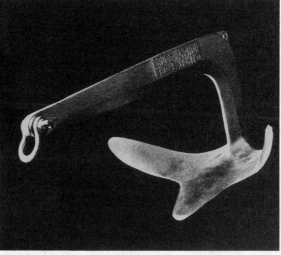

Fig. 10.2: The realistic choices in cruising anchors come down to three types: the plow (above), the fluke-type Danforth (right), and the Bruce (below).

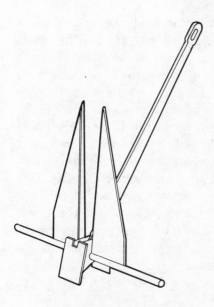

France, maximum drag value was measured at 1,102 pounds. In sand off the beach at Studland Bay, England, it was 1,320 pounds. At sea off Quiberon, France, in mud it measured 1,653 pounds; in a mixture of sand and gravel it was 2,535 pounds; and in compact sand it was 3,086 pounds. In other words, depending on bottom conditions, the same anchor had a maximum drag value that varied by almost 300 percent!

Selecting anchors for your vessel, therefore, is more a matter of matching them to the types of bottoms you are most likely to encounter in your cruising than it is to working out a technical equation. Many cruisers with experience of a wide variety of anchoring situations rely on a good heavy plow as their primary anchor, and they usually go with the CQR brand which is the original of the type. The fluke anchor has been around a long time and some knowledgeable cruisers wouldn't use anything else. I've found it works quite well in hard sand but does not hold well in soft sand or mud and has a problem biting into a grassy bottom. In soft bottoms, it also tends to bring up great gobs of goo with it. But the most serious drawback to the fluke anchor is that if a good-sized chunk of rock or coral—or even its own rode—becomes wedged between one of its flukes and its shank and the anchor rolls over on its back, its long stock prevents it from righting itself and it becomes essentially useless. If you choose a fluke anchor, go with the products of the Danforth division of Rule Industries whose name has become synonymous with the type rather than a less expensive imitation, and buy their top-of-the line Deepset Hi-Tensile® model. It is harder to set than the standard model but it offers a far greater ratio of tensile strength-to-weight. A few cruisers prefer the Bruce, an anchor developed for holding oil rigs in place in the North Sea, on the grounds that if it is deployed in an inverted position, its design forces it to roll over and bite into the bottom. I can't claim personal experience with a Bruce anchor, but its inventor, Peter Bruce, gave me a demonstration with a scale model which convinced me the claim is valid.

Given the wide range of "drag values" or "holding power" of various types of anchors depending on the type of bottom they are set in, choosing anchors of the appropriate size for your vessel is also pretty arbitrary. My recommendations for the amount

® Rule Registered Trademark

of holding power you need to safely anchor different sizes of moderate-to heavy-displacement cruising boats in winds up to about 60 knots are summarized in Fig. 10.3. These recommendations are based strictly on my own experience and that of other seasoned cruisers with whom I have discussed the matter rather than on any scientific evidence.

Secondary Anchors: If for some reason your primary anchor drags and fouls so that it won't reset or you lose it, your secondary anchor is your backup, so it should be a good one.

Most cruisers choose a fluke anchor as a secondary anchor because of the ease of stowing it. Whichever type you choose, your secondary anchor can be one size smaller than your primary anchor (Fig. 10.10), but it also should be carried on the foredeck so that it can be deployed quickly in an emergency. It would be best if your vessel's bow pulpit could accommodate it in a self-deploying roller alongside your primary anchor. A poor second choice is to install a fluke anchor flat on the foredeck in chocks. You will have to walk around it and will probably stub your toe on it more than once, but at least it will be ready when you need it.

However you stow your secondary anchor, it should be attached to its rode. I see a number of cruisers carrying a secondary anchor on the foredeck but not attached to its rode. To me this seems foolish. The times you are likely to need it most are also likely to be times when the foredeck is pitching wildly, the wind is screeching, and the rain is pouring buckets—hardly the

Boat Length	Minimum Holding Power Required	Recommended Primary Anchor Sizes (lbs.)		
		CQR	Danforth*	Bruce
40'–49'	5,500 lbs.	45	41	44
50'–59'	6,500 lbs.	60	60	66
60'–69'	7,500 lbs.	75	90	110

*Deepset Hi-Tensile model

Fig. 10.3: Recommended primary anchors for safely anchoring moderate- to heavy-displacement cruising vessels of 40–69 feet in winds to 60 mph.

best of circumstances in which to be trying to thread a pin into a shackle to attach the anchor to its rode. Still worse is the practice of stowing a secondary anchor in a deck box or belowdecks, even if it is shackled to its rode. In a deck box, it invariably will work its way to the bottom of the box and burrow itself under fenders, dock lines, and shoreside power cords that get tangled up with its rode. If it is stowed below decks, by the time you go down, dig it out, haul it on deck, throw it overboard, and secure its bitter end, your boat may well be on the rocks.

The third or stern anchor should also be a Danforth—for ease of handling—but it can be one size smaller than your secondary anchor. It and its rode can be stowed in a cockpit locker or belowdecks because you are likely to be able to deploy it at your leisure after your primary anchor is well set.

ANCHOR RODES

Primary Rode: If at all possible, the rode on your primary anchor should be entirely of chain rather than rope or a chain-rope combination. The main reason for using an all-chain primary rode is that the key to the holding power of all three types of anchors is keeping the strain on them horizontal rather than vertical. In fact, in order to facilitate their retrieval, they are designed to break out when the angle of pull against them reaches around 10 degrees above the horizontal. When your boat's bow is bobbing up and down wildly in a surge, the sheer weight of an all-chain rode set out with adequate scope makes it stay on the bottom much better than rope and helps keep the strain on the anchor horizontal. Another reason is that anchoring with a rope rode usually requires you to put out a scope of about seven to eight times the water's depth. With an all-chain rode you can get equally good holding under reasonable conditions with a scope of only three to four times the water's depth (more, of course, if the weather is unsettled). Lastly, chain can be handled efficiently by the wildcat of an electric windlass to provide essentially hands-off anchoring, and it is not subject to chafe on rocks and coral.

Installing the massive weight of an all-chain rode in the bow of a planing hull cruiser under about 35 feet in length may unacceptably affect its performance. In that case, the only realistic alternative is to use rope, but it should have at least some chain between it and the anchor to exert a horizontal pull on the anchor and resist chafe. This would be the same arrangement as the secondary rode on a larger vessel, and we'll discuss it in detail when we get to that topic.

If your vessel is capable of carrying an all-chain primary rode, it should be 300 feet long in order to allow you to anchor under normal conditions in up to 100 feet of water with the minimum safe scope of three times the water's depth.

In selecting the chain for a primary anchor rode you want a chain whose "working limit" approximately equals the holding power of the anchor to which it is attached. You want to get that working limit in as light a chain as possible to reduce the amount of weight you have to carry in your vessel's forepeak. Make certain also that the chain you select is compatible with the wildcat of your windlass.

Anchor chain is made from four different grades of wire: proof coil (grade 30); BBB; high-test (grade 40); and alloy (grade 63 or 80). Grade 80 alloy chain usually is referred to as Accoloy, a branded product of American Chain and Cable Company). The four types of chain have vastly differing working load limits according to their sizes and weights (Fig. 10.4).

Proof coil has a low carbon content and should not be used as anchor chain. BBB chain for years was the standard chain used for most recreational boating applications. It has a somewhat higher carbon content than proof coil but pound-for-pound it is not as strong as the newer high-test and alloy chains. It may be fine for light-displacement powerboats, but it's not practical for those of moderate to heavy displacement. In order to get the minimum working load limit required to safely anchor a hefty 40- to 50-foot power cruiser, you must go to the ⅝-inch size. The wildcat of the windlass you normally would install on that size cruiser will not handle chain larger than ½-inch, and 300 feet of BBB chain would weigh over 1,300 pounds.

With the elimination of proof coil and BBB, your practical choices for anchor chain are limited to high-test or Accoloy. The advantages of Accoloy quickly becomes obvious. In order to approximately match the 6,000 to 7,000 pounds of holding power we recommend for the primary anchor of a moderate- to heavy-displacement cruising vessel of about 50 feet in length, for example, you would need to use 300 feet of ⁷⁄₁₆-inch high-test (grade 40) chain which would have a working load limit of 6,600 pounds

Chain Type Trade Size	Working Limit (lbs.)	Wt/100' (lbs.)	Vol/100' (cu.ft.)
Proof Coil			
⅜"	2,625	158	1.14
½"	4,500	278	1.93
⅝"	6,800	410	3.11
BBB			
⅜"	2,750	173	1.14
½"	4,750	296	1.93
⅝"	7,250	447	3.11
High Test (Grade 40)			
⅜"	5,100	157	1.14
⁷⁄₁₆"	6,600	213	1.93
½"	8,200	274	1.93
⅝"	11,500	409	3.11
Accoloy (Grade 80)			
⁹⁄₃₂"	3,250	75	.50
⅜"	6,600	135	1.14
½"	11,250	234	1.93
⅝"	16,500	371	3.11

Fig. 10.4: This chart of the working load limits, weights, and volumes for various types and sizes of anchor chain shows that High Test or Accoloy chain provides far greater strength-to-weight ratios than proof coil or BBB chain.

and weigh 639 pounds, or you could go down a size smaller to ⅜-inch Accoloy chain and get 6,600 pounds of holding power at only 405 pounds of weight.

By combining the recommendations for primary anchors and all-chain rode, we can come up with a computation of the primary anchors and chain sizes needed for moderate- to heavy-displacement power cruisers in three basic size classifications (Fig. 10.5).

Until fairly recently, virtually all anchor chain for use on recreational vessels was BBB chain made to standards set by the

Boat Length	Required Holding Power	Recommended Primary Anchor			Recommended Chain	
		CQR	Danforth*	Bruce	High-Test	Accoloy
40'–49'	5,500	45	41	44	7/16" (6,600)	3/8" (6,600)
50'–59'	6,500	60	60	66	7/16" (6,600)	3/8" (6,600)
60'–69'	7,500	75	90	110	1/2" (8,200)	1/2" (11,250)

*Deepset Hi-Tensile model

(Figures in parentheses are working load limit of chain in pounds)

Fig. 10.5: Recommended chain sizes for various sizes of primary anchors.

International Standards Organization (ISO) which not only established BBB chain's metallic composition but specified the dimensions of its links as well. When U.S. chain manufacturers introduced chain made of high-test and alloy wire, they shifted to a new standard created by the National Association of Chain Manufacturers (NACM) that called for a slightly longer link. From the standpoint of the cruising yachtsman, these longer links have disadvantages: They are more likely to kink, and they are more susceptible to distortion, which interferes with their proper handling by a windlass's wildcat. Further, while they fit the wildcats of windlasses made in the United States, they may not be compatible with the wildcats of some popular windlasses manufactured in England or its former colonies, which still employ the ISO standard. Some of the English manufacturers (for example, Simpson-Lawrence) offer optional wildcats that will handle the longer links; others (such as Maxwell-Nilsson) offer only wildcats that will handle the shorter link of the ISO standard. To further confuse the issue, some U.S. chain manufacturers now make a chain of high-test wire but with a shorter link. It does not, however, conform to the ISO's BBB standard. It is usually designated as short-link or "SL" chain.

The best way to make certain your windlass will efficiently handle your all-chain rode is to buy your chain from the same company that manufactures your windlass; the major U.S. windlass manufacturers have associated chain companies whose products are specifically calibrated to fit their wildcats. If for any reason that solution is impossible or impractical (for example, if you are trying to fit new chain to an existing windlass), be certain you buy your chain from a supplier who is thoroughly familiar with the model of windlass you have and can assure you the two are compatible. In some cases, you may have to remove the wildcat from your windlass and take it to your supplier to make certain his chain will fit. This is especially true if the wildcat you are trying to match is somewhat worn. It may require a larger chain than it was designed to handle when it was new. If you are trying to buy a new windlass or replace the wildcat of an existing windlass, you may have to go the other way and send a sample of your chain to the windlass manufacturer for comparison with the new wildcat. If you do that, send a chain sample that is at least eleven links long, since that much normally is required to go all the way around a wildcat's circumference, and make certain the two mesh properly.

A chain rode should be securely attached to the anchor with a screw pin shackle which has a working load limit at least equal to that of the chain (Fig. 10.6). The pin should be secured to the shackle with stainless-steel wire to eliminate any possibility of its working loose. The bitter end of a chain rode should never be affixed directly to the vessel as there would be no way to cut the vessel loose in an emergency. You should, however, attach a 6-foot piece of ½-inch nylon line to the chain's bitter end with an eye splice and a stainless-steel thimble. Tie the bitter end of the line to an eyebolt securely mounted inside the chain locker. With that arrangement, you won't lose the bitter end of the chain by accident, but in an emergency you can let all the chain run

	Working Load Limit	
Shackle Size	High-Test (Galvanized)	Accoloy (Not Galvanized)
⅜"	2,000 lbs.	2,500 lbs.
½"	4,000 lbs.	5,000 lbs.
⅝"	6,500 lbs.	8,000 lbs.
¾"	10,000 lbs.	N/A
⅞"	13,000 lbs.	N/A
1"	17,000 lbs.	N/A

Fig. 10.6: The working limit of the anchor shackle must be at least equal to that of the chain itself or it becomes literally the weakest link in your ground tackle system.

out, then cut the nylon line once the chain pulls it out of the chain locker onto the deck where you can get at it with a rigging knife. Just make certain the eye splice and thimble connecting the chain and the line are small enough to pass smoothly through your chain locker's deck pipe.

If you use an all-chain primary rode, you will find that when you are in an anchorage subject to heavy surge the chain's weight will tend to cause your boat to jerk unpleasantly and the chain will grate across the bow roller with a most annoying sound. To offset those problems, you might want to rig an anchoring bridle (Fig. 10.7) of the type that both Carleton Mitchell and Frank Glindmeier found useful for anchoring their full-displacement cruisers *Coyaba* and *Summer Wind*.

To construct such a bridle, eye-splice the ends of two 10-

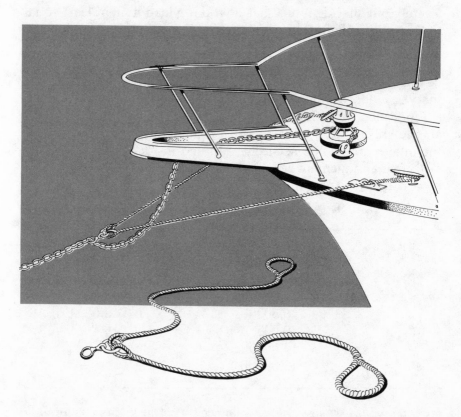

Fig. 10.7: An anchoring bridle made of nylon line can help take the shock out of an all-chain rode and prevent the chain from grating across the anchor roller.

foot lengths of ¾-inch nylon line onto a stout stainless-steel ring. Use a stainless-steel thimble inside the bight to reduce chafe, and weave the splice about 12 inches up into the rope. Also eye-splice into the opposite end of each length of line a loop that is large enough to fit easily over the cleats on each side of your bow. Again, the splice should be worked about 12 inches up into the standing part of the line. Next, attach to the ring a stout stainless-steel sassor, snap shackle, or chain hook, which can hook into or over a link of your anchor chain. Stow the completed bridle in a foredeck box until you need it. Once you are anchored, hook the sassor to the anchor chain, secure the loops on the two ends of the bridle to the bow cleats, and loosen the tension on your windlass to allow slack in the chain. The bridle will take the strain off the bow pulpit. Because the nylon is taking the strain rather than the chain, it will act as a shock absorber and eliminate the sound of the chain grating across the bow roller all night. If you do not use such a bridle every time you anchor, you must install forward of the wildcat a chain stopper or devil's-claw into which you should hook your chain once you are anchored in order to take the strain off the windlass.

In preparing for *Summer Wind*'s voyage from Florida to Alaska and back, Frank Glindmeier came up with another useful idea for anchoring in congested harbors where limited swinging room could prevent him from putting out as much scope of chain as he would like (Fig. 10.8). Frank had a boatyard install a stout eyebolt in the boat's stem about 6 inches above the waterline. He then eye-spliced a 15-foot length of ¾-inch nylon line into the eye with a stainless-steel thimble and eye-spliced a strong snap shackle to the bitter end. Until this rig was needed, the bitter end was tied off to the bow pulpit. When he was forced to anchor on short scope in a crowded harbor, he would untie the bitter end of the rig from the bow pulpit, attach the snap shackle to his anchor chain, then pay out sufficient chain to let the nylon take the strain. As it did so, the snap shackle attaching the nylon to the chain would be about 2 to 4 feet underwater. "The roller in *Summer Wind*'s bow pulpit was eight feet off the water," Frank explains. "With this rig I was able to substantially lower the anchor chain's point of attachment to the boat. If we were anchored in eight feet of water, the rig cut the amount of scope we needed by about a fourth."

Frank offers still another idea: When he and his wife Lee

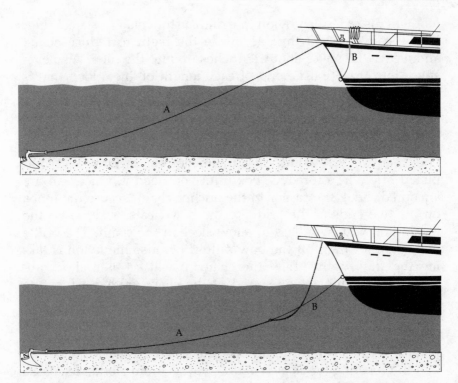

Fig. 10.8: *Frank Glindmeier found this rig useful for anchoring* Summer Wind *in crowded harbors where it was impossible to let out a normal 3:1 scope of all-chain rode.*

were ready to depart an anchorage, Frank would power slowly forward and control the windlass with a separate switch on the flying bridge. Lee would go below and carefully flake the chain down in the chain locker to prevent it from becoming tangled. But after runs where they encountered stiff headwinds, they would get ready to deploy the anchor only to find that the chain had become terribly tangled and would not pay out properly.

"We finally figured out that when we ran into a head sea," Frank says, "the violent up and down motion of the bow was tossing the chain around inside its locker like spaghetti in a bowl. So I bought a truck inner tube, and the next time it looked like we were going to be pounding into a head sea, I stuffed the inner tube into the locker on top of the flaked-down chain and inflated it with a bicycle pump just enough to fill the remaining space in the locker. When we got ready to anchor, we deflated the inner tube, removed it from the locker, and found the chain was still neatly flaked and ready to run out without any problems."

Secondary Rode: While the weight of an all-chain rode is an advantage in getting an anchor to hold properly, it concentrates a great deal of weight in a vessel's forepeak. A stout cruising vessel of around 40 feet should be able to handle the weight of an all-chain primary rode but not the added weight of an all-chain secondary rode as well. For that reason, rope with a length of chain between it and the anchor to resist chafe is the preferred rode for a secondary or a backup anchor and as we said earlier, for the primary rode of a planing hull cruiser under about 35 feet.

Rope used for a rode is properly called "line." It should be made of nylon, which can be stowed wet and resists damage from water, oils, and sunlight better than other materials. It should also be of the hard-laid, three-strand-twist variety. Soft-laid three-strand-twist or braided nylon line is more pleasant to handle, but it does not work as well on the rope drum of a windlass. Braided nylon line is also less elastic than three-strand-twist and therefore does not provide as much shock absorption.

The breaking strength of three-strand-twist nylon line is a function of its diameter (Fig. 10.9). Under the stress of use in cruising, rope is subject to considerable weakening. For that reason, for your anchor rode you should choose new rope with a breaking strength approximately twice the holding power of the anchor to which it will be attached (Fig. 10.10). Replace it when it shows significant fraying or exudes a chalky dust. The latter is a sign its fibers are being broken down by the sun's ultraviolet rays.

Nylon line used as an anchor rode should have six fathoms (36 feet) of chain between it and the anchor to help keep the strain on the anchor horizontal and to resist chafing on rocks or coral. The end of the line that will be attached to this chain should have an eye splice with a stainless-steel thimble of sufficient size to accept the shackle you will use to join them, and the splice should be woven back into the line for at least 12 inches.

To prevent accidentally losing the bitter end of the rope rode on your secondary anchor overboard, it should be whipped and

Diameter	Break Strength (lbs.)	Wt/100' (lbs.)
5/16″	2,550	3
3/8″	3,700	5
7/16″	5,000	6
1/2″	6,400	8
9/16″	8,000	10
5/8″	10,400	12
3/4″	14,200	17
7/8″	23,000	21
1″	28,500	25

Fig. 10.9: *The breaking strength and weight of nylon anchor line vary significantly with its diameter.*

tied by a bowline or anchor hitch to an eyebolt installed inside the rope locker.

WINDLASSES

Few devices aboard your vessel will contribute more to the ease of cruising than a good electric anchor windlass (Fig. 10.11). With it you can deploy and retrieve your primary anchor without any of the strain that inevitably accompanies manual anchoring.

For a moderate- to heavy-displacement cruising power boat in the 30-to-40-foot range, you will need a windlass with at least 350 pounds of line-pull capacity to handle its anchor and combination chain-rope primary rode. It will weigh around 50 pounds.

For a similar boat of 40-to-50-foot LOA, you will need a windlass with at least 500 pounds of line-pull capacity to handle its anchor and all-chain rode, and it will weigh about 80 pounds. For vessels 50 to 60 feet in length, you will need a windlass with about 1,000 pounds of line pull which will weigh about 150 pounds. For vessels of 60 to 70 feet, you will need a windlass with about 1,800 pounds of line pull which will weigh about 200 pounds.

The windlass you select should be capable of handling both

Boat Length	Minimum Holding Power Required	Recommended Secondary Anchor Danforth Deepset Hi-Tensile	Recommended Rode Size* Diameter
40'–49'	3,500	29 (4,000)	9/16" (8,000)
50'–59'	5,000	41 (6,000)	3/4" (14,200)
60'–69'	6,500	60 (7,000)	3/4" (14,200)

*Based on line with a breaking strength approximately twice the holding power of the recommended anchor to offset the effects of line deterioration.

Figures in parentheses are holding power of anchors and breaking strength of line in pounds as rated by their respective manufacturers.

Fig. 10.10: Recommended secondary anchor and anchor-line sizes for moderate- to heavy-displacement cruising vessels 40–69 feet in length.

chain and rope of the size you choose for your primary and secondary anchor rodes. Whether the wildcat and capstan operate vertically or horizontally is a matter of personal choice, but the wildcat should automatically feed the chain into its locker through a deck pipe. You should be able to operate either the wildcat or the capstan independently. You should also be able to release tension on the wildcat with a hand wrench to allow the anchor to fall away freely from its bow roller rather than having to power it down by reversing the direction of the windlass. If your vessel is being carried away from the optimum anchoring point by wind or current, powering down is too slow a process to allow you to place your anchor exactly where you want it.

The windlass should have a foot switch within easy reach of it on the foredeck and a second control station on the flying bridge, but they should be rigged with an off-on switch at the flying bridge position to prevent either from being operated accidentally before you are ready to anchor. After the main power switch has been turned on, the windlass's circuitry should have an automatic cutout switch which allows only one switch to be operated at a time.

Choose a windlass that takes its power at whatever voltage you use for other accessories aboard (usually either 12 or 24 volts, in a few cases 32 volts). Your windlass should be wired from the battery on its own circuit with a breaker in the line to protect

Fig. 10.11: *An electric anchor windlass and an all-chain primary rode can make anchoring virtually a "hands-off" maneuver.*

its electric motor and gearbox from being burned out by an overload.

By combining the information we've assembled to this point, we can construct a chart (Fig. 10.12) for computing the total weight of the primary and secondary anchors, chain and rope rodes, and windlass you will be putting on the bow of your vessel.

One note: Never use your windlass to pull your boat toward its anchor since this can burn out its electric motor. Instead, pull slowly up to the anchor under engine power and use the windlass only to take in the weight of the rode and anchor. For the same reason, never use your windlass to attempt to free a fouled anchor. Instead, use the anchoring bridle described above or a

	Boat Length				
	40′–49′		50′–59′		60′–69′
Primary Anchor Type/Weight	Danforth	41	Danforth	60	CQR 75
Primary Rode* Type/(Size)/Wt.	Accoloy (⅜″) 405		(⅜″) 405		(½″) 702
Secondary Anchor** Weight		29		41	60
Secondary Rode Chain*** Weight		52		52	52
Secondary Rode**** (Size)/Weight	(⁹⁄₁₆″) 30		(¾″) 51		(¾″) 51
Windlass Weight		100		150	200
Total		657		759	1,140

*300′ all-chain
**Danforth Deepset Hi-Tensile
***Six fathoms ⅜″ Accoloy
****Three-strand twist nylon

Fig. 10.12: Depending on the choices you make in primary and secondary anchors and rodes and a windlass, this chart can help you add up the total weight you will be installing on the bow of your vessel.

devil's-claw to take the strain of the anchor chain, then free the anchor using your vessel's engine power.

ANCHORING TECHNIQUE

Most people anchor by approaching their intended point of anchoring from downwind, then cutting the power and letting the boat drift toward the intended anchoring point until it loses all headway. Once their vessel has come to a halt, they drop the anchor and pay out rode as the boat drifts back downwind. When the anchor digs into the bottom, they finish the job by backing down to set it firmly.

Frank Glindmeier says he's figured out a better way.

"When we first started cruising," Frank says, "we used the standard anchoring technique and found it worked about half the time. The other half of the time the anchor got fouled in its rode and we dragged it halfway across the anchorage before we could get it to take hold. Finally I realized that when there was little wind to carry the boat backward, we were dropping the anchor, then dumping the chain right down on top of it, which virtually guaranteed it at least a fifty-fifty chance of fouling. I figured there had to be a better way."

The technique Frank developed works this way:

Once he picks out an anchoring spot, Lee goes to the bow and inserts the wrench in the windlass's tension control to prepare to release it. Frank slowly approaches his intended anchoring spot in the usual manner from downwind but deliberately passes over the spot where he wants to drop the hook. Once he is about 50 feet upwind of his target, he drops both engines into reverse and backs the boat down toward the spot with its engines ticking over just enough to give him about a knot of speed. As the center of the boat is about over the point he wants the anchor to rest, he gives Lee a simple hand signal and she releases the tension to let the anchor and chain run free. Frank continues to back the boat slowly as the chain pays out. When he has all the scope he wants paid out, he signals Lee to tighten up the tension on the windlass. Once the tension is set, the boat's light sternway sets the anchor. Another thirty seconds in reverse at slightly increased engine rpm leaves no doubt that the anchor is well-set.

"What this technique does," Frank says, "is string the chain out behind the anchor rather than dumping it on top of the anchor, which sharply reduces the chances of getting them tangled up."

11

CRUISING TENDERS

While the primary job of a tender is to provide transportation between your anchored vessel and the shore, if you choose the right type of tender and put adequate outboard power on it, you can make it do additional duty as a fishing or diving boat or use it to explore shallow or inland waters you encounter in your cruising.

HARD OR SOFT?

The basic decision you have to make regarding a tender is whether you will select an inflatable or one made of a hard material such as wood or fiberglass. Both have their devoted adherents.

Proponents of hard tenders argue that they handle better in adverse conditions such as a stiff wind or chop, they can be rowed if the outboard quits, and they simply look the way a tender to a proper cruising yacht ought to look, not like an elongated inner tube.

Advocates of inflatable tenders counter that their choice is lighter and easier to handle when hoisted aboard, in a comparable size will carry more load, has much more lateral stability (which is particularly valuable if you will be using your tender as a dive boat), doesn't make noise or scar up your topsides when it bumps into your vessel at anchor, and doesn't skin your shins when you are trying to board it in a rolly anchorage. They also point out that inflatables are now available with a variety of keel and rigid bottom configurations that greatly enhance their handling characteristics.

HARD TENDERS

If you decide on a hard tender, your most obvious choice is a Boston Whaler, which currently dominates this particular segment of the marine market. Boston Whaler makes a fine line of boats that are especially practical for cruising because their internal foam flotation makes them unsinkable. The two Boston Whaler models most often selected for cruising tenders are the 9-foot version, called the Tender, and the slightly larger 11-foot Standard.

The Tender weighs 165 pounds and is designed to carry three people or a total weight, including its outboard and fuel, of 405 pounds. Its list price is $2,500. While the Tender is a nice little craft, in the real world of cruising its limited load-carrying ability can be very inconvenient. If you equip it with even a minimum outboard motor weighing only 30 to 50 pounds and put three people aboard averaging 150 pounds each, you have already exceeded its maximum designed load. And where do you put the groceries? So it is the best choice only where the primary consid-

Fig. 11.1: *Excellent workmanship and internal floatation help make Boston Whaler's 11-foot Standard model the most popular of the hard-cruising tenders.*

eration is the weight and length of a tender when it is hoisted aboard your main vessel.

If your cruising vessel can carry it, a better choice would be Boston Whaler's 11-foot Standard, which weighs 210 pounds and is designed to carry three people or a total load of 560 pounds, including its outboard and fuel. The Standard lists for $2,600, or you can upgrade to the Sport version (Fig. 11.1) that includes wheel steering at a cost of another 40 pounds of weight and an additional $600 in price.

Boston Whaler dealers typically discount their boats only about 10 percent.

In a hard tender, one alternative to the Boston Whaler is a rowing or sailing dinghy. With Carleton Mitchell's extensive sailing background, it's not surprising that as a tender to *Coyaba* he selected a 9-foot Dyer Dhow which he could either take for a recreational sail or push along to the dock with a small outboard. Dyer makes four models of well-constructed fiberglass rowing and sailing dinghies from 7½ to 12½ feet which can be used as yacht tenders. In the standard rowing version, for example, the 135-pound, 10-foot Dyer Dink lists for $2,095. Necessary options such as davit lifting rings put its realistic price at around $2,500. The sailing version lists at $3,625; with necessary options its realistic price is just over $4,000.

INFLATABLE TENDERS

If you decide to consider an inflatable tender, you will find a much wider choice because there are considerable differences in the materials and construction processes used by the manufacturers and there are even greater differences in the price and quality of the boats they produce.

Less expensive inflatables usually are made of polyvinyl-chloride (PVC). They are cheaper to assemble because their seams can be thermobonded electronically on a machine rather than cold-glued by hand. The drawbacks to PVC are that it is not very resistant to ultraviolet light, chafing, or solvents and it can be stained easily by oil and grease. In hot weather it tends to stretch excessively and in cold weather it becomes brittle. In order to make PVC pliable, it must be impregnated with plasticizing oils. Critics of the material say that as it ages these oils work their way to the surface and leach away, causing it to stiffen, crack, and leak air. Some critics also believe these plasticizers attack the glue which is used to attach wooden transoms to some PVC inflatables, causing them to fall off.

The more expensive inflatables are made of a compound of Hypalon—a branded chlorosulfonated polyethylene product created by DuPont—and neoprene. The neoprene is added because adhesives will not stick to pure Hypalon. Inflatables made of the compound are more expensive because the material itself is more costly and seams must be glued by hand.

PVC and Hypalon/neoprene coatings allow inflatables to hold air but neither is very resistant to tears and punctures. The very cheapest of the PVC inflatables (all models of the Sea Eagle brand and Sevylor's Caravelle model, for example) are made of PVC only. They are fine for kids to play with in the pool but should never be considered for a cruising tender. The higher-priced PVC inflatables and all those made of Hypalon/neoprene are reinforced with a fabric backing of polyester or nylon. Reinforcing fabrics can range in density from 840 denier down to 210 denier, with the higher-denier fabrics being the more resistant to tears and punctures.

Inflatables made by France's Zodiac Group under the brand names Zodiac, Bombard, Hurricane, Sevylor, Sea Eagle, and ZED are made of PVC. The Zodiac Group also now owns the German inflatable manufacturer Metzler, which in the past fabricated its boats of a German version of Hypalon but has now shifted to making its boats of PVC.

Manufacturers of upper-end inflatables, such as Avon (Britain), Achilles (Japan), Sillinger (headquartered in France but now also building inflatables in Arizona), and Novurania (Italy), make their boats of some combination of Hypalon and neoprene. Avon, considered the inflatable industry's quality leader, uses nylon fabric sandwiched between two layers of Hypalon/neoprene. Achilles, which has the best reputation for air-retention, uses a nylon core with Hypalon/neoprene on the outside and two layers of neoprene coating on the inside. Sillinger employs the trademarked Orca product of France's Pennel & Flipo which has a Hypalon/neoprene coating on the outside, a polyester fabric core, and two layers of neoprene on the inside. Italy's Novurania, the highest-priced of the major inflatable manufacturers, uses a Trevira polyester fabric core with Hypalon outside and neoprene inside.

If you decide on an inflatable as a tender, go with one of these better-known manufacturers, even though an off-brand may be considerably cheaper.

Inflatables used as tenders come in three basic versions. The least expensive type has an inflatable transom, and in order to accommodate an outboard motor the boat must be outfitted with a bracket. An example would be the 9-foot-3-inch Avon Redcrest (Fig. 11.2), which weighs just 43 pounds and is designed to carry four people or a total of 700 pounds. An outboard bracket and floorboards are included in its $1,125 list price. This type of inflatable normally has a flat bottom.

In the midrange are inflatables with wooden or fiberglass transoms. They usually are fitted with wooden, plastic, or aluminum flooring and some have an inflatable keel which aids materially in their tracking ability. Sillinger and Novurania also offer models in this category that employ a single wooden rib fitted between the floorboards and the fabric bottom to give the bottom a vee-shape. An example of this class of inflatable would be Sillinger's inflatable-keel 420 GTX, which is 13 feet 8 inches long, weighs 172 pounds and is designed to carry six to seven people or a maximum load of 2,204 pounds. Floorboards are included in its list price of $3,280. That same boat with a rib-keel bottom is designated the 420 GRA (Fig. 11.3). It is designed to carry the same maximum loads but weighs 35 pounds more and lists for $4,110.

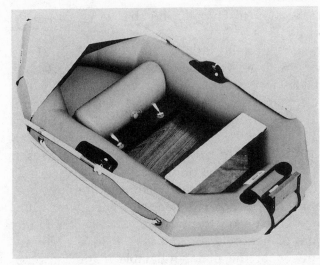

Fig. 11.2: *An inflatable-transom tender is the most economical, but its flat bottom can make it difficult to control in high winds.*

The third type is the rigid inflatable boat (RIB), which has a fiberglass-hull bottom and floor. An example would be Avon's 11-foot 3.40 RIB, which weighs 150 pounds and is designed to carry five people or a maximum load of 1,010 pounds. In its basic configuration it lists for $3,235. For another $445 it can be fitted with optional wheel steering.

Fig. 11.3: *An inflatable bottom with a wooden keel such as Sillinger's 420 GRA helps it track better than an inflatable tender with a flat bottom.*

Most inflatables can be bought from dealers at discounts of 15 to 20 percent, or through the marine catalogs at discounts to 30 percent.

TENDER POWER

In shopping for an outboard for your tender, you'll find that just about all the United States and foreign manufacturers (with the exception of British Seagull) have essentially the same lineup of horsepower sizes. Within a particular horsepower class, they also have almost exactly the same weights. The reason is that regardless of the brand names they carry, they all are built by fewer than a dozen companies in the world. America's OMC Corporation, for instance, makes all the motors that carry the Johnson and Evinrude names. Mercury Marine makes all but one of the Mercury engines and also owns the Mariner brand. Mercury makes all the Mariners over 40 horsepower, but Mariner outboards below 40 horsepower are made in Japan by Yamaha—which also has its own brand. Tohatsu makes its own brand plus the 5-horsepower Mercury and all those that carry the Nissan name. Suzuki and Honda make all their own outboards. This information can be useful since parts often are interchangeable among motors made by a common manufacturer though the brand names are different.

Generally speaking, you can expect a dealer in American and Japanese brands to offer a discount on an outboard for your tender of about 15 percent, perhaps a bit more if he is also selling you the tender itself.

Virtually all outboards in the relevant horsepower categories are available with either standard or long shafts. You'll want the standard-shaft type for use on a tender. Long-shaft outboards are generally necessary only when an outboard is to be used for auxiliary power on a sailboat.

The outboards commonly used to power cruising tenders break down into three basic categories: those under 5 horsepower; those from 8 to 18 horsepower; and those in the 25-to-40-horsepower range.

In the first category, all the major U.S. and foreign brands offer 2.5- and 3.5-horsepower models that have recoil starting, neutral and forward gears (no reverse), a weight of around 27 pounds, and list prices in the $500-to-$650 range. Their 5-horsepower motors have recoil starting; forward, neutral, and reverse gears; a weight around 45 pounds; and a list price in the neighborhood of $1,000. Outboards in the range of 2.5 to 5 horsepower have small fuel tanks built in, and some will also accept fuel from an external tank.

The other entry in this class is the British Seagull line, which includes 2- and 3-horsepower models that have hand rope starting (no recoil) and are direct-forward-drive (no neutral or reverse). They weigh 32 and 34 pounds, respectively, and have list prices of $635 and $675. Seagull also offers a 3-horsepower model with a recoil starter and neutral and forward gears but no reverse. It weighs 37 pounds and lists for $775. The company's 5-horsepower outboard has recoil starting and forward, neutral, and reverse gears; it weighs 52 pounds and lists for $1,045. Seagull outboards have small integral fuel tanks and will not accept fuel from an external tank without modification. They are ugly as sin but tough as nails and will take just about any abuse the cruising life can dish out. Their construction is so simple that any problems that make them stop usually can be repaired by even the least-mechanically-minded member of the crew. If Seagulls are discounted by their dealers at all, it's usually only by about 5 to 10 percent.

The next category of outboards is those with 8, 9.9, 15, and 18 horsepower. Again, all the U.S. and foreign manufacturers have products in these approximate sizes and they all have forward, neutral, and reverse gearing. Outboards of 8 horsepower and above require an external fuel tank. An 8-horsepower outboard weighs about 60 pounds, has recoil starting, and carries a list price of around $1,200 to $1,300. The 9.9-, 15-, and 18-horsepower models all weigh around 80 to 85 pounds and have list prices of about $1,500, $1,800, and $2,000, respectively. They also offer electric starting (but not remote throttle control) as an option that adds about $200 to $250 to their list price.

Above 18 horsepower, you get into the 25-, 30-, and 40-horsepower models. Outboards of 25 and 30 horsepower weigh around 100 pounds, and they list for $2,100 and $2,300, respectively. As an extra, in addition to electric starting, they also offer remote throttle control for use on tenders with wheel steering; the two features together increase their list prices by about $275 to $325. The typical 40-horsepower outboard weighs almost 130 pounds, lists for around $2,400, and offers electric starting and a remote throttle for another $300.

The best size motor to use on the various types of tenders are as follows:

The outboards used on small hard tenders such as the 9-foot Boston Whaler on the Dyer Dink should be limited to not more than 5 horsepower.

Although Boston Whaler recommends that its 11-foot Standard model not be outfitted with an outboard over 10 horsepower, many cruisers power this model with 15 to 18 horsepower. With an outboard of that size, you can use this model for high-speed exploring or even pull a single water skier if he or she weighs no more than 150 pounds and you put some weight in the bow to offset the weight of the operator, the engine, the fuel, and the pull of the skier. With an outboard of either size you pay no weight penalty over a 9.9-horsepower outboard since all three engines weigh around 80 pounds.

Some cruisers outfit this boat with 25- to 40-horsepower engines, but they are flirting with danger. Outboards of those sizes weigh between 100 and 130 pounds, and in order to have reasonable range will require a larger gas tank as well. That weight, plus the weight of an operator, concentrated in the boat's stern without any counterbalancing weight forward can be highly dangerous: If you hit a fair-sized wave at maximum throttle, the boat can flip over backwards. Outboards of that weight also significantly reduce the load of passengers and provisions that the boat can carry safely.

Boston Whaler recommends a maximum of 20 horsepower for its 11-foot Sport model, but it's common for cruisers to put 25- to 30-horsepower outboards on it that weigh about 100 pounds. They seem to have few problems because the Sport model's wheel steering places the operator's weight toward the center of the vessel rather than in the stern. I would not, however, recommend putting a 40-horsepower outboard on this model because of its weight. If the operator is a youngster weighing only about 80 or 90 pounds and he or she runs the boat at full throttle into a stiff chop, it can flip.

Inflatables that do not have hard transoms but must use a bracket to accommodate an outboard should not be fitted with a motor over 5 horsepower; a 2.5- or 3.5-horsepower is really better.

Hard-transom inflatables like the Sillinger 320 usually are fitted with an outboard of up to 9.9 horsepower, although some cruising owners put 15- to 18-horsepower outboards on them.

Because of the stability and load-carrying ability of an inflatable, boats of this size and type perform well with that much power.

An inflatable with a fiberglass bottom, such as the Avon 3.40 RIB, can safely handle an outboard up to 18 horsepower, even if the operator sits in the rear and steers with the outboard's combined throttle/tiller. If an RIB is rigged with remote steering and throttle control that positions the operator's weight farther forward, it can handle up to 25 horsepower.

TENDER REGISTRATION, SALES TAXES, AND INSURANCE

A cruising tender cannot be Federally documented because it does not meet the minimum five-net-tons size requirement. A tender is legally subject to the same state sales and use taxes as any other vessel and may or may not be subject to state registration. You may want to cover your tender under an insurance policy of its own or under a separate schedule of the policy on your main vessel which has a smaller deductible. For details, see our discussion of state sales taxes, registration, and insurance in Chapter 6.

TENDER ANCHORS AND RODES

The best anchor for a hard tender is a 4-pound Danforth. However, the sharp flukes of a Danforth can puncture the fabric of an inflatable tender; for that use, a better choice might be a 3-pound folding anchor. For a tender anchor rode, use about 35 feet of ⅜-inch three-strand-twist nylon line and add 6 feet of ¼-inch chain between it and the anchor to give its small hook a bit more holding power.

TENDER SECURITY

When you are at anchor during your cruising, your tender often will be unattended and tied off to the stern of your main vessel. You also will be leaving it at all manner of places ashore with no one to watch over it. At those times, it can be a tempting target for theft, because in many parts of the world its value will represent several years' income for some passersby. In a number of popular cruising areas, in fact, the locals have become quite adept at the "tender scam," which works this way: At night one fellow will keep a lookout while his friend slips up on an unwatched tender ashore or tied off to the stern of a nice-looking yacht at anchor, cuts its rope painter with the flick of a knife, and disappears with it into the night. The next morning, one of the pair will drop by the anchored vessel, comment on the missing tender, and ask if the owner is offering a reward. If he is, the local will quickly "find" and return the tender. If not, its motor is taken off and sold on one island while the boat, sans its registration numbers, is sold on another.

You will, of course, have your tender identified with your main vessel's name and, if required, its registration numbers painted on its side. For your own protection, take a few additional precautions. First, rely on your rope painter only when tying up ashore where you can easily keep an eye on the tender; or when you are using the tender to explore deserted islands or to go snorkeling or diving. Also, equip your tender with a 10- to 12-foot painter of high-grade ⅛-inch stainless-steel wire encased in plastic. Whereas a rope painter can be cut with a sharp knife, stainless-steel wire can be severed only with bolt cutters, which most potential thieves aren't likely to have handy. Permanently affix one end of the painter to the tender's towing ring with a stainless-steel thimble and a Nico-press fitting. Also Nico-press a stainless-steel thimble into the painter's bitter end and insert into it a stout, high-quality brass or bronze combination lock. Use the lock whenever you leave the tender unattended.

Second, secure your outboard to the tender itself. With motors under 5 horsepower which you might be taking on and off the tender, use plastic-encased stainless-steel wire, Nico-press fittings, and a bronze combination lock as you did on the tender's painter. For larger outboards which you are unlikely to be removing from the tender, use stainless-steel wire and Nico-press fittings to tie the two together so they cannot be separated without considerable effort. It's also a good idea to scratch your name or the name of your cruising vessel on the inside of the outboard's engine cowling. All these motors look pretty much alike. If yours is missing and you find it in someone else's possession, you'll have an easy way to prove to the gendarme that you are its rightful owner.

Third, never leave any loose articles like fishing tackle, snorkeling gear, cameras, or your hand-held VHF in the tender when you are not there to watch over them.

If you make it a habit to follow these simple precautions, you probably will avoid any unpleasant experiences. But if the worst happens and your tender is stolen, at least you should have no worries that your insurance company will try to claim negligence on your part.

TENDER DAVITS

Another important aspect of owning a tender is hoisting it aboard your main vessel, stowing it securely for open-water passages, and putting it back in the water the next time you want to use it—all with a minimum of fuss.

The traditional way of launching and retrieving a tender aboard a modern cruising powerboat of moderate size is to use a strongback or winch boom, both of which suspend the tender's entire weight from a single point. Unless the launching vessel is quite stable or there is someone around to steady the tender, it can easily become unbalanced and tip to one side or the other. On vessels with a motor-yacht configuration, the traditional place for stowing the tender is in a cradle mounted on the aft end of the vessel's cabintop. On a 50- to 60-foot cruising vessel, this means the tender must be lowered and raised anywhere from 12 to 15 feet. On some boats, that distance is even greater because the tender must be lifted an additional 4 feet or so to clear lifelines or safety railings. On boats like the Grand Banks Classics or the Hatteras 42 Long Range Cruiser, the tender is often stowed in a cradle mounted on top of the aft cabin. This location reduces the distance the tender has to be lowered and raised, but it also means it must be swung across at least part of the vessel's beam.

The problem with carrying a tender in either of those locations is that if the yacht is rolling from side to side, launching and retrieving the tender can be quite difficult. In extreme cases, it can be highly dangerous or absolutely impossible.

I'm going to tell a short story here to make my point.

I was the sole guest aboard Frank and Lee Glindmeier's *Summer Wind* during one leg of her shakedown cruise to the Bahamas in preparation for their voyage to Alaska. On our run southwesterly out of Nassau toward Andros, a heavy nor'easter with 30-knot winds set in on our stern, and we surfed down the face of waves that towered over *Summer Wind*'s flying bridge. When we reached Andros, Frank wisely ducked into the first reasonably protected cove he saw. We were able to hunker down behind a headland to get out of the worst of the wind, but the anchorage was still quite rolly. "No problem," said Frank with his typical élan. "We'll just take the dink down and do a bit of bonefishing in the flats."

In view of *Summer Wind*'s planned itinerary on the voyage to Alaska, Frank had decided not to carry a traditional tender but a larger boat that he could use for extensive side trips. For that reason, his "dink" was a 14-foot runabout with a massive 70-horsepower outboard. Together they weighed about 1,200 pounds. Grabbing everything we could find to hold on to, we worked our way to the aft end of the cabintop, stripped off the dink's cover, and rigged it for launching with the strongback. As soon as we had lifted it clear of its cradle, *Summer Wind*'s rolling motion made the tender gyrate wildly from side to side. It did not take Frank long to realize that by the time we got the tender over the side and even with the windows of the main salon which were directly below, *Summer Wind* was likely to lurch and the dink probably would wind up poking into the salon. He properly suggested we secure it and wait for calmer conditions, which we did—for the next three days. At least I got caught up on my reading.

Admittedly that's a rather extreme example, but it illustrates why it makes a great deal more sense to carry a powerboat's tender on davits hung off the stern. That arrangement stows the boat much closer to the water, suspends its weight from at least two points rather than one, and makes launching and retrieving it far easier and less dangerous.

Simpson Davits offers manually operated aft davits for both hard and inflatable tenders that are well constructed of 316 stainless steel and reasonably priced. I personally don't know of any electrically operated davits of this type, but they could be made up by a custom fabricator. If you go to an aft davit setup, you probably will find you have to reinforce your vessel's transom to bear the added weight. You also want to be sure the davits you select pull the tender up snugly against its arms and do not allow it any swinging room.

Some experienced cruisers object to carrying a tender in this fashion because it makes backing into a slip or Mediterranean

mooring more difficult. I can only say that in any kind of cruising beyond marina-hopping you are far more likely to find yourself anchoring out or tying up parallel to a face dock than you
are backing into a slip or a Med moor. In the few instances where
that problem might crop up, I would gladly go to the trouble of
launching the tender before I started backing in order to have
the ease of launching and retrieving it with aft davits the remainder of the time.

John and Mary Matthews use aft davits to carry the 11-foot
Boston Whaler they employ as a tender to their Hatteras 42 Long
Range Cruiser *Rigel.* In the course of a cruise with them from
Savannah, Georgia, to Great Stirrup Cay in the Bahamas, I
watched them launch and retrieve it a number of times. On all
but one occasion they accomplished the task quickly and effort-
lessly. Because the arrangement puts the tender's gunnel almost
10 feet off the water, John says he has never been concerned
that it would be pooped by a big wave and filled with water.

My only criticism of the Matthews' arrangement is that the
davits they selected have a single hoisting line in each arm that
attaches to a spreader bar at a point directly over the tender's
centerline. During launching and retrieval, that configuration allows the tender to tip from side to side. As John cranks it down,
Mary has to stand on the swim platform to steady it. On the one
occasion when they had a problem, it was because the weight of
a full fuel tank shifted and caused the tender to lurch sharply to
one side. I would like to see a davit system in which each arm
incorporated two lifting straps rather than just one. If two straps
on each arm led to lifting eyes in the extreme outboard edge of
the tender's sole, you would have an extremely stable four-point
lifting arrangement that would eliminate the danger of the tender
tipping over on its side as it was being raised or lowered
(Fig. 11.4).

One other alternative for carrying a tender is to use some
sort of pivoting device on the main vessel's swim platform that
allows the tender to be turned up on one gunnel and lashed
across the boat's transom. That is the most practical arrangement
on a cruiser under about 35 feet which doesn't have room to
mount the tender on deck. Edson International makes one such
arrangement called the Flip-Out Inflatable Holder, and versions
for handling small, rigid tenders the same way are made by several companies in the Northwest where the technique is fre-

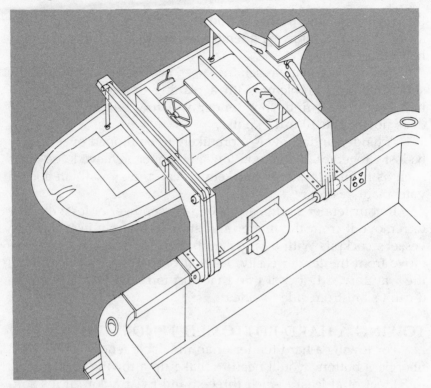

Fig. 11.4: *A pair of aft davits with double lifting straps in each arm would keep the tender stable as it is launched and retrieved.*

quently employed. One is Weaver Industries of Marysville, Washington, which makes the Snap Davit. The main drawback to this approach is that the motor must be removed from the tender each time the tender is brought aboard. Thus, it is practical only if you plan to power your tender with a small, easy-to-remove outboard.

TENDER TOWING

There will be times in your cruising when you would rather tow your tender. Usually it is when you want to move to a new anchorage not far away, and it's daylight and the weather is calm.

There is nothing wrong with towing a tender if you make proper preparations beforehand and take a few sensible precautions. First, the precautions:

Don't tow a tender at night. If it breaks loose, you'll have the devil of a time trying to find it. By daylight it can be miles away. Even when towing a tender during the day, check it every half hour or so.

In a displacement vessel, the speed at which you tow a tender shouldn't be a problem. With a planing or semidisplacement-hull boat, you'll find your tender will tow best if your speed does not exceed 10 to 12 knots.

A tender under tow is more likely to be flipped over than to be lost altogether. Before you tow any tender, remove loose items such as fishing tackle or snorkeling gear and stow them aboard your main vessel.

If your tender's outboard is of 5 horsepower or less, it's best to remove it from the tender and stow it securely in your main vessel's cockpit. With a larger outboard that is too heavy to remove from the tender easily, leave it on the tender but tilt it all the way forward, lock it into that position, and lash it down so it can't slam from side to side.

TOWING A HARD-BOTTOMED TENDER

For towing a hard tender or an inflatable tender with a rigid fiberglass bottom, you'll need to make up a towing line from 40 to 50 feet of at least ½-inch three-strand-twist nylon. If it's soft-laid, it will be easier on your hands. (It's best not to use braided nylon for a tender towing line because it isn't very elastic and therefore doesn't provide much shock absorption.) Eye-splice a stainless-steel sassor large enough to fit the towing eye on your tender into one end of the line and use a stainless-steel thimble to reduce chafing. Whip the bitter end.

You'll also need to rig yourself a towing bridle (Fig. 11.5) that will allow the tender to track as precisely as possible behind the center of your main vessel. It should be made of at least ½-inch three-strand-twist nylon, and the knot in its center should be about 6 to 8 feet off your cruising vessel's transom.

Once your towing line and towing bridle are made up, the next step is to figure out where along the length of the towing line you should join the two to put the tender in the best position for towing. Have someone else operate your main vessel at its normal towing speed so you can work freely in the cockpit. Slowly let the tender's towing line out until the tender's bow is riding on the back of your second stern wave (Fig. 11.6). Note where the towing line crosses the transom, subtract from that

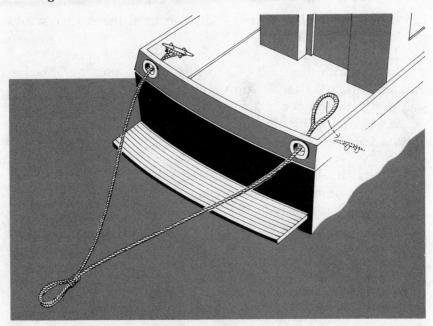

Fig. 11.5:   A towing bridle will help insure that your towed tender will track behind your main vessel in a straight line.

point the 6 feet or so by which the loop in your towing bridle will be behind your stern when everything is in place, and tie the towing line to the center loop in the towing bridle with a bowline. If the tender slews from side to side when you let it back out, that indicates it is not tracking directly behind your main vessel because the knot in your towing bridle is not exactly

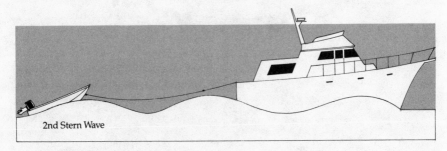

2nd Stern Wave

Fig. 11.6:   A hard tender will tow best if you allow it to ride on the back of your main vessel's second stern wave.

centered. Play with the knot's location until the tender settles down and rides calmly.

Don't forget that whenever you slow down or approach your destination with this kind of a towing rig you must send someone aft to pull the tender up on short scope and fend it off. If you don't, the tender is almost certain to slam into your main vessel's stern, and the towing line will probably wind up wrapped around your props.

TOWING SOFT-BOTTOMED INFLATABLES

Because of its lightness and its lack of a significant keel, the best position in which to tow an inflatable tender with a soft bottom is on the back of the first stern wave your main vessel creates rather than the second. With the tender pulled up that short, it has less room to slew about.

To tow an inflatable tender with a soft bottom, you should have two towing bridles—the one for your main vessel we have already described (though it may need to be a bit longer or shorter), and a second for the tender itself (Fig. 11.7).

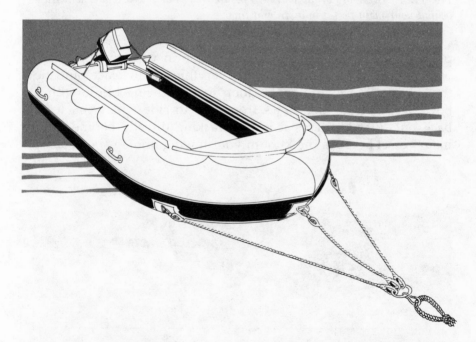

Fig. 11.7: *An inflatable tender should have its own bridle to distribute stress over more than one of its fittings.*

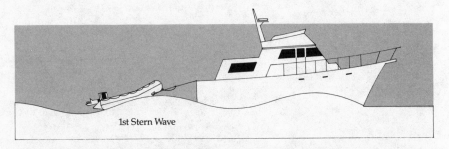

1st Stern Wave

Fig. 11.8: An inflatable tender with a soft bottom tows best if it is pulled up short and rides on the back of your main vessel's first stern wave.

In making up the towing bridle for your main vessel, tie the knot in its center, but instead of making up the loops in the ends, for the time being just tie the ends off to your stern cleats. In towing a soft-bottom tender you won't use a towing line, so you must adjust the distance at which it rides behind your main vessel by adjusting the length of the towing vessel's bridle.

As for the tender's towing bridle, the large hand-hold fitting at the bow of an inflatable is intended primarily for pulling it out of the water and onto the shore. By itself it's not strong enough for towing, so you should have the dealer fit an inflatable with optional rings on either side of its bow just below the rubstrake. When you make up the tender's bridle, its two side lines should take the strain. The center line should have just a little slack but take the strain if either of the fittings accommodating the outside lines separates from the tender.

To determine how long your main vessel's towing bridle should be, put everything in place and have someone operate your vessel at its normal towing speed while you're in the cockpit. Take in or let out the ends of the towing bridle on your main vessel until your inflatable is tracking directly behind your main vessel and riding on the back of the first stern wave it creates (Fig. 11.8). Mark the points at which the ends of the main vessel's towing bridle go around your stern cleats, and make up the end loops as suggested above.

PART III

Staying Safe and Healthy

12

CRUISING SAFETY

On the Ft. Lauderdale-to-Bermuda leg of Don Baumgartner's trans-Atlantic voyage aboard *Trenora*, he and his crew experienced seas he described as being "the size of condominiums" that rolled the vessel as much as 40 degrees off the vertical. On one roll, Don was slammed all the way across the main salon and into a bulkhead. When I met him on the dock at St. George, one eye was swollen almost shut and ringed with deep circles of angry purple. "Even at that," he told me, "I was lucky. If I'd hit

a few feet further aft, I'd have gone right through the window."
As Joe Columbus cruised his 48-footer *Evelyn C.* across the Gulf
of Alaska from Cape Hinchinbrook to Cape Spencer on one of
his annual Anchorage-to-Seattle migrations, he encountered 60-
knot winds and 20-foot seas that sent green water over his flying
bridge. I was in the Abacos a few years ago when one foolish
crew tried to run Whale Cay Passage in the midst of a "rage"
that pitchpoled their 40-foot sailboat. Thanks to the valor of a
native skipper out of Treasure Cay, no lives were sacrificed, but
one woman was seriously injured and the boat was lost.

My point in these brief stories is that the sea is not to be
trifled with. Anytime you plan a voyage that entails an open
water passage, you must have your vessel properly rigged and
equipped to withstand the worst. Making certain that you cruise
in safety as well as comfort involves a great deal more than simply outfitting your vessel with the minimum emergency equipment required for its class by the U.S. Coast Guard.

RIGGING FOR A BLOW

While your vessel is still tied securely in its home slip, imagine what life aboard it would be like in 40-to-50-knot winds and
15-to-20-foot seas, then look for areas that could present problems and figure out how you can prevent potential difficulties.
Based on our discussion of cruising-vessel layout in Chapter 2, I
hope you see in your vessel some very helpful features such as
stout safety railings with an intermediate lifeline; limited expan-
ses of exposed glass; side decks; and interior access to the flying
bridge. Even if all those factors are present, there probably will
be a number of areas where you will need to do some work.

Make certain, for instance, that your vessel has a series of
readily accessible handholds that will allow you and your crew
to go fore and aft safely both inside the vessel and on deck regardless of what the weather is doing. On the interior, those
handholds in the overhead may be fine if you're 6 feet 2 inches
tall, but if your first mate is 5 feet even, you'll need to install
handholds she can reach. As for the exterior, invest in a good
safety harness and figure a way to rig a safety line—often referred to as a "jack" line—along the side decks when the weather
turns really nasty. As nearly as possible it should be continuous
to allow a crewperson wearing a safety harness to clip to it and
walk the length of the deck without having to unclip. If it isn't

continuous, according to Murphy's Law, the few seconds he or she is unattached will be the instant the rogue wave hits and the vessel is knocked on its beam ends. The safety line should run on the inboard side of your decks right up next to the house. During a severe blow, you don't want to have to work your way along your vessel's safety railings, for that would put you to the extreme outside of the vessel in the perfect position to be pitched overboard in a 30- to 40-degree roll. For the same reason, figure a way to run a safety line down the centerline of the foredeck and up to the flying bridge if you must go on deck to reach it.

Bolt down the main pieces of furniture in the main salon so they can't shift. If a vessel is rolling heavily in a seaway, a weighty chair or table can be slammed across the salon with enough force to crush a person's leg. Prepare to lash lighter furniture to a bulkhead with a stout shock cord. Find places to stow loose articles securely, otherwise they can become deadly missiles. Check the galley carefully for positive locks on overhead locker doors that prevent them from being knocked open and spilling their contents on someone's head. On *Trenora*'s Atlantic crossing, Don Baumgartner's bride-to-be Donna Flaxman rigged herself a window-washer's belt in the galley so she would be braced in heavy weather but would still have her hands free to prepare meals.

In Chapter 3 we mentioned the need for an alarm that will alert you to high water in the bilge. It's also a good idea to attach an appropriately sized wooden plug to each of your vessel's through-hull fittings with a piece of light line or wire. If a through-hull fails, having a plug at your fingertips to ram home quickly could help save your vessel. Also have accessible in your engine room several packages of Syntho-Glass, a resin-impregnated fiberglass cloth that is activated with water and sets up in thirty minutes or less. You can use it to stop leaks in broken hoses, wrap temporary patches around broken water, fuel or hydraulic lines, or as a plug (balled up) to fill small holes. Since it is heat-resistant to 1,100°F, it can be used in making temporary repairs to mufflers and exhaust systems.

FIRE PROTECTION

According to U.S. Coast Guard statistics, in one recent five-year period, 1,882 fires and explosions aboard recreational vessels claimed ninety-five lives, inflicted 677 personal injuries, and caused a monetary loss of over $15 million. In preparing any cruising vessel, one of your most basic safety considerations should be preventing the likelihood of a serious fire or explosion. Three key areas you should be especially concerned about are the vessel's fuel and lubricating oil systems, its electrical systems, and its fire-fighting equipment.

Fuel and Lubricating Oil Systems: A four-year study by the Coast Guard and Underwriters Laboratories found that the most common cause of fires in pleasure vessels was the failure of fuel-fill pipes or fuel tanks. Examine all your vessel's fuel-fill hose connections to be certain they are tightly secured at both the underside of the deck fuel fittings and at the top of all tank connections. Check for corrosion or cracking of the hoses and make sure they are double-clamped on both ends. Check fuel-tank vent lines the same way.

Fuel tanks should be of UL-approved fiberglass or heavy-gauge metal with electrically welded seams, never soft-soldered. Solder melts at 1,000°F and the failure of a soldered joint could allow a small fire to become a raging inferno. Metal fuel tanks should be installed with sloping or rounded tops to encourage the runoff of condensation and prevent puddling which can lead to corrosion. Tanks should be installed so they can be inspected visually. Fuel tanks mounted in foam flotation should allow for adequate drainage to prevent moisture-induced corrosion.

Check flexible fuel and lube oil lines for any signs of chafing or deterioration. Check copper injector lines on diesel engines for pitting or corrosion, especially around their termination on the engine block. A high-pressure line spraying fuel or lube oil on a hot engine, turbocharger, manifold, or gearbox can create a voracious monster of a fire in seconds.

Electrical Systems: Many fires aboard recreational vessels are traced to faults in their electrical systems, and the largest single cause of those faults is chafing. Pay particular attention to wiring beneath galley counters where it can be chafed by loose pots and pans.

Since the most effective way to snuff out an electrical fire is to deprive it of oxygen, all circuit and terminal boards should be enclosed in a box of heavy-gauge metal. Be sure all circuits are equipped with circuit breakers appropriate to the load they are designed to carry. Know where your main electrical panel shutdown is located and be sure you can reach and deactivate it in one motion, even in the dark.

Fire-fighting Equipment: We mentioned in Chapter 3 the necessity of having the engine space of a cruising vessel protected with an automatic fire-extinguishing system. In addition to that system, you will need portable fire extinguishers as well.

U.S. Coast Guard regulations require recreational vessels 26 to less than 40 feet in length whose engine spaces are equipped with an automatic fire-extinguishing system to also carry at least one B-I type-approved hand-held fire extinguisher. Vessels 40 to 65 feet in length with fixed fire-extinguishing equipment installed in their engine spaces must carry at least two B-I type-approved hand-held portable fire extinguishers or one B-II type-approved unit. (The "B" refers to the type of fire the extinguisher is designed to fight—flammable liquids—and the I and II refer to the extinguisher's size, with II being the larger.) Recreational vessels 26 to less than 40 feet in length whose engine spaces are not equipped with an automatic fire-extinguishing system must carry at least two B-I type-approved hand-held extinguishers or at least one B-II type-approved unit. Recreational vessels 40 to 65 feet in length whose engine spaces are not equipped with an automatic fire-extinguishing system must carry at least three B-I type-approved units or at least one B-I and one B-II type-approved unit. These portable extinguishers must be mounted in a readily accessible location using an approved quick-release mounting bracket.

For all your portable fire extinguishers you should choose Halon units, which are effective against electrical fires as well as those fueled by flammable liquids. The older, generally less expensive Halon portables use Halon 1211; the newer units use Halon 1301. There is so little difference between the two types that I'd select the one on which I could get the best price. My suggestion would be that you install one B-II type-approved Halon portable extinguisher in a readily accessible location just outside your engine space(s) to extinguish small engine-room fires before they set off your automatic fire-extinguishing system. Also install a B-I type-approved extinguisher that contains at least 5 pounds of active ingredient in each of these spaces: pilothouse, galley, aft end of the salon, passageway to your vessel's forward sleeping quarters, and aft owner's stateroom if your vessel has one.

FIRE-FIGHTING TECHNIQUES

The experience of a friend of mine, Sumner Pingree, who lost his meticulously maintained 53-foot sportfisherman *Roulette* to a turbocharger fire, dramatically illustrates the reality of a fire at sea. A brief review of what happened in his situation will make some valuable points about what to do—and what not to do—if you should experience a fire aboard your vessel.

Roulette was about an hour out of San Juan, Puerto Rico, bound for Palm Beach when mate Joe Berry glanced through an open engine-room door, noticed the fire, and slammed the door shut. "We immediately lost power on the starboard engine and generator," Sumner told me later. "By the time my fourteen-year-old son Richard was halfway up the flying bridge ladder to tell me about the fire, smoke was everywhere. I yanked the port engine back to idle and immediately got off a Mayday call to the Coast Guard. I said I was not declaring an emergency at that moment but had a fire on board and asked them to stand by. We opened the engine-room door to see what was going on. Our Halon system had already gone off and extinguished the fire. But while we were trying to figure out exactly what had happened, the fire reignited with a whoosh. I raced back up to the bridge to call the Coast Guard again, but the fire had already burned through the battery cables and the radio was dead. Within two or three minutes the entire cockpit and main salon were engulfed in flames. I was on the bridge and the flames were all around me. I yelled to everybody to abandon ship. We launched the life raft and leaped into the sea. Ten minutes after we first realized we had a fire aboard, we were swimming. I was amazed how quickly she burned."

Sumner and the crew of *Roulette* were lucky. The fire they had to deal with erupted in daylight, winds were moderate, the seas were calm, and they were in an area where help could reach them quickly. The Coast Guard arrived within an hour and a half of their distress call, and all in the party were rescued without injury. But *Roulette* was a smouldering hulk that quickly disappeared beneath the waves.

Sumner did a number of things right. The instant he realized he had a fire on board, he got off a distress call. If he had waited just two or three minutes while he personally inspected the situation, his radio would have been dead. His engine-room fire extinguisher did its job—it put out the fire. Mate Joe Berry did the right thing by shutting the engine-room door the instant he saw the blaze, which helped starve the fire of oxygen.

But Sumner and his crew did two things—and most of us would have done the same under the circumstances—that proved disastrous. First, he left his port engine at idle while he went below to assess the damage. "I wanted to have the engine to get back to shore on," he says—which sounds reasonable. But that idling engine was sucking Halon out of the engine room and at the same time sucking fresh air into the engine room which was creating the perfect environment for the fire to reignite. The second mistake was in opening the engine-room door before the engine's superheated metal had had a chance to cool below the flash point of the fuel. In fire prevention lingo, Sumner had a "reflash"—and in moments his vessel was gone.

After learning of Sumner's harrowing experience, I interviewed a number of experts in marine fires and developed a consensus of their opinions for fighting a serious fire at sea:

1. At the first suspicion that you have an engine-room fire, shut down all engines, generators, and fans that share that same engine space to prevent them from sucking your fire-suppression chemicals ou. of the engine room and sucking fresh air into the engine room to fuel the fire. This also can help to shut off any fuel or lube oil leaks that might be supplying the fire with flammable liquids.

2. *Immediately*, even before you attempt to assess the damage, get off a distress call giving your exact position, a description of your vessel, and the number of souls on board.

3. Send one crew member aft to stand by the life raft and be prepared to launch it.

4. After your engine-room fire-extinguishing system has discharged, keep all engine-room doors and hatches closed for ten to fifteen minutes to allow the fire suppressant to snuff out the fire completely and the area to cool down below the reflash point. (We mentioned earlier that your engine room should have a viewing port of transparent, heat-resistant material so that you can see what is going on in there without opening the door or raising the hatch.)

5. If you have to open the door or hatch of an engine space where you suspect a fire may be burning, crack it open slowly and keep it between you and the possible fire. The fire may still be smoldering. The instant you open the door and admit oxygen, it can reflash and leap for the source of the oxygen like a tiger.

6. If you have to fight a fire with a hand-held extinguisher, make every effort to get its stream at the base of the fire. Just dumping fire suppressant into the engine space or spraying it at the top of the flames will do little good.

7. Even after you have made certain the fire is out and the area has cooled below the reflash point, before you enter an engine space where a CO_2 system has discharged, allow the area to ventilate for at least fifteen minutes or the stuff can suffocate you. Halon 1301 is safe to breathe in the 5- to 7-percent concentration normally specified for fire suppression.

LIGHTNING PROTECTION

If you are caught in an electrical storm on the water, lightning will be attracted to the highest conductive point in the area— which well could be your boat. The best way to guard against lightning damage is to create a "zone of protection" around it by attracting lightning to a conductor mounted as high on your vessel as possible, then giving the lightning's current a direct, ample, and unimpeded path to run from the conductor to ground—that is, the water.

A lightning protection zone normally will include everything inside a cone-shaped area that has as its apex the highest point of your vessel. The base of the protection zone will be a circle at the water's surface that has a radius approximately twice the height of the conductor (Fig. 12.1).

If your vessel has a metal cruising mast, it should be grounded to your vessel's electrical bonding system with at least a #8 solid copper wire. The wire should run in as straight a line as possible and avoid sharp bends. It also should be run down through your vessel inside a bulkhead to keep crew members

Fig. 12.1: A properly-grounded lightning rod (inset) installed as high as possible can help create a lightning zone of protection around your vessel.

from accidentally coming into contact with it. If your radar antenna is mounted on the mast close to the top, you should protect it by installing on the mast a solid copper rod at least ¼-inch in diameter that extends at least a foot higher than the radar antenna itself.

SAFETY AND SURVIVAL EQUIPMENT

U.S. Coast Guard regulations require virtually all recreational vessels registered in the United States to carry certain safety and survival equipment on board. We'll concentrate here on the requirements for recreational vessels 26 to 65 feet in length. Required equipment must be "Coast Guard–approved," which means only that the Coast Guard has approved that particular equipment to meet one of its specific legal requirements. The fact that a particular device is not Coast Guard–approved does not necessarily mean it is not good equipment, only that it will not satisfy a specific Coast Guard regulation. The Coast Guard's requirements are nothing more than the absolute minimum in the way of lifesaving and safety equipment that should be aboard your vessel. There are additional items that you should consider to be equally, if not more, important.

The most comprehensive research into marine safety and survival being done today is that of the Safety of Life at Sea (SOLAS) Convention of the International Maritime Organization. While much of SOLAS's work is directed toward commercial shipping and fishing interests, its standards in many cases are equally applicable to cruising. While by law you must conform to the U.S. Coast Guard regulations on safety and survival equipment, I strongly urge you wherever possible to equip your vessel to meet the more stringent—and in many cases more realistic—standards set by SOLAS. (SOLAS, incidentally, does not inspect and approve safety devices. It simply issues standards and it's up to manufacturers who want to meet them to see that their products comply. For that reason, in referring to such equipment we'll use the term "SOLAS-qualified" rather than "SOLAS-approved.")

PERSONAL FLOTATION DEVICES

Wearable Personal Flotation Devices (PFD's): Coast Guard regulations require you to carry one Type I, II, or III wearable PFD for each person on board.

Even if you will be venturing into open water only occasionally, all the wearable PFD's you carry should be of Type I (Fig. 12.2), which is intended for offshore use and is designed to turn an unconscious person from a face downward position in the water to a vertical or slightly backward face-up position and to provide at least 22 pounds of buoyancy. A number of experienced cruisers loathe and despise Type I PFD's. They argue that their bulkiness makes them not only difficult to store but so uncomfortable to wear, so difficult to work in, and so unattractive, that no one will use them. They also argue—and rightly so— that Type I PFD's are not sufficiently buoyant: The wearer does not float high enough in the water to avoid ingesting seawater. Tests conducted showed that Type I PFD's will turn an unconscious person into a face-up position only about 70 percent of the time.

For several reasons, despite all their limitations, I still think Type I PFD's should be carried aboard a cruising powerboat. First, though they are not foolproof, they still offer the highest proba-

Fig. 12.2: *Though it is bulky and not particularly stylish, a Type I Personal Floatation Device is the best choice for the offshore cruiser.*

bility of turning an unconscious person over and floating him or her in a face-up position of any life jacket that satisfies Coast Guard requirements. Second, I think the point about them being so uncomfortable and hard to work in that no one will wear them is valid aboard a cruising sailboat, where the entire crew is often on deck in bad weather and may frequently have to go forward. But on the vast majority of powerboats, most people ride out bad weather in the pilothouse or the main salon. The only time they put on life jackets is when they have to go on deck. Even then they are outside only a few minutes and take them off as soon as they come back inside. Under those conditions, I don't see that the Type I's bulkiness is really a problem. Third, even the Type I's critics will admit that it provides far more protection in the water than a Type II or Type III substitute.

I do agree that the Type I's buoyancy is inadequate and think it is wise to supplement it with a good-quality personal inflatable life ring. There are several such units on the market, but the best one I have seen is the Seacurity unit produced by Survival Technologies Group. When inflated by a manually fired CO_2 cartridge, this device deploys a horseshoe ring of polyurethane-coated nylon which provides an additional 35 pounds of buoyancy. It is packed in a leather pouch designed to be worn on the belt, but I'd prefer to see it attached directly to the life jacket. (STG offers the unit affixed to a USCG type-approved Type III PFD but not to a Type I.) The Seacurity unit weighs 17 ounces, has a list price of $69.95, and is available through a limited number of boating supply stores or the company's catalog (101 16th Avenue South, St. Petersburg, FL 33701).

There is a strong movement in some quarters of the PFD industry to persuade the Coast Guard to allow inflatable life jackets to satisfy its PFD requirements for recreational vessels. Inflatable life jackets that provide 35 pounds of buoyancy have been accepted by marine regulatory agencies in Europe for years. The Coast Guard, however, refuses to go along with the idea on the basis that inflatable life jackets require too much maintenance to ensure that they will function properly in an emergency. (The Coast Guard does approve a Type V "special purpose" inflatable life jacket, but only for use aboard commercial vessels working in inland or coastal waters. A Type V jacket will not meet its requirement for pleasure vessels.) I don't often agree with the Coast Guard's regulatory bureaucracy, but in this case I do. For an inflatable life jacket to work, it has to be inflated by a CO_2 cartridge. As a certified scuba diver, and I think a fairly conscientious one, I have carried CO_2 cartridges as emergency backups on my buoyancy compensator for years. I have dutifully replaced the cartridge every year or so, but, instead of simply discarding the old one, I usually fire it just to make certain the mechanism still works. I haven't kept records on the failure rate but at least I can say that it's too high for me to trust my life to a CO_2-inflatable life jacket. (Actually, the failure usually is not in the CO_2 cartridge itself but in the firing mechanism due to corrosion, jamming, a broken firing pin, or a poor attachment in which the firing pin has not pierced the membrane of the cartridge.)

If you are one of those who object so strenuously to the Type I PFD's that you simply refuse to have them on your vessel, you might want to carry Type II life jackets on board to satisfy the Coast Guard but actually use one of the extremely light inflatable vests. The Mustang vest made in the United States, the Crewsaver from England, and the Autoflug vest from Germany are all well made but also are expensive. With manual activation of the CO_2 cartridge they run $135 to $165; those activated by seawater are around $185. The Mustang lists for $281 but also includes a sewn-in safety harness.

Whichever type PFD you choose, make sure you carry enough of them to accommodate the largest number of people you are likely to have aboard at any one time, and that they are of the appropriate sizes to accommodate the anticipated number of adults and children. (In this context, anyone who weighs over 90 pounds is considered an adult.) If the wearable PFD's you buy don't have patches of reflective tape affixed to the front of the shoulder area on each side and across the back, buy the kits available for this purpose and mark them yourself.

You are required to stow wearable PFD's so that they are "readily accessible," which doesn't mean stuffed down in the bottom of a belowdecks hanging locker. The best place to carry them is in the seat lockers of your flying bridge. Hang them on individual hooks installed at the top of the back of the locker so they don't wind up underneath whatever else you stow there.

If you will be cruising in cold-water areas above about 40 degrees North, you will need to provide immersion suits for all on board. They are expensive and you are not required by the Coast Guard to carry them, but in water below 60 degrees, survival times without them can be limited to an hour or less.

Wearable PFD Accessories: You also should securely attach to each of your PFD's a signaling whistle such as the ACR/WW-3 and a personal rescue light. In personal rescue lights, you'll have a choice of three basic types: xenon strobes; steady or flashing incandescents; and cylume lights.

Xenon strobes give off a brilliant flash of 250,000 peak lumens about once each second. They are especially good at penetrating rain or fog. The best unit of this type on the market is ACR's Firefly Rescue Light, which retails for $69.95 and is available through marine catalogs for under $50. My criticism of that unit is that it must be manually activated. I would prefer to have a light that would activate automatically when it comes in contact with seawater rather than having to be switched on by the person in trouble who may be unconscious or may panic and simply forget to turn it on quickly. The manual switch does allow the user to turn the light off and save its battery when no potential rescuer is in sight. In continuous operation, its integral battery will power the unit for about nine hours.

Rescue lights of the steady or flashing incandescent type were developed originally as marshaling lights for the victims of vessel sinkings or aircraft ditchings rather than as alert/locate lights for man-overboard situations. They provide only about 6 candela, which their manufacturers say makes them visible over a 3-square-mile area. That might be true on a clear, totally dark night. But in moonlight, rain, or fog the distance over which they are visible can be limited to no more than a few hundred yards—if that. On most of these units the battery is water-activated, but only after you pull a ring to remove two small sealing plugs. That seems to me to nullify the water-activated feature; again, the person might be unconscious or might panic and fail to pull the plugs. The best light of this type is ACR's L8-2, which lists for $19.95.

The only type of cylume light that should even be considered as a personal rescue light is the heavy-duty version; it is about 6 inches long and is activated by squeezing a jaw-like device to crush its inner vial and allow its chemicals to mix. These units produce only about three candela but they are the cheapest of the three—about $9.

Some experts in marine search-and-rescue object to xenon strobes with the argument that their flash is so rapid that the human eye has difficulty perceiving its exact location which makes it difficult to vector in on. A report on xenon research issued by Britain's Royal Navy a couple of years ago said that xenon strobes could actually cause short circuits in the human brain and induce epileptic seizures—even in people who don't suffer from the disease. In the industry, that report is still regarded with a heavy dose of skepticism.

Despite these criticisms and its greater expense, I still feel the xenon strobe is the superior choice for a personal rescue light. Its range of visibility over the widest variety of circumstances offers the best chance of enabling airborne or seaborne searchers to locate the person wearing it. I have discussed the matter with pilots and crewmen on Coast Guard search-and-rescue helicopters. They say they use strobes themselves, they recommend them, and they have no difficulty vectoring in on them.

Especially if you will be cruising with only two people on board, you might consider Survival Technologies' man-overboard alarm which includes a small water-activated transmitter worn on a life jacket and an on-board receiver that sounds an alarm. The company is extending the concept to offer an optional null meter to vector in on the signal and also have the transmitter automatically deploy a man-overboard pack.

We'll discuss emergency position-indicating radio beacons (*EPIRB*'s) in detail later in this chapter. Here we'll mention that you could go to the additional expense of equipping your PFD's with a Class B mini-EPIRB such as the ACR RLB-21. It weighs 15 ounces and is powered by a lithium battery with a ten-year storage life. It lists for $315 but is sold by most of the marine catalogs for under $200. Putting one of these units on each of your PFD's would be expensive, but if it could save a life it would be well worth the cost.

Throwable PFD's: In addition to wearable PFD's, Coast Guard regulations also require that recreational vessels 26 to 65 feet in length carry one throwable Type IV PFD which can be a type-approved floating cushion, ring buoy, or horseshoe buoy. Actually, regardless of the size of your vessel, you should carry one Type IV PFD on either side of its forward half and one at the stern. Use ring or horseshoe buoys rather than cushions. Each should be carried in brackets for immediate use and should be fitted with a 75-foot floating safety line. It would be ideal if all three could be horseshoe buoys because they are easier for a person who has fallen overboard to get into than a ring buoy. However, for appearance's sake, most cruisers carry ring buoys in brackets on the port and starboard sides of the pilothouse and a horseshoe buoy in the cockpit. They should have attached safety lines, but most don't.

Type IV throwable PFD's should also be equipped with strobe lights (though few cruisers do it) that automatically activate when they are immersed in seawater. ACR produces such a light (model 566), which lists for about $95 but is available through the marine catalogs for around $60.

Ring or horseshoe buoys are hard to throw accurately for any distance. Though the heaving lines encased in a weighted bag that are available through most marine catalogs are not Coast Guard type-approved and will not satisfy the Type IV requirement, you might also consider carrying one or more aboard. Survival Technologies also produces its Seaid unit—a life ring in a throwable plastic container that is automatically inflated by a CO_2 cartridge when it hits the water.

Man-Overboard Packs: Several companies make man-overboard packs which contain a man-overboard pole topped by a flag or light, a horseshoe buoy, drouge, whistle, strobe light, and dye marker (Fig. 12.3). They are mounted on a vessel's stern and release their contents by gravity when someone on board yanks a lanyard or releases a shock cord. If you follow the recommendations above regarding PFD's, anyone aboard your vessel who goes overboard while wearing a life jacket will already have with him everything but the man-overboard pole and dye pack. If you don't care to follow the PFD suggestions, a man-overboard package would be a good idea; I like STG's idea of having it automatically deployed when a life-jacket-mounted transmitter is immersed in the sea.

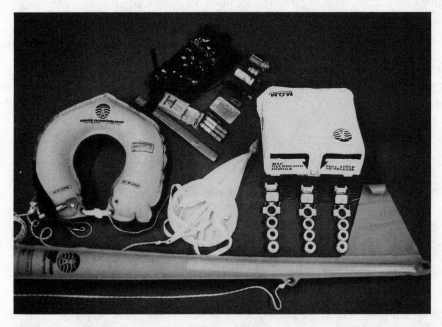

Fig. 12.3: *A man overboard module mounted on your vessel's stern is one quick way to get help to anyone unfortunate enough to fall or be swept off your vessel.*

SEARCHLIGHTS

If someone goes overboard at night, you can't save him until you can see him. Many sizable cruising powerboats have one or more searchlights on the forward edge of the flybridge that can be controlled from the pilothouse or the bridge steering station. While these units are useful for spotting navigation markers and other stationary objects ahead of your vessel, they can be somewhat slow and cumbersome to operate and their range of motion is limited. They are difficult if not impossible to train on a person in the water, especially since that person is likely to be aft of amidships and more likely at the stern while your crew is trying to get him back on board. For search-and-rescue work, you'll find that a more practical arrangement would be to mount three hand-held 12-volt halogen searchlights with long accordion-type cords on your vessel. I'd suggest you put one in the pilothouse, one on the flying bridge, and one in the cockpit. Several units with highly focused beams of up to 400,000 candlepower are available through the marine catalogs for under $100; they can be mounted in brackets and can be wired to utilize any of the 12-volt plugs on board your vessel. A poor second choice would be a battery-powered unit such as ACR's Super Beam Gun, which produces a 22,000-candlepower beam off a 6-volt lantern battery. It lists for $69.95 but sells through the marine catalogs for about $40.

VISUAL DISTRESS SIGNALS

Coast Guard regulations require all U.S.-registered recreational vessels over 26 feet in length to carry type-approved daytime and nighttime visual distress signals (VDS's). To meet the minimum requirement for a daytime VDS, you can use an orange flag with square-and-disk, three orange smoke signals (floating canister or hand-held type), or three red flares (hand-held, meteor, or parachute type). To meet the minimum requirement for a nighttime VDS you can carry an electric SOS light or three red flares (hand-held, meteor, or parachute type).

For open-water voyaging, of course, you will want to exceed those minimums considerably.

Daytime VDS's: The most popular daytime VDS's are hand-held orange smoke flares that burn for about fifty seconds. A package

of three lists for just over $25 but is available through the cata-
logs for under $20. A potential problem with a hand-held smoke
flare is that you are most likely to use it in a life raft where there
is a good chance the smoke will blow right back into the raft—
which may have a fixed canopy. While they are more expensive
(around $60), you'll be better off with the SOLAS-qualified float-
ing smoke canisters which have a much greater burn-time—about
three minutes.

Nighttime VDS's: Red hand-held flares made to U.S. Coast Guard
specifications burn for about two minutes and have about 500
candlepower. A package of three sells through the catalogs for
around $12. While they satisfy the Coast Guard requirement for
a nighttime VDS (three required), you have to strike them like
matches to ignite them, which can be impossible in a driving
rain or in a lifeboat with seawater slopping in the sides. They
also drip hot slag. A much better choice is the SOLAS-qualified
type which is fired by ramming home a mechanical plunger and
does not drip slag (Fig. 12.4). It burns for only one minute rather

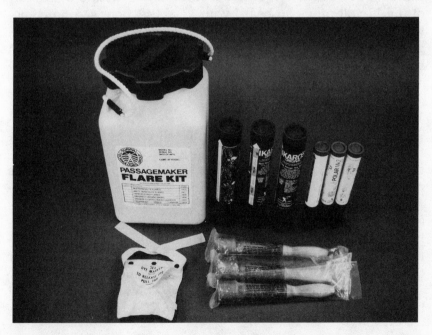

Fig. 12.4: *SOLAS-qualified flares are more dependable and safer to use than
the standard type.*

than two as with the USCG-approved type but does so with thirty times the brilliance—15,000 candela. They sell for around $15 each. Some, but not all, SOLAS-qualified hand-held red flares are also USCG-approved.

For offshore voyaging you also want to lay in a good supply of red aerial flares which come in two basic varieties, meteor and parachute.

Meteor Flares: Some meteor flares can be fired from their own casing while others require a pistol-type launcher. The small Skyblazer is fired from its own casing, reaches an altitude of about 250 feet, and burns for about eight seconds. The catalogs sell a package of three for about $12. Because the Skyblazer is compact, waterproof, and inexpensive it's a good idea to stick one in the pocket of your foul-weather jacket. But because the Skyblazer's signal is limited to 500 candela, it should not be relied on as your primary aerial flare. Experts who use them regularly in boating safety demonstrations tell me their firing mechanism is prone to a high failure rate.

Meteor flares, which are fired from a pistol-type launcher, are either 12-gauge or 25 mm. The 12-gauge type reach an altitude of about 250 feet and burn at 10,000 to 15,000 candlepower for about six seconds. The 25-mm type are preferable to the 12-gauge type because, although they have the same six-second burn-time, they reach a greater altitude (about 375 feet) and their 30,000 candlepower is more than twice as bright. A 25-mm launcher can also be used to fire parachute flares whereas a 12-gauge launcher cannot.

Parachute Flares: The Coast Guard approves parachute flares that are fired from a pistol-type launcher, but they do not meet SOLAS standards. The 25-mm launcher is the most popular size. Pistol-launched parachute flares reach an altitude of about 1,000 feet, burn at 10,000 to 20,000 candlepower for about thirty seconds, and (theoretically) are visible for up to forty miles. They sell for about $20 and their launchers cost about $40. The best value is Olin's 25-mm kit which lists for about $135 but sells regularly at retail for about $90. It includes a launcher, three red hand-held flares, three red meteor flares, and one parachute flare. You should add at least two more parachute flares to it.

A better choice than the pistol-launched parachute flare is

the SOLAS-qualified red parachute flare, which is fired from its own canister. The units made by Ikaros and Pains-Wessex are also USCG-approved. They reach an altitude of 1,000 feet, burn at 30,000 candlepower for forty seconds, and sell through the catalogs for about $45 each.

I would also suggest you have on board at least one or two SOLAS-qualified white illumination parachute flares for search-and-rescue situations. Like the red parachute flares, white illumination flares also are fired from their own canister and reach a 1,000-foot altitude. They burn for only thirty seconds but do so at 80,000 candela which can light up 2 square miles of ocean. They retail for about $70 each.

Whichever types of flares you choose to carry aboard your vessel, remember that they all will be stamped with an expiration date and must be replaced before that date passes. If the Coast Guard inspects your vessel and finds your VDS's are out of date, they will issue a citation.

EMERGENCY POSITION-INDICATING RADIO BEACONS

When activated in a distress situation either automatically or manually, emergency position-indicating radio beacons (EPIRB's) transmit signals to alert rescuers and guide them to the individual's location. Recreational vessels are not required to carry EPIRBs, but you should never venture offshore without at least one aboard. Those most practical for recreational use come in four classes:

Class A EPIRB's (Fig. 12.5) are designed primarily for offshore use aboard commercial vessels but can be used by recreational vessels as well. They are bracket-mounted on the exterior of a vessel, float free if the vessel sinks, and activate automatically.

Class B EPIRB's (Fig. 12.6) are designed for offshore use aboard recreational vessels, are bracket-mounted inside the vessel, and must be manually activated and deployed. Class B also includes the mini-B unit which is designed to be attached to a life jacket or survival craft.

Class S is a mini-EPIRB (Fig. 12.7) designed for use on the survival craft required to be carried by certain commercial vessels but they also may be used on life rafts aboard recreational vessels. The difference between the Class B mini-EPIRB and the

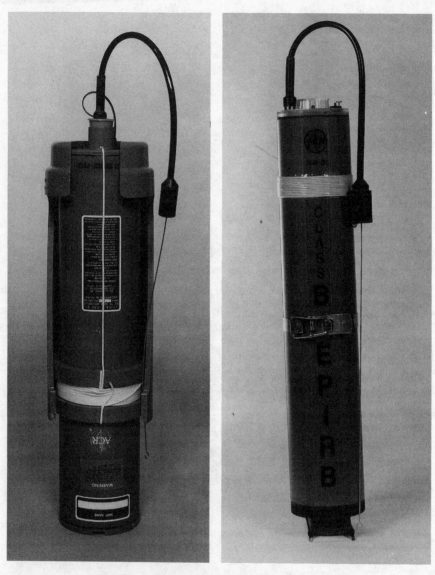

Fig. 12.5: *A Class A EPIRB installed on your vessel's exterior will automatically float free and activate in the event of a sinking.*

Fig. 12.6: *A Class B EPIRB is carried inside your vessel and must be manually activated and deployed.*

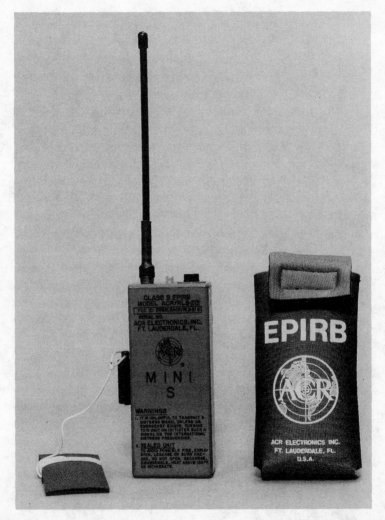

Fig. 12.7: *A Class S mini-EPIRB would be a valuable addition to your life raft supplies.*

Class S unit is that whereas the mini-B unit must be activated manually, the Class S unit is attached to the raft and is activated automatically when the raft inflates.

Class A, Class B (including the mini-B model), and Class S EPIRB's transmit carrier signals on 121.5 and 243.0 MHz which are picked up primarily by the joint U.S.-Soviet network of COSPAS/SARSAT orbiting satellites which relay them to rescue services on the ground. Currently there are four satellites in the

COSPAS/SARSAT network, each of which orbits the earth every ninety minutes. The two frequencies were chosen for EPIRB signals because 121.5 MHz is the primary emergency frequency for commercial aviation and 243.0 MHz is the primary guard frequency for military aviation. If the crews of either type of aircraft are monitoring the frequencies, they can pick up the signals as well.

Class C EPIRB's are designed for use aboard recreational vessels in inland or coastal waters. They should not be used aboard bluewater cruising boats since they do not transmit on 121.5 MHz or 243.0 MHz but only on 156.75 MHz (VHF channel 15) and 156.8 MHz (VHF channel 16). Their signals cannot be picked up by overflying aircraft or satellites, only by a VHF radio. Their maximum range is advertised as twenty miles, but with their antenna at or close to water level, I doubt that would be dependable. Even if you plan to do only coastal cruising, I recommend that you carry a Class B EPIRB rather than a Class C.

For offshore voyaging, you should carry a Class A EPIRB for your primary unit. I'd suggest the ACR RLB-14 which has a magnesium battery with a shelf life of six years. The unit weighs under 6 pounds and lists for $495, though it can be bought through the marine catalogs for under $300. Replacement batteries cost around $60. It should be mounted on your vessel's exterior in a position that will allow it to float free if the vessel goes down.

If you don't like the idea of mounting an EPIRB on your vessel's exterior and want a Class B unit, I'd recommend the ACR RLB-20 which has an alkaline battery with a four-year shelf life, weighs just over 4 pounds, lists for $370, and sells through the catalogs for around $200. Replacement batteries cost around $40. It should be mounted in its bracket just inside the door of your pilothouse. If you need it, you'll have to yank it from its bracket, turn it on, release its antenna, and hurl it into the sea.

As mentioned above, you should also equip your vessel's life jackets with a Class B mini-EPIRB. By using Type I life jackets and outfitting them with Class B mini-EPIRB's, reflective patches, a whistle, and a personal safety light; making certain anyone who has to go on deck in heavy weather is wearing an inflatable horseshoe; and equipping your boat with one or more weighted heaving lines and powerful hand-held searchlights, you would have the optimum system for saving the life of anyone who has the misfortune of falling overboard or being swept off your vessel into the sea (Fig. 12.8).

You should also outfit your life raft with a Class B mini-EPIRB or a Class S unit such as ACR's RLB-21S. It presently lists at $415 but is heavily discounted through the marine catalogs. The Coast Guard is considering a new regulation that would require Class S EPIRB's to incorporate a transponder to emit a signal that would show up as a target on the radar of search-and-rescue craft. If that change is required, it is expected to drive the price of the Class S unit up into the $1,000-to-$1,400 range.

Type 406 EPIRB: Two factors—a vast number of false alarms from the current generation of EPIRB's being inadvertently activated, and sharp cutbacks in the Coast Guard's budget—have made that service reluctant to launch full-scale air/sea rescue efforts until it is reasonably sure an EPIRB signal indicates a gen-

Fig. 12.8:   *You can help keep an accident from turning into tragedy by providing everyone on board your vessel with a Type I PFD fitted with reflective patches, a whistle, a personal rescue light, a mini-EPIRB and an inflatable life ring. Your vessel should also have a powerful hand-held searchlight and a weighted heaving line.*

uine emergency. (The cost of operating a Coast Guard C-130 rescue aircraft is now around $7,000 an hour, and the average delay between the time an EPIRB signal is received and a full-scale search effort is launched is *twenty-six* hours.)

This situation has led to the development of a new type of EPIRB referred to loosely as the "Type 406" (Fig. 12.9) because it transmits signals on both 406 MHz and 121.5 MHz. The 406-MHz alerting component of the new EPIRB broadcasts a 121-bit serial number that is distinctive to it alone. When that serial number is received by a COSPAS/SARSAT satellite and relayed to a ground station, it is run through a computer at the National Oceanic and Atmospheric Administration (NOAA) which can identify the type and size of the vessel on which that particular EPIRB was installed. The computer file is based on information

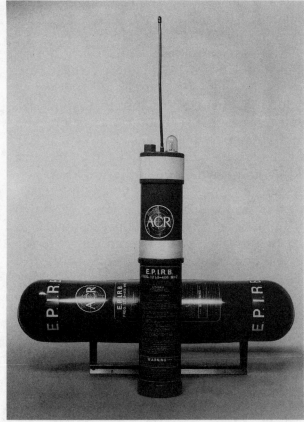

Fig. 12.9: *The new Type 406 EPIRB transmits a signal which is unique to the vessel on which it is installed.*

provided by the purchaser of the EPIRB through the return of a mandatory registration card. Once a search is launched in the general area indicated by the 406-MHz signal, rescuers home in by using the unit's 121.5-MHz signal and strobe light.

Though the 406 EPIRB system has been in operation in Europe since 1987, so far it is mandatory in the United States only aboard commercial fishing vessels. This is in response to the devastating loss of life among commercial fishermen in recent years (some four hundred Alaska fishermen have died in accidents at sea in the past five years). Type 406 EPIRB's can be carried voluntarily aboard any vessel that is equipped with a VHF radio.

The 406 is offered in Category 1 and Category 2 units whose features are comparable to the Class A and B EPIRB's. Category 1 units must be installed on the exterior of the vessel, must be capable of being launched by a hydrostatic release, and must be activated automatically. Category 2 units can be mounted inside the vessel and are manually launched and activated.

ACR is now marketing its RLB-23 unit which meets Category 1 requirements. It is 20 inches long and 4.25 inches in diameter and has a 12-inch antenna. With a battery (which must be replaced every 5 years) it weighs 7.8 pounds and is designed to operate for at least forty-eight hours. It comes in a cylindrical, hydrostatically released canister that is about 35 inches long and 6.4 inches in diameter. The complete unit retails for around $3,000. ACR's RLB-24 meets Category 2 requirements; it is the same size and weight as the RLB-23 and has the same operating characteristics, but it does not require a canister. It retails for around $2,000.

Because of their expense, the 406 EPIRB's have not shown up in any significant numbers in the recreational boating field yet, but over the next two to three years we can expect to see them drop in price to the point that they will become attractive to that market.

Under the rules of the FCC, since EPIRB's transmit radio signals, they must be licensed. You can request this when you file the Form 506 application for your regular ship station license. EPIRB's do not require any kind of operator permit.

Note: The batteries in EPIRB's are marked with an expiration date after which less than half their shelf life remains. If you carry an EPIRB aboard your vessel, you must replace its battery prior to its expiration date or you will be subject to a Coast Guard citation.

LIFE RAFTS

Should you suffer the ultimate catastrophe and wind up in the water with your ship sunk or destroyed by fire, the most immediate danger you face is hypothermia—loss of body heat. Even 75- or 80-degree seawater can rob the body of dangerous amounts of heat in a few hours. For that reason, the essential lifesaving equipment of every cruising vessel must include a sturdy life raft to keep everybody out of the water until help arrives.

Life rafts come in two basic configurations, coastal and offshore.

The coastal models are suitable only for vessels that will stay reasonably close to shore and in areas where help is likely to reach them within about a day. They have only a single inflation ring and a single floor, and list for around $2,000 to $2,500.

For offshore voyaging, you will want to carry a good ocean life raft large enough to accommodate at least the greatest number of people you could reasonably expect to have on board. It's really best to increase that number by two additional people. Life rafts are designed to provide only 4 square feet of space per persons. The occupants of a life raft filled to capacity would become terribly cramped in a matter of hours—not to mention days or weeks—and there would be no extra space to stow an abandon-ship bag or any other items you might be fortunate enough to salvage off your main vessel before it goes down.

The price of a good six-person ocean life raft ranges from around $3,500 to about $5,000, depending on features. Since your life could well depend on it, get one with the most features you can afford. Here's what I'd suggest you look for:

Your raft should have double flotation rings that are inflated automatically by a CO_2 cartridge within a maximum of thirty seconds after launching. It also should have a double floor (usually an extra-cost option) to provide its occupants additional protection against hypothermia.

The major difference among the more popular life rafts sold for use on recreational vessels is the stabilization system their manufacturers employ to keep them from capsizing. For years, most life rafts offered on the recreational boating market were lightly ballasted and exhibited a dangerous tendency to ride up on the crest of a wave and tilt, which allowed wind to sweep underneath and capsize them. Once a life raft is capsized, its occupants have to get into the water to right it, exposing themselves to the effects of hypothermia. If the canopy floods during the capsize, righting the raft can be almost impossible. A number of Government agencies and private companies have tried to develop life-raft stabilization systems to help correct this tendency.

The more expensive life rafts on the market utilize heavier ballasting. Switlik's six-person search-and-rescue model (Fig. 12.10) uses a toroidal (think of a doughnut) ballast pocket that encircles the perimeter of the raft's bottom. With a double floor, it lists for around $4,100. Switlik SAR life rafts are used aboard most U.S. Coast Guard vessels. Givens's six-person model employs a full, round-bottomed ballasting chamber. Its list price with a double floor is $4,450. Of the two, the Switlik seems to offer the more consistent quality, primarily because the company does all it own manufacturing in-house, whereas Givens subcontracts a good deal of its production to others.

The life rafts made by Avon, Viking, BFA, and a number of

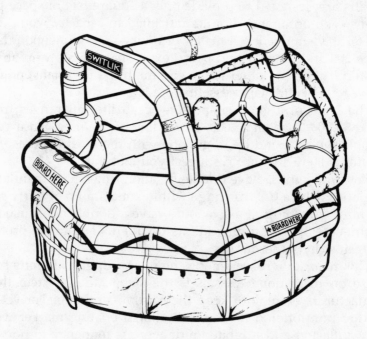

Fig. 12.10: *The Switlik SAR life raft's torroidal ballasting system gives it exceptional stability.*

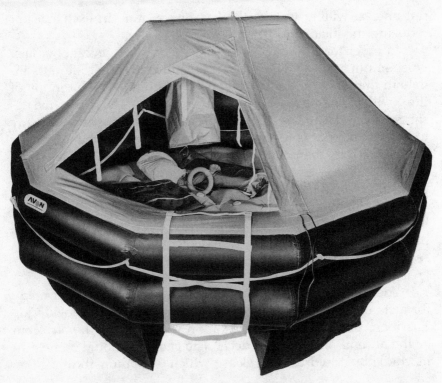

Fig. 12.11: A number of life-raft manufacturers such as Avon employ the ballast pockets called for by the Icelandic ballasting system.

other manufacturers are designed to meet the Icelandic Standard developed by the International Maritime Organization. This stabilization system utilizes a series of ballast pockets in conjunction with a sea anchor. Avon's six-person Mark III model (Fig. 12.11) is typical of this type of raft and with a double floor lists for $3,750. Winslow offers an offshore life raft but I would not recommend you consider it; in my judgment, its construction and materials are not adequate for its purpose.

Advocates of life rafts designed to the Icelandic Standard argue that since they present less resistance to wave pressure, they subject their occupants to less banging around. They say that life rafts that employ a toroidal system or a full-ballasting system present so much resistance to wave pressure that their occupants have a rougher ride. For offshore voyaging, I'll happily spend the extra money for the toroidal or the fully ballasted raft and be willing to take the banging around in exchange for reducing the likelihood of capsizing.

In order for a life raft to be USCG-approved, its canopy must erect automatically when the raft is launched. Most life rafts inflate in that fashion. In its standard configuration, the canopy of the Switlik SAR must be erected manually. The company designs its standard rafts this way because it believes the best way to board a life raft is to jump directly into it rather than jumping into the water, then climbing aboard. Switlik argues that if the canopy is already erected, those who board it first are more likely to be injured by those who jump into it after them. To me, the argument makes sense. I also like the option of being able to lower the canopy in fair weather to air it out and give the occupants a horizon to look at, which can materially cut down on seasickness. (Switlik makes the same raft with an automatic-erection canopy that is Coast Guard–approved.)

Your life raft should be mounted on deck in a canister ready for instant use (Fig. 12.12), never in a valise stowed belowdecks. The most popular mounting location is the top of the aft cabin or the aft end of the upper deck. The canister should be held in its cradle by a hydrostatic release which will automatically allow

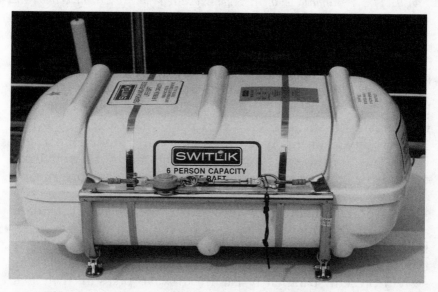

Fig. 12.12: *Your life raft should be carried on deck in a canister held in place by a hydrostatic release.*

it to float free if your vessel sinks before anyone on board has time to launch it. Hydrostatic releases are activated by water pressure when they are submerged about 3 to 10 feet below the surface.

As mentioned above, you should also equip your life raft with one of the Class S or Class B mini-EPIRB's.

Even the most expensive life raft is useless if it is not in seaworthy condition and you don't know how to launch it properly. Be sure to have your raft inspected once a year by a qualified service technician who should check its CO_2 cartridge, test the ability of its air chambers to remain inflated, and replace any supplies that are out of date. If you stick around during one of these inspections, you'll find it an interesting and informative experience. You should also plan exactly what you would do in the event you needed to launch your raft, and you should conduct drills periodically to make certain everyone on board knows what their responsibilities would be in an abandon-ship situation.

Chances are your life raft will never do anything more than sit on deck in its canister. But if the time ever comes when you need it, you'll be glad you took the time to buy a good one, learned how to use it, and kept it ready to save your life.

THE ABANDON-SHIP BAG

The E-pack emergency kits that come with even the most expensive life rafts are a joke. They contain no food, only minimal signaling and first-aid equipment, and only a pint of water per person, which is sufficient to keep one person alive for only about five to seven days. To make matters worse, the water is packed in a can that must be opened with a can opener and can't be resealed except with a flimsy plastic lid. Since the canister most life rafts are packed in doesn't allow space for adequate additional survival supplies, you should rig a separate abandon-ship bag, stow it in a readily accessible location, and make it the first thing that goes overboard after you launch your raft. You can buy abandon-ship bags especially designed for the purpose or use one of the large waterproof plastic bags sold for canoeing. A list of minimum suggested contents for an offshore abandon-ship bag is given in Fig. 12.13.

The most important thing you need in your supplemental life-raft supplies is additional water. You can purchase water in

OFFSHORE ABANDON-SHIP BAG

Signaling Equipment

41 Class B mini-EPIRB (if not packed in life-raft canister) ——

3 SOLAS-type hand-held red parachute flares ——

3 SOLAS-type hand-held white parachute flares ——

3 SOLAS-type hand-held red meteor flares ——

2 Solas-type orange smoke canisters ——

12 cylume chemical light sticks ——

Waterproof flashlight with spare batteries ——

Waterproof compass ——

Fishing Equipment

1 filet knife in scabbard ——

1 spool 30-pound test fishing line ——

20 feet wire leader ——

3 medium fishing spoons ——

1 16-inch spear gun ——

1 wire saw ——

2 propane cigarette lighters ——

Provisions

Hand-operated watermaker or solar still ——

One-gallon folding plastic jug ——

Two pkgs. freeze-dried food per person ——

Clothing

1 long-sleeve shirt per person ——

1 sun visor or billed cap per person ——

1 pair sunglasses per person ——

1 thermal blanket per person ——

2 rolls toilet paper in self-sealing plastic bag ——

Medical Supplies

1 vial seasickness pills ——

2 tubes sunburn cream ——

1 jar petroleum jelly ——

1 tube antiseptic ointment ——

1 vial Demerol pain pills ——

1 roll bandages ——

1 roll adhesive tape ——

Fig. 12.13

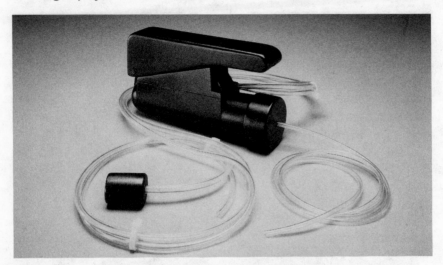

Fig. 12.14: *This hand-operated reverse osmosis unit provides one of the most essential ingredients in life raft survival—fresh water.*

sealed packets for your abandon-ship bag (eight per person) or tether plastic jugs of water to your life raft (at least a half-gallon per person). You also could put a solar still in your abandon-ship bag, but I've never found one that works very well. What I have found that works is the new Survivor hand-operated reverse-osmosis watermaker developed by Recovery Engineering (Fig. 12.14). By operating its hand pump to force seawater through its reverse-osmosis membrane at thirty strokes a minute, you can make a cup of fresh water from seawater in about fifteen minutes. The unit weighs less than 4 pounds and sells in the STG catalog for $525.

Most of the commercially available abandon-ship bags have built-in flotation. If you prepare your own, rig it with sufficient flotation to keep it afloat until you can get it in the life raft, and attach a 50-foot floating line to give you a better chance to grab on to it.

There will be certain items you probably won't want to put in the abandon-ship bag but would need if you had to leave your main vessel. These would include such items as any special medications you require, eyeglasses, your passport, and a few greenbacks. When Carleton Mitchell cruised aboard *Coyaba*, he kept these items in a plastic bag near his bunk so if necessary he could quickly grab them on the way out.

13

CRUISING HEALTH

You are plowing into a stiff head sea fifty miles offshore. One of your anchors appears to be working its way loose from its bow roller and a guest goes forward to secure it. He slips on the wet foredeck. His head strikes a bow cleat, knocking him unconscious and inflicting a nasty gash on his head. Would you have the knowledge and supplies aboard to deal with such a serious medical emergency until you could get him to professional help?

Most of us in the United States suffer from the 911 syndrome; we take for granted that emergency medical assistance is always just moments away. But at sea, you are on your own. Emergency medical personnel call the first sixty minutes following a medical trauma the Golden Hour because treatment administered—or not administered—during that brief time can be literally a matter of life or death. As a skipper responsible for the well-being of your crew, you have a moral (and potentially legal) obligation to prepare and equip yourself to deal with virtually any medical emergency that might arise aboard your vessel.

EMERGENCY MEDICAL TRAINING

At the very least, you should attend an eight-hour Red Cross basic first-aid course. Try to find a chapter that offers the new Standard First Aid Course rather than the old Multi-Media course; it provides more hands-on learning and includes much more thorough instruction in cardiopulmonary resuscitation (CPR). Some Red Cross chapters offer it for free, others charge a nominal fee of around $25. An even better idea is to attend a Red Cross Advanced First Aid Course. This fifty-three-hour course is designed primarily for "first responder" personnel such as firefighters and law enforcement officers who might be the first to reach the scene of an accident. It covers the rudiments of handling everything from wounds and shock to broken bones and poisoning. It also would be wise to have a crew member attend one of these courses with you in case *you* are the victim.

Even the Advanced First Aid Course doesn't cover everything you need to know, because it is based on the assumption that in the situations its graduates are likely to encounter, professional medical help will be less than an hour away. In cruising, especially if you like to explore the backwaters, you could easily find yourself in situations where even airborne medical help is twenty-four or more hours away (in extreme cases a lot more). One school of thought says that if amateurs try to perform more involved medical procedures than those covered in the Advanced First Aid Course, they are likely to do more harm than good. That school of thought also worries that anyone who goes beyond the procedures he has been certified to perform is exposing himself to potential legal liabilities. My attitude is that if the doctor is many hours (perhaps even days) away and a life is hanging in the balance, anything I can do to help save that life is better than letting the person die. On the legal side, I'd trust in a provision of the Federal Boat Safety Act of 1971 called the Good Samaritan Act which protects individuals who render aid to the victims of boating accidents from being held liable for civil damages so long as they acted as a reasonably prudent person might under similar circumstances. For those reasons, if I were embarking on an extensive voyage to remote areas, I'd get a friendly physician to show me the correct way to do such things as administer an injectible painkiller or antibiotic, deal with major airway problems, and stop serious bleeding. Another way to get much of the instruction you might find valuable is the course offered by Medical Advisory Systems, Inc. which we'll mention when we cover emergency medical communications.

EMERGENCY MEDICAL SUPPLIES AND EQUIPMENT

The medical supplies aboard your vessel should be appropriate to the type of cruising you will be doing, should be stowed in their own containers, and the containers should be stowed in their own lockers with their locations clearly marked on the outside. Everyone on board should know where your vessel's medical supplies are kept, but no one should go into them without informing you so you can keep track of their contents and replace consumed items as soon as possible. In Appendix III you'll find a suggested list of all the medical supplies you should consider having on board for both coastal and offshore cruising.

In coastal cruising, you should at least carry a true first-aid kit to allow you to deal with medical emergencies until you can get the victim to professional medical assistance. You can make up your own, using the list in Appendix III as a guide, or buy one of the prepackaged versions available through the marine catalogs. Even the best of the latter will need to be extensively supplemented.

For offshore cruising, you should also carry a trauma kit to deal with serious injuries until you reach professional medical assistance or until a doctor or paramedic can reach you. Again, you can make up your own trauma kit or buy one of the pre-packaged varieties. Some of the basic items required in a comprehensive trauma kit are provided in the Soft Pack Responder Kit (Fig. 13.1) listed in the Survival Technologies Group catalog for $175, but it will require a number of additions. The best trauma kits for extended offshore cruising are the Stat Kits produced by Banyan International Corporation, P. O. Box 1779, Abilene, Texas 79604-1779. Even Banyan's largest kit, which lists for about $700, doesn't contain all the supplies you will need for cruising in the boondocks, but it's a good start. Because it contains a number of prescription medications, you will have to arrange to purchase it through your physician, who can also supply you with prescriptions for the other medications you should have on board.

In most cases, it will be possible to carry the medications you should have on board without getting into "controlled substances." Should you have a legitimate need to carry controlled substances, however, you can do so quite legally provided your

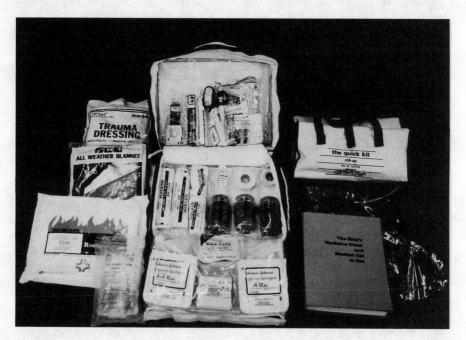

Fig. 13.1: *You can buy a commercially available trauma kit such as this Soft Responder from Survival Technologies Group or make up one of your own.*

vessel is documented. Under the Code of Federal Regulations, Part 21, Section II, a U.S.-licensed physician may legally write prescriptions for controlled substances that are made out to the name of a documented vessel and marked "Ship's Stores." The physician must notify the Drug Enforcement Administration of his prescription of such substances by filing DEA Form 222. He also must file an annual report with the DEA of the disposition of such substances. (Physicians who regularly prescribe such medications file both reports as a matter of course. You would not be asking the physician from whom you request such prescriptions to go to a great deal of trouble just for you.) Information regarding controlled-substance medications prescribed in this manner must be entered in the ship's log, and the controlled substances themselves must be kept under lock and key. As the vessel's captain, you may dispense those medications, but only under the control of a licensed physician (radio contact has been interpreted as meeting this requirement), and you must enter into the log the date, the quantity, and the name of the individual to whom you dispensed them.

When clearing customs in some countries, you may be required to declare any controlled substances on your vessel and should most certainly do so. But handling them in this manner conforms to the regulations of the International Maritime Organization to which the United States is a signatory and should help keep you from running afoul of the laws regarding them in any nation that is also an IMO signatory.

EMERGENCY MEDICAL REFERENCE

Be sure to have on board a good book on handling medical emergencies. The most detailed I've seen is *Ship's Medicine Chest and Medical Aid at Sea*, published by the U.S. Public Health Service. This is a hard-cover, loose-leaf book written for amateurs who are charged with medical responsibilities aboard U.S.-registered merchant vessels and covers everything from ankle sprains to zinc deficiency. It is available from the Superintendent of Documents, U.S. Government Printing Office, Washington, D.C. 20402 as stock number 917-010-00000-5. If you charge to a major credit card, you can also order it by telephone (202-783-3238). The cost, which includes periodic updates for an indefinite period, is $44.

If you will be cruising tropical waters, you should carry a reference to potential dangers from such marine creatures as jellyfish and stingrays and the treatment of any injuries they inflict. The best work I have seen on the subject is *A Medical Guide to Hazardous Marine Life* by Paul S. Auerbach, M.D. It is available through the Dolphin Book Club, Camp Hill, PA 17012.

SCUBA-DIVING EMERGENCIES

If anyone aboard your vessel will be scuba diving, you should make certain he or she is properly certified and never dives without a buddy. You should also brush up on the proper handling of a diver with a suspected air embolism (place the person on his left side so the heart is at the lowest part of the body, elevate the feet, and administer pure oxygen) and know the location of the nearest recompression chamber in the area you will be cruising. An excellent not-for-profit organization of which any cruising diver should be a member is Diver's Alert Network (DAN, Box 3823, Duke University Medical Center, Durham, NC 27710), which covers the United States, Canada, and the Caribbean. For a $15 annual membership fee, DAN offers a twenty-four-hour hotline—call 919-684-8111—through which it can provide medical advice and assistance on handling diving accidents and coordinate the evacuation of a diving-accident victim to the nearest hyperbaric chamber. In a diving emergency, even nonmembers can use the number, and the organization will accept collect calls. For $25 per year, DAN also offers an insurance policy that pays up to $15,000 of any medical expenses involved in treating the effects of a diving-related accident; since they often involve air-ambulance evacuation and lengthy treatment, such accidents can be horrendously expensive.

IMMUNIZATIONS

If you will be visiting other countries in your cruising, you and your crew will require certain immunizations and may want to have others even though they are not required. Once you have drawn up your cruising itinerary, there are a number of sources for up-to-date information regarding the immunizations required or recommended for the countries you will be visiting. If your family physician can't provide the information, your local health department should have a copy of *Health Information for*

International Travelers, published by the U.S. Public Health Service, and should receive the periodic bulletins the PHS mails out to update it. You can also get current information from PHS Quarantine Stations in New York, Miami, Chicago, Los Angeles, San Francisco, Seattle, and Honolulu. If all else fails, call the Foreign Travel Division of the U.S. Public Health Service's Centers for Disease Control in Atlanta, Georgia (404-639-2572).

Make certain to find out which immunizations you'll need well in advance of your planned departure since some of them could require a series of shots that must be given as much as two to six weeks apart. Immunization shots normally can be given by your family physician or county health department. Make sure you get a record of your vaccinations and the dates they were administered in the form of a validated International Certificates of Vaccination which is approved by the World Health Organization; keep it with your passport.

MEDICAL CHECKUPS

Before embarking on any extensive cruise to areas where medical services may not be immediately available, you should be certain all crew members (and invited guests) undergo an up-to-date physical exam, inform you of any medical problems they have, and carry sufficient supplies of any special medications they require. Vital medications should be carried in sealable plastic bags next to their bunks so they can grab them rapidly should you have to abandon ship. You and your crew should also have dental checkups and attend to any sensitive teeth that might cause problems. A toothache at sea is hell.

EMERGENCY MEDICAL COMMUNICATIONS

The steps outlined above should prepare you to deal with most medical emergencies you are likely to encounter in cruising. But what if you are in the boondocks and someone on board your boat has a life-threatening emergency you really can't handle yourself, say, a heart attack or a ruptured appendix? The best thing you can do is make sure you can communicate with a doctor from wherever you might be. One way to do that is to subscribe to Medical Advisory Systems, Inc., Pleasure Craft Division, P.O. Box 193, Pennsylvania Ave. Ext., Owings, MD 20736

(301-855-8070). This is a private company that serves primarily merchant ships and the offshore oil industry but also operates a program for recreational boaters in cooperation with the Medic Alert Foundation in California. For a lifetime membership fee of $100 plus $30 each time you use the service, Medic Alert maintains your medical history in its computerized file and MAS provides you with a twenty-four-hour hotline through which you can reach its attending physicians who are on round-the-clock standby at its headquarters or a network of other physicians who work with them around the world. You can access the hotline through a Coastal or High Seas radiotelephone operator or call the company directly over single sideband radio. The company continuously monitors 2182.0 kHz and 16590.0 kHz and every five seconds automatically scans five other SSB frequencies: 4983.0 kHz, 7952.0 kHz, 12327.0 kHz, 16450.0 kHz, and 22722.0 kHz. With the exception of 2182.0 kHz, these are not marine SSB frequencies, but under special terms of the operating license granted to MAS by the FCC, yachtsmen may use them as "adjacent" frequencies to deal with medical emergencies. The company's physicians can also be contacted by maritime satellite with the two-digit emergency code "MD."

For additional fees, MAS can also provide you with a list of recommended medical supplies that should be carried on your vessel depending on its size and the number in its crew, a guide to their use, the supplies themselves, and a basic emergency medical procedures manual. For $495 you can also participate in a three-day advanced first-aid training course which MAS stages periodically in various cities around the country. I have not attended the course personally but understand it is excellent. "In three days," says MAS President Ron Pickett, "we take first responders aboard merchant vessels and teach them how to handle ninety-five percent of the situations they are likely to encounter." The company also offers a less-expensive two-day basic first-aid course.

Another possible means of getting in contact with medical help in a hurry is to get yourself an amateur radio operator's license and carry a radio aboard that is capable of operating over the ham frequencies. Ham operators can be pretty fantastic friends in a crunch. They have disaster networks that deal with emergencies and physicians they can get to in a hurry. Often a ham radio operator will be able to connect you with medical help quicker than any Government agency.

EMERGENCY MEDICAL EVACUATION

Don't slack off on your emergency preparations on the theory that if anyone on board your vessel has a serious medical problem he or she can be evacuated quickly to a hospital by helicopter. Because air/sea rescue helicopters have a fairly limited range, there are many prime cruising areas that they simply cannot reach. Further, helicopter evacuation is a potentially hazardous operation for the patient, the vessel's crew and the helicopter crew and should be used only as a last resort to prevent death or permanent injury. Should you ever be involved in evacuating someone off your vessel by helicopter, here are some things you should know.

PREPARING FOR HELICOPTER EVACUATION

1. Once you've arranged for helicopter evacuation and know the chopper is on its way, maintain a continuous guard on VHF channel 16, SSB frequency 2182.0 kHz, or any other frequency the rescue coordinating base or helicopter pilot may request.

2. While the chopper is in transit, work out a step-by-step evacuation plan and make certain everyone who will be assisting in the evacuation knows exactly what they are to do. Also establish a set of simple hand signals to communicate. Once the helicopter is overhead, the noise on deck will be deafening and even shouted conversation will be impossible. Make sure everyone who will be on deck during the operation is wearing a life jacket and, if you have them on board, inflatable life rings.

3. Clear a suitable hoist area, preferably on your vessel's highest, aft-most deck of any loose gear and potential obstructions such as booms and antennas. If you will have to bring the helicopter litter from the hoist area to a patient inside your vessel, clear a wide pathway of any potential obstructions.

4. Reduce your vessel's headway to the slowest speed at which you can maintain steerage. Take up the course that allows your vessel to ride easiest, but if you have a choice put the wind on your port bow. Due to the clockwise rotation of a chopper's blades, it is easiest for the pilot to hover with the wind striking his craft from the port forward quarter. Maintain your course,

speed, and heading unless directed otherwise by the chopper pilot or crew.

5. Tag the patient with information about any medication you have administered and any known applicable medical condition or history. Move the patient as close as possible to the hoist area and, if the injury permits, put him or her in a life jacket.

6. If the evacuation is conducted at night, fire flares only if the coordinating base or helicopter pilot requests you to do so. Once the chopper is in your vicinity and begins its approach to your vessel, shine a light on any permanent obstructions on your vessel such as a mast or radar antenna of which the pilot should be aware, but do not shine a light in the helicopter's direction since it could blind the pilot or the hoist man.

HOISTING PROCEDURES

1. Once your evacuation preparations are complete and the helicopter is hovering over your vessel, signal the pilot to "come on" with your arms.

2. The hoist man will probably drop a light trail line to allow you to guide the litter down to the hoist area. You can safely touch this line as it will not cause static shock, but keep it free-running at all times and do not attach it to or allow it to become entangled with your vessel.

3. As the litter is lowered from the helicopter and you guide it to the hoist area with the trail line, allow it to touch your vessel before anyone on board touches it in order to discharge static electricity.

4. Once the litter is on deck, be prepared to unhook it quickly from the hoist cable if the pilot requests you to (in severe weather he may need freedom to maneuver while you strap the patient in) or if you must take it inside the vessel to load the patient. Never attempt to move the litter without unhooking it from the hoist cable. If you do unhook the litter, keep the hoist cable free and do not attach it to your vessel or allow it to become entangled with it.

5. Once the patient is strapped into the litter and is in the hoist area ready for pickup, signal the helicopter to drop the hoist cable but allow it to touch the vessel before anyone on board touches it to avoid static shock. Once the hoist cable is attached to the litter, make sure everyone on deck is clear before giving a "thumbs-up" signal for the hoist man to haul it in. If a trail line is attached, use it to steady the litter as it is hoisted but make certain it does not become entangled with your vessel.

Even your most elaborate preparations cannot prepare you to face every medical emergency you conceivably could encounter in cruising, but taking these basic steps should help you deal with most situations you are likely to face. And if all else fails, at least you will know you did your best.

14

CRUISING SECURITY

All the violence in the news of late brings up the question of the steps you should take to protect yourself, your property, your crew, and your guests, especially if you are planning to venture far off the beaten path.

The topic of cruising security need not be of particular concern. In most cruising situations, you will find you are safer than if you were walking down a dark street in many major American cities. There are, however, a few things simple common sense indicates you should do.

SECURE YOUR VESSEL

For security at anchor, round-the-world sailor Joshua Slocum spread tacks on the decks of *Spray* to discourage natives from creeping aboard in the dark of night. I knew one experienced sail-cruising couple who, before retiring in a lonely cove at night, would crisscross open hatches with black thread attached to a tin pie plate and a large spoon separated by about 4 inches. The separation was enough to compensate for normal roll and surge, but anyone trying to slip aboard at least announced his presence soon enough to allow them to get out the rolling pin. You'll want to be a bit more elaborate in making sure your vessel is protected from uninvited guests when you are away from it or asleep on board.

First, protect all salon or pilothouse doors with a stout deadbolt lock. On sliding doors, install the lock at a top corner and place it vertically rather than horizontally, with its deadbolt going into the overhead plate. You could go to the extreme of installing one of the commercially available marine alarm systems that set off a loud horn if anyone tries to enter your vessel without disarming it (though most cruisers I know don't use one).

If you are planning to cruise remote areas and intend to leave deck hatches open at night for ventilation, you might be wise to cover them with stout stainless-steel grates you can secure from the inside.

We cruising yachtsmen treasure our independence, but it is only common sense to file at least a general float plan with friends at home whom you talk to regularly over radiotelephone or with cruising friends you meet along the way. As you prepare to depart a port, if you've met some fellow cruisers you feel you can trust, make certain they can give an accurate description of your vessel, tell them where you plan to make your next stop, and set a deadline by which you will contact them to say you've arrived safely.

The most obvious precaution you can take is to stay away

from potential trouble spots. There is no reason today to hesitate to embark on a cruise of either the Caribbean or Pacific coasts of Central America, but stay well offshore—thirty to fifty miles would not be excessive—of countries that are involved in political turmoil such as Nicaragua and El Salvador. Likewise, you need have no undue concern about cruising most of the Bahamas, but plan your itinerary to avoid anchoring off the west coast of Andros Island, which is a favorite base of those running drugs into South Florida.

At an unfamiliar dock, be suspicious of anyone who displays excessive interest in your immediate cruising plans, especially if they involve a night run off a deserted coast. If you will be leaving shortly, tell him you intend to stay for several days, then slip out to sea at first light. In paying shoreside expenses, don't flash large rolls of cash. That's an open invitation for the wrong people to pay unwanted attention to you and your plans.

Under no circumstances allow anyone aboard your boat whose bona fides you cannot not check thoroughly, even if he is only 4 feet tall, blind, and says he is only trying to reach the bedside of his dying mother on the next island.

At anchor in remote areas, be cautious about inviting the natives aboard. Some of them are fascinated by the glittering toys of modern society and they might possibly walk off with one or two of them. If you do invite natives aboard, first put away everything small and easily portable, invite them in small groups you can keep an eye on, limit their time aboard, and be chary of spreading around too much hospitality (soft drinks are better than anything alcoholic). One easy way to make friends in truly primitive areas is to carry along a large supply of inexpensive ballpoint pens (the kind that go "click") and an instant-developing camera with plenty of film.

WEAPONS: YES OR NO?

The topic of cruising security always raises the debate about whether or not you should carry firearms aboard. My rule of thumb is, if you are comfortable around guns ashore, know how to use them, and believe you could save your life with one, then carry one. If not, you probably will shoot yourself in the foot while getting it out of the case and should leave it at home. If you are uncomfortable having firearms aboard your vessel, bear in mind that a pistol-fired or canister-launched aerial flare dropped into the cockpit or onto the foredeck of a threatening vessel might well keep its crew occupied while you figure out your best avenue of escape.

If you do decide to carry weapons aboard you will need to consider rifles, shotguns, and handguns. Their exterior surface should be stainless steel or hard-chrome plated to protect them from the corrosive marine environment, and you should clean and oil them regularly. Keep them loaded with appropriate ammunition, but be sure their safety is engaged, make certain all adults cruising with you know where they are stowed, and keep them well out of the reach of any curious children who might come on board.

An important question regarding firearms on board a cruising vessel is what you do about declaring them when you enter other countries. In most cases I would declare them, especially in Venezuela and Guadeloupe. In those countries, detailed searches are common, and if you are found to be carrying undeclared weapons you will be arrested and your entire vessel confiscated. You may carry rifles and shotguns into Canada if you declare that they are to be used for hunting. If you declare a handgun, Canadian authorities will either seal it in a pouch that must be presented—unopened—when you exit the country, or they will impound it and you can pick it up on your way back across their border. I learned the hard way about the Canadians' lack of tolerance for visitors who fail to declare handguns. I tried it once and for my trouble had the gun confiscated, was hit with a heavy fine, and now have a framed document on my wall which officially declares me a smuggler.

In most of the countries you will visit, the customs official will simply take note of the presence of any weapons you declare and tell you not to carry them on desk or ashore. In a few countries—Cuba and the Netherlands Antilles islands of Aruba, Bonaire, and Curaçao being prime examples—the customs officials will impound your weapons during your visit and hand them back to you—along with your dock lines—when you depart. In entering a few countries, I would not declare any weapons on board my vessel but would bury them deep—really deep. In countries like Mexico and Jamaica, any weapons you declare will be confiscated and you will not get them back. You also may be arrested and your entire vessel can be confiscated. If you are carrying weapons aboard your vessel and decide not to declare them, remember also to keep their ammunition and any descriptive literature or cleaning apparatus well out of sight. The best up-to-date advice regarding the declaration of weapons in the various countries you will visit will come from other cruisers who have visited those countries recently.

IF YOU ARE BOARDED

The escalating war on drugs makes it increasingly likely that if you cruise extensively, sooner or later you will be boarded and your vessel subjected to a search for illegal drugs.

American yachtsmen returning to the United States from such areas as the Bahamas and Mexico are experiencing a sharp increase in random boardings by the U.S. Coast Guard and U.S. Customs in search of drugs. In addition, you can expect more blockades like Operation Glass Eye in which, during one summer weekend, fifteen Coast Guard boats, two Customs boats, and four boats from the New York Harbor Police stopped *every* vessel transiting the Verrazano Narrows on the way into New York harbor.

Like most law-abiding Americans, I'm all for stemming the flood of illegal drugs being smuggled into our country, but with the increase in boardings we need to be aware of our position under the law and the possible penalties we face should we transgress that law, even without meaning to do so.

On land, as American citizens we have all manner of Fourth Amendment rights against unreasonable search and seizure. In most cases, law-enforcement personnel must have "probable cause" to suspect we are breaking the law before they stop and search us. It would not be unreasonable to think we carry those same rights when we go to sea.

Not so. When it comes to our legal rights in a boarding situation, the blunt truth is we don't have any. Under 14 U.S. Code 89, the Coast Guard has the right to stop and search any U.S. flag vessel anywhere (even outside U.S. territorial waters) and any time, whether or not it has reason to believe any U.S. law is being violated. The same goes for U.S. Customs if the vessel (whether of U.S. or foreign registry) is within our nation's twelve-mile customs zone.

If you are shown a blue light by either of these agencies,

you must stop. You cannot refuse to allow their personnel to board your vessel, nor can you stop them from searching every nook and cranny of your vessel (including ripping out bulkheads and the like), or even searching your person and that of everyone else aboard.

"So what?" you say. "I'm not breaking any law. Being stopped may be a nuisance and delay my trip by a few minutes, but that would be my only concern."

That's exactly what one friend of mine thought as he was bringing his sportfishing yacht back to Florida from a trip to the Bahamas. Upon entering U.S. waters he was stopped by the Coast Guard and his vessel searched. Beneath a forward bunk the boarding party found 3 pounds of marijuana a crew member had bought in the islands intending to sell it to his friends back home. My friend did not know the substance was aboard, but as the master of the vessel he was held legally responsible. He was arrested on the spot and handcuffed, as was everyone else aboard. The Coast Guard boarding party assumed control of his boat and took it into the nearest U.S. port where it was turned over to Customs and seized.

Once the case reached the courts and the crew member testified that the owner knew nothing, the criminal charges against my friend were dropped. He went down to reclaim his boat which had been in the Customs impound lot for over two months. He was certain that since the charges had been dropped, Customs would return his boat without a hassle.

Again, not so. Customs had seized his boat under an administrative procedure that does not involve any court review. My friend finally got his boat back, but it cost him over $8,000 in legal fees and repair bills for damage done to the boat while it was in the impound lot.

Under the Coast Guard's more recent Zero Tolerance policy, the same thing can happen even if the quantity of illegal drugs found aboard your vessel is minuscule. The moral of the story is that you need to be extremely careful about what you allow anyone to bring on board your vessel, particularly if you are reentering the United States from another country.

So much for being boarded by U.S. authorities. What if you are stopped by authorities of another country?

On *Summer Wind*'s voyage to Alaska, Frank and Lee Glindmeier were making a night run about twenty miles off the coast of Nicaragua when a blip appeared on their radar and started to close in on them. The vessel refused to answer Frank's call on VHF, and he had to change course twice to avoid a collision. It turned out to be a Nicaraguan gunboat with a soldier manning a 50-mm machine gun on its bow. Frank finally was able to shout across the water in broken Spanish that he was a peaceful American yachtsman. The gunboat backed off but escorted them until ten o'clock the next morning when they reached the border.

Since hearing Frank's rather harrowing tale, I've done a good bit of thinking of how I would handle such a situation. You will have your own ideas, but these are mine:

Most nations of the world claim a territorial limit of three miles off their shores and a customs zone of twelve miles. Other nations claim up to a 200-mile territorial limit. The military forces of governments that are threatened by armed insurrection frequently patrol one hundred miles or more off their shores and stop any vessel they encounter. If my cruise plan called for me to run off the coast of a nation I knew was in political turmoil, I would inform the U.S. Coast Guard of my schedule and set a deadline by which, if I didn't contact them with an "all-clear," they would at least know I was missing. I would make my run at night, stay as far offshore as possible, and know at all times exactly how far I was off the coast in case the matter came into dispute later. I'd also make the run without lights and remove my radar reflector.

If in the course of the run I was approached by an official vessel of another country, I would try to raise it on VHF. If I got no response, I would carefully note my position and contact the Coast Guard or anyone else I could reach to tell them what was going on. If the vessel kept coming toward me and it was at night, I'd turn on my running lights and shine a light on my American ensign. I would maintain speed and course until ordered to stop or until the approaching vessel blocked my path. If they called me on the radio or hailed me over a loudspeaker, I would appear on deck but show no firearms.

If ordered to, I would stop, but I would make every effort to argue them out of boarding my vessel. If they insisted on boarding, I would have little choice but to allow it but would be coolly indignant while arguing my right to cruise in international waters without interference. I'd drag out my U.S. passport and my vessel's documentation papers. If asked if I was armed, I'd declare any weapons on board. Hopefully, once they'd checked me out and found I wasn't trying to smuggle M-16's to the guerrillas, they'd let me go on my way. If they insisted that I put into the nearest port, I'd go into my indignant act again. If they continued to insist, I'd try to argue them out of placing any of their personnel on my boat, arguing that in light of their superior speed and firepower, I had little choice but to follow them.

If all argument failed, I would do as ordered but only under the severest protest, liberally invoking the name of my brother the senator, my uncle the president, and any other fiction I could dream up on the spot. I'd also keep trying to contact the Coast Guard until ordered away from my radio at the point of a gun.

If I were forced into port, either under tow or under my own power, the minute I touched land I'd raise hell to see the nearest U.S. consul, rousting him out of bed if necessary. If that was refused, I'd demand to see the superior of the individual I was dealing with and start my indignation routine all over again.

As a last resort, I'd steal a spoon and try to dig my way out of jail.

CLEARING FOREIGN
CUSTOMS

If you have never before cleared a boat through customs and immigration in another country, the first few times you go through the process you may find you are in for an interesting experience.

It's a sad fact of the cruising life, particularly in poorer third-world nations, that customs and immigration officials are paid less than a living wage precisely because their bosses know they will make up any shortfall by hitting up visitors for either cash or a "gift" of goods that are hard to come by in their own country. Yachtsmen are often favorite targets, so you need to know the ropes.

When you enter a foreign country for the first time, make certain your initial landfall is a legal point of entry. In many countries, the smaller fishing villages closest to the border don't have customs or immigration offices. If you go ashore looking for one, technically you have entered the country illegally and might have some rather complicated explaining to do when you finally locate an official farther down the coast. Your best source of information on where to clear is a good cruising guide or other cruising folks who have been there before you.

Try to time your arrival so that you enter a legal port—with your yellow quarantine flag flying—between 9:00 A.M. and about 3:00 P.M. Monday through Friday, except on religious or political holidays or the president's birthday, or during the siesta hours of noon to 2:00 P.M. The point is that if you try to clear on weekends or after normal business hours, you probably will be hit with fairly stiff overtime charges. "Normal business hours," of course, are whatever the guy with the badge on his chest and the gun on his hip jolly well says they are.

Once you reach a legal port of entry, anchor in the harbor or tie up to the dock and just relax for an hour or so. Chances are the dockmaster, the harbormaster, or a helpful fellow yachtsman will come along to tell you what to do next. If no one turns up in a reasonable length of time, the captain or owner should go ashore alone, taking along the ship's papers, some local currency, the crew's passports, and vaccination records, and a crew list—preferably typed—which gives the name, nationality, and home address of all on board. Experienced cruising people either have several copies of their crew list run off before leaving home or, if their crew will vary en route, carry along a portable typewriter and plenty of carbon paper.

If the clearance process is conducted in the customs office ashore, chances are it will be crisp, efficient, and quickly over. If the customs officer wants to come aboard your boat, tell your crew to make themselves scarce belowdecks until he is gone, then spread out your documents on the salon table. Be polite and friendly, but not overly so, and try to keep things on a businesslike basis and get the procedure over with quickly. If the official seems inclined to chat, offer him a seat. If he seems impressed by your boat, say something like, "Yes, she is nice," but don't offer a tour unless one is requested. That's an open invitation for him to start opening drawers and poking into lockers.

Up to this point, keep the booze out of sight. If the official seems in no hurry to get down to business, offer him some "refreshment," not "a drink." If he accepts, rattle off your list of options from soft drinks to beer and whiskey and let him make the choice. If he has a couple of thirsty-looking corporals with him, don't offer them anything without clearing it with the commandante, then provide soft drinks rather than beer or liquor.

As early as possible, nudge your papers forward a bit and hope he will take the hint and get on with the business at hand. If he ignores the move, be on your guard. Chances are he will eventually take a cursory glance at your papers and start talking about "problems," most likely that you are trying to enter after normal business hours—even though it's eleven o'clock on an otherwise unremarkable Thursday morning. Try to get the difficulty stated clearly. If there is a real problem, try to get it cleared up quickly. If he continues to be vague, he's probably just looking for his *mordita* or *baksheesh* or whatever it's called where you happen to be, so give a deep but silent sigh and say something like, "If there is anything I can do to get this problem straightened out . . ." That gives him the opening he's looking for to hit you for a few bucks without directly asking you for a payoff. The average hit will run around $5 to $25, disguised as a "fee" of some sort. As soon as you fork it over, all "problems" will magically disappear. But don't expect a receipt.

Once your papers are stamped, he may continue the chat and admire the quality of your Scotch which is your cue to offer him another drink. If he persists in hanging about after that, offer him the rest of the bottle and try to work him toward the door. Some experienced cruising people carry along a case of rotgut for just such occasions and keep the good stuff hidden.

After he's gone, relax. Strike your quarantine flag, hoist the courtesy flag of the country you are visiting, and get the good stuff out of the bottom galley drawer. Forget the rip-off, and enjoy your visit.

PART IV

Final Preparations

16

SPARES AND REPAIRS

The night is dark and violent. You have been warned that the entrance lights marking the unfamiliar channel you are trying to negotiate are unreliable, so you are picking your way through carefully on the compass course given in your cruising guide.

Suddenly your compass goes dark. All it needs is a fifty-cent lightbulb. Did you remember to put spares aboard? If so, where are they? In your toolbox? In that catch-all drawer in the galley? And where's that tiny screwdriver you need to get inside the compass in the first place? In this situation, having the spare part you need and the tools to fix it aboard and being able to lay your hands on them quickly can mean the difference between arriving inside the harbor or arriving on the rocks.

LEARN THE MECHANICS

Unless you are well experienced with diesel engines, before you strike off on an extended voyage you might want to audit selected sessions of a diesel mechanics course at your local community college or vocational school. If you're unable to invest that much time, at least ask a friendly mechanic to show you how to clear an air lock in a diesel engine, diagnose a simple electrical problem, or replace a clogged fuel injector.

While you are at it, also get someone to show you how to replace a water-pump impeller and the valves in a marine toilet. Those are two skills that will almost certainly come in handy.

THE CRUISING TOOL KIT

Put together a first-rate tool kit that includes a good ½-inch-drive socket-wrench set and open-end and box wrenches that will handle bolt heads up to about an inch in diameter. Your socket-wrench set should have at least a 12-inch extender. Aside from a good assortment of screwdrivers and the other tools you'd normally carry, you'll need some specialized tools such as two pairs of large Channel Lock pliers whose jaws open up to about 3 inches (to keep your stuffing box nuts tight), a pair of Vise-Grip pliers, and a good volt-ohm meter to run down electrical problems. Another handy gadget to include is a small mirror with an angled handle that will let you look into all manner of hard-to-get-to places such as the underside of your main and generator engines. You'll find a more extensive list of recommended tools to carry in Appendix IV.

MANUALS TO ASSEMBLE

You should assemble from the manufacturers of all the basic equipment aboard your vessel not only their owner/operator manuals but shop manuals, schematic drawings, and a complete parts list as well. Also make sure you have an up-to-date list of their servicing dealers in the areas you plan to cruise and find out if they have a twenty-four-hour hotline you can call if you need to have a part shipped in or run into a problem you can't puzzle through. Some manufacturers of marine equipment also list in their literature a particular single sideband marine radio channel they monitor.

Organize all this information into a couple of stout ring binders either alphabetically or with a table of contents so you can find information quickly.

DEVELOP A MAINTENANCE SCHEDULE

The owner's manuals will give you a list of recommended maintenance procedures that should be performed on each piece of gear aboard your vessel at particular intervals. Organize all that information into a maintenance calendar and make it a part of your ship's log.

GATHER THE SPARES

For coastal cruising, you need at the minimum to carry backups for those items whose failure would completely disable your vessel, its key navigation and communiations equipment, or its tender. On a twin-engine vessel, the thing most likely to disable both engines at the same time would be contaminated fuel that clogged the primary and secondary filters on both engines, and you should carry a generous supply of replacements for each. On a single-engine vessel, you would be wise to carry a spare engine generator or alternator and its drive belt, a thermostat and gasket, an impeller for the raw water pump, an injector and the tools you need to install it, a valve cover gasket, and a spare ignition switch. I personally would also have a spare starter motor aboard and be sure I knew how to install it. Also carry backup fuses for at least your VHF radio, depth-sounder, and radar, and a spark plug and ignition kit for your tender's outboard.

For voyaging into the boondocks, your spare parts inventory will need to be much more extensive and should include such items as a spare shaft, prop, strut and rudder (on a vessel with twin engines, two of each is even better), along with a wheel puller and all the nuts, bolts, washers, cotter pins, and lubricants you'll need to install them. Also be certain you take along an extra-generous supply of the replacement items you're likely to need, such as oil, fuel, and water filters (three times the number you think you could possibly need usually works out about right), hoses and clamps of appropriate diameters, gaskets, belts, pump impellers, light bulbs, fuses, and the like.

Many owner's manuals for marine equipment also include a recommended list of spare parts you should carry with you. Make certain all those are aboard along with a complete spare bilge pump, fuel pump, alternator, and a couple of spare injectors. A more complete list of spares you should have aboard is in Appendix V.

A SPARES INVENTORY SYSTEM

The most elaborate inventory of spare parts aboard a vessel is useless unless you can lay your hands on the part you need quickly. The best system I've seen for doing that was one Frank Glindmeier developed for *Summer Wind*. He emptied the vessel of everything—and I mean everything—and identified every locker, bin, nook, and cranny aboard it where he might be able to stow spares. He assigned each space a designator of three or four letters and numbers (PHD3, for instance, referred to "pilothouse drawer, third from the top") and listed them in a notebook. As he put an item into each stowage space, he dutifully noted a description of it and the quantity. He then cross-referenced that information alphabetically by item. Each time he used an item, he reduced its quantity in the inventory system appropriately.

This system gave Frank several advantages. If he needed a particular spare part, a quick check of the notebook told him exactly where it was stowed and how many he had on board. When he reached a major port, he could quickly tell exactly what items he needed to replace and in what quantity. The system also meant he didn't forget to pick up a replacement for the pump diaphragm he used in Venezuela or the allen wrench that fell overboard in Ketchikan.

PERFORM ROUTINE MAINTENANCE

Before departing on a major cruise aboard a used vessel, have a qualified mechanic tune up your main and generator engines and check any systems you are doubtful about. Perform all routine maintenance, even that which might not be quite due, and pay extra attention to replacing any doubtful pump impellers, slightly frayed alternator belts, rusted clamps, suspicious fuel and water hoses, and the like. Put new bulbs in all your running lights.

Also be sure to check all the electrical connections you can get at and clean and tighten any that appear to be corroded or loose. Thoroughly scrape down your battery terminals, make certain they are tight, and coat them with petroleum jelly to help cut down corrosion. Also check and lubricate all the sea cocks on your vessel's through-hull fittings and make sure its raw-water strainers are clean.

TAKE A SHAKEDOWN CRUISE

Before you depart on an extensive cruise with either a new or a used vessel, I'd strongly advise you to take a shakedown cruise of at least a week before you head to the boondocks. Operate all the vessel's systems, make careful notes, and attend to any problems before you head out on your main voyage.

If you are not well versed in night cruising, plan to include at least one overnight passage in familiar waters. Everything looks different at night, and the overnight run will help you work out a watch system. Before you go, update yourself on the new lighting regulations. It's nice to know if that object out there with the funny lights on it headed your way is a freighter bearing down on you at 20 knots or a slow-moving tug towing a barge behind it on a half-mile of steel cable.

ENGINE-OIL ANALYSIS

Prior to departing on an extended cruise, send a sample of your engine oil to a good testing laboratory and have them perform an engine-oil analysis; this can be a valuable benchmark for monitoring your engine's condition. If you submit follow-up samples after every 3,000 miles or so of cruising and compare the results, the lab might alert you to developing problems which you can correct before they get too serious. This precaution is especially important if your cruising will take you to the lower Caribbean, South America, or Mexico where diesel fuel often is not as highly refined as the fuel we are familiar with in the United States. It often contains high levels of sulphur which can eat away at your engines' valves and piston rings and damage the interior cylinder walls. The first time you take on fuels in these areas, reduce your interval between engine oil and oil filter changes by one third. The first time you change lubricating oil that was used with that load of fuel, submit a sample to your testing laboratory. The results may well indicate you should further reduce your interval between oil and oil filter changes by another third.

DEALING WITH DIESEL FUEL

The diesel fuel you take aboard your vessel is likely to be full of all manner of contaminants. In addition to rust from storage tanks, sludge, and plain old dirt, the most troublesome of these contaminants are algae, fungi, and other microorganisms that live off nutrients in the fuel itself. If their growth is not prevented or checked, they can congregate together in large strings, clumps, or mats of black, brown, or green "slime" which clog your primary and secondary fuel filters and damage metal fuel tanks and rubber gaskets. At best, this buildup will require you to change your filters much more frequently than if you were working with clean fuel; at worst it can actually shut off your engine's fuel supply which—under Murphy's Law—will happen when you are trying to navigate a twisting, poorly marked channel at night in the midst of a raging storm.

Contamination results basically from haphazard procedures at the refinery and poor handling practices by fuel distributors and dealers, so there is not much you can do improve the quality of the fuel you buy. You can, however, make sure you start with clean tanks, maintain good fuel-handling procedures, and treat your fuel with biocides to inhibit microorganism growth.

The fuel tanks of a new boat just off the manufacturing line are likely to be clean. A used vessel, however, or even a new boat that has been sitting at a dealer's dock for months, may already have significant microorganism growth in its tanks. If the vessel you buy has dark globules in its fuel filters or its engine room has a faint odor of rotten eggs, it probably has slime buildup in its tanks. You can also check for the presence of microorganisms in diesel fuel with test kits. If your fuel dealer can't sell you a good one, you can order the SaniCheck kit from Fuel Quality Services, Inc., P.O. Box 317, Buford, Georgia 30518, or the Microb Monitor Test Kit from Boron Oil Co., 1876 Guildhall Building, Cleveland, Ohio 44115.

If your vessel shows signs of significant microbial buildup, you must thoroughly clean its tanks before you embark on an extended voyage. The best way to do that is to drain and discard all the fuel and have the tanks thoroughly cleaned with pressurized steam. If the vessel's tanks don't have clean-out ports or are otherwise inaccessible, fill them with fresh fuel. (If necessary, drain off enough fuel to allow you to add at least one third of each tank's capacity in fresh fuel to allow proper mixing and dilution of the biocide you are going to add.) As the fuel is flowing in, add to it a biocide in the proportions directed by its manufacturer. In the case of Biobor JF from U.S. Borax, for example, the concentration should be 270 parts per million (2.8 fluid ounces per 100 gallons of each tank's capacity). Another good biocide is Kathon FP 1.5 from Rohm and Haas, but note that its recommended concentrations are half those of Biobor JF. Do not exceed the biocide manufacturer's recommended concentrations. Allow the biocide to work at least twenty-four hours, preferably forty-eight hours, before operating your vessel. As you burn the fuel, the biocide will circulate through your vessel's entire fuel system to clean it. As you burn this load of treated fuel, the microorganisms destroyed by the biocide will migrate to your fuel filters. If you have a severe case of microbial buildup, it could shut down your fuel system entirely. Restrict your first several hours of operation to fair weather and areas where you can deal with a shutdown, if it occurs, until you can clear it. Carry at least a case of fresh primary filter elements and half a case of secondary filter elements on board, check your fuel filters at least every half hour, and change them out if they begin to clog.

Even with clean tanks, your battle against microorganisms

isn't over. They can still get into your tanks in fuel you bring on board and condense into your fuel from the air that flows into your tanks through their vents.

Though these bedeviling little critters subsist on nutrients in the fuel itself, they cannot exist without water. Therefore, your first line of defense is keeping water out of your fuel. Since diesel fuel is the lighter of the two fluids, most of the water it contains or that evaporates out of the air in the tank and mixes with it will eventually settle to the bottom of the tanks of a vessel at rest. It would be wonderful if your fuel tanks had bottom sumps which would allow you to drain off water as it accumulates—as aircraft pilots are able to do from the tanks in their craft—but few yacht builders include such a convenience. Of course you will prevent the water in your fuel from reaching your engine by trapping most of it in the fuel/water separators on your engine(s), but that doesn't do anything to prevent water getting into your tanks in the first place. One way to do that would be to install fuel/water separators between your fuel inlet and your tanks to separate as much water (and other contaminants) as possible out of the fuel before it ever gets into your tanks. I know few cruisers who do that, but it's an idea that could pay big dividends—particularly for the long-distance cruiser who must take on fuel in remote ports that contains God-only-knows what.

Some cruisers add isopropyl alcohol to their fuel as a water precipitant. This is not a good idea, particularly in vessels with fiberglass fuel tanks built prior to about 1980, as it can deteriorate the resins used up until then. Isopropyl alcohol in concentrations of 1 pint per 124 gallons of fuel is appropriate only to prevent diesel fuel from freezing during the winter in northern climates.

Your second line of defense is to keep your fuel treated with a biocide to inhibit the growth of any bugs that get into it. For this you can use a lower level of concentration than is needed for a cleanup. In the case of Biobor JF, this maintenance level would be 135 ppm or 1.4 fluid ounces per 100 gallons of fuel. The owner who operates his boat only about twenty-five hours a month should add biocide at a maintenance level to every load of fuel he takes on. The owner doing extended cruising who consumes fuel considerably faster needs to add biocide at a maintenance level to only about every third or fourth load of fuel he takes aboard.

A biocide is about the only additive you should put in your fuel on a regular basis. In particular, stay away from any additives that contain heavy concentrations of isopropyl alcohol or metallic substances such as barium. If you are getting heavy carbon buildup on your diesel engine's injectors which causes it to run rough or emit heavy smoke, the first step is to have a good mechanic check their fuel flow adjustment. If that doesn't solve the problem, ask him about using a detergent dispersant which eases the surface tension of the molecules in fuel and helps prevent particulate matter from conglomerating. Some cruisers favor STP's Concentrated Injector Cleaner for this purpose, but I would not add it to my fuel without the advice of a diesel mechanic I trusted.

Some of these preparations may seem a bit excessive, but at least they can help make your cruise relaxed and enjoyable. At best, they could save your life.

17

MONEY AND MAIL

If you are planning an extended cruise through the boon-docks which will keep you out of touch with home for extended periods of time, there are some basics concerning mail, money, and legal matters you'll want to attend to before you leave.

COVER THE HOME FRONT

First, update your will and leave a witnessed, notarized copy with your attorney or a trusted relative or friend. Don't make the mistake of leaving the only copy of your will in a safe-deposit box. In the event something happens to you, the authorities are likely to seal the box and your survivors will have to go to court to get it opened. Normally it can be opened only when Federal and state revenue agents are present to list its contents for possible estate taxes.

It's also a good idea to leave your power of attorney with your lawyer or a trusted relative or friend in case something serious requires your legal authorization at a time when it is difficult or impossible for you to get home.

If you expect to have regular income such as dividend, social-security, or pension checks coming in while you are gone, arrange to have them deposited directly to your bank account. You may also need to make provisions for regular payment of such things as insurance premiums, your home mortgage, and estimated taxes. You can arrange for most such payments to be drafted from your bank account. If not, the trust department of most banks will make them for you, or you can ask your CPA or a trusted friend or relative to handle them for you. Whomever you ask to handle financial matters for you at home, put your instructions in writing. Then, if something goes wrong, you both will have a base of reference as to what you agreed to.

If you have stock options that need to be exercised, bond coupons that need to be clipped, certificates of deposit that need to be rolled over, or investment decisions that need to be executed in your absence, don't forget to set up an arrangement with your banker, accountant, stockbroker, or that trusted friend or relative. Again, put your instructions in writing.

THE CRUISING KITTY

I was visiting aboard the boat of some cruising friends in the Caribbean several years ago, and the husband withdrew a small square of paper from his wallet, handed it to me, and said, "If you can figure that out, it's worth around twenty-five thousand dollars to you." On the paper were about ten lines of undecipherable letters and numbers. After I had puzzled over it for a few minutes he took it back and said with a laugh, "We're carrying about twenty-five thousand dollars in U.S. currency aboard which is broken up into packages of three to five thousand dollars each, wrapped in plastic and hidden in various places around the boat. This piece of paper is to remind me where I've hidden it."

I suppose that's one way to handle the matter of cruising funds, but I'd suggest you handle your cruising kitty somewhat differently.

Certainly, it's a good idea to have some ready cash aboard in both U.S. funds and the currencies of the countries you'll be visiting. You can't very well give a customs official who wants his *mordita* a check, you might need fuel, provisions, or repair services in some out-of-the-way place where cash is the only acceptable means of exchange. I suggest you keep a cushion of at least $2,000 to $2,500 available at all times in case you encounter a major expense that can be handled only with cash, but I wouldn't carry more than about $5,000 in cash aboard at any one time. If your vessel is robbed or sinks, most marine insurance policies won't cover the loss of cash. Carry most of your cruising cash in U.S. dollars, preferably in bills no larger than a twenty since in many foreign countries breaking larger denominations can be a problem. For the rest of your cash, go to a large national or regional bank and get $100 or so in small denomintions of the currencies of each country you plan to visit. You may have to pay customs and duty fees before you can go ashore to make a currency exchange. Like my friend, break your cash up into several packages, stash them in various locations around your boat, and make yourself a cue card to help you remember where they are. If your vessel is broken into, at least maybe the robbers won't find all of them.

Carry the bulk of your cruising kitty in traveler's checks so you can get it back if the checks are lost or stolen, but be sure to keep the receipt apart from the checks themselves. If the U.S. dollar is rising against the currencies of the countries you plan to visit, get your traveler's checks in U.S. funds. If it's falling against those currencies, get traveler's checks in those currencies. Most large national and regional banks can provide traveler's checks in British pounds, French francs, Spanish pesos, or the other currencies that might be most useful in the particular areas you plan to cruise.

You generally will find that banks are the best place to convert U.S. dollars to another currency or to cash traveler's checks. In many countries abroad, banks have limited hours of operation, and catching them when they are open can call for a bit of extra planning, but their exchange rate usually will be better than you'll get in currency-exchange houses which are open longer hours. When changing money at a bank, shop for the best rates, since even bank rates can vary a percentage point or two.

Carry a wide variety of credit cards and use them whenever possible to pay major expenses such as fuel bills, repair services, and shoreside expenses. In my travels to some thirty-five countries around the world, I have found Mastercard, Visa, Diner's Club, and Carte Blanch the most widely accepted. American Express is also widely recognized, but many smaller merchants refuse to honor it because it carries a higher discount rate. When you pay a bill rendered in a foreign country with a credit card, and then pay the credit card charge in U.S. dollars, the rate of exchange will be the one in effect the day the charge is posted to your account. I've done this a number of times and never felt I was treated unfairly on the exchange rate.

The best arrangement for replenishing your cruising funds during an extended voyage is to maintain an account in a large international bank that has branches in the countries you plan to visit. With today's sophisticated banking computers, you often can get cash within hours, even though you are thousands of miles from home, and pay little or nothing for the service.

In areas where these banks do not have offices of their own, they usually maintain correspondent relationships with local banks. Get a list of your bank's correspondents and try to work through one of them when you need a fresh infusion of funds or have an emergency. You are likely to get quicker service than you will at a noncorrespondent bank and probably will save money in the bargain. With this kind of a setup, your home bank can send you money by wire transfer to their correspondent bank in about two days and the transaction usually will cost you only about ten dollars.

In my experience, the two U.S. banks with the most foreign branches are Chase Manhattan and Citibank. Another international bank with widespread offices is Barclays.

Some cruisers carry a letter of credit from their home bank and draw against it at a local bank when they need money. Others carry cashier's checks from their home bank. I've tried both arrangements and found neither satisfactory. The local bank normally will want to process the transaction and collect the funds from your stateside bank before they release money to you. The process can take a week to ten days—even more in especially remote areas—and processing fees can run the equivalent of $25 U.S. or more, plus the costs of telegrams or telex messages.

FORWARDING MAIL

The best way to get important mail to catch up with you while you're cruising is to have whoever is keeping up with it send a package to any guests who might be coming to visit about three days before their departure and ask them to bring it down with them.

If you have a fairly firm itinerary, an alternative is to give the person handling your mail the addresses of marinas, yacht clubs, and resorts you plan to visit along the way and your approximate arrival dates at each. Have him gather together only the important items from a month or so worth of mail, put it in a sturdy envelope, and mail it to your destination marked with your name, the name of your vessel, and "Hold for Arrival." Caution him, however, to allow as much as two weeks for surface mail to arrive at its destination and not to include checks, cash, or other items of value. If you have an American Express card, its offices will hold mail for you; or you may be able to set up the service through your bank's offshore branches or their correspondent institutions.

If you prefer not to ask a relative or friend to handle mail forwarding for you, several companies that advertise in the major boating magazines will do it for you—for a fee of course.

Don't forget to tell key contacts at home how to reach you through VHF marine or High Seas radiotelephone operators as we outlined in chapter 9.

18

CRUISE PLANNING

During a recent September some friends of mine arrived in Road Town, Tortola, eagerly anticipating a dream cruise through the British Virgin Islands aboard a charter vessel. They had scheduled their trip during the "off season," because the charter rates were significantly lower then than during the other months of the year.

The only problem was that the charter service had failed to

remind them that September is the height of the hurricane season in the Caribbean. As my friends waited for a checkout of
their boat, they learned that a severe tropical storm was building
up 350 miles southeast of Grenada and was headed their way.
Their boat was almost ready and they could go aboard in a couple of hours, they were told, but their checkout would be delayed. All the company's personnel were busy ferrying its
remaining yachts to safe harbor to avoid the storm's possible
onslaught.

There is no doubt that the charter company was irresponsi-
ble in not informing my friends of the weather conditions they
were likely to encounter in the Caribbean at that time of the year
and in allowing them to depart with a storm brewing. But my
friends were also unwittingly guilty of poor cruise planning.

A few years ago in Fort-de-France, Martinique, I made a
similar sort of cruise-planning mistake—but in reverse. At the
end of a beautiful week's run down the Windwards from Antigua, I got up before dawn to pack for an early-morning flight
home. As the sun peeked over the mountains, I began to hear
the strains of a steel band drifting in through the porthole. I
stuck my head out to find the wharf jammed with dancing natives. When I asked one of the revelers what was doing on, he
beamed and said, "Why, Mon, it's the first day of Carnival!"
After a couple of frantic calls back stateside to persuade a somewhat irritated editor to revise a deadline, I was able to extend
my stay for long enough to join in at least part of the festivities.
With a little better planning, I would have scheduled my cruise
for a week longer to participate fully in the celebration, and the
last-minute schedule change would not have been necessary.

As you plan your next voyage, dig out the pilot charts and
a calendar early to make certain you don't miss something special or run into conditions you'd just as soon avoid.

CONSIDER THE WEATHER

The first consideration in cruise planning, of course, is the
weather. You wouldn't strike out across the Atlantic in November, nor would you attempt to cross the Pacific at the height of
the cyclone season, but what is the best time to go? You may be
like a farmer friend of mine who says the best time to plant his
garden is "when I got time, and it ain't too wet to plow," but if

you have a little leeway in your schedule, here are a few suggestions:

First, consult the pilot charts for the area you plan to visit to find out about typical temperatures, wind strengths, and sea states month by month. That information would suggest, for instance, that you should plan to cruise the Bahamas, the Gulf of Mexico, and the Caribbean sometime other than August and September since that is the worst of their hurricane season. From mid-December to mid-January, the Windwards and Leewards normally experience "Christmas winds" which can blow 40 knots or better for days on end. The best time to cruise those areas is February through April before the heat really begins to bear down in May, or in November after the likelihood of tropical storms has passed.

If you dream of cruising the South Pacific, try to avoid January and February which is the heart of their cyclone season. For areas such as Australia which are below the equator, remember that their seasons are the reverse of those in the Northern Hemisphere: in summer—roughly November through March—winds tend to be variable and the rains can be drenching. The best time for cruising an area like the Great Barrier Reef is May through August—the Australian winter—when winds are more dependable and the climate is drier.

For cruising the east or west coasts of the United States and Canada above 40 degrees North (roughly anything above New York and San Francisco), plan on May through September or pack your warm woollies. The same goes for any place in Europe north of the English Channel.

CHECK OUT CELEBRATIONS

Once you've figured out the best time of year to cruise the area you have in mind, check with the national, state, and local tourist boards for the dates of any special events that you can tie into your schedule. A great many foreign nations have tourist offices in New York, and their staffs tend to be competent and helpful. To enjoy Carnival, for example, try to wind up in heavily Catholic countries just before Lent.

I'm a great one for clipping and filing magazine articles on other folks' cruises, and picking up local handouts wherever I go. A quick check of the files tells me when to plan a visit to

Chesapeake Bay to coincide with the greatest number of crab festivals, when to visit the Gulf Coast for Jambalaya or Jamaica for Goombay.

CHARTS AND CRUISING GUIDES

Once you know the approximate route your cruise will follow, start assembling a complete collection of up-to-date charts, coastal pilots, and cruising guides to the areas you will be visiting.

Between NOAA and the Defense Mapping Agency in the United States, the British Admiralty, and the French and Canadian hydrographic services, there is hardly a spot on earth that hasn't been charted, though the information on some of the more remote areas may not have been updated since the days of the whaling ships. Choose the smallest-scale charts you can find as they will show more detail. Pay particular attention to harbor charts, even for places a bit off your route that you don't actually plan to visit. In severe weather, you might have to duck into some unintended harbors or anchorages, and you don't want to be running an entrance channel blind.

Coastal pilots, usually hard-bound volumes published by the same government agencies that produce maritime charts, provide valuable information about the weather you can expect to encounter in an area at various times of the year, and also include elaborately detailed sailing directions for entering various harbors and anchorages. Their prose is usually dry and bureaucratic, but when you are feeling your way through unfamiliar waters they can be worth their weight in gold.

Cruising guides can be marvelous storehouses of information about the areas you will be visiting and often will bring to your attention a bit of history or an out-of-the-way sight worth visiting. Some are big and filled with glossy photographs, others may be thin, printed on cheap paper, and crudely illustrated, but having them is far better than visiting an area with no guide at all.

DON'T FORGET PASSPORTS AND VISAS

If your cruising plans will take you outside the United States, make certain your passport and those of your crew are up to date or make plans to renew them.

More and more countries now require advance applications for visas rather than simply granting them at their borders. Once you have figured out which countries you will be visiting, check with a good travel agency or the U.S. State Department early to find out if any of them require advance visa applications. If they do, file early since processing through normal channels can take up to two months. If you get in a time bind, there are several companies in Washington, D.C., that for a fee will hand-carry visa applications through the bureaucratic maze for you and can cut the time to a week or less. Ask your travel agent to recommend a good one, based on the countries you plan to visit.

If you plan to rent automobiles for shoreside sightseeing during your cruise, get an International Driving Permit which is honored in countries ranging from Afghanistan to Zimbabwe. In the United States they are issued by the American Automobile Association. You will need a passport photo to go along with your application. The permit is valid only if you also have a valid U.S. driver's license, and you must carry both documents with you.

SCHEDULING GUESTS

Once you have a cruising plan in mind, it's a good idea to go ahead and make out at least a rough itinerary with major stopover points penciled in. Be sure to include plenty of layover time along your route to account for weather and mechanical delays.

Once you have an itinerary, you can begin working out a schedule with family members or friends you might ask to join you along the way. Early planning is necessary to give them time to look into work and school vacations, and arrange their own passports, visas, and travel schedules. Guests who are not familiar with visiting aboard cruising vessels will find it helpful if you write out for them step-by-step instructions covering what they need to do in advance, how to pack (lightly, and in soft luggage which is easier to stow on board), and the clothes they should bring, including boating shoes with nonslip soles. (Either in that memo or as soon as they arrive on board, make certain to tell them exactly what they can and cannot dispose of in your marine head.)

The earlier you get your schedule of guest visits worked out, the earlier you can start your own planning for provisioning your vessel to make sure you have everything you need on board when they arrive.

PROVISIONING

One of the best provisioning systems for an extended cruise I have run across was developed by Frank and Lee Glindmeier for their voyage from Florida to Alaska and back aboard *Summer Wind*. They knew that throughout the Caribbean and in South and Central America, reprovisioning with good-quality meats at reasonable prices would be difficult if not impossible. Because of that, they wanted to leave home carrying all the meat they would need for the first leg of the voyage from Florida to San Diego. In San Diego, they would reprovision for the San Diego–Glacier Bay–San Diego leg, then again as they prepared for the run back to Florida. In order to preserve that much meat, Frank had a company that specializes in marine refrigeration replace the vessel's standard household-type refrigerator/freezer in the galley with a well-insulated holding-plate unit and install a large holding-plate freezer in the vessel's cockpit.

Since Frank and Lee planned to have a number of family members and friends join them along the way for anywhere from a week to a month at a time, they worked out well in advance a fairly detailed cruise plan so their guests could arrange their vacations. Once the cruise plan was set, Lee knew how many people she would have aboard each week of the entire eighteen-month journey and planned her menus accordingly. She then purchased all the meat she would need for the first leg of the voyage in bulk and had it cut, wrapped, and labeled to her specifications. (She had the butcher trim off almost all the fat and remove bones to reduce weight and volume.) She started with the final week of the first leg of the cruise and worked backward. All the meat for that week went into its own freezer bag, labeled by contents and quantity, and that bag went into the bottom of the big cockpit freezer. Similar bags for prior weeks went into the big freezer in successive order. Each Sunday evening, Lee transferred the meat for the coming week from the cockpit freezer to the galley freezer. This not only meant that the meat for each week was convenient to hand in the galley but that the cockpit freezer was opened only once a week which helped keep down its energy consumption.

A couple of other provisioning hints: Lee knew that when *Summer Wind* was at anchor miles from the nearest grocery store she would hardly be able to run out for a forgotten jar of minced garlic or chili powder, so she developed an equally practical process for dealing with *Summer Wind*'s canned and dry food stores. Once she had made out her menus, she computed the quantity of each item she would need. She then identified every nook, cranny, and cubbyhole on the vessel which could be used to store provisions and assigned each a three- or four-character identifier which she listed in a looseleaf notebook. As she filled each compartment, she listed its contents, then cross-referenced each item by its quantity and location. When she was through, she had an alphabetical list of every can of beans and box of spaghetti on board, knew how many she had and exactly where to find them. As she used an item, she reduced its quantity in her inventory appropriately. When she found the next market, she knew exactly what provisions she needed to replenish and in what quantity. "In the entire eighteen months," Frank says, "I can't think of a time when we ran out of any dry or canned stores we really wanted or needed."

About six months before Charlie and Nancy Bowen departed on their year-long voyage through the Caribbean aboard their 40-foot displacement cruiser *Takabrake III*, Nancy drew up a list of all the canned and dry stores she felt she could justify purchasing by the case. "In provisioning for earlier cruises," she says, "I had joined various clubs which allow you to buy in case lots. But for that trip, I took my list to the manager of the local grocery store I usually deal with which is part of a major chain. Every time the chain had a special on one of the items on my list, the manager bought whatever I needed and sold it to me for only about a four percent markup. I got particularly good prices on items which carried the store's own brand."

DAILY CRUISING SCHEDULE

Ideally, each day that you'll be under way you'll be able to depart the dock or anchorage around 10:00 A.M. and get the hook set in the next beautiful spot by around 4:30 P.M. (not much later in tropical areas since coral heads and reefs can be almost impossible to spot when the sun is low in the sky).

There will, of course, be times when your vessel's speed

and the distance to be traveled won't allow you to cover all of a run in daylight hours. In those instances, time your departure in the dark if necessary, but plan to arrive at your destination during daylight hours, preferably between midmorning and mid-afternoon. Trying to feel your way into an unfamiliar harbor or anchorage in the dark is no way to ensure a trouble-free cruise.

With some careful advance planning, you can make certain your cruising will be enjoyed under sunny skies with the wind at your back and timed to allow you to take part in the best your cruising area has to offer. Without careful cruise planning, like my friends in Tortola, you may find yourself setting out into a gale or hearing the line I encounter every time I go fishing: "You shoulda' been here last week!"

Epilog

DO IT!

In the course of this book, we've considered hundreds of the questions you'll face in selecting and outfitting a cruising powerboat appropriate to the type of voyage on which you yearn to embark, and we've discussed many of the things you need to know before you cast off your lines. If I did my job well, you're a lot better prepared now to take on the challenges and excitements of the cruising life than you were when we started.

I have only one final bit of advice: Do it!

Many of us put off launching our cruising dreams until we can afford exactly the boat we want, outfit it down to the last luxury we possibly could want aboard, and have all the money we could conceivably need tucked away in the bank. Prudence is fine—to a point. But carried too far, it can mean "someday" never comes.

Let the sound of the waves lapping against that rocky coast in Maine or that beach in the Caribbean make you a little crazy. Set yourself a timetable and say, "By then, by God, we will go!" and do whatever you must to meet it. Find a boat you can afford in the realizable future. Within the limits of safety and reasonable comfort we've discussed, rig her with only the basics if you have to. But make your plans and take off. Some of the happiest cruisers—in fact, the happiest *people*—I've ever met were aboard minimal boats and had no ice for their drinks. But they were on the water and *living* their dreams, not just planning for them.

When you pull into Casco Bay up in Maine, or English Harbour down in Antigua, or Elfin Cove in Alaska, if you spot a nifty little cruiser named *Ladye Anne* quietly tucked away in a corner, that'll be me. Drop by and say hello.

Until then, bon voyage.

POWERBOAT HULL FORMS

DISPLACEMENT/LENGTH RATIO

One of the best rules of thumb for determining how much heft the builder of a particular boat you are considering has built into his product is to determine the boat's Displacement/Length ratio with the formula:

$$D/L = \frac{\text{Displacement (in long tons)}}{\left(\frac{\text{LWL}}{100}\right)^3}$$

(To convert displacement in pounds into long tons, divide it by 2,240.)

The smaller a boat's load waterline length, the larger its D/L ratio should be.

In a displacement-hull boat with an LWL of around 50 feet intended for extensive bluewater cruising, look for a D/L ratio of at least 250. A boat of that type with an LWL of around 40 feet should have a D/L ratio of 320 or better.

In semidisplacement or planing hulls, the D/L ratio for cruisers with an LWL of around 50 feet should be not less than 180, and 200 is even better. Those type boats with LWLs of around 40 feet should have a D/L ratio of 220 or higher.

We are now seeing on the market a number of planing-hull

boats in the 40-foot range which their builders advertise as "high performance family cruisers." In order to keep down weight and thus increase speed, these boats are constructed with cored hulls and all manner of lightweight materials, which in many cases result in D/L ratios of 160 or less. They may be acceptable for family outings close to home in fair weather, but they are far too lightly built to stand up to the conditions you sooner or later are certain to encounter in serious cruising.

SPEED/LENGTH RATIO

One of the basic facts of life in yacht design is that at a speed in knots equal to 1.34 times the square root of its LWL, the hull of a vessel moving through water produces a wave equal in length to its own LWL. If the vessel is sufficiently powered to exceed this theoretical hull speed, it will create a bigger bow wave, which will cause the bow to rise and force its stern to sink deeper into its own wake. A vessel will continue to operate in this fashion until it reaches a speed in knots equal to at least twice the square root of its LWL, at which point it will begin to overcome the resistance of its bow wave and begin to plane on top of the water rather than plow through it.

This principle clearly affects the basic hull design and propulsion packages of the three types of pleasure-yacht hulls discussed in the text: displacement-hull yachts are designed to operate below their theoretical hull speed; planing-hull yachts are designed to operate in excess of it; and semidisplacement-hull boats are designed to operate on both sides of the "hump."

Understanding the principle of S/L ratios is a key to analyzing the hull form of any cruising vessel you might consider, regardless of its type.

In analyzing semidisplacement or planing hulls designed to operate in excess of their hull speed, flat sections aft are a plus. In the critical speed range between 1.34 and twice the square root of their LWL, they help resist the stern's tendency to sink as the bow rises to overcome the bow wave, which assists the boat to come up on plane faster. Boats with excessive (over about 16 degrees) dead rise aft cut into the water rather than providing this countering resistance, which is why it takes them longer to come up on plane.

In analyzing a displacement vessel designed solely for cruising below its hull speed, smooth, well-rounded sections aft ease the flow of water past the hull. This contributes to the vessel's operating efficiency, but also gives it a more exaggerated fore-and-aft pitching motion in a head sea. As the bow rises on a wave, the rounded sections aft create little countering resistance and can cause the vessel to "hobby horse." Well-rounded stern sections also do nothing to help resist that type hull's tendency to roll. A displacement-hull vessel with relatively flat sections in the aft fourth of its hull will roll considerably less while giving up only a minimal amount of efficiency. In a head sea, those flat sections aft provide some resistance to the bow's attempt to rise to a wave and results in less pitching.

MARINE DIESEL ENGINES

ENGINE DESIGNATIONS

The designations of marine diesel engines manufactured by Detroit Diesel Corporation (formally a division of General Motors but now privately owned) such as 4-53 or 8V-71TI describe several of the engine's key characteristics. The first number describes the number of cylinders. If that number is followed by the letter V, the cylinders are inclined alternately at a vee-angle; if not, they are in line. The number after the dash indicates the displacement of each of the engine's cylinders in cubic inches. If that number is followed by the letter T, the engine is turbocharged. If the T is followed by the letter I, it is intercooled; if by the letter A, it is aftercooled. The letter N or the absence of a letter indicates the engine is naturally aspirated. All Detroit Diesel engines designated in this fashion are two-cycle and are available in both left-hand (the flywheel, viewed from forward of the engine, rotates counterclockwise) and right-hand rotations.

Detroit Diesel more recently has introduced the 6.2L (162 SHP) and 8.2T (211 SHP) engines for pleasure marine use. Both are eight-cylinder, four-cycle diesels. The numbers in their designation refer to the (approximate) total displacement of all eight cylinders in liters. The 6.2L is naturally aspirated and the L indicates it is available in left-hand rotation only. The T following the 8.2 designation indicates that the engine is turbocharged. It is available in both left-hand and right-hand rotations.

The designations of Ford-Lehman marine diesels, which are four-cycle engines, describe their brake-horsepower ratings.

The designations of the four-cycle marine diesels made by Caterpillar, Perkins, Cummins, and Volvo are essentially model numbers and tell you little if anything about their basic characteristics.

HORSEPOWER RATINGS

As you compare the horsepower ratings of marine diesel engines, make sure you know which horsepower you are considering. Engine manufacturers and boat builders normally refer to an engine in terms of its brake horsepower (BHP)—the maximum horsepower it develops with no load applied. For cruising applications, it's more realistic to compare shaft horsepower (SHP), which is the maximum horsepower an engine actually delivers to a vessel's shaft and propeller after allowing for the loss of power in its marine transmission. In some engine specification sheets, shaft horsepower also reflects the loss of power needed to drive the engine's raw-water pump and its generator or alternator. The difference between an engine's brake and shaft horsepower normally is around 3 percent.

Shaft horsepower is further reduced by propeller load—the horsepower consumed by the engine's associated shaft and prop. At low engine rpm, where torque is high, propeller load can consume on the order of 75 percent of the engine's shaft horsepower. As engine rpm are increased, propeller torque (and thus its load) gradually is reduced to the point of being negligible at the engine's maximum rpm.

The horsepower ratings of marine diesels are further defined by the type of service in which the engine is employed.

The marine continuous rating refers to the net horsepower available at the transmission when the engine is operated at 90 percent or more of its maximum rpm for more than 1,000 hours a year. That rating normally is applied to engines installed in commercial workboats and is a level of operation few owner-operators of pleasure vessels would attain.

The marine intermittent rating refers to the net horsepower available at the marine transmission when the engine normally is operated at not more than 90 percent of its maximum rpm and is operated at its maximum rpm for not more than 10 percent of its total operating hours. This rating usually is applied to engines installed in privately owned long-distance cruising vessels which are operated for not more than 1,000 hours a year.

The marine maximum rating typically is defined the same way as the marine intermittent rating, but total engine hours normally are limited to 500 hours per year. This rating usually is applied to engines installed in privately owned high-performance boats where speed is a primary consideration and overall load factors are low.

ENGINE SPECIFICATION SHEETS

By studying a specification sheet's performance curve for a particular engine at the rating appropriate to the way you intend to use the engine, you can determine a great deal about the actual horsepower you will have to work with at different rpm settings and the amount of fuel it will consume per hour. In studying performance curves, realize that the figures assume essentially "laboratory conditions": that the engine is installed in an efficient hull with a clean bottom which is carrying about half the weight of water, fuel, and stores it is designed to carry and is operating under ideal weather conditions. A particularly inefficient hull, a fouled bottom, excessive weight, or heavy seas can reduce all the power ratings and increase the fuel consumption figures by 25 percent or more.

As an example, let's study the performance curve of a Detroit Diesel 6V-71TA marine diesel (Fig. II.1). Note first that (1) all the figures given allow for the power consumed by the engine's marine gear, raw-water pump, and a 75 amp. generator. At 2,300 rpm, the maximum speed at which the engine is designed to operate, it will develop 375 brake horsepower and 365 shaft horsepower (2). The cruising speed of a diesel engine normally will be 200 rpm below its maximum speed. At 2,100 rpm, as the top curve on the spec. sheet shows, the engine will develop a shade over 350 shaft horsepower (3). The lower curve indicates that at its maximum speed it will consume 20 gallons of fuel per hour (4). But after allowing for propeller load, at 2,100 rpm it will actually deliver only 280 SHP (5) and consume about 15.5 gallons of fuel per hour (6).

One gallon of fuel per hour develops 18 shaft horsepower. Therefore, a quick way to figure fuel consumption in gallons per hour (gph) for a marine diesel is to divide the shaft horsepower

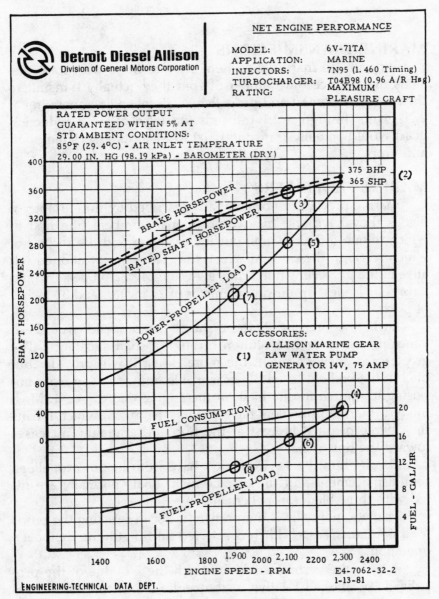

NET ENGINE PERFORMANCE

Detroit Diesel Allison
Division of General Motors Corporation

MODEL:	6V-71TA
APPLICATION:	MARINE
INJECTORS:	7N95 (1.460 Timing)
TURBOCHARGER:	T04B98 (0.96 A/R Hsg)
RATING:	MAXIMUM
	PLEASURE CRAFT

RATED POWER OUTPUT
GUARANTEED WITHIN 5% AT
STD AMBIENT CONDITIONS:
85°F (29.4°C) - AIR INLET TEMPERATURE
29.00 IN. HG (98.19 kPa) - BAROMETER (DRY)

375 BHP (2)
365 SHP

BRAKE HORSEPOWER

RATED SHAFT HORSEPOWER

POWER-PROPELLER LOAD

ACCESSORIES:
ALLISON MARINE GEAR (1)
RAW WATER PUMP
GENERATOR 14V, 75 AMP

FUEL CONSUMPTION

FUEL-PROPELLER LOAD

SHAFT HORSEPOWER

FUEL - GAL/HR

ENGINE SPEED - RPM

E4-7062-32-2
1-13-81

ENGINEERING-TECHNICAL DATA DEPT.

it develops at a particular rpm by 18. In the case of the 6V-71TA engine above, at 1,900 rpm—after allowing for propeller load—it will develop about 208 shp (7) and consume right at 11.5 gph (8).

MARINE TRANSMISSIONS

Virtually all marine diesel engines are fitted with transmissions that reduce the number of rpm they actually transmit to their associated shaft and propeller. A diesel engine operating at 2,200 rpm through a 2:1 transmission (also called a reduction gear) would actually transmit 1,100 RPM to its associated shaft and prop.

MARINE PROPELLERS

Marine propellers normally are described by the number of blades they have and by two additional numbers, the first of which refers to their overall outside diameter and the second of which refers to the pitch at which the blades are positioned relative to the propeller's hub. Thus a 4-blade 24 × 32 propeller would have four blades, an outside diameter of 24 inches, and 32 inches of pitch.

Pitch, theoretically, is the distance the propeller would advance if rotated one revolution through a solid substance. The greater a propeller's pitch, the more thrust it will provide. But pitch must be held to within reasonable limits to keep from imposing too much torque load on the engine that drives it. Most modern marine propellers have progressive pitch, which means the degree of pitch is least at the hub and gradually increases toward the tips.

Planing-hull boats normally have four-blade propellers; semidisplacement and full-displacement boats normally are fitted with three-blade propellers.

Diameter normally is the primary factor in selecting the props for a particular vessel. Pitch is selected for fine-tuning the boat's operation.

Rake is the vertical angle at which the aft edge of the propeller is positioned relative to the centerline of the hub. Props with minimum rake (where the angle between the centerline of the hub and the aft edge of the blade is closest to 90 degrees) tend to raise a vessel's stern. Props with rearward rake tend to raise the vessel's bow. The props on planing-hull cruisers typically have 3 to 5 degrees of aft rake, where props on semidisplacement and full-displacement hulls typically have little if any rake.

Marine propellers come in right-hand and left-hand versions. A right-hand propeller, viewed from the stern of the vessel to which it is attached, rotates clockwise. (Thus, a right-handed engine must be fitted with a left-hand propeller.)

On twin-screw vessels, the top of each propeller normally rotates toward the outboard side.

RECOMMENDED MEDICAL SUPPLIES

FIRST-AID KIT

Item	*Quantity*
Alcohol	2 bottles, 16 oz. ea.
Ammonia inhalents	12
Analgesic ointment	4 tubes, 2 oz. ea.
Analgesics	600 tablets/capsules
Antacid	2 bottles, 16 oz. ea.
Antibiotic ointment	4 tubes, 1 oz. ea.
Antidiarrhea compound	2 bottles, 16 oz. ea.
Antiemetic compound	2 bottles, 16 oz. ea.
Bandages, adhesive	2 large boxes of assorted sizes
Bandages, elastic	4, 4 inches × 4 feet ea.
Bandage scissors	1 pair
Bee-sting kit	1
Benadryl	50 tablets, 25 mg. ea.
Benzocaine toothache gel	4 tubes, 1/3 oz. ea.
Betadine scrub brushes	24
Betadine solution	2 bottles, 4 oz. ea.
Bronchodilators	2

Cake decorating gel	4 tubes, 16 oz. ea.
Charcoal, liquid activated	2 bottles, 16 ozs. ea.
Chemical heat packs	24
Chemical ice packs	24
Chlorine bleach	2 bottles, 16 oz. ea.
Ear drops, nonprescription	2 bottles, 1 oz. ea.
Ear syringe	1
Eye drops, nonprescription	4 bottles, 1 oz. ea.
Gauze pads	1 box of 100, 4 inches × 4 inches ea.
Ipecac	2 bottles, 16 oz. ea.
Lip balm, medicated with sun- screen	10 tubes, 1.5 oz. ea.
Meat tenderizer	2 bottles, 4 oz. ea.
Mineral oil	1 bottle, 16 oz.
Needle-nose tweezers	1 pair
Nosebleed packs	6
Oral thermometers	2
Penlight	1 (with extra batteries)
Safety pins	24 in assorted sizes
Scopolamine patches	1 box of 50
Snakebite kit	1
Sunscreen lotion containing PABA	4 bottles in assorted strengths
Sunburn lotion	6 bottles, 8 oz. ea.
Throat lozenges	100
Tape, waterproof	
1″	100 feet
2″	100 feet
Vinyl gloves	1 box of 50 ea.

TRAUMA KIT

The following recommendations are intended as a general guide to the equipment that would be required aboard a vessel

intended for offshore cruising to allow an appropriately trained
crew member to provide basic trauma life support for at least 24
hours until the victim can be transported to professional medical
assistance. Specific items should be employed only after appropriate training in their use has been completed and, if at all possible, only under the direction of a qualified physician. Purchases
of the recommended equipment should be made through a competent surgical supply house that can ensure that necessary
equipment and systems are compatible and complete. The recommendations cover only adults. If small children will be aboard,
sizes and dosages must be altered appropriately.

Item	*Quantity*
General Supplies:	
Alcohol wipes	1 box of 200
Bandages, elastic	4, 4 inches × 6 feet ea.
Bandages, elastic, self-adhering pressure	4
Bandages, roller	12
Bandages, triangular	4
Betadine brushes	25
Blanket, disposable emergency	2
Blood pressure cuff	1
Burn sheet	2
Dressings, multitrauma sterile	24
Eye irrigation kit	1
Eye patches	22
Food wrap, plastic	2 boxes
Gloves, sterile	2 pair
Lubricant, water-soluble	1 tube
Ointment, antiseptic	4 tubes, 2 oz. ea.
Pads, compression	4
Pads, gauze	
4" × 4"	1 box of 50
8" × 8'	1 box of 50
Pads, petroleum gauze	1 box of 50

Item	Quantity

General Supplies:

Shears, emergency	1 pair
Stethoscope	1
Tape, waterproof	
2″	100 feet
4″	100 feet
Tongue depressors	1 box of 100
Tourniquets	2

Airway, Breathing, Circulation Supplies:

Airway Kit

*Oxygen	1 D cylinder with integral pressure regulator and tubing
Bag-valve-mask device	1
Pocket mask w/oxygen inlet	1
Oxygen mask	1
Oxygen cannula	1
Oxygen tubing	2 sets
Portable suction unit and tubing	1
Oral airways	1 set with 7 sizes
McGill forceps	1 pair

Fracture-, Neck-, and Spinal-injury Supplies:

Ladder or air splints	1 kit of asorted types and sizes
Cervical collars	1 kit with 3 sizes
Sandbags	2 of 3 pounds ea.
Long spine-board or scoop stretcher	1

Severe Bleeding/Circulation Supplies:

Scissors, surgical	1 pair
Steri-strips	2 boxes in assorted sizes
Suture kit	
4/0 nylon and needles	4 kits

| *Item* | *Quantity* |

Severe Bleeding/Circulation Supplies:

Curved forceps	1 pair
Hemostats	2 pair
Xylocaine, topical	2 aerosol cans
Military Antishock Trousers (MAST)	1 pair

Body-Fluid Replacement Supplies:

| Arm board | 1 |
| Large-bore IV catheter with large-bore tubing | 4 sets in various sizes |

MEDICATIONS KIT

| *Item* | *Quantity* |

Codeine
| Oral | 50 caps, 30 mg. ea. |
| Injectable | 10 prefilled syringes, 60 mg. ea. |

Demerol
| Oral | 50 caps., 25 mg. ea. |
| Injectable | 10 prefilled syringes, 100 mg. ea. |

| Dextrose, 50% solution | 6 bags, 1000cc ea. |

Epinephrine (1:1000 type)
| Injectable | 10 prefilled syringes, 0.5 mg. ea. |

Morphine
Injectable	10 prefilled syringes, 10 mg. ea.
Narcan (IV push)	4 prefilled syringes, 0.4 mg. ea.
Nitroglycerine	50 tablets, 0.4 mg. ea.
Oxygen	12 E cylinders, 22 cu. ft. ea.

Penicillin
| Oral | 50 caps., 500 mg. ea. |
| Injectable | 10 prefilled syringes, 1.2 million units ea. |

Item	Quantity
Plasmanate	6 bags, 250cc ea.
Ringer's lactate	6 bags, 1000cc ea.
Tetanus toxoid	5 prefilled syringes, 0.5 mg. ea.

*Oxygen, one of the most effective substances available for sustaining life in a trauma situation, legally is a drug and must be prescribed by a physician. One E cylinder containing 22 cu. feet of oxygen at 2,000 psi will provide a typical 5 liter/min. flow for approximately two hours. With a regulator to reduce its pressure to 50 psi, it will weigh approximately 12 pounds. (To compute the usage rate in minutes of an oxygen cylinder: multiply its capacity in cubic feeet by 28.32 [liters/cu. ft.], subtract 50 to account for pressure-regulator consumption, then divide the result by the liters per minute of flow.) Oxygen must be stored away from excess heat and clearly marked with a warning sign prohibiting smoking, open flames, or electrical sparks.

Note: Never use medications past their expiration date as their chemical composition may have altered.

For further reading on emergency medical procedures and supplies, see *Basic Trauma Life Support*, 2nd ed., John E. Campbell et al., Prentice-Hall, 1988.

Appendix IV

THE CRUISING TOOL KIT

For coastal cruising in areas where you are likely to have access to shoreside experts and facilities to handle major problems aboard your vessel, you should carry a good tool kit that includes the following:

Basic Hand Tools/Supplies

Socket wrench set:
 1/2-inch drive
 3/16-inch to 1-inch sockets
 12-inch rotating extender arm

Open-end wrench set:
 1/4-inch to 1-inch

Crescent wrenches:
 10 inches
 16 inches

Allen wrench set:
 1/16-inch to 1/4-inch

Standard pliers

Channel Lock pliers:
 10 inches
 16 inches

Vise-grip pliers

Needle-nose pliers

Screwdriver kit:
 Straight and Phillips
 4 inches to 16 inches each

Hand or cordless electric drill

High-carbon drill bit set:
 1/16-inch to 1/2-inch

Retractable metal tape measure:
 25-foot

Carpenter's hammer

Ball-peen hammer

Rubber mallet

Hand saw

Hacksaw

Trouble light

Angled mirror on extendable handle

Utility knife

Funnel

Oil-can spout

Assorted-grit sandpaper

Assorted metal files

Assorted screws, nuts, bolts, and washers

Wire brush

Epoxy glue

Electrical Tools/Supplies

Solder iron or gun

Rosin-core solder

Volt-ohm meter

Snap-on ammeter

Polarity tester

Test light

Assorted test leads with alligator clips each end

Battery cables

Electrician's cutter/stripper/crimper tool

Assorted electrical terminals

Assorted electrical wire

Electrician's tape

Duct tape

Spray can of moisture inhibitor

Special Tools/Supplies

Injector timing tool

Injector nut wrench

Manual air-pump, pressure gauge, and needle

Inflatable patch kit

Syntho-glass

Assorted wooden thru-hull plugs

For offshore voyaging where you are likely to have to attend to virtually all repairs yourself with the tools you have on board, in addition to the items above you should also consider carrying:

Wheel puller

Torque wrench, 100-pound capacity

Copper pipe and joints
Pipe solder
Butane torch

PVC pipe and joints
Pipe adhesive

Manual or electric oil-transfer pump

Fiberglass patch kit

Feeler gauge set

Installed workbench vise

Small crowbar

Maintenance supplies:
   Polyurethane varnish
   Urethane or epoxy paint

Assorted nylon-bristle paint brushes
Paint solvent
Chrome polish
Brass polish
Vinyl cleaner/protector
Boat polish/wax

Appendix V

SPARE PARTS AND SUPPLIES

As you assemble your spare-parts inventory for either coastal or offshore cruising, here is a list of replacement items and supplies you should at least consider having on board:

Engine

Alternator or generator

Drive belts

Starter motor

Starter switch

Starter solenoid

Raw-water pump

Fuel pump

Thermostat and gasket

Injectors

Valve cover gasket

Mechanical gauges and
   sensors
   RPM

Coolant temperature
Oil pressure

Fuel filters
   Prmary
   Secondary

Fuel biocide

Oil

Oil filters

Fuel-line hose and fittings

Oil-line hose and fittings

Transmission

Oil or fluid

Mechanical drive oil-termpera-
   ture gauge

Underwater Gear

Shaft

Strut and bearings

Propeller

Rudder

Appropriate nuts, bolts, washers, shaft keys, lubricants, and sealants

Shaft zincs

Rudder zincs

Hydraulic System

Hydraulic line and fittings

Hydraulic valve

Hydraulic pump

Hydraulic fluid

AC Electrical System

Generator relay

Generator circuit board

Generator starter switch

Generator starter solenoid

Circuit breakers
120 volt of appropriate amperage ratings
240 volt of appropriate amperage ratings

Air conditioning/heating unit relay

Refrigeration compressor relay

Incandescent light bulbs

Fluorescent light tubes

120-volt light switch

120-volt receptacle

DC Electrical System

Circuit breakers of appropriate amperage ratings

Fuses appropriate to all onboard DC equipment

Electronic compass sensor

Light switch

Pump switch

Marine head switch

Windlass switch

Depth-sounder transducer

Water/Waste System

Marine-head seal kits

Marine-head supply pump

Marine-head macerator pump

Watermaker supply pump

Bilge pump

Water pump

Impellers appropriate to all onboard water pumps

Water heater element

Water hoses, fittings, and clamps

Water pipes and fittings

Water purification tablets

Assorted plumbing washers

Tender/Outboard

Outboard spark plug

Outboard ignition kit

Coil

Condenser

Outboard motor oil

Outboard fuel supply line

Steering cable, clamps, and pulleys

PHOTO CREDITS

Fig. 1 2—Viking Yachts
Fig. 1.4—Detroit Diesel Corporation
Fig. 1.5—Detroit Diesel Corporation
Fig. 1.6—Grand Banks Yachts, Ltd.

Fig. 5.2—Hatteras Yacht Co.

Fig. 8.8—Digital Marine Electronics Corp.
Fig. 8.11—Magnavox Advanced Products and Systems Company
Fig. 8.16—Furuno USA, Inc.
Fig. 8.17—Laser Plot, Inc.

Fig. 9.9—ICOM, Inc.
Fig. 9.14—Hal Communications Corp.
Fig. 9.15—Raytheon Corporation

Fig. 10.2—Jay Stuart Haft Co.; Mooring, Inc.; Danforth Division of Rule Industries, Inc.

Fig. 11.1—Boston Whaler, Inc.; Chris Cunningham
Fig. 11.2—Imtra Corporation
Fig. 11.3—Sillinger Inflatable Boats & Imports USA, Inc.
Fig. 12.3—Survival Technologies Group
Fig. 12.4—Survival Technologies Group
Fig. 12.5—ACR Electronics Corp.
Fig. 12.6—ACR Electronics Corp.
Fig. 12.7—ACR Electronics Corp.
Fig. 12.9—ACR Electronics Corp.
Fig. 12.10—Switlik Parachute Co.
Fig. 12.11—Imtra Corporation
Fig. 12.12—Switlik Parachute Co.
Fig. 12.13—Survival Technologies Group
Fig. 12.15—Survival Technologies Group

Fig. 13.1—Survival Technologies Group

INDEX